THEY
WALKED
WITH
GOD

THEY WALKED WITH GOD

Compiled and Introduced by James S. Bell, Jr.

MOODY PRESS

CHICAGO

READER'S NOTE

In compiling this devotional I reviewed more than fifty volumes by twelve different authors. Forty-six were applicable to the subject matter. All are numbered within the Colportage Library, the earliest line of books in what eventually would become Moody Press, though many are now out of print. The heading at the top of each page refers to the book title from which the selection originates. The subheading usually corresponds to the given chapter within the above book title. Occasionally I have substituted a subheading closer to the meaning of the text when the chapter title did not seem to fit. The author of the selection is listed at the bottom. The bibliography at the end of this volume lists every work, including those still being published by Moody Press.

JAMES S. BELL, JR.

PREFACE

In the 1890s they greatly encouraged believers in America, England, and Scotland, their words and writings calling Christians to the consecrated life and sinners to a new life. In the 1990s, they continue to speak. You will find their illustrations and statements in devotionals, magazines, and perhaps in sermons by your pastor. Their names now represent the Christian zeal that today we are trying to recapture in the West, even as hunger for spiritual depth has swept into the Commonwealth of Independent States (the former Soviet Union) and Eastern Europe.

They are F. B. Meyer, D. L. Moody, George Mueller, Andrew Murray, and Charles Spurgeon, among others. Amazingly, at one time they all wrote for a single publisher, Moody Press, as part of Moody's illustrious Colportage Library. The Colportage Library, a series of more than five hundred titles, first appeared one hundred years ago as part of the Bible Institute Colportage Association (BICA). After the death of Dwight L. Moody in 1899, the school he founded was renamed the Moody Bible Institute, and the publishing house he founded, BICA, eventually became Moody Press.

With gratitude to God for one hundred years of service, Moody Press is pleased to present *They Walked with God*, 365 readings from more than forty titles in our classic Colportage Library.

As a pastor who preached weekly for seventeen years, I always appreciated the writings of men of previous eras, such as Spurgeon, Murray, and Henry Ironside. Serving now as president of Moody Bible Institute, I have come to appreciate the insightful writings of three of my predecessors, James M. Gray, R. A. Torrey, and, of course, D. L. Moody. I know you will find the words of these preachers, teachers, and evangelists as helpful today as they were a century ago.

Two distinctives of titles in the Colportage Library were their cost and distribution. D. L. Moody wanted to produce inexpensive yet quality books that would proclaim the gospel clearly and draw believers close to their Lord Jesus Christ. As a result, all the books were uniform in size, bound with paper covers, and addressed such themes as salvation, the Christian life, prayer, Bible study, and evangelism. The books were distributed door to door by colporters, who, like the Fuller Brush men, were traveling salesmen whose products consisted of books, Bibles, and gospel tracts.

As you read *They Walked with God*, I know the zeal of these godly men and women will challenge you to greater service to our Lord. They will cause you to look inward to your heart's condition and outward to the condition of others—the spiritually lost all around us.

Moody Press editorial director James Bell has compiled an inspiring anthology from the works of these twelve writers; he has been ably assisted in planning this project by general manager William Thrasher and Greg Thornton, Moody Press's executive editor. With them, I trust that this volume will encourage and inspire you as you walk with God.

JOSEPH M. STOWELL

INTRODUCTION

It is said that we "stand on the shoulders of giants" in reference to the spiritual legacy of saints gone before us. Though this term is often ascribed to the Reformers and Puritans, I believe it can also apply to a select group of individuals who walked with God at the turn of this century. Like Whitefield and Wesley, this group had a passion for the conversion of souls. They also had a zeal for holy living, to combat both the cold formalism of religion in the Victorian era and the outright lawlessness of an expansive frontier.

God was well able to meet the spiritual needs of that generation both in the USA and the United Kingdom through the ministries of His chosen instruments, many of whose writings are found in this volume. What further contributes to their "giant" stature is that the writings of this group still have an impact on our generation today—one hundred years later.

Of course D. L. Moody and Charles H. Spurgeon are credited with spearheading the growth of evangelical Christianity during this period, and their writings figure prominently here. Yet others have by no means been forgotten, for their works continue to flow through Christian bookstores year after year. These include the household names of Andrew Murray, F. B. Meyer, and George Mueller. Finally, I've included another group that *should* remain a part of our Christian publishing heritage. Indeed, most have some books still in print. Their ministries and books shaped not only that original generation but subsequent ones as well. You may recognize the names C. I. Scofield, R. A. Torrey, Frances Ridley Havergal, Henry (Harry) A. Ironside, J. C. Ryle, Horatius Bonar, and James M. Gray.

Do not expect these daily devotional selections to meet today's felt needs. They won't, as other Christian books do, help you to go on a diet or straighten out your teenager. One hundred years ago Christian books focused on our relationship with God—His magnificent love and our utter unworthiness. In other words, they contain excellent matter to begin your day devoted to His service. These readings go back to the basics in how to get right with God, how to grow in holiness, and how to tell others of your faith.

The surprisingly contemporary language and use of anecdotes is no accident. Like modern Christian publishers, D. L. Moody sought to reach as many typical believers in the pew as possible. Yet the down-to-earth style serves as a reminder that it is possible to reach the unbeliever through the written word as well. Hopefully some of these entries will inspire a new burden for the lost in the mind and heart of the daily reader.

The purpose of this volume is not only to edify the reader but also to commemorate the rich spiritual heritage with which God has blessed Moody Press. The esteemed servants of Christ whose works are contained in these pages represent the "first fruits" in the early years of the Moody Colportage Library—together in one volume for the first time to celebrate one hundred years of humbly attempting to be the name you can trust in Christian publishing.

These individuals, like us, were not perfect. Yet, though they are all dead, their words and deeds still speak to our lives. Though we are often obsessed with what is new, we neglect to our own detriment this "cloud of witnesses" who can minister to our timeless spiritual needs. They did not all claim to be trained theologians but wished to practice the presence of God and to walk with Him consistently, separate from the world. I trust this volume will daily inspire you to do the same.

JAMES S. BELL, JR.

FULL ASSURANCE

Moving Forward

The Christian life is never static. One must either grow in grace, or there will be backsliding and deterioration. "The backslider in heart shall be filled with his own ways" (Proverbs 14:14). He who does not go on with God, but allows himself to drift, is almost sure to lose the joy of his salvation. Examine yourself as to this matter, and if you find that you have been careless in regard to the study of your Bible, careless as to your prayer life, careless as to the proper use of the means of grace, confess all this to God and give diligence to walk with Him in days to come, that you may develop a stronger Christian character.

Last of all, let me remind you that any known sin condoned in your life will rob you of the joy and assurance of your salvation. "If I regard iniquity in my heart, the Lord will not hear me." Many believers have gone on happily with Christ for some time, but, through toying with sin, have become ensnared and entrapped into something that has so grieved the Spirit of God that they have lost their sense of acceptance in Christ. See to it that there is no unconfessed sin in your life. Be sure that you are not tolerating any secret sin that is draining you of spiritual power and hindering your communion with God.

Worldliness, carnal indulgence of any kind, unfaithfulness as to your Christian responsibilities, the harboring of malice or ill-will toward others—all or any of these things are calculated to destroy your sense of assurance. If guilty of any of them, face things honestly in the presence of God, remembering that He has said, "If we confess our sins, he is faithful and just to forgive us our sins, and to cleanse us from all unrighteousness."

Do not accept the suggestion of the tempter that you are powerless to break away from evil habits. Remember, it is not a question of your own power, but when you honestly repent of the wrongdoing and turn to the Lord for divine help to overcome your besetting sin, He will undertake for you. As you reckon yourself to be dead indeed unto sin, but alive unto God through Jesus Christ our Lord, the Holy Spirit will work in you and through you. He will cause you to triumph over tendencies toward evil and enable you to live victoriously to the glory of the God who has saved you.

HENRY A. IRONSIDE

WEIGHED AND WANTING

A Blessing or a Curse

I believe it to be literally true that our temporal condition depends on the way we act upon this commandment: "Honor thy father and mother (which is the first commandment with promise), that it may be well with thee, and that thou mayest live long on the earth." The Scriptures express the outcome of this command in many ways: "Honor thy father and thy mother, as the Lord thy God hath commanded thee; that thy days may be prolonged, and that it may go well with thee, in the land which the Lord thy God giveth thee." "Cursed is he that setteth light by his father or mother." "Whoso curseth his father or mother, his lamp shall be put out in obscure darkness."

It would be easy to multiply texts from the Bible to prove this truth. Obedience and respect at home prepare the way for obedience to the employer, and they are joined with other virtues that help toward a prosperous career, crowned with a ripe, honored old age. Disobedience and disrespect for parents are often the first steps in the downward track. Many a criminal has testified that this is the point where he first went astray. I have lived over sixty years, and I have learned one thing if I have learned nothing else—that no man or woman who dishonors father or mother ever prospers.

Young man, young woman, how do you treat your parents? Tell me that, and I will tell you how you are going to get on in life. When I hear a young man speaking contemptuously of his gray-haired father or mother, I say he has sunk very low indeed. When I see a young man as polite as any gentlemen can be when he is out in society, but who snaps at his mother and speaks unkindly to his father, I would not give the snap of my finger for his religion.

If there is any man or woman on earth that ought to be treated kindly and tenderly, it is that loving mother or that loving father. If they cannot have your regard through life, what reward are they to have for all their care and anxiety? Think how they loved you and provided for you in your early days.

D. L. MOODY

FIVE "MUSTS" OF THE CHRISTIAN LIFE

The "Must" of the Decreasing Self

Some of us can never forget the hymn composed by the late Pastor Theodore Monod of Paris in his first radiant vision of a life hidden in Christ with God:

> *All of Self and none of Thee!*
> *Some of Self and some of Thee!*
> *Less of Self and more of Thee!*
> *None of Self and all of Thee!*

"Reckon yourselves to be dead indeed unto sin, but alive unto God, through Jesus Christ our Lord."

We must receive more of the grace of the Holy Spirit. In Romans 7, the apostle Paul complains of being tied and bound by the self-life. He is like a caged bird, which beats its breast against the bars of its cage in vain aspirations for liberty. Then, suddenly, in Romans 8, he changes his note and cries: "There is now no more of this self-condemnation, for those who are in Christ Jesus, who walk and live after the Spirit, because the law of the Spirit of life, in Christ Jesus, has made them free from the law of sin and death."

Let us stand together on the deck of an ocean-bound steamer and watch the flight of a seagull. There is, of course, the downward pull of gravitation; but, for every pull downward, there is a stroke of the live bird's wing on the elastic air; and this more than compensates for the downward pull. That stroke, we know, is due to the spirit of life, which throbs in the bird's breast.

So, by the Holy Spirit, who indwells our spirit, there is given to each one of us the very life of our glorious Savior. The regularity, immediacy, and quality of the Christ-life are more than sufficient to counteract the downward pull of sin. At the first slight suggestion of sin, the Holy Spirit resists the self-life, so that we may not do the things that we otherwise would; nor shall we fall into those sins of will and thought and act, which were once natural to us. "If we live by the Spirit, by the Spirit let us walk." (See Galatians 5:16–26.) The Spirit will lust against the flesh and obtain absolute victory, which will fill our hearts with joy. Indeed, temptation may even promote a stronger character by making Jesus a more living reality.

F. B. MEYER

THE EMPTY TOMB

All Shall Rise

The doctrine of the resurrection teaches that all men will rise again—not a certain portion of the race, not a few thousand persons, but all men. It might be easier to believe in an Elijah, who should raise a dead man occasionally, or in a Christ, who should call back to life a young man at the gates of Nain or raise a Lazarus or say, "Talitha cumi" to a little deceased girl. But hard for reason is the doctrine that *all* shall rise—the myriads before the Flood, the multitudes of Nineveh and Babylon, the hosts of Persia and of Media, the millions that followed at the feet of Xerxes, the hosts that marched with Alexander, and all the innumerable millions that fell beneath the Roman sword.

Think of the myriads who have passed away in countries like China, swarming with men, and conceive of these throughout six thousand years fattening the soil. Remember those who have perished by shipwreck, plague, earthquake, and worst of all, by bloodshed and war; and remember that all these will rise without exception; not one of woman born shall sleep on forever, but all the bodies that ever breathed and walked this earth shall live again. "O, monstrous miracle," says one. "It wears the aspect of a thing incredible." Well, we shall not dispute the statement but will give even yet more reason for it.

The wonder increases when we remember in what strange places many of these bodies now may be. For the bodies of some have been left in deep mines where they will never be reached again; they have been carried by the wash and swell of tides into deep caverns of the ancient main; there they lie, far away on the pathless desert where only the vulture's eye can see them, or buried beneath mountains of fallen rock. In fact, where are not man's remains? Who shall point out a spot of earth where the crumbling dust of Adam's sons is not? Blows there a single summer wind down our streets without whirling along particles of what once was man? Is there a single wave that breaks upon any shore that holds not in solution some relic of what was once human? They lie beneath the meadow grass; yet surely from anywhere, from everywhere, the scattered bodies shall return, like Israel from captivity.

As certainly as God is God, our dead shall live, and stand upon their feet, an exceeding great army.

CHARLES H. SPURGEON

WEIGHED AND WANTING

To Wish a Man Dead

Let us look once again at the Sermon on the Mount, that men think so much of, and see what Christ had to say: "Ye have heard that it has been said by them of old time, Thou shalt not kill; and whosoever shall kill shall be in danger of the judgment: but I say unto you, that whosoever is angry with his brother without a cause shall be in danger of the judgment: and whosoever shall say to his brother, Raca [an expression of contempt], shall be in danger of the council: but whosoever shall say, Thou fool [an expression of condemnation], shall be in danger of hell fire."

As someone has said, Jesus described "three degrees of murderous guilt, all of which can be manifested without a blow being struck: secret anger, the spiteful jeer, [and] the open, unrestrained outburst of violent abusive speech."

Again, what does John say? "Whosoever hateth his brother is a murderer; and ye know that no murderer hath eternal life abiding in him."

Did you ever in your heart wish a man dead? That was murder. Did you ever get so angry that you wished any one harm? Then you are guilty. I may be addressing someone who is cultivating an unforgiving spirit. That is the spirit of the murderer, and it needs to be rooted out of your heart.

We can only read men's acts—what they have done. God looks down into the heart. That is the birthplace and home of the evil desires and intentions that lead to the transgression of all God's laws.

Listen once more to the words of Jesus: "From within, out of the heart of men, proceed *evil thoughts, adulteries, fornications, murders, thefts, covetousness, wickedness, deceit, lasciviousness, an evil eye, blasphemy, pride, foolishness* . . ."

May God purge our hearts of these evil things, if we are harboring them! Ah, if many of us were weighed now, we should find Belshazzar's doom written against us: *"Tekel"*—Wanting!

D. L. MOODY

FULL ASSURANCE

Assurance Forever

God refuses to compromise His own character for the sake of anyone, much as He yearns to have all men to be saved.

It was this that stirred the soul of Luther, and brought new light and help after long, weary months of groping in the darkness, trying in vain to save himself in conformity to the demands of blind leaders of the blind. As Luther was reading the Latin Psalter, he came across David's prayer, "Save me in thy righteousness." Luther exclaimed, "What does this mean? I can understand how God can damn me in His righteousness, but if He would save me it must surely be in His mercy!" The more he meditated on it, the more the wonder grew. But little by little the truth dawned upon his troubled soul that God Himself had devised a righteous method whereby He could justify unrighteous sinners who came to Him in repentance and received His word in faith.

Isaiah stresses this great and glorious truth throughout his marvelous Old Testament unfolding of the gospel plan. In unsparing severity, the prophet portrays man's utterly lost and absolutely hopeless condition apart from divine grace. "The whole head is sick, and the whole heart faint. From the sole of the foot even unto the head there is no soundness in it; but wounds and bruises and putrefying sores: they have not been closed, neither bound up, neither mollified with ointment" (Isaiah 1:5–6). It is surely a revolting picture, but nevertheless it is true of the unsaved man as God sees him. Sin is a vile disease that has fastened upon the very vitals of its victim. None can free himself from its pollution or deliver himself from its power.

But God has a remedy. He says, "Come now, and let us reason together, saith the Lord: though your sins be as scarlet, they shall be as white as snow; though they be red like crimson, they shall be as wool" (verse 18). It is God Himself who can thus purge the leper from all his uncleanness, and justify the ungodly from all his guilt. And He does it, not at the expense of righteousness, but in a perfectly righteous way.

HENRY A. IRONSIDE

THE OVERCOMING LIFE

True Wisdom

Notice that all those who have made a deep impression on the world, and have shone most brightly, have been men who lived in a dark day. Look at Joseph; he was sold as a slave into Egypt by the Ishmaelites; yet he took his God with him into captivity, as Daniel afterwards did. And he remained true to the last; he did not give up his faith because he had been taken away from home and placed among idolaters. He stood firm, and God stood by him.

Look at Moses, who turned his back upon the gilded palaces of Egypt and identified himself with his despised and downtrodden nation. If a man ever had a hard field it was Moses; yet he shone brightly and never proved unfaithful to his God.

Elijah lived in a far darker day than we do. The whole nation was going over to idolatry. Ahab and his queen and all the royal court were throwing their influence against the worship of the true God. Yet Elijah stood firm and shone brightly in that dark and evil day. How his name stands out on the page of history!

Look at John the Baptist. I used to think I would like to live in the days of the prophets; but I have given up that idea. You may be sure that when a prophet appears on the scene, everything is dark and the professing church of God has gone over to the service of the god of this world. So it was when John the Baptist made his appearance. Eighteen centuries have rolled away, and yet the fame of that wilderness preacher shines brighter than ever. He was looked down upon in his generation, but he has outlived all his enemies; his name will be revered and his work remembered as long as the church is on the earth.

Talk about your field being a hard one! See how Paul shone for God as he went out, the first missionary to the heathen, telling them of the God whom he served, and who had sent His Son to die a cruel death in order to save the world. Men reviled him and his teachings; they laughed him to scorn when he spoke of the crucified One. But he went on preaching the gospel of the Son of God. He was regarded as a poor tentmaker by the great and mighty ones of his day; but no one can now tell the name of any of his persecutors, or of those who lived at that time, unless their names happen to be associated with his and they were brought into contact with him.

D. L. MOODY

FIVE "MUSTS" OF THE CHRISTIAN LIFE

The "Must" of Service

There are three possible plannings for human life. We may be guided by our senses—"We like this or do not like that." We may be guided by our own will and choice. But, best of all, we may be guided, as our Lord was, by constantly waiting for the indication of God's purpose. That indication is like a deep-toned bell ringing in our heart-depths, but finally corroborated by circumstances and certainly vindicated by results.

One Sunday morning, I was sitting on the porch of Mr. Moody's home, looking down on the Connecticut River. We were talking of the ways of God, and he recalled a sermon of Dr. Andrew Bonar on the words, repeated five times in Scripture, "See that thou make all things according to the pattern shown thee on the Mount." Dr. Bonar described the tabernacle pattern as woven out of sunbeams; and Moses walked with God from one part to another of the ethereal structure, learning the specific reason for each. When, for instance, they viewed the altar of sacrifice, God explained that in process of time Calvary would bear the weight of the dying Savior; and, as they looked on the laver, God would explain that the soul, redeemed by the blood of Christ, would always need cleansing. So also the significance of the altar of incense, the veil, the ark, and the mercy-seat. When presently Moses returned to the people, he discovered that for everything that had been revealed in the vision there was exact and adequate provision in the gifts of the people.

This is a most helpful lesson. The first thing for any of us is not to run hither and thither, consulting people or soliciting their help, but to be perfectly assured that we are in the mind of the Lord and that He will supply all our need, according to His riches in glory by Christ Jesus.

It must never be forgotten that none of those that live in God's purposes need ever be ashamed. His delays are not denials. "[From of old,] men have not heard, nor perceived by the ear, neither hath eye seen, O God, beside Thee, what He hath prepared for him that waiteth for Him" (Isaiah 64:4).

F. B. MEYER

WEIGHED AND WANTING
God Speaks

If it were known that God Himself was going to speak once again to man, what eagerness and excitement there would be. For nearly nineteen hundred years He has been silent. No inspired message has been added to the Bible for nearly nineteen hundred years. How eagerly all men would listen if God should speak once more. Yet men forget that the Bible is God's own Word, and that it is as truly His message today as when it was delivered of old. The law that was given at Sinai has lost none of its solemnity. Time cannot wear out its authority or the fact of its authorship.

I can imagine someone saying, "I won't be weighed by that law. I don't believe in it."

Now men may dispute as much as they like about other parts of the Bible, but I have never met an honest man who found fault with the Ten Commandments. Infidels may mock the Lawgiver and reject Him who has delivered us from the curse of the law, but they can't help admitting that the commandments are right. Renan said that they are for all nations and will remain the commandments of God during all the centuries.

If God created this world, He must make some laws to govern it. In order to make life safe we must have good laws; there is not a country the sun shines upon that does not possess laws. Now this is God's law. It has come from on high, and infidels and skeptics have to admit that it is pure. Legislatures nearly all over the world adopt it as the foundation of their legal systems.

"The law of the Lord is perfect, converting the soul: the testimony of the Lord is pure, making wise the simple: the statutes of the Lord are right, rejoicing the heart: the commandment of the Lord is pure, enlightening the eyes."

Now the question for you and me is—are we keeping these commandments? If God made us, as we know He did, He had a right to make that law; and if we don't use it rightly it would have been better for us if we had never had it, for it will condemn us. We are found wanting. And being found condemned, we have only one hope for deliverance—Jesus Christ the righteous.

D. L. MOODY

KEPT FOR THE MASTER'S USE

Our Lips Kept for Jesus

Yes, it is true enough that we should show forth His praise not only with our lips but in our lives; but with very many Christians the other side of the prayer wants praying—they want rousing up even to wish to show it forth not only in their lives but with their lips. I wonder how many, even of those who read this, really pray, "O Lord, open Thou my lips, and my mouth shall show forth Thy praise!"

And when opened, oh, how much one does want to have them so kept for Jesus that He may be free to make the most of them, not letting them render second-rate and indirect service when they might be doing direct and first-rate service to His cause and kingdom. It is terrible how much less is done for Him than might be done, because we think that if what we are doing or saying is not bad, we are doing good in a certain way, and therefore may be quite easy about it. People are not converted by this sort of work; at any rate I never met or heard of anyone.

"He thinks it better for his quiet influence to tell!" said an affectionately excusing relative of one who had plenty of special opportunities of soul winning, if he had only used his lips as well as his life for his Master.

"And how many souls have been converted to God by his quiet influence all these years?" was my reply. And to that there was no answer. For the silent shining was all very beautiful in theory, but not one of the many souls placed specially under his influence had been known to be brought out of darkness into marvelous light. If they had, they must have been known, for such light can't help being seen.

When one has even a glimmer of the tremendous difference between having Christ and being without Christ; when one gets but one shuddering glimpse of what eternity is and what it may mean without Christ; when one gets but a flash of realization that all these neighbors of ours, rich and poor alike, will have to spend that eternity either with Him or without Him—it is hard, very hard, indeed, to understand how a man or woman can believe these things at all and make no effort for anything beyond the temporal elevation of those around.

FRANCES R. HAVERGAL

THE EMPTY TOMB

The Resurrection Credible

I would desire, if I might have my way, to be drawn to my grave by white horses or to be carried on the shoulders of men who would express joy as well as sorrow in their dress, for why should we sorrow over those who have gone to glory and inherited immortality? Sound the gladsome trumpet! The conqueror has won the battle; the king has climbed to his throne.

"Rejoice," say our brethren from above, "rejoice with us, for we have entered into our rest." "Blessed are the dead which die in the Lord from henceforth. Yea, saith the Spirit, that they may rest from their labors, and their works do follow them." Bless God evermore that over the pious dead we sing His living promises!

Let us, in the next place, cheer our hearts in prospect of our own departure. We shall soon pass away. There is a place where you shall sleep, perhaps in a lone grave in a foreign land, or perhaps in a niche where your bones shall lie side by side with those of your ancestors; but to the dust return you must. Well, let us not repine. It is but for a little, a rest on the way to immortality. Let us meet death not only with equanimity but with expectation, since it is to resurrection that we aspire.

Then again, if we are expecting a blessed resurrection, let us respect our bodies. Let not our members become instruments of evil. Be pure. In your baptism, your bodies were washed with pure water to teach you that henceforth you must be clean from all defilement. Put away from you every evil thing.

Lastly, the ungodly are to rise again, but it will be to a resurrection of woe. Their bodies sinned, and their bodies will be punished. "Fear him," says Christ, "who is able to destroy both soul and body in hell." He will cast both of them into a suffering that shall cause perpetually enduring destruction to them. This is terrible indeed. To slumber in the grave would be infinitely preferable to such a resurrection—"the resurrection of damnation," as the Scripture calls it.

A certain Acilius Aviola was seized with an apoplexy, and, his friends conceiving him to be dead, carried him to his funeral pyre. But when the heat had warmed his body, he awoke to find himself hopelessly encircled with funeral flames. In vain he called for deliverance; he could not be rescued, but passed from torpor into intolerable torment. Such will be the dreadful awakening of every sinful body when it shall be aroused from its slumber in the grave. The body will start up to be judged, condemned, and driven from God's presence into everlasting punishment.

May God grant that it may never be your case or mine, but may we believe in Christ Jesus now, and so obtain a resurrection to life eternal. Amen.

CHARLES H. SPURGEON

FIVE "MUSTS" OF THE CHRISTIAN LIFE

The "Must" of Spiritual Worship

Our Savior tells us that the Father "seeketh" such to worship Him; and the grave question for us all is whether He ever bends over us, as we kneel, receiving as grateful incense the ascriptions of our worshiping love. He hears us babble in petitions, which we may have uttered for years! He hears our intercessions for others, which are the expression of human affection! But does He often hear the outburst of worship and praise from hearts that have obeyed the psalmist's injunction to join the universal chant arising from the unfallen universe? To this the psalmist calls us when he says: "O come, let us sing unto the Lord; let us make a joyful noise to the rock of our salvation. O come, let us worship and bow down; let us kneel before the Lord our Maker."

Let us kindle our hearts to praise by listening, as Isaiah did to the chant of the seraphim—"Holy, holy, holy, is the Lord of hosts, the whole earth is full of his glory"; or by listening to the song of the virgin-mother: "My soul doth magnify the Lord, and my spirit hath rejoiced in God my Saviour"; or by listening as John did to the out-circling song of heaven, beginning with the inner circle of the redeemed, and reaching out to every created thing, which is in the heaven, and on the earth, and on the sea! "Unto Him that sitteth on the throne, and unto the Lamb, be the blessing and the honour, and the glory, and the dominion, for ever and ever. And the four living creatures said, Amen! And the elders fell down and worshipped" (Revelation 5:13–14, RV).

In order to incite our sluggish souls to worship, we may recite aloud the Psalms, or the *Te Deum*, or any of the great hymns of the church. But, best of all, it is for the soul to pour out its adoring gratitude and love in its own glad words. "We give Thee thanks for our creation, preservation, and for all the good things in our lives, but above all for the redemption of our world by our Lord Jesus Christ and for our own adoption into eternal union with Thyself."

F. B. MEYER

SHORT TALKS

Separation from the World

Wherefore come out from among them, and be ye separate, saith the Lord, and touch not the unclean thing; and I will receive you. And I will be a Father unto you, and ye shall be my sons and daughters, saith the Lord Almighty" (2 Corinthians 7:17–18).

I do not believe that there is any doctrine more needed today in the Christian church in America than the doctrine of separation. We have lost power because the line between the church and the world has been almost obliterated. A good many people profess Christianity, but their profession does not mean much; the result is that the world does not know what Christians really believe. For every unconverted man that reads the Bible, a hundred read you and me; and if they see us hand-in-glove with the ungodly they are not going to have any confidence in our professions.

"Be not unequally yoked together with unbelievers." How is it with matrimony? How many ministers would marry a godly woman to an ungodly man? Why not take a stand and say you will not be a party to it? The courts are filled with divorce cases because Christian men and women have been yoked with unbelievers. Look at the mothers whose children have been unequally yoked with infidels and men of the world! My friends, if we want the power of God we must obey God's Word, cost us what it may.

How is it with your life? Are you hand-in-glove with the world? If you are, how can you expect God to fill you with the Holy Spirit? I believe that the cause of Christ is suffering more from this one thing than any other ten things put together. God cannot give us power because we are allied with the ungodly. The mirth that satisfies the world will not satisfy the true child of God, and yet how many of us are just looking to the world for our pleasure.

If we walk with God, we will not be asking, "What is the harm of this and that?" The question will be, "What is the good?" If a thing does not help us we will give it up for something better.

D. L. MOODY

KEPT FOR THE MASTER'S USE

Beautiful Feet

Our Lord has many uses for what is kept for Himself. How beautiful are the feet of them that bring glad tidings of good things! That is the best use of all, and I expect the angels think those feet beautiful, even if they are cased in muddy boots or galoshes.

Once the question was asked, "Wherefore wilt thou run, my son, seeing that thou hast no tidings ready?" So if we want to have these beautiful feet, we must have the tidings ready which they are to bear. Let us ask Him to keep our hearts so freshly full of His good news of salvation that our mouths may speak out of their abundance. If the clouds be full of rain, they empty themselves upon the earth. May we be so filled with the Spirit that we may have much to pour out for others.

Besides the privilege of carrying water from the wells of salvation, there are plenty of cups of cold water to be carried in all directions; not to the poor only—ministries of love are often as much needed by a rich friend. But the feet must be kept for these; they will be too tired for them if they are tired out for self-pleasing. In such services we are treading in the blessed steps of Christ, who went about doing good.

Then there is literal errand-going—just to fetch something that is needed for the household or something that a tired relative wants, whether asked or un-asked. Such things should come first instead of last, because these are clearly our Lord's will for us to do, by the position in which He has placed us; what seems more direct service may be after all not so directly apportioned by Him.

"I have to go and buy some soap," said one with a little sigh. The sigh was a waste of breath, for her feet were going to do her Lord's will for that next half-hour much more truly than if they had carried her to her well-worked district, and left the soap to take its chance.

FRANCES R. HAVERGAL

SHORT TALKS

An Unwelcome Visitor

You read of His going up to the annual feast at Jerusalem; you never read of Jerusalem giving Him a welcome. Although Christ had wrought many miracles, and many parables had fallen from His lips, although the most wonderful sermons that were ever preached on this earth were preached by Him, there was hardly anyone speaking a kind word for Him. Almost a universal hiss was going up against Him.

In one place you read that He looked around Him and saw death and woe and misery, while so few people were willing to let Him bless them, and then looked to that world where all knew Him and honored Him and loved Him, where He had never been mistrusted or called a blasphemer or impostor, which was common all around Him when He was on earth. I can just imagine how, as He looked toward that world, He sighed and longed to get back. In another place it says He had been lifting up the standard very high, and many of His disciples "went back, and walked no more with Him." It is one of the sad scenes in His life.

In another place it says: "Every man went to his own house, and Jesus went to the Mount of Olives." He didn't have any house to go to. He that was once rich became poor for your sake and mine. He that created all things had emptied Himself and become one of the poorest of the land. On an occasion like that He uttered the words: "The foxes have holes, and the birds of the air have nests; but the Son of Man has nowhere to lay His head." His cradle was a borrowed one. He hadn't a inch of ground that He could call His own. When He went to the Mount of Olives, the ground was His bed, the sod was His pillow. I can see Him with His locks wet with the dew of the night.

I often think if I had been living in those days I would like to have had a home in Jerusalem, I would have liked that very night to have asked Him to my home. But I presume my house would have been closed against Him like the others in the city of Jerusalem.

D. L. MOODY

SATAN AND THE SAINT

Christ's Credentials

Think of the gracious revelation of God's purpose and power in the healing of the man born blind (John 9). Think of his case, and in many another that might be named. Away back in the councils of eternity God determined to redeem the human race, putting the iniquity of us all upon the Person of His own Son, our Savior Jesus Christ. It was necessary that the Son should take upon Himself our human nature; that He should come to earth; and that He should be known and identified when He came, by the works He should do, that men might believe on Him.

And so, for your redemption, and mine, and that of the whole world, God caused this child to be born blind. The impairment brought sorrow to his parents and to himself. Day after day, week after week, month after month, year after year he sat there. All Jerusalem knew him; thousands of people from Judea and Galilee knew him and knew he had been born blind.

And now the reason for it all! The Son of Man has left the glory He had with the Father before the world was; He has come down to earth to suffer and die; and He is about to be identified as the Son of God and the Savior of the world. On this memorable day He is passing by the temple gate and, seeing this man, speaks to him the word of power that gives him the sight he never had. The man returns to his home, and it is known there—and in all Jerusalem and in all Judea and in all the world—that God did it to certify to the well-beloved One, whose blood cleanseth us from all sin.

Was it not worth the while of that man to have been born blind and to have suffered so? Was it not worth while for his parents to have suffered? Does God ever put suffering upon His faithful witnesses when reward does not follow it? It was well worth his while, not only for his own sake, but for that of millions of redeemed souls who have been won to God through Jesus Christ. They are in His presence now, because of the testimony he bore to Him by sitting at the temple gate until He restored his sight.

JAMES M. GRAY

FIVE "MUSTS" OF THE CHRISTIAN LIFE

Fellowship with Christ in Service

It is a beautiful privilege to work along with Christ, but we shall not serve in that blessed apprenticeship long without learning this lesson: that He has no pleasure in service rendered to Himself or others that does not cost us blood! This is characteristic of His own service to the world, and you will find that He will soon drop you out unless you are prepared, in your measure, to surrender yourself to the blood-letting, which alone counts in the service of humanity.

As we look out on society today we can understand why so many lives are unhappy. They have never learned that the one secret of happiness is to give to the point of self-denial and self-sacrifice. As Phillips Brooks has put it, "They need something to happen which shall force them out on the open ocean of complete self-sacrifice. If only a slow quiet tide or a furious storm would come and break every rope that binds them to the wooden wharves of their own interests and carry them clear out to sea! The soul that trifles and toys with self-sacrifice can achieve neither its true joy nor power. Only the soul that gives itself up forever to the life of others can know the delight and peace which surrender gives."

This trace of blood in our actions is a matter that we can never talk about. When it is being shed, we must anoint our head and wash our face, that men may have no inkling of what is happening. Neither the right hand nor the left hand must know, nor divulge the secret. It should be remembered, also, that we have no right to deprive wife or child of whatever is necessary. It must be a personal act, affecting no one but yourself. You must be the one who gives the blood, not they! Keep happy and smiling! When Jesus was performing this miracle, there was no strain or effort, no wrinkle on His forehead, no cloud upon His smile. He drew no attention to Himself, needed no thanks, and stole away unrecognized, at least for the moment, as the giver.

Of course, there is no merit in such actions. The blood we shed cannot atone, cannot save, cannot cleanse. Only His blood can do that. But, also, it is true that the great soulwinners of the world have faced the blood of martyrdom and counted not their lives dear unto themselves.

F. B. MEYER

THE OVERCOMING LIFE

Humility

Have we been decreasing of late? Do we think less of ourselves and of our position than we did a year ago? Are we seeking to obtain some position of dignity? Are we wanting to hold on to some title, and are we offended because we are not treated with the courtesy that we think is due us?

Some time ago I heard a man in the pulpit say that he should take offense if he was not addressed by his title. My dear friend, are you going to take the position that you must have a title and that you must have every letter addressed with that title or you will be offended? John did not want any title, and, when we are right with God, we shall not be caring about titles. In one of his early epistles Paul calls himself "the least of all the apostles." Later on he claims to be "less than the least of all saints," and again, just before his death, he humbly declares that he is the "chief of sinners." Notice how he seems to have grown smaller and smaller in his own estimation. So it was with John. And I do hope and pray that as the days go by we may feel like hiding ourselves and let God have all the honor and glory.

"When I look back upon my own religious experience," says Andrew Murray, "or round upon the church of Christ in the world, I stand amazed at the thought of how little humility is sought after as the distinguishing feature of the discipleship of Jesus. In preaching and living, in the daily activities of the home and social life, in the more special fellowship with Christians, in the direction and performance of work for Christ—alas, how much proof there is that humility is not esteemed the cardinal virtue, the only root from which the graces can grow, the one indispensable condition of true fellowship with Jesus."

See what Christ says about John. "He was a burning and shining light." Christ gave him the honor that belonged to him. If you take a humble position, Christ will see it. If you want God to help you, then take a low position.

I am afraid that if we had been in John's place, many of us would have said, "What did Christ say about me? I am a burning and shining light!" Then we would have had the recommendation put in the newspapers and would have sent them to our friends, with that part marked in blue pencil.

D. L. MOODY

SATAN AND THE SAINT

Suffering Worthwhile

It is worthwhile being a saint of God, and worthwhile suffering for Him. Do you remember what Paul says concerning this? He says that we are witnesses for God not only in the eyes of men, but angels. God's angels throughout all His universe are looking down upon the church and magnifying the wisdom, the grace, the power, and the love of God, as manifested in His dealings with His people through Jesus Christ. Job was bearing witness not only before men, but angels, evil and holy angels both. He was testifying by his fidelity that God's grace is sufficient and that He can keep the feet of His saints.

When trial comes upon us, regenerated Christian men and women, instead of causing our hands to hang down and our knees to become weak, such trial should have the opposite effect. Let us lift up our heads and throw back our shoulders and strengthen our hearts and count ourselves happy that God has thought us worthy to suffer for Him. Let us trust Him though He slay us!

Does it pay to serve God? "Godliness is profitable unto all things, having promise of the life that now is, and of that which is to come" (1 Timothy 4:8). It paid Job to serve Him, for his latter end was better than the beginning. And Jesus says that no man hath left father or mother, or brother or sister, or wife or children, or houses or lands, for His sake and the gospel's, who shall not receive a hundredfold now in this present time, and in the time to come, life everlasting!

As we go out to face whatever is before us, may we do so with the courage and patience and hope born of the knowledge that we are His, and that He is ours, through faith in the once crucified, but now glorified, Redeemer.

JAMES M. GRAY

FIVE "MUSTS" OF THE CHRISTIAN LIFE

The Day of Pentecost

Let us then take the following steps, suggested by Andrew Murray:

1. I believe that there is a Pentecostal blessing to be received—the anointing of the Holy Spirit and the enduement with power [a filling of Holy Spirit-power described in Ephesians 5:18].
2. I believe it is for me!
3. I have never received it; or, if I received it once, I have lost it.
4. I long and desire to secure it at all cost; and am prepared to surrender whatever hinders.
5. I do now humbly and thankfully open my heart to receive all that I believe my Savior is waiting to give; and even if there be no resulting emotion, I will still believe that I have received according to Mark 11:24.

If there is any difficulty in making a full surrender (see step 4 above), I suggest that if you have not been willing to give up the key of some special door, tell Him that you are willing to be made willing, and cast on Him the responsibility of dealing with that special difficulty. When dealing with your own case or the case of others, the one matter that claims imperative and primary consideration is the will. When that takes Christ's side, you may trust Him to deal with every hindrance or sin; and He will.

As to steps, I trust that I may not be charged with egotism, if I reprint part of a tract by Dr. Chapman: "Two or three years ago Mr. Moody invited me to breakfast at his home in Northfield. I got to the house before the breakfast hour and met Dr. Meyer beneath a great tree in front of the house. I said to him, 'What is the matter with me? So many times I seem half empty, and so many times utterly powerless; what is the matter?' He put his hand on my shoulder, and said: 'Have you ever tried to breathe out three times without breathing in once?' I wondered if he was referring to some new breathing exercise, so I said, 'I do not think I have,'

"'Well,' he said, 'try it.' So I breathed out once, and then I had to breathe in again. Then he said: 'You must always breathe in before you can breathe out, and your breathing out must always be in proportion to your breathing in.' Then he said: 'Good morning,' and I went on into Mr. Moody's house. But I had had my lesson and knew that I had been trying to breathe out more than I had breathed in."

There must be a constant inhalation of the Spirit of Pentecost!

F. B. MEYER

WEIGHED AND WANTING

Consolation in God Alone

There is no satisfaction for the soul except in the God of the Bible. We come back to Paul's words, and get consolation for time and eternity: "We know that an idol is nothing in the world, and that there is none other God but one. For though there be that are called gods, whether in heaven or in earth (as there be gods many, and lords many), yet to us there is but one God, the Father, of whom are all things, and we in him; and one Lord Jesus Christ, by whom are all things, and we by him" (1 Corinthians 8:4–6).

My friend, can you say that sincerely? Is all your hope centered on God in Christ? Are you trusting Him alone? Are you ready to step into the scales and be weighed against this first commandment?

God will not accept a divided heart. He must be absolute monarch. There is not room in your heart for two thrones. Christ said: "No man can serve two masters; for either he will hate the one and love the other, or else he will hold to the one and despise the other. Ye cannot serve God and Mammon." Mark you, He did not say—"No man *shall* serve . . . Ye *shall* not serve . . ," but "No man *can* serve . . . Ye *cannot* serve . . ." That means more than a command; it means that you cannot mix the worship of the true God with the worship of another god any more than you can mix oil and water. It cannot be done. There is not room for any other throne in the heart if Christ is there. If worldliness should come in, godliness would go out.

The road to heaven and the road to hell lead in different directions. Which master will you choose to follow? Be an out-and-out Christian. "Him only shalt thou serve." Only thus can you be well pleasing to God. The Jews were punished with seventy years of captivity because they worshiped false gods. They have suffered nearly nineteen hundred years because they rejected the Messiah. Will you incur God's displeasure by rejecting Christ too? He died to save you. Trust Him with your whole heart, for with the heart man believeth unto righteousness. I believe that when Christ has the first place in our hearts—when the kingdom of God is first in everything—we shall have power, and we shall not have power until we give Him His rightful place. If we let one false god come in and steal our love away from the God of heaven, we shall not have peace or power.

D. L. MOODY

FULL ASSURANCE

Queen Victoria Decides the Question

There is an apparently authentic story told of the great Queen Victoria, so long ruler of Britain's vast empire. When she occupied her castle at Balmoral, Scotland, she was in the habit of calling, in a friendly way, upon certain cottagers living in the neighborhood. One aged Highland woman, who felt greatly honored by these visits and who knew the Lord, was anxious about the soul of the queen. As the season came to a close one year, Her Majesty was making her last visit to the humble home of this dear child of God. After the good-byes were said, the old cottager timidly inquired, "May I ask Your Gracious Majesty a question?"

"Yes," replied the queen, "as many as you like."

"Will Your Majesty meet me in heaven?"

Instantly the royal visitor replied, "I will, through the all-availing blood of Jesus."

That is the only safe ground for assurance. The blood shed on Calvary avails for all classes alike.

When Israel of old was about to leave Egypt, and the last awful plague was to fall on that land and its people, God Himself provided a way of escape for His own. They were to slay a lamb, sprinkle its blood on the doorposts and lintel of their houses, go inside, and shut the door. When the destroying angel passed through that night, he would not be permitted to enter any blood-sprinkled door, for Jehovah had said, "When I see the blood, I will pass over you." Inside the house, some might have been trembling and some rejoicing, but all were safe. Their security depended, not on their frames of mind or feelings, but on the fact that the eye of God beheld the blood of the lamb and they were sheltered behind it. As they recalled the word that He had given concerning it and truly believed it, they would have much assurance.

So it is today! We cannot see the blood shed so long ago for our redemption on Calvary, but there is a sense in which it is ever before the eye of God. The moment a repentant sinner puts his trust in Christ, he is viewed by God as sheltered behind the blood-sprinkled lintel.

HENRY A. IRONSIDE

SHORT TALKS

The Precious Blood

The blood of Christ is precious, because it justifies me. "Being now justified by his blood, we shall be saved from wrath through him" (Romans 5:9).

I haven't been able to climb up to the height of that word, *justified*. Do you know what it means? It is better than pardon. Justification means that there isn't a charge against you. Your sins are completely wiped out; they are not to be remembered; they are not to be mentioned. Think of it! God says He puts them out of His memory.

I have been running up an account down at the grocery store for some years, and I haven't any money to pay. I go down there, and the storekeeper says: "Mr. Moody, I have good news for you. A friend of yours came here today and paid the whole bill; it is all settled."

That is justification. "Who shall lay anything to the charge of God's elect? It is God that justifieth." God won't do it; He would be a strange judge if He justified a man and then brought a charge against him.

"Who is he that condemneth? It is Christ that died, yea, rather that is risen again." Thank God for the precious blood that justifies me. No wonder when that truth dawned on Martin Luther, he rose and he shook all Europe.

It is precious because it cleanses me. "If we walk in the light, as he is in the light, we have fellowship one with another, and the blood of Jesus Christ his Son cleanseth us from all sin" (1 John 1:7).

The blood of Jesus Christ cleanses from all sin. Think of it. Not a part of our sin, but *all*. We Christians ought to be the happiest people in the world.

And it is precious because it is going to give me boldness in the day of judgment. Isn't that good?

Do you know I pity these people who live all their lifetime under the bondage of death. If I am behind the blood of the Son of God, judgment is already passed; it is behind me; it is not before me. Know you not that you shall judge the world? People live in constant dread of the great white throne judgment. When that comes, I am going to be with Christ on the throne; I am not going to be judged!

D. L. MOODY

FIVE "MUSTS" OF THE CHRISTIAN LIFE

Reckon on God's Faithfulness

Reckon, or depend, on God for answers to prayer. Once you have handed the matter over to God, thoughtfully and deliberately, you must dare to believe that He has taken it in hand and that, though He may keep you waiting, He will not be at rest until He has finished it. The Lord will perfect that which concerneth me: His mercy endureth forever: He will not forsake the work of His own hands.

Prayer is the cooperation of the human spirit with the divine. As a slight noise will sometimes dislodge an avalanche, so the prayer of faith sets in motion the power of the ascended Christ. Believing prayer supplies the fulcrum on which God rests the lever of His omnipotence. In prayer there is union between the divine and the human so that, as the human body of our Lord provided the channels along which the divine life-power was able to reach us, the prayer of faith opens a wide channel by which God's grace and providence may come to man.

Effective prayer has two characteristics. First, we must allow the Holy Spirit to winnow away what is inconsistent with God's will. We cannot impose our will on God, but must wait for the solution of our life problems, which He will most certainly grant, sometimes by a flash, at other times by the slow unfolding of His will. When we cannot solve our problem in our own way, we must trust Him to deal with it in a better way; and He cannot fail. Second, we must cease to worry. However long the interval, however strong the combination of adverse circumstances, we may still our hearts, in the patience of unwavering faith, sure that our Lord will not rest until He has finished the matter in hand, which we have entrusted to Him.

Never forget to reckon on God's faithfulness! That anchorage will never fail to hold.

F. B. MEYER

SALVATION FROM START TO FINISH

The Nature of Growth

The Holy Spirit is a great teacher, who when He begins a subject completes it. That is the reason we should always study a text in the light of its context in order to learn the mind of the Spirit.

For example, in 2 Peter 1 He not only tells us the basis and the means of Christian growth, but also describes its nature. In the simplest terms He reveals how we may know whether it is being accomplished in us or not:

"And beside this, giving all diligence, add to your faith virtue; and to virtue, knowledge; and to knowledge, temperance; and to temperance, patience; and to patience, godliness; and to godliness, brotherly kindness; and to brotherly kindness, charity" (verses 5–7).

Here is a superstructure of seven stories we are to erect upon the great, broad, deep foundation of our faith.

This faith has been given us of God underlying our whole spiritual life, and now we are to add to it virtue. This does not mean that we can add to it by our own strength or ability, but only through the grace of God assisting us; and yet nevertheless, there is a real and important sense in which the work is ours, or we could not be exhorted to it in this way.

The Revised Version states it thus: "Yea, and for this very cause, adding on your part all diligence, in your faith supply virtue."

That is, on account of these "exceeding great and precious promises" of God, because of their help to you, because of what they are meant to accomplish in comforming you to the divine nature, because of your need of them to escape "the corruption that is in the world through lust," Peter tells us, "for this very cause, adding on your part all diligence."

That which we add, in other words, is not virtue but diligence. The first comes from God, but the latter is the means we should exercise to obtain it. We add the diligence and the result is a "supply" of virtue.

JAMES M. GRAY

THE OVERCOMING LIFE

The Complete Victor

Ye are of God, little children, and have overcome them, because greater is he that is in you, than he that is in the world." The only man that ever conquered this world—was complete victor—was Jesus Christ. When He shouted on the cross, "It is finished!" it was the shout of a conqueror. He had overcome every enemy. He had met sin and death. He had met every foe that you and I have to meet and had come off victor. Now if I have got the spirit of Christ, if I have got that same life in me, then it is that I have got a power that is greater than any power in the world, and with that same power I overcome the world.

Notice that everything human in this world fails. Every man, the moment he takes his eye off God, has failed. Every man has been a failure at some period of his life. Abraham failed. Moses failed. Elijah failed. Take the men that have become so famous and that were so mighty—the moment they got their eye off God, they were weak like other men; and it is a very singular thing that those men failed on the strongest point in their character. I suppose it was because they were not on the watch.

Abraham was noted for his faith, and he failed right there—he denied his wife. Moses was noted for his meekness and humility, and he failed right there—he got angry. God kept him out of the promised land because he lost his temper. I know he was called "the servant of God" and that he was a mighty man and had power with God, but, humanly speaking, he failed and was kept out of the promised land. Elijah was noted for his power in prayer and for his courage, yet he became a coward. He was the boldest man of his day and stood before Ahab and the royal court and all the prophets of Baal; yet when he heard that Jezebel had threatened his life, he ran away to the desert and under a juniper tree prayed that he might die.

Peter was noted for his boldness, and a little maid scared him nearly out of his wits. As soon as she spoke to him, he began to tremble, and he swore that he didn't know Christ. I have often said to myself that I'd like to have been there on the day of Pentecost alongside of that maid when she saw Peter preaching.

D. L. MOODY

SATAN AND THE SAINT

The Kingdom of Darkness

Satan is the head of a kingdom of great power, called in the Scriptures "the kingdom of darkness." In this kingdom there are legions of evil angels and demons who do his will. For instance, in Colossians 2:14–15, Paul describes Christ as "blotting out the handwriting of ordinances that was against us, which was contrary to us, and took it out of the way, nailing it to his cross; and having spoiled principalities and powers." By *principalities and powers* is meant those evil areas of which Satan is the head. But we are also told that Christ "made a show of them openly, triumphing over them in it," that is, in the cross. The idea seems to be that these evil principalities and powers laid hold of Christ, if possible to prevent His going to the cross for our redemption. And that Christ, as the result of His faith in God, overcame them, or, as the Revised Version puts it, "threw them off from him," as though they were hanging on to Him in their desperate determination that He should not do the will of His Father.

What is said of Christ in this connection is said of us who are members of Christ: "For we wrestle not against flesh and blood, but against principalities, against powers, against the rulers of the darkness of this world, against spiritual wickedness in high places" (Ephesians 6:12). This means those "heavenly places" where we found Satan himself in the book of Job. These same rulers of darkness are those with whom we, as the saints of God and disciples of Christ, are contending today in our spiritual conflict.

In Revelation 12, we find that a day is coming when there shall be a war in those heavenly places, when those evil principalities and powers, with Satan at their head, shall be in conflict with the hosts of light with the archangel Michael at their head. As the result, Satan and his hosts shall be cast down to this earth. Then it is that the culmination of iniquity on this earth shall take place, which can be put away only by the coming of the Son of Man Himself.

JAMES M. GRAY

THE OVERCOMING LIFE

Internal Foes

If you really want to get control, I will tell you how, but you won't like the medicine. Treat it as a sin and confess it. People look upon it as a sort of a misfortune. One lady told me she inherited it from her father and mother. Supposing she did; that is no excuse for her.

When you get angry again and speak unkindly to a person, and when you realize it, go and ask that person to forgive you. You won't get mad with that person for the next twenty-four hours. You might do it in about forty-eight hours, but go the second time, and after you have done it about half a dozen times, you will get out of the business, because it makes the old flesh burn.

A lady said to me once, "I have got so in the habit of exaggerating that my friends accuse me of exaggerating so that they don't understand me."

She said, "Can you help me? What can I do to overcome it?"

"Well," I said, "the next time you catch yourself lying, go right to that party and say you have lied, and tell him you are sorry. Say it is a lie; stamp it out, root and branch; that is what you want to do."

"Oh," she said, "I wouldn't like to call it lying." But that is what it is.

Christianity isn't worth a snap of your finger if it doesn't straighten out your character. I have got tired of all mere gush and sentiment. If people can't tell when you are telling the truth, there is something radically wrong, and you had better straighten it out right away. Now, are you ready to do it? Bring yourself to it whether you want to or not. Do you find someone who has been offended by something you have done? Go right to the person and say you are sorry. "But I'm not to blame," you say. Never mind, go right to them and tell them you are sorry. I have had to do it a good many times. An impulsive man like myself has to do it often, but I sleep all the sweeter at night when I get things straightened out.

Confession never fails to bring a blessing. I have sometimes had to get off the platform and go down and ask a man's forgiveness before I could go on preaching. A Christian man ought to be a gentleman every time; but if he is not, and he finds he has wounded or hurt someone, he ought to go and straighten it out at once.

D. L. MOODY

SALVATION FROM START TO FINISH

Christ, Our Sin Bearer

The great Huxley is reported to have said that if there were some being, or some power, to whom he could turn over his nature, by which of course, he meant his will, to have it regulated like a clock, and kept regulated, he would hand it over immediately and absolutely.

This agnostic did not know that there was such a Being to whom his nature, or his will, might be thus surrendered, to be set right and to be kept right.

That Being is the eternal Son of God, who cries to the needs of Huxley and others: "Come unto me, all ye that labor and are heavy-laden, and I will give you rest. Take my yoke upon you, and learn of me; for I am meek and lowly in heart: and ye shall find rest unto your souls" (Matthew 11:28–29).

The man who believes in Jesus Christ in the gospel sense of that term commits and surrenders himself to Him absolutely, eternally, irreversibly. And Jesus Christ takes him and regenerates him. And the man finds rest, and he has peace.

If his will were still his own, the risk of loss would be his own. But since his will has been handed over to Jesus Christ, he is "persuaded that he is able to keep that which has been committed unto him against that day" (2 Timothy 1:12).

But there is something more than bare commitment and preservation here. The One to whom we are returned is "the Shepherd and Bishop of our souls." A shepherd not only keeps his sheep, but tends and feeds them. He causes the sheep to lie down in green pastures and leads them beside still waters. He restores the sheep when wounded. He comforts them in danger. He defends them when attacked. He showers his love upon them. His goodness towards them never fails.

All this our reconciled God and Savior is, and does, to us. All this is involved in our being returned to Him; all this is included in the work of the atonement, and all this has been purchased for us by the merits of His shed blood. Who would not commit himself unto Him to be saved and to be kept?

JAMES M. GRAY

SHORT TALKS

Heavenly Fire

From the time God met Moses at the burning bush, Moses became one of the greatest leaders this world ever had. But first, Isaiah and Job and Jeremiah and Moses—all of them had to fall before God and see their utter unfitness for the work.

Have you who have gone into Christian work ever had any such experience? Have you ever passed through the furnace and been taught by the Spirit of God that your natural gifts go for naught unless you have the fire of heaven in your soul? You can't go on heavenly missions without heavenly fire. When Isaiah saw the vision of God's glory he said, "Woe is me! for I am undone; because I am a man of unclean lips, and I dwell in the midst of a people of unclean lips; for mine eyes have seen the King, the Lord of Hosts." Death to self; that is what it means. The first step to a higher service is the end of self. God's way up is down. God never yet lifted up a man high that He did not cast down first. Self must be annihilated. When we get to the end of our own power, then the power of God can be manifested in us.

People say they haven't strength and wisdom, therefore they should lean upon God's strength and God's wisdom!

You ask, "How am I to humble myself and get to the end of myself?" I will tell you. One look at God does the work. Isaiah saw God lifted high on His throne; and what a blessing he has been all these centuries. Why? Because he was purified by the God of heaven and received a divine call.

Let this purifying process go on. If there is something wrong in your life, make up your mind you are going to get right, first of all. No man or woman is ready to receive the gifts of God until the heart is right.

D. L. MOODY

THE CHRIST-LIFE FOR THE SELF-LIFE

A Castaway

But we must begin at the bottom; we must begin at the root of our self-confidence. The prime cause of all failure in private life as well as in public ministry is the assertion of self. As long as men and women think it is all right with them, nothing can be done for them. It is only when there is excited within them a fear that, after all, things may not be quite so well as they seem, a dread that, after all, they may have made a mistake and be self-deceived —only then, in the secret of their own chambers, they begin to ask God: "Am I just what I expected?" It is then that the heart is laid open, and they are brought to understand how a man may be almost a castaway and yet be taken back to the bosom of Christ as Peter was; for within six weeks the man who was nearly cast away became the Apostle of Pentecost.

Paul said, "Lest . . . I myself should be a castaway." He knew he had a perfect right to go to an idol temple, but chose not to go for fear that other men seeing him might follow him, and that what might be innocent to him might be death to them. He knew he had rights as a Christian, but chose to abstain rather than possibly ruining a man's soul by going. He may well have thought, *I have a perfect right, if I choose, to take a wife; but I shall not do it. I will live a bachelor life, and toil with my hands, because by being lonesome myself I may touch some other man who is lonesome too, and by working with my own hands I shall stay upon the bench beside others who will be drawn to me by sympathy. There are many things this body of mine may have in innocence, but I shall not take them because I wish to keep my body under, lest it should master me and cause me to be a castaway.*

Christ waits—the sweet, strong, pure Son of God, His heart yearning over men and yearning to pour itself through us to save them. But many of us have choked Him, resisted Him, thwarted Him. One feels like asking the whole audience to fall before Him in confession and to ask that this holy day may not pass until He has restored us to fellowship with Himself.

F. B. MEYER

THE SCHOOL OF OBEDIENCE

The Life of Full Obedience

Christ revealed the new law of love to be merciful as the Father in heaven, to forgive just as He does, to love enemies and to do good to them that hate us, and to live lives of self-sacrifice and beneficence. This was the religion Jesus taught on earth.

When we are provoked or ill-used, let us look upon an unforgiving spirit, upon unloving thoughts and sharp or unkind words, upon the neglect of the call to show mercy and do good and bless, all as so much disobedience. As such, our disobedience must be felt and mourned over and plucked out like a right eye; only then can the power of a full obedience be ours.

Christ spoke much of self-denial. Self is the root of all lack of love and obedience. Our Lord called each disciple to deny him- or herself and to take up the cross, forsake self and become the servant of all. Christ issued the call because self—self-will, self-pleasing, self-seeking—is simply the source of all sin.

When we indulge the flesh in such a simple thing as eating and drinking, when we gratify self by seeking or accepting or rejoicing in what indulges our pride, when self-will is allowed to assert itself and we make provision for the fulfillment of its desire, we are guilty of disobedience to His command. This gradually clouds the soul and makes the full enjoyment of His light and peace an impossibility.

Christ claimed for God the love of the whole heart. For Himself He equally claimed the sacrifices of all to come and follow Him. The Christian who has not definitely at heart made this his aim, who has not determined to seek for grace so to live, is guilty of disobedience. There may be much in his religion that appears good and earnest, but he cannot possibly have the joyful consciousness of knowing that he is doing the will of his Lord, and keeping His commandments.

ANDREW MURRAY

SOVEREIGN GRACE

Penance for Sin

A nd what have we that we can offer to God in return for His free gift of salvation? Less than nothing. We must come and take salvation in God's way.

There is no merit in taking a gift. If a beggar comes to my house and asks for bread to eat, and I give him a loaf of bread, there is no merit in his taking the bread. So if you experience the favor of God, you have to take it as a beggar. Someone has said, "If you come to God as a prince, you go away as a beggar; if you come as a beggar, you go away as a prince." It is to the needy that God opens the wardrobe of heaven and brings out the robe of righteousness.

Paul says again: "If by grace, then it is no more of works; otherwise grace is no more grace. But if it be of works, then it is no more grace; otherwise work is no more work." Paul is reasoning in this way: if I work for a gift or attempt to give money for it, it ceases to be a gift. The only way to get a gift is to take it as a gift.

An old man got up in one of our meetings and said, "I have been forty-two years learning three things." I pricked up my ears at that; I thought that if I could find out in about three minutes what a man had taken forty-two years to learn, I should like to do it. The first thing he said he had learned was that he could do nothing toward his own salvation. "Well," said I to myself, "that is worth learning." The second thing he had found out was that God did not require him to do anything. Well, that was worth finding out too. And the third thing was that the Lord Jesus Christ had done it all, that salvation was finished, and that all he had to do was to take it.

Dear friends, let us learn this lesson; let us give up our struggling and striving and accept salvation at once.

D. L. MOODY

THE SECRET OF GUIDANCE

The Mystery

Christ is in the believer. He indwells the heart by faith, as the sun indwells the lowliest flowers that unfurl their petals and bare their hearts to its beams. Not because we are good. Not because we are trying to be whole-hearted in our consecration. Not because we keep Him by the tenacity of our love. But because we believe, and in believing we have thrown open all the doors and windows of our nature. And He has come in.

He probably came in so quietly that we failed to detect His entrance. There was no footfall along the passage. The chime of the golden bells at the foot of His priestly robe did not betray Him. He stole in on the wing of the morning, or like the noiselessness with which nature arises from her winter's sleep and arrays herself in the robes that her Creator has prepared for her. But this is the way of Christ. He does not strive, nor cry, nor lift up or cause His voice to be heard. His tread is so light that it does not break bruised reeds; His breath so soft that it can re-illumine dying sparks. Do not be surprised, therefore, if you cannot tell the day or the hour when the Son of Man came to dwell within you. Only know that He has come. "Know ye not as to your own selves, that Jesus Christ is in you, unless indeed ye be reprobate?" (2 Corinthians 13:5 RV).

It is very wonderful. Yes; the heavens, even the heavens of heavens, with all their light and glory, alone seem worthy of Him. But even there He is not more at home than He is with the humble and contrite spirit that simply trusts in Him. In His earthly life, He said that the Father dwelt in Him so fully that the words He spoke and the works He did were not His own but His Father's. Further, He desires to be in us as His Father was in Him, so that the outgoings of our life may be channels through which He, hidden within, may pour Himself forth upon men.

F. B. MEYER

HEAVEN

Heaven—Its Certainty

Rejoice not that the spirits are subject unto you; but rather rejoice because your names are written in heaven." This brings us face to face with the doctrine of assurance.

I find a great many people up and down Christendom who do not accept this doctrine. They believe it is impossible for us to know in this life whether we are saved or not. If this be true, how are we going to get over what Christ has said as we find it here recorded? If my name is written in heaven, how can I rejoice over it unless I know it? These men were to rejoice that their names were already there, and the name of each one who is a child of God is there, sent on for registry ahead of our arrival there.

A few years ago a party of Americans on their way from London to Liverpool decided that they would stop at the Northwestern Hotel, but when they arrived they found the place had been full for several days. Greatly disappointed, they took up their baggage and were about to start off when they noticed a lady of the party preparing to remain.

"Are you not going, too?" they asked.

"Oh, no," she said, "I have good rooms all ready."

"Why, how did that happen?"

"Oh," she said, "I telegraphed on ahead, a few days ago."

Now that is what the children of God are doing; they are sending their names on ahead; they are securing places in the mansions of Christ in time. If we are truly children of God our names have gone on before, and there will be places awaiting us at the end of the journey. You know we are only travelers down here. We are away from home. When war is going on, the soldiers on the battlefield want nothing better to live in than tents. They long for the war to close that they might go home. They care nothing to have palaces and mansions on the battlefield. Well, there is a terrible battle going on now, and by and by, when the war is over, God will call us home. The tents are good enough for us while journeying through this world. It is only a night, and then the eternal day will dawn.

D. L. MOODY

LIGHT ON LIFE'S DUTIES

Repentance

True repentance shows itself in eager care not to offend again. This care prompts the sinner to go back on his past life to discover how it was that he came to sin, and to avoid the cause.

Is it a friendship? Then he will cut the tender cord, though it were the thread of his life.

Is it an amusement? Then he will forever absent himself from that place, those scenes, and that companionship.

Is it a profitable means of making money? Then he will rather live on a crust than follow it a moment longer.

Is it a study, a pursuit, a book? Then he will rather lose hand or foot or eye than miss the favor of God, which is life.

Is it something that the church permits? Nevertheless, to him if it be sin, he will discard it.

If you cannot walk on ice without slipping or falling, it is better not to go on at all. If you cannot digest certain food, it is better not to put it into the mouth. It may seem impossible to extricate yourself from certain entanglements that have woven themselves about you. Nevertheless, remember Him who said, "Let my people go, that they may serve me." He cut the knot for them, and if you trust Him, He will cut it for you. Or if He does not cut it at a single blow, He will untie it by the patient workings of His providence.

Take any public step that may be necessary. It is not enough to confess to God; you must also confess to man, supposing that you have sinned against him. Leave your gift at the altar and go to be reconciled to thy brother. If you have done him a wrong, go and tell him so. If you have defrauded him, whether he knows or not, send him the amount you have taken or kept back, and add to it something to compensate him for his loss.

F. B. MEYER

THE WAY OF LIFE

The Great Arbitration Case

Neither is there any arbitrator betwixt us, that might lay his hand upon us both" (Job 9:33). What Job desired to have, the Lord has provided for us in the person of His own dear Son, Jesus Christ. We cannot say with Job that there is no arbitrator who can lay his hand upon both, because there is now "one mediator between God and man, the man Christ Jesus." In Him let us rejoice, if indeed we have an interest in Him; and if we have not yet received Him, may almighty grace bring us even now to accept Him as our advocate and friend.

There is an old quarrel between the thrice holy God and His sinful subjects, the sons of Adam. Man has sinned; he has broken God's law in every part of it and has wantonly cast off from him the allegiance that is due to his Maker and his King. There is a suit against man, which was formally instituted at Sinai and must be pleaded in court before the Judge of the quick and the dead. God is the great plaintiff against His sinful creatures, who are the defendants. If that suit be carried into court, it must go against the sinner. There is no hope whatever that at the last tremendous day any sinner will be able to stand in judgment if he shall leave the matter of his debts and obligations toward his God unsettled until that dreadful hour.

Sinner, it would be well for thee to "agree with thine adversary quickly while thou art in the way," for if you be once delivered up to the great Judge of all the earth, there is not the slightest hope that thy suit can be decided otherwise than to thine eternal ruin. "Weeping, and wailing, and gnashing of teeth," will be the doom adjudged thee forever if thy case before the living God shall ever come to be tried at the fiery throne of absolute justice. But the infinite grace of God proposes an arbitration, and I trust you are not anxious to have your suit carried into court but are willing that the appointed arbitrator should stand between you and God and lay His hand upon both and propose and carry out a plan of reconciliation. Though you be a bankrupt sinner, there is hope for you. You may yet find peace with God. There is a way by which your debts may yet be paid. That way is a blessed arbitration in which Jesus Christ shall stand as the arbitrator.

CHARLES H. SPURGEON

SOVEREIGN GRACE

Worthiness

In Luke's gospel we read of the centurion who had a sick servant. He felt as though he were not worthy to go himself and ask Christ to come to his house, so he asked some of his friends to beseech the Master to come and heal his servant. They went and delivered the centurion's message, saying, "He is worthy for whom thou shouldest do this: for he loveth our nation, and he hath built us a synagogue." The Jews could not understand grace; so they thought Christ would grant the request of this man because he was worthy. "Why," they said, "he hath built us a synagogue!" It is the same old story that we hear today. Let a man give a few thousand dollars to build a church and he must have the best pew; "he is worthy." Perhaps he made his money by selling or making strong drink: but he has put the church under an obligation by this gift of money, and he is considered "worthy." The same spirit was at work in the days of Christ.

The Master immediately started for the centurion's house, and it looked as though He was going because of his personal worthiness. But if He had done so, it would have upset the whole story as an illustration of grace. As the Savior was on the way, out came the Roman officer himself and told Jesus that he was not worthy to receive Him under his roof. He had a very different opinion of himself to that of his Jewish friends. Suppose he had said, "Lord, you will be my guest; come and heal my servant because I am worthy: I have built a synagogue." Do you think Christ would have gone? I do not think He would. But he said, "I am not worthy that Thou shouldst enter under my roof. Neither thought I myself worthy to come unto Thee, but say in a word, and my servant shall be healed."

Jesus marveled at the man's faith. It pleased Him wonderfully to find such faith and humility. Like the Syro-Phoenician woman, he had low thoughts of himself and high thoughts of God; therefore he was in a condition to receive the grace of God.

Let us learn a lesson from this man and take a humble position before God, crying to Him for mercy; then help will come.

D. L. MOODY

THE CHRIST-LIFE FOR THE SELF-LIFE

Christ, the Living, Bright Reality

Spirit of God, infill, *infill* my entire being, deeper, deeper, deeper yet. In the depth of my nature, when I am least thinking about it, go on day by day as the antiseptic of my flesh or self-life. Antagonize it, work against it, keep it out of sight, keep it under Christ."

The Holy Ghost will do it.

But you say: "Mr. Meyer, I am so afraid that if I am always dealing with the self-life, it will hurt me. It will be like standing by a bier and seeing death disintegrate a corpse."

I reply—and this is the beauty of it—that while the Spirit of God in the depth of your heart is antagonizing the self-life, He does it by making Jesus Christ a living, bright reality. He fixes your thoughts upon Jesus. You do not think about the Spirit, you hardly think about self, but you think much about your dear Lord; and all the time that you are thinking about Him, the process of disintegration and dissolution and death of self is going on within your heart.

A dear sister said to me once: "I am going to spend a whole day praying for the Holy Ghost."

She went to a hut in a wood, and she came back to me at night and said, "I have had a grand day, but I am a bit disappointed. I do not feel that I have more of the Holy Ghost now than I did."

"But," I said, "is Jesus much to you?"

"Oh," she replied, "Jesus never was so sweet and precious as He is now."

"Why, my dear woman," I said, "that is the Holy Ghost, because He glorifies Christ, and when the Holy Ghost works most, you do not think about the Holy Ghost, but you think about your dear Lord."

The Holy Spirit may make you know what it is to have Jesus as the center and origin of your life. The fountain hitherto has been self. O, cursed self! The world says: "Not Christ, but Barabbas, self." The Christian says: "Not Barabbas, but Christ." Let us send Barabbas to the cross. Let us free Christ to live in us.

F. B. MEYER

SOWING AND REAPING

We Reap What We Sow

Do we desire the love of our fellows in our seasons of trial? Then we must love them when they need its cheering influence most. Do we long for sympathy in our sorrow and pain? Then we shall have it if we have also wept with those who weep. Are we hoping to reap eternal life? Then we must not sow to the flesh, or we shall reap corruption. Instead, let us sow to the Spirit so that we shall reap its immortal fruits, as God's Word promises.

Dr. Chalmers has drawn attention to the difference between the act of sowing and the act of reaping. "Let it be observed," he says, "that the act of indulging in the desires of the flesh is one thing and the act of providing for the indulgence is another. When a man, on the impulse of sudden provocation, wreaks his resentful feelings upon the neighbor who has offended him, he is not at that time preparing for the indulgence of a carnal feeling, but actually indulging it. He is not at that time sowing, but reaping (such as it is) a harvest of gratification.

"This distinction may serve to assist our judgment in estimating the ungodliness of certain characters. The rambling voluptuary who is carried along by every impulse, and all whose powers of mental discipline are so enfeebled that he has become the slave of every propensity, lives in the perpetual harvest of criminal gratification. A daughter whose sole delight is her rapid transitions from one scene of expensive brilliancy to another, who dissipates every care and fills every hour among the frivolities and fascinations of her volatile society— she leads a life that cannot prepare her for the coming judgment or the coming eternity. Yet she reaps rather than sows."

According to Chalmers, often it is her father who has sown. "He sits in busy and brooding anxiety over his speculations, wrinkled, perhaps, by care and sobered by years into utter distaste for the splendors and insignificances of fashionable life. The father sows, and he reaps in his daughter's life."

D. L. MOODY

THE SECOND COMING OF CHRIST
Seen of All

Handle me, and see; for a spirit hath not flesh and bones, as ye see me have." This same Jesus, with a material body, is to come in the clouds of heaven. In the same manner as He went up, He shall come down. He shall be literally seen. The words cannot be honestly read in any other way: "Every eye shall see Him."

Yes, I do literally expect to see my Lord Jesus with these eyes of mine, even as that saint expected who long ago fell asleep, believing that though the worms devour his body, yet in his flesh should he see God, whom his eyes should see for himself, and not another. There will be a real resurrection of the body, though the moderns doubt it; such a resurrection that we shall see Jesus with our own eyes. We shall not find ourselves in a shadowy, dreamy land of floating fictions, where we may perceive but cannot see. We shall not be airy nothings, mysterious, vague, impalpable; but we shall literally see our glorious Lord, whose appearing will be no phantom show or shadow dance. Never day more real than the day of judgment; never sight more true than the Son of Man upon the throne of His glory.

We are getting too far away from facts nowadays and too much into the realm of myths and notions. However, "every eye shall see Him"; in this there shall be no delusion.

Note well that He is to be seen of all kinds of living men; every eye shall see Him; the king and the peasant, the most learned and the most ignorant. Those that were blind before shall see when He appears. I remember a man born blind who loved our Lord most intensely, and he was wont to glory in this—that his eyes had been reserved for his Lord. He said, "The first whom I shall ever see will be the Lord Jesus Christ. The first sight that greets my newly-opened eyes will be the Son of man in His glory."

CHARLES H. SPURGEON

THE SCHOOL OF OBEDIENCE

The Obedience of Faith

When I read the gospel story and see how ready the sick and the blind and the needy were to believe Christ's word, I often ask myself what it was that made them so much more ready to believe than we are. The answer I get in the Word is this, that one great difference lies in the honesty and intensity of the desire. They did indeed desire deliverance with their whole heart. There was no need of pleading with them to make them willing to take His blessing.

Alas, that it should be so different with us! All indeed wish, in a sort of way, to be better than they are. But how few there are who really "hunger and thirst after righteousness"; how few intensely long and cry after a life of close obedience and the continual consciousness of being pleasing to God.

There can be no strong faith without strong desire. Desire is the great motivating power in the universe. It was God's desire to save us that moved Him to send His Son. It is desire that moves men to study and work and suffer. It is alone the desire for salvation that brings a sinner to Christ. It is the desire for God and the closest possible fellowship with Him, the desire to be just what He would have us be and to have as much of His will as possible, that will make the promised land attractive to us. It is this that will make us forsake everything to get our full share in the obedience of Christ.

And how can the desire be awakened?

Shame on us that we need to ask the question, that the most desirable of all things—likeness to God in the union with His will and doing it—has so little attraction for us. Let us stake it as a sign of our blindness and dullness and beseech God to give us by His Spirit "enlightened eyes of the heart," that we may see and know "the riches of the glory of our inheritance" waiting upon the life of true obedience. Let us turn and gaze, in this light of God's Spirit, and gaze again on the life as possible, as divinely blessed, until our faith begins to burn with desire, and to say: "I do long to have it. With my whole heart will I seek it."

ANDREW MURRAY

THE EMPTY TOMB

Old Testament Resurrections

We only catch glimpses of the doctrine of the resurrection now and then in the Old Testament, but the saints of those days evidently believed in it. Nearly two thousand years before Christ, Abraham rehearsed His sacrifice on Mount Moriah when he obeyed God's call to offer up Isaac. Referring to this Paul writes: "accounting that God was able to raise [Isaac] up, even from the dead: from whence also he received him in a figure." Five hundred years later, we find God saying unto His servant Moses: "I kill, and I make alive."

Later still, Isaiah wrote, "He will swallow up death in victory, and the Lord God will wipe away tears from off all faces." Isaiah also declared, "Thy dead men shall live; together with my dead body shall they rise. Awake and sing, ye that dwell in the dust; for thy dew is as the dew of herbs, and the earth shall cast out the dead." Ezekiel's vivid description of the resurrection of dry bones, setting forth in prophecy the restoration of Israel, is other evidence.

When David lost his child, he said he could not call the little one back to him, but that he would go and be with the child. At other times he wrote, "As for me, I will behold thy face in righteousness; I shall be satisfied when I awake with thy likeness"; and "God will redeem my soul from the power of the grave; for he shall receive me."

The patriarch Job comforted himself with the same glorious hope in the hour of his deep sorrow. He who had asked, "What is my strength that I should hope? and what is mine end that I should prolong my life?" said, "I know that my Redeemer liveth, and that he shall stand at the latter day upon the earth; and though after my skin worms destroy this body, yet in my flesh shall I see God; whom I shall see for myself, and mine eyes shall behold, and not another." Job must have firmly believed that his body was to be raised to life again, hereafter but not on earth, for "there is hope for a tree," he said again, "if it be cut down, that it will sprout again, and that its tender branch will not cease. Though its root wax old in the earth, and its stalk die in the ground, yet at the scent of water it will bud, and bring forth boughs like a plant."

D. L. MOODY

THE SECOND COMING OF CHRIST

Occupy Till I Come

What is the present duty of all Christ's professing disciples? When I speak of present duty, I mean, of course, their duty between the period of Christ's first and second advents. I find an answer in the words of the nobleman, in the parable, to his servants, "He delivered them ten pounds, and said unto them, Occupy till I come."

Few words are more searching and impressive than these four: "Occupy till I come." They are spoken to all who profess and call themselves Christians. And they address everyone who has not formally turned his back on Christianity. They ought to stir up all hearers of the gospel to examine themselves whether they are in the faith and to prove themselves. For your sake, remember, these words were written: "Occupy till I come."

The Lord Jesus bids you to "occupy." By that He means that you are to be "a doer" in your Christianity and not merely a hearer and professor. He wants His servants not only to receive His wages and eat His bread and dwell in His house and belong to His family—but also to do His work. You are to "let your light so shine before men that they may see your good works." Have you faith? It must not be a dead faith; it must "work by love." Do you love Christ? Prove the reality of your love by keeping Christ's commandments.

Do not forget this charge to "occupy." Beware of an idle, talking, gossiping, sentimental, do-nothing religion. Think not because your doings cannot justify you, or put away one single sin, that therefore it matters not whether you do anything at all. Away with such a delusion! Cast it behind you as an invention of the devil. As ever you would "make your calling and election sure," be a doing Christian.

J. C. RYLE

SOVEREIGN GRACE

Peace, Grace, and Glory

There is a great deal of difference between law and grace. "Being justified by faith we have peace with God through our Lord Jesus Christ; by whom also we have access by faith into this grace wherein we stand, and rejoice in hope of the glory of God." There are three precious things here: peace for the past; grace for the present; and glory for the future. There is no peace until we see the finished work of Jesus Christ—until we can look back and see the cross of Christ between us and our sins. When we see that Jesus was "the end of the law for righteousness," that He "tasted death for every man," that He "suffered, the just for the unjust," then comes *peace*. Then there is "the *grace* wherein we now stand." There is plenty of grace for us as we need it—day by day, and hour by hour.

Then there is *glory* for the time to come. A great many people seem to forget that the best is before us. Dr. Bonar says that everything before the true believer is "glorious." This thought took hold of my soul; and I began to look the matter up and see what I could find in Scripture that was glorious hereafter. I found that the kingdom we are going to inherit is glorious: our crown is to be a "crown of glory"; the city we are going to inhabit is the city of the glorified; the songs we are to sing are the songs of the glorified; we are to wear garments of "glory and beauty." Furthermore, our society will be the society of the glorified; our rest is to be "glorious"; the country to which we are going is to be full of "the glory of God and of the Lamb."

Many are always looking on the backward path and mourning over the troubles through which they have passed. They keep lugging up the cares and anxieties they have been called on to bear and are forever looking at them. Why should we go reeling and staggering under the burdens and cares of life when we have such prospects before us?

If there is nothing but glory beyond, our faces ought to shine brightly all the time.

D. L. MOODY

THE CHRIST-LIFE FOR THE SELF-LIFE

Holy Spirit Power

They tell me that George Macdonald, wanting to teach his children honor and truth and trust, places on the mantel of the common room in their house money enough for the whole use of his family. If the wife wants money she goes for it, if the boys and girls want money they go for it; whatever want there is in that house is supplied from that mantelshelf deposit. So God put in Jesus everything the soul can want, and He says: "Go and take it. It is all there for you."

Are you in sorrow? In Christ there is joy. Are you tempted? In Christ there is solace. Are you at the end of your strength? In Jesus there is might. I recall those words, however, because you might think that God gives this or that apart from Christ. Let me put it more correctly: you take Christ, and He is the supply of your want, your need, so that you are blessed with all spiritual blessings in Christ in heavenly places. All that you want is in Christ, and I think it is a good thing to have want in order to learn what there is in Christ.

When I was a boy my mother never took so much notice of me as when I was disappointed, weak, ill, and worn. I think sometimes I used to sham a bit because my mother always did so much for me then. It is when you are weak and weary, and your faith has gone, and your strength is exhausted, and your hopes are vanishing, and everything around is passing from your grasp—it is then that God comes and says: "Child, I have put into Jesus everything your spirit wants"; and though, like Madam Guyon, you have to spend ten years in jail, Christ will be friends and comfort and strength and society—and all you want.

Would that people might understand what Jesus can be to the soul. For in Jesus they have mountains and lakes and rivers and streams and treasures and cornfields and olive yards—everything a soul can want to make it blessed. Spirit of God, take of the things of Christ and reveal them to every waiting heart.

F. B. MEYER

THE STORY OF THE PRODIGAL

The Turning Point

There is a time with sinners when even their old companions seem to say, "We do not want you. You are too miserable and melancholy. Why don't you go home?" They sent him to feed swine, and the very hogs grunted, "Go home!" When he picked up those carob husks and tried to eat them, they crackled, "Go home." His hungry belly and his faintness cried, "Go home." Then he thought of his father's face and how kindly it had looked at him, and it seemed to say, "Come home!" He remembered the bread enough and to spare, and every morsel seemed to say, "Come home!" He pictured the servants sitting down to dinner and feasting to the full and every one of them seemed to look right away over the wilderness to him, and to say, "Come home! Thy father feeds us well. Come home!"

Everything said, "Come home!" Only the devil whispered, "Never go back. Fight it out! Better starve than yield! Die game!"

"No; I will arise and go to my father."

Oh, that you would be equally wise! What is the use of being damned for the sake of a little pride? Yield, man! Down with your pride! You will not find it so hard to submit if you remember that dear Father who loved us and gave Himself for us in the person of His own dear Son. You will find it sweet to yield to such a friend. And when you get your head in His bosom and feel His warm kisses on your cheek, you will soon feel that it is sweet to weep for sin— sweet to confess your wrongdoing, and sweeter still to hear Him say, "I have blotted out thy sins like a cloud, and like a thick cloud thy transgressions." "Though your sins be as scarlet, they shall be as white as snow; though they be red like crimson, they shall be as wool."

CHARLES H. SPURGEON

TO THE WORK!

The Spirit of Revival

My experience has been that those who are converted in a time of special religious interest make even stronger Christians than those who were brought into the church at ordinary times. One young convert helps another, and they get a better start in the Christian life when there are a good many together.

People say the converts will not hold out. Well, they did not all hold out under the preaching of Jesus Christ: "Many of his disciples went back and walked no more with him." Paul mourned over the fact that some of those who made profession were walking as the enemies of the cross of Christ. The master taught in His wonderful parable that there are various kinds of hearers: those represented by the wayside hearers, the stony ground hearers, the thorny ground hearers, and the good ground hearers; they will remain to the end of time.

I have a fruit tree at my home, and every year it has so many blossoms that if they should all produce apples the tree would break down. Nine-tenths, perhaps, of the blossoms will fall off, and yet I have a large number of apples. So there are many who make a profession of Christianity who fall away. It may be that those who seemed to promise the fairest turn out the worst, and those who did not promise so well turn out best in the end. God must prepare the ground and He must give the increase. I have often said that if I had to convict men of sin I would have given up the work long ago. That is the work of the Holy Ghost. What we have to do is to scatter the good seed of the Word and expect that God will bless it to the saving of men's souls.

Of course, we cannot expect much help from those who are all the time talking against revivals. I believe many young disciples are chilled through by those who condemn these special efforts. If the professed converts sometimes do not hold out, it is not always their own fault.

D. L. MOODY

ANSWERS TO PRAYER

How to Read the Scriptures

If anyone should ask me how he may read the Scriptures most profitably, I would advise him: Above all, he should seek to have it settled in his own mind that God alone, by His Spirit, can teach him, and that therefore it becomes him to seek God's blessing previous to reading, and also while reading.

Second, he should have it settled in his mind that, although the Holy Spirit is the best and sufficient teacher, yet this teacher does not always teach immediately when we desire it, and that, therefore, we may have to entreat Him again and again for the explanation of certain passages; but He will surely teach us at last, if indeed we are seeking for light prayerfully, patiently, and with a view to the glory of God.

Third, it is of immense importance for the understanding of the Word of God, to read it in course, so that we may read every day a portion of the Old and a portion of the New Testament, going on where we previously left off. This is important because (1) it throws light upon the connection, and a different course, according to which one habitually selects particular chapters, will make it utterly impossible ever to understand much of the Scriptures; (2) while we are in the body, we need a change even in spiritual things, and this change the Lord had graciously provided in the great variety that is to be found in His Word; (3) it tends to the glory of God, for leaving out some chapters here and there is practically saying that certain portions are better than others, or that here are certain parts of revealed truth unprofitable or unnecessary; and (4) it may keep us, by the blessing of God, from erroneous views, as in reading thus regularly through the Scriptures we are led to see the meaning of the whole and also kept from laying too much stress upon certain favorite views.

Finally, the Scriptures contain the whole revealed will of God, and therefore we ought to seek to read from time to time through the whole of that revealed will. There are many believers, I fear, in our day, who have not read even once through the whole of the Scriptures; and yet in a few months, by reading only a few chapters every day they might accomplish it.

GEORGE MUELLER

THE SCHOOL OF OBEDIENCE

Entry into the School of Obedience

Though externally Christ's obedience unto death came at the end of His life, the spirit of His obedience was the same from the beginning. Whole-hearted obedience is not the end but the beginning of our school life. The end is fitness for God's service, when obedience has placed us fully at God's disposal. A heart yielded to God in unreserved obedience is the one condition of progress in Christ's school and of growth in the spiritual knowledge of God's will.

Remember God's rule: all for all. Give Him all—He will give you all. Consecration avails nothing unless it means presenting yourself as a living sacrifice to do nothing but the will of God. The vow of entire obedience is the entrance fee for him who would be enrolled by no assistant teacher, but by Christ Himself, in the school of obedience.

This unreserved surrender to obey, as it is the first condition of entering Christ's school, is the only fitness for receiving instruction as to the will of God for us.

There is a general will of God for all His children, which we can, in some measure, learn out of the Bible. But there is a special individual application of these commands—God's will concerning each of us personally—that only the Holy Spirit can teach. And He will not teach it, except to those who have taken the vow of obedience.

This is the reason why there are so many unanswered prayers for God to make known His will. Jesus said, "If any man wills to do His will, he shall know of the teaching, whether it be of God." If a man's will is really set on doing God's will, that is, if his heart is given up to do, and he as a consequence does it as far as he knows it, he shall know what God has further to teach him.

It is what is true of every scholar with the art he studies, of every apprentice with big trade, of every man in business: doing is the one condition of truly knowing. And so obedience, the doing of God's will as far as we know, and the will and the vow to do it all as He reveals it, is the spiritual organ for receiving the true knowledge of what is God's will for each of us.

ANDREW MURRAY

SOWING AND REAPING

God and Us Working Together

The "working out of salvation" is man's part in the work of salvation. God will not repent for the man, nor believe for the man, nor lead a holy life for the man. God works inwardly; man works outwardly. And this outward human work is as necessary as the inward divine work."

God works in us, and then we work for Him. If He has done a work in us, we certainly ought to go and work for others. A man must have this salvation, and must know it, before he can work for the salvation of others.

Many of you have tried hard to save yourselves; but what has been the end of it all? I remember a lady in northern England who became quite angry when I made this remark publicly: "No one in this congregation will be saved till they stop trying to save themselves." Down she came from the gallery and said to me: "You have made me perfectly miserable."

"Indeed," I said, "how is that?"

"Why, I always thought that if I kept on trying, God would save me at some time, and now you tell me to stop trying. What, then, am I to do?"

"Why, let the Lord save you."

She went off in something like a rage. It is not always a bad sign when you see a man or a woman wake up cross, if it is the Word of God that wakes them up. A day or two afterwards she came and thanked me. She said she had been turning over in her mind what I had said; and at last the truth dawned upon her that, though she had worked long, though she had formed a good many resolutions, she had made no progress. So she gave up the struggle; and then it was that the Lord Jesus saved her.

I want to ask you this question: If sin needs forgiveness—and all sin is against God—how can you work out your own forgiveness? If I stole $100 from a friend, I could not forgive myself, could I? No act of mine would bring about forgiveness, unless my friend forgave me. If I want forgiveness of sin, it must be the work of God. If we look at salvation as a new life, it must be the work of God. God is the author of life: you cannot give yourself life. That is what I read in the Bible—salvation is a gift.

D. L. MOODY

THE SECRET OF GUIDANCE
Waiting for God's Plan to Unfold

We must wait the gradual unfolding of God's plan in providence. God's impressions within and His Word without are always corroborated by His providence around, and we should quietly wait until these three focus into one point.

Sometimes it looks as if we are bound to act. Everyone says we must do something; and, indeed, things seem to have reached so desperate a pitch that we must. Behind are the Egyptians; right and left are inaccessible precipices; before is the sea. It is not easy at such times to stand still and see the salvation of God; but we must. When King Saul compelled himself and offered sacrifice, because he thought that Samuel was too late in coming, he made the greatest mistake of his life.

God may delay to come in the guise of His providence. There was delay while Sennacherib's host lay like withered leaves around the Holy City. There was delay while Jesus came walking on the sea in the early dawn or hastened to raise Lazarus. There was delay before the angel sped to Peter's side on the night before his expected martyrdom. He stays long enough to test patience of faith, but not a moment behind the extreme hour of need. "The vision is yet for an appointed time, but at the end it shall speak, and shall not lie; though it tarry, wait for it, because it will surely come; it will not tarry."

It is very remarkable how God guides us by circumstances. At one moment the way may seem utterly blocked, and then shortly afterward some trivial incident occurs, which might not seem much to others but which to the keen eye of faith speaks volumes. Sometimes these signs are repeated in different ways in answer to prayer. They are not haphazard results of chance, but the opening up of circumstances in the direction in which we should walk. And they begin to multiply as we advance toward our goal, just as lights do as we near a populous town when darting through the land by night express.

F. B. MEYER

SOWING AND REAPING

Be Not Deceived: God Is Not Mocked

Many a weeping wife has come to me about her husband, saying, "He is good at heart." The truth is, that is the worst spot in him. If the heart was good, all else would be right. Out of the heart are the issues of life. Christ said: "From within, out of the heart of men, proceed evil thoughts, adulteries, fornications, murders, thefts, covetousness, wickedness, deceit, lasciviousness, an evil eye, blasphemy, pride, foolishness." That is Christ's own statement regarding the unregenerate heart.

Some years ago a remarkable picture was exhibited in London. As you looked at it from a distance, you seemed to see a monk engaged in prayer, his hands clasped, his head bowed. As you came nearer, however, and examined the painting more closely, you saw that in reality he was squeezing a lemon into a punchbowl!

What a picture that is of the human heart! Superficially examined, it is thought to be the seat of all that is good and noble and pleasing in a man. In reality, until regenerated by the Holy Ghost, it is the seat of all corruption. "This is the condemnation, that light is come into the world, and men loved darkness rather than light."

A Jewish rabbi once asked his scholars what was the best thing a man could have in order to keep him in the straight path. One said a good disposition; another, a good companion; another said wisdom was the best thing he could desire. At last a scholar replied that he thought a good heart was best of all.

"True," said the rabbi, "you have comprehended all that the others have said. For he that hath a good heart will be of a good disposition, and a good companion, and a wise man. Let everyone, therefore, cultivate a sincerity and uprightness of heart at all times, and it will save him an abundance of sorrow." We need to make the prayer of David our own: "Create in me a clean heart, O God, and renew a right spirit within me!"

D. L. MOODY

THE CHRIST-LIFE FOR THE SELF-LIFE

His Best for Each

Do you think God has made a mistake in your life? If instead of being a poor man you had been rich, if instead of being a lone woman you had had one to call you wife and little children to clutch your dress and call you mother, if instead of being tied to the office stool you had been a minister or missionary, you think that you would have been a better, sweeter character. But I want you to understand that God chose for you your lot in life out of myriads that were open to Him, because just where you are you might realize your noblest possibilities. Otherwise God would have made you different from what you are. But your soul, born into His kingdom, was a matter of care and thought to Him, how best He might nurture you; and He chose your lot with its irritations, its trials, its difficulties, all the agony that eats at your nature.

Though men and women do not guess it, He chose your soul just as it is, because in it, if you will let Him, He can realize the fairest life within your reach. Look at the potter's wheel with the clay lump spinning round. I begin to manipulate the clay. It rises beneath my hand till I come to one certain point where, either through some flaw in the clay, a bubble or a fault, it resists me. Leaving that point, I put my hand around again, and in some other direction endeavor to secure my purpose, and then come back to that one point, but again I meet that obstruction that thwarts me. The genius of my brain as an artist is complete; the power of my hand to manipulate is unrivaled; it is the clay that thwarts me, until presently, because I have been frustrated again and again, the work is a marred, spoiled thing.

Now is not that true of you?

The one trouble of my life, years ago, was just this about which I am speaking now. God was dealing with me. I suppose He wanted to make me a vessel fit for His use. But there was one point in my life where I fought God as the clay fights the hand of the potter. I fought God; I will not say for how long. God help me! The only benefit that I can get now out of those years the cankerworm has eaten is to discover the secret in other lives while they, too, are standing still, and then to take them to the Christ to whom I went myself. There I shall encourage them to hope that He who years ago took up a spoiled and marred life and made a little of it, will take other men and women and will find out where they have thwarted Him. If they let Him, He will touch them there, and as they yield to Him they will be made again.

F. B. MEYER

HEAVEN

We Shall Live Forever

I cannot agree with some people that Paul has been sleeping in the grave and still here, after the storms of eighteen hundred years. I cannot believe that he who loved the Master, who had such a burning zeal for Him, has been separated from Him in an unconscious state.

"Father, I will that they also, whom thou has given me, be with me where I am; that they may behold my glory, which thou hast given me." This is Christ's prayer.

Now when a man believes on the Lord Jesus Christ, he receives eternal life. A great many people make a mistake right there. The apostle John said that the person who believes on the Son has, *has* eternal life. John did not say that the person shall have it when he comes to die; it is in the present tense; it is mine now—if I believe. It is the gift of God, that is enough. You cannot bury the gift of God; you cannot bury eternal life. All the gravediggers in the world cannot dig a grave large enough and deep enough to hold eternal life; all the coffin-makers in the world cannot make a coffin large enough and strong enough to hold eternal life; it is mine. It *is* mine!

When Paul said "to be absent from the body and present with the Lord," he meant what he said: that he was not going to be separated from Him for eighteen hundred years. The spirit that was given him when he was converted he had from a new life and a new nature, and they could not lay that away in the sepulcher. Even the body shall be raised. This body, sown in dishonor, shall be raised in glory; this body that has known corruption shall put on immortality. It is only a question of time.

Paul said, "If our earthly house of this tabernacle were dissolved, we have a building of God, a house not made with hands, eternal in the heavens."

D. L. MOODY

THE SECRET OF GUIDANCE

Fact, Faith, and Feeling

The lack of feeling does not always indicate that we are wrong. It may be that Christ would teach us to distinguish between love and the emotion of love, between joy and the rapture of joy, between peace and the sense of peace. Or perhaps He may desire to ascertain whether we cling to Him for Himself or for His gifts.

Children greet their father from the window, as he turns the corner and comes down the street. He hears the rush of their feet along the passage as he inserts his latchkey in the door. But one day he begins to question whether they greet him for the love they bear him or for the gifts with which he never forgets to fill his pockets. One day, therefore, he gives them due notice that there will be no gifts when he returns at night. Their faces fall, but when the hour of return arrives they are at the window as usual, and there is the same trampling of little feet to the door. "Ah," he says, "my children love me for myself," and he is glad.

Our Father sometimes cuts off the supply of joy and suffers us to hunger, that He may know what is in our hearts and whether we love Him for Himself. If we still cling to Him as Job did, He is glad and restores comforts to His mourners with both hands.

Seek feeling, and you will miss it. Be content to live without it, and you will have all you require. If you are always noticing your heartbeats, you will bring on heart disease. If you are ever muffling against cold, you will become very subject to chills. If you are perpetually thinking about your health, you will induce disease. If you are always consulting your feelings, you will live in a dry and thirsty land, where no water is.

Be indifferent to emotion. If it is there, be thankful; if it is absent, go on doing the will of God, reckoning on Him, speaking well of Him behind His back, and, above all, giving no signs of what you are suffering, lest you be a stumbling block to others. Then joy will overtake you as a flood. He will make you sit at His table and gird Himself to come forth and serve you.

F. B. MEYER

THE STORY OF THE PRODIGAL

The Best Robe

I know what it is you want. You want the best robe without your Father's giving it to you, and the shoes on your feet of your own procuring. You do not like going in a beggar's suit and receiving all from the Lord's loving hand. But this pride of yours must be given up, and you must get away to God, or perish forever. You must forget yourself, or only remember yourself so as to feel that you are bad throughout and no more worthy to be called God's son. Give yourself up as a sinking vessel that is not worth pumping, but must be left to go down, and get you into the lifeboat of free grace. Think of God your Father and of His dear Son, the one Mediator and Redeemer of the sons of men. There is your hope—to fly away from self and to reach your Father.

Sinner, your business is with God. Hasten to Him at once. You have nothing to do with yourself or your own doings or what others can do for you. The turning point of salvation is "He arose and came to his father." There must be a real, living, earnest, contact of your poor guilty soul with God, a recognition that there is a God and that God can be spoken to, and an actual speech of your soul to Him through Jesus Christ, for it is only God in Christ Jesus that is accessible at all. Going thus to God, we tell Him that we are all wrong, and want to be set right; we tell Him we wish to be reconciled to Him and are ashamed that we should have sinned against Him; we then put our trust in His Son, and we are saved.

O soul, go to God; it matters not that the prayer you come with may be a very broken prayer, or even if it has mistakes in it, as the prodigal's prayer had when he said, "Make me as one of thy hired servants"; the language of the prayer will not matter so long as you really approach God. "Him that cometh to me," says Jesus, "I will in no wise cast out"; and Jesus ever liveth to make intercession for them that come to God through Him.

CHARLES H. SPURGEON

SOVEREIGN GRACE

An Unforgettable Lesson

I met a man once in Scotland who taught me a lesson that I shall never forget. A Christian friend wanted me to go and have a talk with him. He had been bedridden for many years. This afflicted saint comforted me and told me some wonderful things. He had fallen and broken his back when he was about fifteen years of age and had lain there on his bed for some forty years. He could not be moved without a good deal of pain, and probably not a day passed all those years without suffering. If anyone had told him he was going to lie there and suffer for forty years, probably he would have said he could not do it. But day after day the grace of God has been granted to him; and I declare to you it seemed to me as if I were in the presence of one of God's most highly-favored children.

When I was in that man's chamber, it seemed as though I was about as near heaven as I could get on this earth. Talk about a man's face shining with the glory of the upper world! I seldom see a face that shines as did his. I can imagine that the very angels when they are passing over the city on some mission of mercy come down into that man's chamber to get refreshed. There he lay all those years, not only without a murmur, but rejoicing all the while.

I said to him: "My friend, does the devil never tempt you to doubt God and to think He is a hard master?"

"Well now," he said, "that is just what he tries to do. Sometimes, as I look out of the window and see people walking along in health, Satan whispers: 'If God is so good, why does He keep you here all these weary years? Why, if He loved you, instead of lying here and being dependent on others, you might now have been a rich man and riding in your own carriage.'"

"What do you do when the devil tempts you?"

"Oh, I just take him up to the cross; and he had such a fright there eighteen hundred years ago that he cannot stand it; and he leaves me."

I do not think that bedridden saint has much trouble with doubts; he is so full of grace. And so if we will only come boldly to God, we shall get all the help and strength we need. There is no a man or woman alive but may be kept from falling, if they will let God hold them up in His almighty arms.

D. L. MOODY

THE SECRET OF GUIDANCE

Standing and Experience

Perhaps you do not distinguish between your standing in Christ and your experience. Our experiences are fickle as April weather; now sunshine, now cloud; lights and shadows chasing each other over miles of heathery moor or foam-flecked sea.

But our standing in Jesus changes not. It is like Himself—the same yesterday, today, and forever. It did not originate in us, but in His everlasting love, which, foreseeing all that we should be, loved us notwithstanding all. It has not been purchased by us, but by His precious blood, which pleads for us as mightily and successfully when we can hardly claim it as when our faith is most buoyant. It is not maintained by us, but by the Holy Spirit. If we have fled to Jesus for salvation, sheltering under Him, relying on Him, and trusting Him, though with many misgivings, as well as we may, then we are one with Him forever.

We were one with Him in the grave; one with Him on Easter morn; one with Him when He sat down at God's right hand. We are one with Him now as He stands in the light of His Father's smile, as the limbs of the swimmer are one with the head, though it alone is encircled with the warm glory of the sun, while they are hidden beneath the waves. And no doubt or depression can for a single moment affect or alter our acceptance with God through the blood of Jesus, which is an eternal fact.

You have not realized this, perhaps, but have thought that your standing in Jesus was affected by your changeful moods. As well might the fortune of a ward of the court be diminished or increased by the amount of her spending money. Our standing in Jesus is our invested capital. Our emotions at the best are but our spending money, which is ever passing through our pocket or purse, never exactly the same. Cease to consider how you feel, and build on the immovable rock of what Jesus is and has done and will do for you.

F. B. MEYER

SHORT TALKS
Born Again

How solemn these words are: "Except a man be born again, he cannot see the kingdom of God" (John 3:3), much less inherit it. If this thing be true, it is a most solemn truth, and you and I cannot afford to be deceived. Let us put the question here to ourselves: Have I really been born of the Spirit?

I just as much believe that a man has got to be born from above before he wants to go to heaven as I believe that I exist. Take an unregenerated man and put him under the shadow of the tree of life, and it would be hell to him. Take the carnal man, or the natural man, and put him on the crystal pavements of heaven, and it would be hell to him. Man has got to have a divine nature before he will want to go to heaven. If he has this low nature, he doesn't want to go there. He would be out of his element, he would be out of his atmosphere, if he got there.

Make sure that you are in the kingdom, that you have been born into it. We have a law in this country that no man can be president of the United States unless he was born here. I never heard any foreigner complain of that law. I want to know if the God of heaven hasn't a right to say who shall come into His kingdom. Does He have a right to say how they all enter it? I think He has.

This is an awfully solemn question. Put it now to yourself: "Have I been born again? Have I received the gift of God, which is eternal life?"

D. L. MOODY

ANSWERS TO PRAYER
The Book Above All Books

L ike many believers, I practically preferred, for the first four years of my divine life, the works of uninspired men to the oracles of the living God. The consequence was that I remained a babe, both in knowledge and grace. In knowledge I say; for all true knowledge must be derived by the Spirit, from the Word. And as I neglected the Word, I was for nearly four years so ignorant that I did not *clearly* know even the fundamental points of our holy faith. And this lack of knowledge most sadly kept me from walking steadily in the ways of God.

For it is the truth that makes us free (John 8:31–32), by delivering us from the slavery of the lusts of the flesh, the lust of the eyes, and the pride of life. The Word proves it. The experience of the saints proves it; and also my own experience most decidedly proves it. For when it pleased the Lord in August 1829 to bring me really to the Scriptures, my life and walk became very different. And though ever since that I have very much fallen short of what I might and ought to be, yet, by the grace of God, I have been enabled to live much nearer to Him than before.

If any believers read this who prefer other books to the Holy Scriptures, and who enjoy the writings of men much more than the Word of God, may they be warned by my loss. I shall consider this book to have been the means of doing much good, should it please the Lord, through its instrumentality, to lead some of His people no longer to neglect the Holy Scriptures, but to give them the preference, which they have hitherto bestowed on the writings of men.

My dislike to increase the number of books would have been sufficient to deter me from writing these pages had I not been convinced that this is the only way in which the brethren at large may be benefited through my mistakes and errors, and been influenced by the hope that, in answer to my prayers, the reading of my experience may be the means of leading them to value the Scriptures more highly and to make them the rule of all their actions.

GEORGE MUELLER

SOWING AND REAPING

Ignorance of the Seed Makes No Difference

I f a farmer neglects to plant in the springtime, he can never recover the lost opportunity. Nor can you, if you neglect yours. Youth is a seedtime, and if it is allowed to pass without good seed being sowed, weeds will spring up and choke the soil. It will take bitter toil to uproot them.

An old sage said that when a good farmer sees a weed in his field he has it pulled up. If it is taken early enough, the blank is soon filled in, and the crop waves over the whole field. But if allowed to run too late, the bald patch remains. It would have been better if the weed had never been allowed to get root.

Beware of letting some secret sin get the mastery over you, binding you hand and foot. Every sin grows. When I was speaking to five thousand children in Glasgow some years ago, I took a spool of thread and said to one of the largest boys, "Do you believe I can bind you with that thread?"

He laughed at the idea. I wound the thread around him a few times, and he broke it with a single jerk. Then I wound the thread around and around, and by and by I said, "Now get free if you can."

He couldn't move hand or foot. If you are slave to some vile habit, you must either slay that habit or it will slay you.

My friend, what kind of seed are you sowing? Let your mind sweep over your record for the past year. Have you been living a double life? Have you been making a profession without possessing what you profess? If there is anything you detest, it is hypocrisy. Do you tell me God doesn't detest it also? If it is a right eye that offends, make up your mind that you will pluck it out; or if it is a right hand or a right foot, cut it off. Whatever the sin is, make up your mind that you will gain the victory over it without further delay.

D. L. MOODY

KEPT FOR THE MASTER'S USE

Our Lives Kept for Jesus

What a long time it takes us to come to the conviction, and still more to the realization, that without Christ we can do nothing, but that He must work all our works in us! This is the work of God, that you believe in Him whom He has sent. And no less must it be the work of God that we go on believing and that we go on trusting. Then, dear friends, who are longing to trust Him with unbroken and unwavering trust, cease the effort and drop the burden, and now entrust your trust to Him! He is just as well able to keep that as any other part of the complex lives we want Him to take and keep for Himself.

And do not be content with the thought *Yes, that is a good idea; perhaps I should find that a great help.* But, now, then, do it. It is no help to the sailor to see a flash of light across a dark sea, if he does not instantly steer accordingly.

Consecration is not a religiously selfish thing. If it sinks into that, it ceases to be consecration. We want our lives kept, not that we may feel happy, and be saved the distress consequent on wandering, and get the power with God and man, and all the other privileges linked with it. We shall have all this, because the lower is included in the higher; but our true aim, if the love of Christ constrains us, will be far beyond this. Not for "me" at all, but "for Jesus"; not for my comfort, but for His joy; not that I may find rest but that He may see the travail of His soul and be satisfied!

Yes, for Him I want to be kept. Kept for His sake; kept for His use; kept to be His witness; kept for His joy! Kept for Him, that in me He may show forth some tiny sparkle of His light and beauty. By being kept in Him I shall be able to do His will and His work in His own way.

FRANCES R. HAVERGAL

THE OVERCOMING LIFE

Are Your Children Safe?

The command of the Scripture given to Noah for his own safety and that of his household I now ask as a question for each father and mother: "Are your children in the ark of God?" You may scoff at it, but it is a very important question. Are all your children in? Are all your grandchildren in? Don't rest day or night until you get your children in. I believe my children have fifty temptations where I had one. I believe that in the great cities there is a snare set upon the corner of every street for our sons and daughters; and I don't believe it is our business to spend our time in accumulating bonds and stocks. Have I done all I can to get my children in? That is the question.

Now, let me ask another question: What would have been Noah's feelings if, when God called him into the ark, his children would not have gone with him? If he had lived such a false life that his children had no faith in his word, what would have been his feelings? He would have said: "There is my poor boy on the mountain. Would to God I had died in his place! I would rather have perished than had him perish." David cried over his son: "Oh, my son Absalom, my son, my son Absalom, would God I had died for thee." Noah loved his children and they had confidence in him.

Someone sent me a newspaper a number of years ago containing an article that was marked. Its title was "Are all the children in?" An old wife lay dying. She was nearly one hundred years of age, and the husband who had taken the journey with her sat by her side. She was just breathing faintly, but suddenly she revived, opened her eyes, and said, "Why! It is dark."

"Yes, Janet. It is dark."

"Is it night?"

"Oh, yes! It is midnight."

"Are all the children in?"

There was that old mother living life over again. Her youngest child had been in the grave twenty years, but she was traveling back into the old days, and she fell asleep in Christ asking, "Are all the children in?"

D. L. MOODY

ALL OF GRACE
Why Saints Persevere

The hope that filled the heart of Paul concerning the Corinthian brethren was full of comfort to those who trembled as to their future. But why was it that he believed that the brethren would be confirmed unto the end?

I want you to notice that he gives his reasons. Here they are: "God is faithful, by whom ye were called unto the fellowship of his Son, Jesus Christ" (1 Corinthians 1:9).

The apostle does not say, "*You* are faithful." Alas! The faithfulness of man is a very unreliable affair; it is mere vanity. He does not say, "You have faithful ministers to lead and guide you, and therefore I trust you will be safe." Oh, no! If we are kept by men we shall be but ill kept. He puts it, "God is faithful." If we are found faithful, it will be because God is faithful. On the faithfulness of our covenant God the whole burden of our salvation must rest. On this glorious attribute of God the matter hinges.

We are variable as the wind, frail as a spider's web, weak as water. No dependence can be placed upon our natural qualities or our spiritual attainments; but God abides faithful. He is faithful in His love; He knows no variableness, neither shadow of turning. He is faithful to His purpose; He does not begin a work and then leave it undone. He is faithful to His relationships; as a Father He will not renounce His children, as a friend He will not deny His people, as a Creator He will not forsake the work of His own hands. He is faithful to His promises and will never allow one of them to fail to a single believer. He is faithful to His covenant, which He has made with us in Christ Jesus and ratified with the blood of His sacrifice. He is faithful to His Son and will not allow His precious blood to be spilt in vain. He is faithful to His people to whom He has promised eternal life and from whom He will not turn away.

This faithfulness of God is the foundation and cornerstone of our hope of final perseverance. The saints shall persevere in holiness, because God perseveres in grace. He perseveres to bless, and therefore believers persevere in being blessed. He continues to keep His people, and therefore they continue to keep His commandments.

CHARLES H. SPURGEON

THE WAY TO GOD

What Spiritual Regeneration Is Not

Now, let me say what regeneration is not. It is not going to church. Very often I see people and ask them if they are Christians. "Yes, of course I am; at least, I think I am: I go to church every Sunday." Ah, but this is not regeneration. Others say, "I am trying to do what is right—am I not a Christian? Is not that a new birth?" No. What has that to do with being born again? There is yet another class—those who have "turned over a new leaf" and think they are regenerated. No; forming a new resolution is not being born again.

Nor will being baptized do you any good. Yet you hear people say, "Why, I have been baptized; and I was born again when I was baptized." They believe that because they were baptized into the church, they were baptized into the kingdom of God. I tell you that it is utterly impossible. You may be baptized into the church and yet not be baptized into the Son of God. Baptism is all right in its place. God forbid that I should say anything against it. But if you put that in the place of regeneration—in the place of the new birth—it is a terrible mistake. You cannot be baptized into the kingdom of God. "Except a man be *born again*, he cannot see the kingdom of God" (John 3:3). If any one reading this rests his hope on anything else—on any other foundation—I pray that God may sweep it away.

Another class says, "I go to the Lord's Supper; I partake uniformly of the sacrament." Blessed ordinance! Jesus hath said that as often as ye do it ye commemorate His death. Yet, that is not being "born again"; that is not passing from death unto life. Jesus says plainly—and so plainly that there need not be any mistake about it—"Except a man be born . . . of the Spirit, he cannot enter into the kingdom of God" (verse 5). What has a sacrament to do with that? What has going to church to do with being born again?

Another man comes up and says, "I say my prayers regularly." Still I say that is not being born of the Spirit. It is a very solemn question, then, that comes up before us; and oh that every reader would ask himself earnestly and faithfully: "Have I been born again? Have I been born of the Spirit? Have I passed from death unto life?"

D. L. MOODY

BACK TO BETHEL

Holiness to the Lord

Never forget that holiness is not an attainment but an attitude. It is the opening of the heart to the balmy air and sunlight of God's nature, which, entering in, fill the spirit of man or woman.

In Exodus 28:36, the high priest stands before you vested in his full white robes, with breastplate of gold. On the frontlet of his forehead, the legend *Holiness to the Lord* is inscribed, so that wherever he goes to and fro, he bears upon his brow that sacred text.

Suppose I should turn from him and, speaking to you, say that I want you to meet Christ in glory bearing that frontlet upon your brow and have that holy legend inscribed upon you. It might be you would shrink back and say, "No, no, I will never be a hypocrite. I do trust in Christ and desire to be like Him. But I dare not arrogate to myself that sacred frontlet, that holy legend. I am not *Holiness to the Lord.*"

Then, my friend, you are putting away from you the privilege of this dispensation, of which Zechariah says that in this age there shall be so much Holy Spirit given to the men and women who believe in Christ that *Holiness to the Lord* shall be engraved upon their heads, that the common vessels in their homes shall have the same legend upon them, and be as holy as the vessels in the Lord's house: "In that day shall there be upon the bells of the horses, HOLINESS UNTO THE LORD; and the pots in the Lord's house shall be like the bowls before the altar" (Zechariah 14:20).

I remember so well spending some winter days in the city of Boston. I shall never forget the blue sky and the crisp white snow, the absence of the rumbling of wheels, and everywhere the sweet music of the sleigh bells. The bells of all our life—the dinner bell, the rising bell, the bell summoning us to our daily work, the telephone bell asking us to hold conversation with another—all the bells ringing in our lives are to have these words inscribed so that our whole life shall have this as its keynote.

F. B. MEYER

CHARGE THAT TO MY ACCOUNT

Outside the Camp

J ust as Christ's place in glory is our place, so His place on earth is our place, as we go through this sinful world. What is His place down here? It is the place of rejection, for "He came unto His own, and His own received Him not." These two expressions of "His own" are not absolutely the same in the original. The first is the neuter; the second is personal. Thus the passage may be rendered: "He came unto His own things and His own people received Him not."

Think of it, He came to His own city, Jerusalem, the city of the great King. If there was any place on earth where He might have expected to be received with gladness and acclaim, it was Jerusalem. He came unto His own temple; every whit of it uttered His glory, the very veil spoke of His perfect humanity, and every piece of furniture pictured Him. There was the altar, the laver, the candlestick, the table of showbread, and everything spoke of Him; but as He came to His own things, the very priests in the temple joined in the cry "Away with Him, away with Him, crucify Him!" and they led Him outside the gate, the rejected One.

There were two candidates that day, Christ and Barabbas. The people chose the murderer and rejected the Savior. He accepted the place they gave Him, and with lowly grace allowed them to lead Him outside the city, away from the temple, away from the palace, outside the gates, unto the place called Calvary.

As far as the world is concerned, it has never reversed that judgment. He is still the rejected One, and the place the world has given Him should determine the place that you and I will take. He was rejected, not merely by the barbarian world, not merely by those who were living low, degraded lives, but also by the literary world, the cultured world, the religious world. It was the religious leaders of the people who demanded His death, and all the world acquiesced. The world still continues to do so. It has its culture, its refinements, its civilization (often mistaken for Christianity), its religion (one that has no place for the cross of Christ or the vicarious atonement or His glorious resurrection), but our blessed Lord is apart from it all, and the word to us is this: "Let us go forth therefore unto him without the camp, bearing His reproach."

HENRY A. IRONSIDE

THE OVERCOMING LIFE

Rest

Casting all your care upon Him for He careth for you" (1 Peter 5:7). We would have a victorious church if we could get Christian people to realize that. But they have never made the discovery. Christ is the sin-bearer, but they do not realize that He is also the burden-bearer. "Surely he hath borne our griefs and carried our sorrows." It is the privilege of every child of God to walk in unclouded sunlight.

Some people go back into the past and rake up all the troubles they ever had, and they look into the future and anticipate that they will have still more trouble, and they go reeling and staggering all through life. They give you the cold chills every time they meet you. They put on a whining voice and tell you what "a hard time they have had." I believe they embalm them and bring out the mummy on every opportunity. The Lord says, "Cast all your care on Me. I want to carry your burdens and your troubles." What we want is a joyful church, and we are not going to convert the world until we have it. We want to get this long-faced Christianity off the face of the earth.

Take these people that have some great burden and let them come into a meeting. If you can get their attention upon the singing or preaching, they will say, "Oh, wasn't it grand! I forgot all my cares." And they just drop their bundle at the end of the pew. But the moment the benediction is pronounced they grab the bundle again. You laugh, but you do it yourself. Cast your care on Him.

Sometimes they go into their closet and close their door, and they get so carried away and lifted up that they forget their trouble; but they just take it up again the moment they get off their knees. Leave your sorrow now; cast all your care upon Him. If you cannot come to Christ as a saint, come as a sinner. But if you are a saint with some trouble or care, bring it to Him. Saint and sinner, come! He wants you all. Don't let Satan deceive you into believing that you cannot come if you will. Christ says, "Come unto me all ye that labour and are heavy laden." With the command comes the power.

D. L. MOODY

CALVARY'S CROSS

The Significance of the Cross

From the day of Christ's crucifixion the cross became a power in the earth —a power which went forth like the light, noiselessly yet irresistibly— smiting down all religions alike, all shrines alike, all altars alike; sparing no superstition or philosophy; neither flattering priesthood nor succumbing to statesmanship; tolerating no error, yet refusing to draw the sword for truth; a power superhuman, yet wielded by human, not angelic hands; "the power of God unto salvation."

This power remains; in its mystery, its silence, its influence it remains. The cross has not become obsolete; the preaching of the cross has not ceased to be effectual. There are men among us who would persuade us that in this late age the cross is out of date and out of fashion, time-worn, not time-honored; that Golgotha witnessed only a common martyr scene; that the great sepulchre is but a Hebrew tomb; that the Christ of the future and the Christ of the past are widely different. But this shakes us not. It only leads us to clasp the cross more fervently and to study it more profoundly, as embodying in itself that gospel that is at once the wisdom and the power of God.

Yet the cross is not without its mysteries or, as men would say, its puzzles, its contradictions. It illuminates, yet it darkens; it interprets, yet it confounds. It raises questions, but refuses to answer all that is raised. It solves difficulties, but it creates them too. It locks as well as unlocks. It opens, and no man shuts; it shuts, and no man opens. It is life, and yet it is death. It is honor, yet it is shame. It is wisdom, but also foolishness. It is both gain and loss; both pardon and condemnation; both strength and weakness; both joy and sorrow; both love and hatred; both medicine and poison; both hope and despair. It is grace, and yet it is righteousness. It is law, yet it is deliverance from law. It is Christ's humiliation, yet it is Christ's exaltation. It is Satan's victory, yet it is Satan's defeat. It is the gate of heaven and the gate of hell.

Let us look at the cross as the divine proclamation and interpretation of the things of God; the key to His character, His Word, His ways, His purposes; the clue to the intricacies of the world's and the church's history.

HORATIUS BONAR

SOWING AND REAPING

When a Man Sows, He Expects to Reap

Sowing to the flesh" does not mean simply taking due care of the body. The body was made in the image of God, and the body of a believer is a temple of the Holy Ghost, and we may be sure that due care for the image is well-pleasing to God. The expression refers rather to pandering to the lusts of the body, pampering it, providing gratification for its unlawful desires at the expense of the higher part of a man, indulging the animal propensities that in their excess are sinful. "Sowing to the flesh" is scattering the seeds of selfishness, which always must yield a harvest of corruption.

"When we were in the flesh, the motions of sins . . . did work in our members to bring forth fruit unto death." And what does Paul say are the works of the flesh? "Adultery, fornication, uncleanness, lasciviousness, idolatry, witchcraft, hatred, variance, emulations, wrath, strife, sedition, heresies, envying, murders, drunkenness, revelings, and such like."

I was at the Paris exhibition and I noticed there a little oil painting, only about a foot square, and the face was the most hideous I have ever seen. On the paper attached to the painting were the words "Sowing the tares," and the face looked more like a demon's than a man's. As he sowed these tares, up came serpents and reptiles, and they were crawling up on his body, and all around were woods with wolves and animals prowling in them. I have seen that picture many times since. Ah! The reaping time is coming. If you sow to the flesh you must reap to the flesh. If you sow to the wind you must reap the whirlwind.

And yet it must not be thought that indulgence in the grosser vices is the only way of sowing to the flesh. Every desire, every action that has not God for its end and object is seed sown to the flesh. If a man is sowing for a harvest of money or ambition, he is sowing to the flesh and will reap corruption, just as surely as the liar and adulterer. No matter how "polite" and "refined" and "respectable" the seed may be, its true nature will out, the blight of corruption will be upon it.

D. L. MOODY

THE TRUE VINE

Abide in My Love

The love of the Father to the Son is not a sentiment—it is a divine life, an infinite energy, an irresistible power. It carried Christ through life and death and the grave. The Father loved Him and dwelt in Him and did all for Him. So the love of Christ to us, too, is an infinite living power that will work in us all He delights to give us. The feebleness of our Christian life is that we do not take time to believe that this divine love does really delight in us and will possess and work all in us. We do not take time to look at the vine bearing the branch so entirely, working all in it so completely. We strive to do for ourselves what Christ alone can, what Christ oh so lovingly longs to do for us.

And this now is the secret of the change we spoke of, and the beginning of a new life, when the soul sees this infinite love willing to do all and gives itself up to it. "Abide ye in my love." To believe that it is possible so to live moment by moment; to believe that everything that makes it difficult or impossible will be overcome by Christ Himself; to believe that love really means an infinite longing to give itself wholly to us and never leave us; and in this faith to cast ourselves on Christ to work it in us; this is the secret of the true Christian life.

And how to come to this faith? Turn away from the visible if you would see and possess the invisible. Take more time with Jesus, gazing on Him as the heavenly Vine, living in the love of the Father, wanting you to live in His love. Turn away from yourself and your efforts and your faith, if you would have the heart filled with Him and the certainty of His love. Abiding means going out from everything else to occupy one place and stay there.

ANDREW MURRAY

THE WAY TO GOD

The Cross of Christ Speaks of the Love of God

After I became a father, and for years had an only son, as I looked at my boy I thought of the Father giving His Son to die, and it seemed to me as if it required more love for the Father to give His Son than for the Son to die. Oh, the love that God must have had for the world when He gave His Son to die for it! "God so loved the world, that he gave his only begotten Son, that whosoever believeth in him should not perish, but have everlasting life" (John 3:16). I have never been able to preach from that text. I have often thought I would, but it is so high that I can never climb to its height; I have just quoted it and passed on. Who can fathom the depth of those words: "God *so* loved the world"? We can never scale the heights of His love or fathom its depths. Paul prayed that he might know the height, the depth, the length, and the breadth of the love of God, but it was past his finding out. It "passeth knowledge" (Ephesians 3:19).

Nothing speaks to us of the love of God like the cross of Christ. Come with me to Calvary and look upon the Son of God as He hangs there. Can you hear that piercing cry from His dying lips: "Father, forgive them; for they know not what they do!" and say that He does not love you? "Greater love hath no man than this, that a man lay down his life for his friends" (John 15:13). But Jesus Christ laid down His life *for His enemies.*

Another thought is this: He loved us long before we even thought of Him. The idea that He does not love us until we first love Him is not to be found in Scripture. In 1 John 4:10 it is written: "Herein is love, not that we loved God, but that he loved us, and sent his Son to be the propitiation for our sins." He loved us before we even thought of loving Him. You loved your children before they knew anything about your love. And so, long before we ever thought of God, we were in His thoughts.

What brought the prodigal home? It was the thought that his father loved him. Suppose the news had reached him that he was a cast-off and that his father did not care for him anymore. Would he have gone back? Never! But the thought dawned upon him that his father loved him still: so he rose up, and went back to his home. Dear reader, the love of the Father ought to bring us back to Him. It was Adam's calamity and sin that revealed God's love. When Adam fell, God came down and dealt in mercy with him. If any one is lost it will not be because God does not love him; it will be because he has resisted the love of God.

D. L. MOODY

THE IMPORTANCE AND VALUE OF PROPER BIBLE STUDY

Study the Bible Microscopically

Study the Bible, really study it. That comes out in Acts 17:11—they "searched the Scriptures daily, whether those things were so." Note carefully the word "searched," or as it is translated in the Revised Version, "examining" the Scriptures. The Greek word translated "searched" in the Authorized Version and "examining" in the Revised Version, is a very strong word. It means "to search after by looking through, to investigate, to examine, to inquire into, to scrutinize, to sift." It means the closest and most minute study.

The Bible, being God's book, is full of meaning in its minutest word and is worthy of not merely the cursory, superficial reading, the careless skimming that most people give to it. That is all most of the other books, men's books, deserve; any closer study than that is a waste of time. But the Bible, being God's book, God's own perfect Word, God's inexhaustible storehouse of truth, in which are hidden the infinite treasures of the wisdom and knowledge of God, is worthy of the closest and minutest study. And it abundantly rewards such study, and that is one of the countless proofs that the Bible really is God's Word. The more closely and microscopically you study this book, the more you see and the more wonderful the blessing you get. The Bible should be studied with the closest and most concentrated attention. Here is where more people miss the fullest blessing in their study of the Bible than anywhere else. They are looking at the Bible with their bodily eyes, but their minds are off in a dozen other places.

When you study the Bible, resolutely shut everything else out, shut the door of your mind to everything else, and shut yourself up with God alone. It may take time to cultivate this habit of concentrated attention, but any Christian can accomplish it. If you find your mind wandering, go back and fasten your eyes and your mind on that verse again, and chew every word. Remember what Jeremiah said, "Thy words were found and I did eat them; and Thy words were unto me a joy and the rejoicing of my heart" (Jeremiah 15:16 RV).

R. A. TORREY

HEAVEN
Avoid Idolatry

What we need to do is to obey the voice of the Master, and instead of laying up treasures on earth, lay them up in heaven. If we do that, bear in mind, we shall never be disappointed.

It is clear that idolaters are not going to enter the kingdom of God. I may make an idol of business; I may make an idol of the wife of my bosom; I may make idols of my children. I do not think you need go to heathen countries to find men guilty of idolatry. I think you will find a great many right here who have idols in their hearts. Let us pray that the spirit of God may banish those idols from our hearts, that we may not be guilty of idolatry; that we may worship God in spirit and in truth. Anything that comes between me and God is an idol—anything, I don't care what it is; business is all right in its place, and there is not danger of my loving my family too much if I love God more; but God must have the first place; and, if He has not, then the idol is set up.

Not the least of the riches of heaven will be the satisfaction of those wants of the souls, which are so much felt down here but are never found—such as infinite knowledge, perfect peace, and satisfying love. Like a beautiful likeness that has been marred, daubed all over with streaks of black, and is then restored to its full beauty of color when it is washed with the blood of Jesus Christ. The senseless image on the canvas cannot be compared, however, in any other way with the living, rational soul.

Could we but see some of our friends who have gone on before us we would very likely feel like falling down before them. The apostle John had seen so many strange things, yet, when one of the bright angels stood before him to reveal some of the secrets of heaven, he fell down to worship him. He says in the last chapter of Revelation:

And I John saw these things, and heard them. And when I had heard and seen, I fell down to worship before the feet of the angel which shewed me these things. Then saith he unto me, See thou do it not: for I am thy fellow servant, and of thy brethren the prophets, and of them which keep the sayings of this book: worship God. (Revelation 22:8-9)

D. L. MOODY

CALVARY'S CROSS

The Blood Shed for Many

The blood of Jesus has an intimate connection with remission of sins. The Bible says, "This is my blood of the new [testament] covenant, which is shed for many for the remission of sins" (Matthew 26:28). Jesus, suffering, bleeding, dying, has produced for sinners the forgiveness of their sins.

Of what sins?

Of all sins of every sort and kind, however heinous, aggravated, and multiplied. The blood of the covenant takes every sin away, be what it may. There was never a sin believingly confessed and taken to Christ that ever baffled His power to cleanse it. This fountain has never been tried in vain. Murderers, thieves, liars, and adulterers have come to Jesus by penitence and faith, and through the merit of His sacrifice for their sins have been put away.

Of what nature is the remission?

It is pardon, freely given, acting immediately and abiding forever, so that there is no fear of the guilt ever being again laid to the charge of the forgiven one. Through the precious blood our sins are blotted out, cast into the depths of the sea, and removed as far from us as the east is from the west. Our sins cease to be. They are made an end of. They cannot be found against us anymore forever. Yes, hear it, hear it, oh wide earth! Let the glad news startle your darkest dens of infamy; there is absolute remission of sins! The precious blood of Christ cleanses from all sin; yes, turns the scarlet into a whiteness that exceeds that of the newly fallen snow—a whiteness that never can be tarnished. Washed by Jesus, the blackest sinners shall appear before the judgment seat of the all-seeing Judge without spot.

How is it that the blood of Jesus effects this?

The secret lies in the vicarious, substitutionary character of our Lord's suffering and death. Because He stood in our place, the justice of God is vindicated, and the threatening of the law is fulfilled. It is now just for God to pardon sin. Christ's bearing the penalty of human sin instead of man has made the moral government of God perfect in justice, has laid a basis for peace of conscience, and has rendered sin immeasurably hateful, though its punishment does not fall upon the believer.

This is the great secret, this is the heavenly news, the gospel of salvation, that through the blood of Jesus, sin is justly put away.

CHARLES H. SPURGEON

SOVEREIGN GRACE

Grace Enough

I find that many Christians are in trouble about the future; they think they will not have grace enough to die by. It is much more important that we should have grace enough to *live* by. It seems to me that death is of very little importance in the meantime. When the dying hour comes, there will be dying grace; but you do not require dying grace to live by. If I am going to live perhaps for fifteen or twenty years, what do I want with dying grace? I am far more anxious about having grace enough for my present work.

I have sometimes been asked if I had grace enough to enable me to go to the stake and die as a martyr. No, what do I want with martyr's grace? I do not like suffering; but if God should call on me to die a martyr's death, He would give me martyr's grace. If I have to pass through some great affliction, I know God will give me grace when the time comes; but I do not want it till it comes.

There is a story of a martyr in the second century. He was brought before the king and told that if he did not recant they would banish him. Said he, "O king, you cannot banish me from Christ; for He has said, 'I will never leave thee nor forsake thee!' The apostle John was banished to the island of Patmos; but it was the best thing that could have happened: for if John had not been sent there, probably we should never have had that grand book of Revelation. John could not be separated from his Master."

So it was with this brave martyr, of whom I was speaking. The king said to him, "Then I will take away your property from you."

"You cannot do that, for my treasure is laid up on high, where you cannot get at it."

"Then I will kill you."

"You cannot do that; for I have been dead these forty years: 'My life is hid with Christ in God.'"

The king said, "What are you going to do with such a fanatic as that?"

Let us remember that if we have not grace enough for service, we have no one to blame but ourselves. We are not deprived in God; He has abundance of grace to qualify us to work for Him.

D. L. MOODY

ABSOLUTE SURRENDER

Surrendering to God

I am sure there is many a heart that says, "Ah, but that absolute surrender implies so much!" Someone says: "Oh, I have passed through so much trial and suffering, and there is so much of the self-life still remaining, and I dare not face the entire giving of it up, because I know it will cause so much trouble and agony."

Alas! Alas! That God's children have such thoughts of Him, such cruel thoughts. Oh, I come to you with a message, fearful and anxious one. God does not ask you to give the perfect surrender in your strength or by the power of your will; God is willing to work it in you. Do we not read, "It is God that worketh in us, both to will and to do of His good pleasure"? And that is what we should seek for—to go on our faces before God, until our hearts learn to believe that the everlasting God Himself will come in to turn out what is wrong, to conquer what is evil, and to work what is well-pleasing in His blessed sight. God Himself will work it in you.

Look at the men in the Old Testament, like Abraham. Do you think it was by accident that God found that man, the father of the faithful and the friend of God, and that it was Abraham himself, apart from God, who had such faith and such obedience and such devotion? You know it is not so. God raised him up and prepared him as an instrument for His glory.

Did not God say to Pharaoh, "For this cause have I raised thee up, for to show in thee my power?" And if God said that of him, will not God say it far more of every child of His?

Oh, I want to encourage you, and I want you to cast away every fear. Come with that feeble desire; and if there is the fear that says, "Oh, my desire is not strong enough, I am not willing for everything that may come, I do not feel bold enough to say I can conquer everything"—I pray you, learn to know and trust your God now. Say, "My God, I am willing that Thou shouldst make me willing." If there is anything holding you back, or any sacrifice you are afraid of making, come to God now and prove how gracious your God is and be not afraid that He will command from you what He will not bestow.

ANDREW MURRAY

KEPT FOR THE MASTER'S USE

Our Moments Kept for Jesus

While we have been undervaluing these fractions of eternity, what has our gracious God been doing in them? How strangely touching are the words, "What is man, that . . . thou shouldest set thine heart upon him, and that thou shouldest visit him every morning, and try him every moment?" Terribly solemn and awful would be the thought that He has been trying us every moment, were it not for the yearning gentleness and love of the Father revealed in that wonderful expression of wonder "What is man, that thou shouldest set thine heart upon him?" Think of that ceaseless setting of His heart upon us, careless and forgetful children as we have been! And then think of those other words, none the less literally true because given under a figure: "I, the Lord, do keep it; I will water it every moment."

We see something of God's infinite greatness and wisdom when we try to fix our dazzled gaze on infinite space. But when we turn to the marvels of the microscope, we gain a clearer view and more definite grasp of these attributes by gazing on the perfection of His infinitesimal handiwork. Just so, whereas we cannot realize the infinite love that fills eternity, and the infinite vistas of the great future are dark with excess of light even to the strongest telescopes of faith, we see that love magnified in the microscope of the moments, brought very close to us, and revealing its unspeakable perfection of detail to our wondering sight.

But we do not see this as long as the moments are kept in our own hands. We are like little children closing our fingers over diamonds. How can they receive and reflect the rays of light, analyzing them into all the splendor of their prismatic beauty, while they are kept shut up tight in the dirty little hands? Give them up! Let our Father hold them for us, and throw His own great light upon them. Then we shall see them full of fair colors of His manifold loving-kindnesses.

Let Him always keep them for us, and then we shall always see His light and His love reflected in them.

FRANCES R. HAVERGAL

THE WAY TO GOD

Heartfelt Repentance

Heaven is a prepared place for a prepared people. If your boy has done wrong and will not repent, you cannot forgive him. You would be doing him an injustice. Suppose he goes to your desk and steals ten dollars and squanders it. When you come home, your servant tells you what your boy has done. You ask if it is true, and he denies it. But at last you have certain proof. Even when he finds he cannot deny it any longer, he will not confess the sin but says he will do it again the first chance he gets. Would you say to him, "Well, I forgive you," and leave the matter there? No! Yet people say that God is going to save all men, whether they repent or not—drunkards, thieves, harlots, whoremongers, it makes no difference. "God is so merciful," they say. Dear friend, do not be deceived by the god of this world. Where there is true repentance and a turning from sin unto God, He will meet and bless you; but He never blesses until there is sincere repentance.

David made a woeful mistake in this respect with his rebellious son, Absalom. He could not have done his son a greater injustice than to forgive him when his heart was unchanged. There could be no true reconciliation between them when there was no repentance. But God does not make these mistakes. David got into trouble on account of his error of judgment. His son soon drove his father from the throne.

Speaking of repentance, Dr. Brookes, of St. Louis, well remarks: "Repentance, strictly speaking, means 'a change of mind or purpose'; consequently it is the judgment which the sinner pronounces upon himself, in view of the love of God displayed in the death of Christ, connected with the abandonment of all confidence in himself and with trust in the only Savior of sinners. Saving repentance and saving faith always go together; and you need not be worried about repentance if you will believe.

"Some people are not sure that they have 'repented enough.' If you mean by this, that you must repent in order to incline God to be merciful to you, the sooner you give over such repentance the better. God is already merciful, as He has fully shown at the cross of Calvary; and it is a grievous dishonor to His heart of love if you think that your tears and anguish will move Him, 'not knowing that the goodness of God leadeth thee to repentance.' It is not your badness, therefore, but His goodness that leads to repentance; hence the true way to repent is to believe on the Lord Jesus Christ, 'who was delivered for our offences, and was raised again for our justification.'"

D. L. MOODY

TEN REASONS THE BIBLE IS THE WORD OF GOD
Old Testament Prophecy

There are two classes of prophecies in the Bible—first, the explicit, verbal prophecies; second, those of the types.

In the first we have the definite prophecies concerning the Jews, the heathen nations, and the Messiah. Taking the prophecies regarding the Messiah as an illustration, look at Isaiah 53, Micah 5:2, and Daniel 9:25–27. Many others might be mentioned, but these will serve as illustrations. In these prophecies, written hundreds of years before the Messiah came, we have the most explicit statements as to the manner and place of His birth, the manner of His reception by men, how His life would end, His resurrection, and His victory over death. When made, these prophecies were exceedingly improbable and seemingly impossible of fulfillment; but they were fulfilled to the very minutest detail of manner and place and time. How are we to account for it? Man could not have foreseen these improbable events—they lay hundreds of years ahead. But God could, and it is God who speaks through these men.

But the prophecies of the types are more remarkable still. Everything in the Old Testament—history, institutions, ceremonies—is prophetical. The high-priesthood, the ordinary priesthoods, the Levites, the prophets, priests, and kings are all prophecies. The tabernacle, the brazen altar, the laver, the golden candlestick, the table of showbread, the veil, the altar of incense, the ark of the covenant, the very coverings of the tabernacle are prophecies. In all these things, as we study them minutely and soberly in the light of the history of Jesus Christ and the church, we see, wrapped up in the ancient institutions ordained of God to meet an immediate purpose, prophecies of the death, atonement, and resurrection of Christ, the day of Pentecost, and the entire history of the church. We see the profoundest Christian doctrines of the New Testament clearly foreshadowed in these institutions of the Old Testament. The only way in which you can appreciate this is to get into the Book itself and study all about the sacrifices, feasts, and so on, till you see the truths of the New Testament shining out in the Old.

R. A. TORREY

BACK TO BETHEL
Worthy of Our Calling

The epistle to the Ephesians is the epistle of "In-ness." That is, it is the epistle in which from first to last Paul uses the little preposition "in," and tells us what we are in Christ Jesus. Just as this whole creation slept in the mind of God to be elaborated step by step to its consummation, so the whole church of Jesus Christ lay in the mind of God before the mountains were brought forth or ever He had formed the earth. And you and I were appointed to a definite place in that wonderful body. What that place was will not be made fully clear to us until we stand before God in the eternal light, but it is comforting to know that there was a definite place in the purpose of God for you and me.

Doesn't that give a new meaning and dignity to your life, that it is the working out of the conception of God and that every day you must try so to walk as to realize the purpose that was in the mind of God when He created you in Christ Jesus? As one looks out upon men and women and things, life seems so full of commonplaces and little anxieties, worries, troubles, and misfortunes that one is apt to get into the way of supposing it does not matter very much how he lives. But if we remember that there is an eternal purpose in Christ in our regeneration, we shall always try to act worthily of our great calling in Christ Jesus.

The greatest thing you can do in this world is to live a saintly, holy, lovely life. All the small things of your life—the worries, anxieties, the troubles, your location and environment, the lines you are compelled to follow—all these have been contrived by God to give you the best opportunity possible to become what He wants you to be. God could have made you anything He liked. He could have made that woman a queen; He could have made that man a millionaire or a prince. But out of all the myriad opportunities of this world God Almighty chose for you just that position in which you find yourself today because He knew that was the one place in which you could come nearest His ideal.

F. B. MEYER

CHARGE THAT TO MY ACCOUNT

Two Aspects of Peace

Sometimes people use expressions that will not always bear the test of Scripture. Let me give an instance of this:

A number of years ago an earnest young Christian and I went to a mission in San Francisco. At the close of the meeting, a kind, motherly woman came to me and asked, "Are you a Christian, sir?"

I replied immediately, "Yes, I am."

"Thank God," she said, and then turning to my friend, she asked, "And have you made your 'peace with God,' sir?"

Rather to my astonishment, he answered, "No, madam, I have not."

I knew he was a Christian, and I wondered at his replying in that way.

She said to him rather severely, "Well, if you don't make your 'peace with God,' you will be lost forever."

With a bright, happy smile on his face, he replied, "Madam, I can never make my 'peace with God,' and I never expect to try; but I am thankful that the Lord Jesus Christ has settled that for me, and through what He did for me I shall be in heaven for all eternity."

He then put the question to her, "Have you never read that remarkable passage, 'Having made peace by the blood of his cross'?"

As he went on to explain it to her, the truth gripped my own soul. I saw then, and have realized it ever since, that sinners are saved through the "peace" that He made at the cross. And so we read in Romans 5:1, "Therefore being justified by faith, we have peace with God through our Lord Jesus Christ." This peace is not of our making—and is not of our keeping either. We enjoy the peace He made as we accept by faith the testimony of His Word.

But we also read, "My peace give I unto you." What does the Lord Jesus mean by this? It is another aspect of peace altogether. It is that quiet rest of soul that was ever His in the midst of the most trying circumstances. He shares His peace with us. It is of this we read in Philippians 4:6–7: "Be careful for nothing [or, in nothing be anxious, RV], but in everything by prayer and supplication with thanksgiving, let your requests be made known unto God. And the peace of God, which passeth all understanding, shall keep your hearts and minds through Christ Jesus."

HENRY A. IRONSIDE

THE WAY HOME
Christ's Boundless Compassion

There was a time (during the Civil War) when many thought that Abraham Lincoln had too much compassion. Many of our soldiers did not understand army discipline and consequently were court-martialed and condemned to be shot; but Lincoln would always pardon them. At length the nation rose up against him and said that he was too merciful, and ultimately they got him to agree that if a man was court-martialed he must be shot. There would be no more reprieves.

A few weeks after this, news came that a young soldier had been sleeping at his post. He was court-martialed and condemned to be shot. The boy wrote to his mother, "I do not want you to think I do not love my country, but it came about this way: My comrade was sick, and I went out on picket for him. The next night he ought to have come, but being still sick I went out for him again, and without intending it I fell asleep. I did not intend to be disloyal."

It was a very touching letter. The mother and father said there was no chance for him, there were to be no more reprieves. But there was a little girl in that home, and she knew that Abraham Lincoln had a little boy and how he loved that boy; and she thought if Abraham Lincoln knew how her father and mother loved her brother he would never allow him to be shot. So she took the train to go and plead for her brother.

When she got to the president's mansion, with genuine tears and pleadings she got past the sentinel, the secretary, and the other officials. She succeeded in getting, unobstructed, into Lincoln's private room, and there were the senators and ministers busy with state affairs.

The president saw the child and called her to him and said, "My child, what can I do for you?"

She told him her story. The big tears rolled down his cheeks. He was a father, and his heart was full; he could not stand it. He treated the girl with kindness, reprieved the boy, gave him thirty days furlough, and sent him home to see his mother. His heart was full of compassion.

Let me tell you, Christ's heart is more full of compassion than any man's. You are condemned to die for your sins; but if you go to Him He will say, "Loose him, and let him go." He will rebuke Satan. Go to Him as that little girl went to the president, and tell Him all. Keep nothing from Him, and He will say, "Go in peace."

D. L. MOODY

CALVARY'S CROSS

What Think You of the Cross?

The cross means that Christ died for sinners upon the cross, that He made atonement for sinners by His suffering for them on the cross—a complete and perfect sacrifice for sin, which He offered up when He gave His own body to be crucified. This is the meaning in which Paul used the expression, when he told the Corinthians, "The preaching of the cross is to them that perish foolishness" (1 Corinthians 1:18), and when he wrote to the Galatians, "God forbid that I should glory save in the cross." He simply meant, "I glory in nothing but Christ crucified as the salvation of my soul."

This is the subject he loved to preach about.

He was a man who went to and fro on the earth, proclaiming to sinners that the Son of God had shed His own heart's blood to save their souls, that Jesus Christ had loved them and died for their sins upon the cross. Mark how he says to the Corinthians, "I delivered unto you first of all that which I also received, how that Christ died for our sins" (1 Corinthians 15:3). He—a blaspheming, persecuting Pharisee—had been washed in Christ's blood. He could not hold his peace about it. He was never weary of telling the story of the cross.

This is the subject he loved to dwell upon when he wrote to believers.

It is wonderful to observe how full his epistles generally are of the sufferings and death of Christ. He enlarges on the subject constantly. He returns to it continually. It is the golden thread that runs through all his doctrinal teaching and practical exhortation. He seems to think that the most advanced Christian can never hear too much of the cross.

This is what he lived upon all his life, from the time of his conversion. He tells the Galatians, "The life that I now live in the flesh I live by the faith of the Son of God, who loved me and gave himself for me" (Galatians 2:20). What made him so strong to labor, so willing to work, so unwearied in endeavoring to save some, so persevering and patient? The secret of it all was that he was always feeding by faith on Christ's body and Christ's blood. Jesus crucified was the meat and drink of his soul.

J. C. RYLE

PLEASURE AND PROFIT IN BIBLE STUDY

The Old and New Testaments

I want to show how absurd it is for anyone to say he believes the New Testament and not the Old. It is a very interesting fact that of the thirty-nine books of the Old Testament, it is recorded that our Lord made quotations from no less than twenty-two. Very possibly He may have quoted from all of them; for we have only fragments reported of what He said and did. You know the apostle John tells us that the world could scarcely contain the books that could be written, if all the sayings and doings of our Lord were recorded. About 850 passages in the Old Testament are quoted or alluded to in the New; only a few occurring more than once.

In the gospel of Matthew there are more than a hundred quotations from twenty of the books in the Old Testament. In the gospel of Mark there are fifteen quotations taken from thirteen of the books. In the gospel of Luke there are thirty-four quotations from thirteen books. In the gospel of John there are eleven quotations from six books. In the four gospels alone there are more than 160 quotations from the Old Testament.

You sometimes hear men saying they do not believe all the Bible, but they believe the teaching of Jesus Christ in the four gospels. Well, if I believe that, I have to accept these 160 quotations from the Old Testament. In Paul's letter to the Corinthians there are fifty-three quotations from the Old Testament; sometimes he takes whole paragraphs from it. In Hebrews there are eighty-five quotations—in that one book of thirteen chapters. In Galatians, sixteen quotations. In the book of Revelation alone there are 245 quotations and allusions.

A great many want to throw out the Old Testament. It is good historic reading, they say, but they don't believe that it is a part of the Word of God and don't regard it as essential in the scheme of salvation. The last letter Paul wrote contained the following words: "And that from a child thou hast known the holy scriptures, which are able to make thee wise unto salvation through faith which is in Christ Jesus." All the Scriptures that the apostles possessed were the Old Testament.

D. L. MOODY

KEPT FOR THE MASTER'S USE

Our Voices Kept for Jesus

If you only knew, dear hesitating friends, what strength and gladness the Master gives you when you loyally sing forth the honor of His name, you would not forgo it. Oh, if you only knew the difficulties it saves! For when you sing "always and only for your King," you will not get much entangled by the King's enemies. Singing an out-and-out sacred song often clears one's path at a stroke as to many other things. If you only knew the rewards He gives, very often then and there, the recognition that you are one of the King's friends by some lonely and timid one, the natural openings to speak a word for Jesus to hearts which, without the song, would never have given you the chance of the word.

If you only knew the joy of believing that His sure promise "My word shall not return unto me void" will be fulfilled as you sing that word for Him! If you only tasted the solemn happiness of knowing that you have indeed a royal audience, that the King Himself is listening as you sing! If you only knew—and why should you not know? Shall not the time past of your life suffice you for the miserable, double-hearted calculating service? Let Him have the whole use of your voice at any cost, and see if He does not put many a totally unexpected new song into your mouth.

I am not writing all this to great and finished singers, but to everybody who can sing at all. Those who think they have only a very small talent are often most tempted not to trade with it for their Lord. Whether you have much or little natural voice, there is reason for its cultivation and room for its use. Place it at your Lord's disposal, and He will show you how to make the most of it for Him; for not seldom His multiplying power is brought to bear on a consecrated voice.

FRANCES R. HAVERGAL

THE WAY TO GOD

Our Spiritual Need of Christ

While looking through some papers I once read this wonderful description of Christ. I do not know where it originally came from, but it was so fresh to my soul that I should like to give it to you:

"Christ is our Way; we walk in Him. He is our Truth; we embrace Him. He is our Life; we live in Him. He is our Lord; we choose Him to rule over us. He is our Master; we serve Him. He is our Teacher, instructing us in the way of salvation. He is our Prophet, pointing out the future. He is our Priest, having atoned for us. He is our Advocate, ever living to make intercession for us. He is our Savior, saving to the uttermost. He is our Root; we grow from Him. He is our Bread; we feed upon Him. He is our Shepherd, leading us into green pastures. He is our true Vine; we abide in Him. He is the Water of Life; we slake our thirst from Him. He is the fairest among ten thousand; we admire Him above all others. He is 'the brightness of the Father's glory, and the express image of His person'; we strive to reflect His likeness. He is the upholder of all things; we rest upon Him. He is our wisdom; we are guided by Him. He is our Righteousness; we cast all our imperfections upon Him. He is our Sanctification; we draw all our power for holy life from Him. He is our redemption, redeeming us from all iniquity. He is our Healer, curing all our diseases. He is our Friend, relieving us in all our necessities. He is our Brother, cheering us in our difficulties."

Here is another beautiful extract; it is from Gotthold:

"For my part, my soul is like a hungry and thirsty child; and I need His love and consolation for my refreshment. I am a wandering and lost sheep; and I need Him as a good and faithful shepherd. My soul is like a frightened dove pursued by the hawk; and I need His wounds for a refuge. I am a feeble vine; and I need His cross to lay hold of, and to wind myself about. I am a sinner; and I need His righteousness. I am naked and bare; and I need His holiness and innocence for a covering. I am ignorant; and I need His teaching: simple and foolish; and I need the guidance of His Holy Spirit. In no situation, and at no time, can I do without Him. Do I pray? He must prompt, and intercede for me. Am I arraigned by Satan at the divine tribunal? He must be my Advocate. Am I in affliction? He must be my Helper. Am I persecuted by the world? He must defend me. When I am forsaken, He must be my support; when I am dying, my life; when mouldering in the grave, my Resurrection. Well, then, I will rather part with all the world, and all that it contains, than with Thee, my Saviour."

D. L. MOODY

THE SCHOOL OF OBEDIENCE
Obedience to the Last Command

In which way ought we to give to Christ Jesus? I fear many, many give as if they were free to give what they choose, what they think they can afford. The believer to whom the right, which the purchase price of the blood has acquired, has been revealed by the Holy Spirit, delights to know that he is the bond slave of redeeming love, and to lay everything he has at his Master's feet, because he belongs to Him.

Have you ever wondered that the disciples accepted the great command so easily and so heartily? They came fresh from Calvary, where they had seen the blood. They had met the risen one, and He had breathed His Spirit into them. During the forty days "through the Holy Ghost he had given his commandments unto them." Jesus was to them Savior, Master, Friend, and Lord. His word was with divine power; they could not but obey. Oh, let us bow at His feet and yield to the Holy Spirit to reveal and assert His mighty claim, and let us unhesitatingly and with the whole heart accept the command as our one life-purpose: the gospel to every creature!

The last great command has been so prominently urged in connection with foreign missions that many are inclined exclusively to confine it to them. This is a great mistake. Our Lord's words, "Make disciples of all nations; teaching them to observe all things whatsoever I have commanded you," tell us that our aim is to be nothing less than to make every man a true disciple, living in holy obedience to all Christ's will.

What a work there is to be done in our Christian churches and our so-called Christian communities ere it can be said that the command has been carried out! And what a need that the whole church, with every believer in it, realize that to do this work is the sole subject of its existence! The gospel brought fully, perseveringly, savingly to every creature: this is the mission, this ought to be the passion, of every redeemed soul. For this alone is the Spirit and likeness and life of Christ formed in you.

ANDREW MURRAY

SOWING AND REAPING

A Man Expects to Reap the Same Kind as He Sows

If I should tell you that I sowed ten acres of wheat last year and that watermelons came up, or that I sowed cucumbers and gathered turnips, you wouldn't believe it. It is a fixed law that you reap the same kind of seed you sow. Plant wheat and you reap wheat, plant an acorn and there comes up an oak, plant a little elm and in time you have a big elm.

One day, the master of Lukman, an Eastern writer of fables, said to him, "Go into such a field, and sow barley."

Lukman sowed oats instead. At the time of harvest his master went to the place, and, seeing the green oats springing up, asked him: "Did I not tell you to sow barley here? Why, then, have you sown oats?"

He answered, "I sowed oats in the hope that barley would grow up."

His master said, "What foolish idea is this? Have you ever heard of the like?"

Lukman replied, "You yourself are constantly sowing in the field of the world the seeds of evil and yet expect to reap in the resurrection day the fruits of virtue. Therefore, I thought, also, I might get barley by sowing oats."

The master was abashed at the reply and set Lukman free.

Like produces like in vegetation, and like produces like in labor. If a man has learned the trade of a carpenter, he does not expect to excel as a watchmaker. If he has toiled hard to acquire a knowledge of the law, he does not expect to practice medicine for a livelihood. Men expect to reap in the occupation they have learned.

This law is just as true in God's kingdom as in man's kingdom; just as true in the spiritual world as in the natural world. If I sow tares, I am going to reap tares; if I sow a lie, I am going to reap lies; if I sow adultery, I am going to reap adulterers; if I sow whiskey, I am going to reap drunkards. You cannot blot this law out; it is in force. No other truth in the Bible is more solemn.

D. L. MOODY

MOODY'S LATEST SERMONS
Work After Worship

After the transfiguration on the mountain, Jesus and the disciples came down and met a father who had a son possessed with a devil (Mark 9:14-29). When the father went to bring his son to Jesus the devil tripped him up. Like a bad tenant, he tried to do as much harm as he could before leaving. The devil knew that he was going to get orders to leave, so he gave the boy such a throw that he nearly killed him. The disciples could not cast the devil out. The boy was deaf and dumb, and I presume the disciples said: "Oh, you know, that is a hopeless case. If he could only tell us how he feels, or if we could only shout into his ear, we might get at him; but we cannot make him hear or speak, and we cannot do anything."

They lacked faith. But the Lord came down, and that father came to Christ. "Mark you," Spurgeon says, "he (the father) was a poor theologian when he came to Christ. He came and said, 'If thou canst do anything,' and the Lord rebuked him right there. He said, 'If thou canst believe.' He put the 'if' in the right place. 'All things are possible to him that believeth; bring him unto me.'"

You may have some brother or father or friend whom you want to be converted. You have brought them to Christians, and the devil has not been cast out. Listen! What did Christ say to His Father? "Bring him unto me."

There is a great deal of joy in the thought that Christ has power over the devils. Remember that "all power in heaven and earth" is given to Him, and don't think for a moment that any man is beyond the reach of God's mercy. Don't you think that your brother who is a slave to strong drink is beyond the reach of God. "Bring him to Me," says Christ. Get beyond your church, your society and go right to the master Himself.

When that mother came and told Elisha that her child was dead (2 Kings 4:8-37), the prophet said to his servant, "Take that stick and lay it out on that dead child." Away went the servant. But that woman was wiser than Elisha; she would not leave him. She was not going to trust in that staff or that servant, she wanted the prophet himself. Some people think that it will do to love Christ without giving themselves to the work. No. Sometimes your whole life must be given to win a person. Make up your mind that if it costs you your life, you are going to do it.

D. L. MOODY

THE EMPTY TOMB

Their Souls Sleep Not

Oh, how we should rejoice—we who hang our salvation wholly upon Christ, who beyond a doubt is "risen from the dead."

"But now is Christ risen from the dead, and become the firstfruits of them that slept." The representations of 1 Corinthians 15:20 are twofold. Death is here compared to a sleep: "The first fruits of them that slept." However, it is compared also to a sowing, for Christ is pictured as being "the first-fruits." Now, to obtain a harvest there must have been a sowing. If the resurrection of Christ be the firstfruits, then the resurrection of believers must be looked upon as a harvest, and death would therefore be symbolized by a sowing.

First, then, we have before us the picture so commonly employed in Scripture of death as a sleep. We must not make a mistake by imagining that the soul sleeps. The soul undergoes no purification or preparative slumber; beyond a doubt, "Today shalt thou be with me in paradise" is the whisper of Christ to every dying saint. They sleep in Jesus, but their souls sleep not. They are before the throne of God, praising Him day and night in His temple—singing hallelujahs to Him who has washed them from their sins in His blood. It is the body that sleeps so deeply in its lonely bed of earth, beneath the coverlet of grass, with the cold clay for its pillow.

But what is this sleep? We all know that the surface idea connected with sleep is that of resting. That is doubtless just the thought that the Holy Spirit would convey to us. The eyes of the sleeper ache no more with the glare of light or with the rush of tears. His ears are teased no more with the noise of strife or the murmur of suffering. His hand is no more weakened by long protracted effort and painful weariness. His feet are no more blistered with journeyings to and fro along a rugged road. There is rest for aching heads, and strained muscles, and overtaxed nerves, and loosened joints, and panting lungs, and heavy hearts, in the sweet repose of sleep.

On yonder couch the laborer shakes off his toil, the merchant his care, the thinker his difficulties, and the sufferer his pains. Sleep makes each night a Sabbath for the day. Sleep shuts the door of the soul and bids all intruders tarry for a while, that the royal life within may enter into its summer garden of ease.

So it is with the body while it sleeps in the tomb. The weary are at rest.

CHARLES H. SPURGEON

MOODY'S LATEST SERMONS
Fresh Supplies

Turn to Acts 4:31 and you will find He came a second time, and at a place where they were, so that the earth was shaken, and they were filled with this power. The fact is, we are leaky vessels, and we have to keep right under the fountain all the time to keep full of Christ, and so have a fresh supply.

I believe this is a mistake a great many of us are making; we are trying to do God's work with the grace God gave us ten years ago. We say, if it is necessary, we will go on with the same grace. Now, what we want is a fresh supply, a fresh anointing and fresh power, and if we seek it, and seek it with all our hearts, we will obtain it. The early converts were taught to look for that power. Philip went to Samaria, and news reached Jerusalem that there was a great work being done in Samaria, with many converts; and John and Peter went down, and they laid their hands on them, and they received the Holy Ghost for service. I think that is what we Christians ought to be looking for—the Spirit of God for service—that God may use us mightily in the building up of His church and hastening His glory.

When the inquiry was made if they had received the Holy Ghost since they believed, twelve men at Ephesus answered, "We have not so much as heard whether there be any Holy Ghost" (Acts 19:2). I venture to say there are very many, who, if you were to ask them, "Have you received the Holy Ghost since you believed?" would reply, "I don't know what you mean by that." They would be like those twelve men who had never understood the peculiar relation of the Spirit to the sons of God in this dispensation. I firmly believe that the church has just laid this knowledge aside, mislaid it somewhere, and so Christians are without power. Sometimes you can take one hundred members into the church, and they don't add to its power. Now that is all wrong. If they were only anointed by the Spirit of God, there would be great power if one hundred saved ones were added to the church.

D. L. MOODY

SATAN AND THE SAINT

When Christ Comes

What will be the effect or the consequences of Christ's second coming in the history of the earth and the human race?

In answering this, let me say that the great event is not limited to a single point of time, but in a sense covers a long period of time. The second coming, in other words, might be spoken of as a drama with several acts, or as an act with several scenes.

The first scene will be the translation of the church to meet Christ in the air, according to the words of Paul: "The Lord himself shall descend from heaven with a shout, with the voice of the archangel, and with the trump of God, and the dead in Christ"—not all the dead, but those who have fallen asleep in Christ—"shall rise first; then we which are alive and remain shall be caught up together with them in the clouds, to meet the Lord in the air" (1 Thessalonians 4:13–18).

Some think too strange, too mysterious to be possible, the translation of the church into the air! But God has shown us what it means. In the age before the Flood, "Enoch walked with God and was not; for God took him"; or, as the New Testament says: "He was translated, having never seen death." In the Mosaic age we have a demonstration in Elijah. Walking with Elisha across the Jordan, dry shod, when they reached the other shore the chariot of fire came down and took Elijah in a whirlwind into heaven. He never saw death. What God can do with one He can do with millions when the time comes.

It is written in the Scriptures: "It is appointed unto men once to die, and after this the judgment" (Hebrew 9:27); and I have heard it rendered as though it read: "It is appointed unto all men once to die." But this is not true. There is one generation of men that, living on earth, shall never see death. That generation is the one just referred to, who, believing on the Lord Jesus Christ and waiting for His coming, shall be caught up to meet Him in the air when He comes.

JAMES M. GRAY

THE OVERCOMING LIFE

Confessing Christ

If you are converted, the next step is to confess it openly. Paul told his listeners, "If thou shalt confess with thy mouth the Lord Jesus Christ, and shalt believe in thine heart that God hath raised him from the dead, thou shalt be saved. For with the heart man believeth unto righteousness; and with the mouth confession is made unto salvation" (Romans 10:9–10).

Confession of Christ is the culmination of the work of true repentance. We owe it to the world, to our fellow Christians, to ourselves. He died to redeem us, and shall we be ashamed or afraid to confess Him? Religion as an abstraction, as a doctrine, has little interest for the world, but what people can say from personal experience always has weight.

I remember some meetings being held in one place where bitter and reproachful things were being said about the work. One day, one of the most prominent men in the place rose and said, "I want it to be known that I am a disciple of Jesus Christ; and if there is any criticism to be cast on His cause, I am prepared to take my share of it." It went through the meeting like an electric current, and a blessing came at once to his own soul and to the souls of others.

Men come to me and say: "Do you mean to affirm, Mr. Moody, that I've got to make a public confession when I accept Christ; do you mean to say I've got to confess Him in my place of business, and in my family? Am I to let the whole world know that I am on His side?"

That is precisely what I mean. A great many are willing to accept Christ, but they are not willing to publish it, to confess it. A great many are looking at the lions and the bears in the way. Now, my friends, the devil's mountains are only made of smoke. He can throw a straw into your path and make a mountain of it. He says to you, "You cannot confess to your family; why, you'll break down! You cannot tell it to your shopmate; he will laugh at you." But when you accept Christ, you will have power to confess Him.

D. L. MOODY

GOD'S WAY OF HOLINESS

The Root and Soil of Holiness

The apostles trusted the gospel with the sinner, and the sinner with the gospel, so unreservedly, and (as many in our day would say) unguardedly. "To him that worketh not, but *believeth* . . . his faith is counted for righteousness" (Romans 4:5) was a bold statement. It's a statement by one who had great confidence in the gospel that he preached; who had no misgivings as to its unholy tendencies, if men would but give it fair play. He himself always preached it as one who believed it to be the power of God unto holiness no less than unto salvation.

That this is the understanding of the New Testament, the "mind of the Spirit," requires no proof. Few would in words deny it to be so; only they state the gospel so timorously, so warily, so guardedly, with so many conditions, terms and reservations, that by the time they have finished their statement, they have left no good news in what they had once announced as "the gospel of the grace of God."

The more fully that the gospel is preached, in the grand old apostolic way, the more likely is it to accomplish results similar to those in apostolic days. The gospel is the proclamation of free love, the revelation of the boundless charity of God. Nothing less than this will suit our world; nothing else is so likely to touch the heart, to go down to the lowest depths of depraved humanity, as the assurance that the sinner has been loved—loved by God with a righteous love and with a free love that makes no bargain as to merit or fitness or goodness.

"Herein is love, not that we loved God, but that he loved us," declares the apostle John in his first letter. With nothing less than this free love will the Lord trust our fallen race. He will not trust them with law or judgment or terror (though these are well in their place); but He will trust them with His love! Not with a stinted or conditional love; with half pardons or an uncertain salvation or a doubtful invitation or an all but impracticable amnesty. With these He will not mock the weary sons of men. He wants them to be holy, as well as safe; and He knows that there is nothing in heaven or earth so likely to produce holiness, under the teaching of the Spirit of holiness, as the knowledge of His own free love.

HORATIUS BONAR

THE CHRIST-LIFE FOR THE SELF-LIFE
The Son Revealed to Us

W hen it pleased God, who separated me from my mother's womb, and called me by his grace, to reveal his Son in me, that I might preach him among the heathen, immediately I conferred not with flesh and blood" (Galatians 1:15–16). Paul wrote that "it pleased God to reveal his Son in me." Now, "to reveal" means "to undrape." There is a statue, covered with a veil. It is there, but it's hidden. I take off the veil, and you see it. When you were regenerated, Christ came unto you: that is what regeneration means— Christ born into your spirit. But Christ came in as a veiled figure, and you who are regenerate but who have never seen the Christ as He truly is behold Him as a veiled figure, even though He is in you. When Jesus died, the veil of the temple was rent in two from the top to the bottom; and when the soul appreciates the death of Christ as its own death to sin, the veil is rent in two from the top to the bottom, and the Holy Ghost reveals Jesus as the substitute for the self-life.

"It pleased God to reveal his Son in me." O, my God, I thank Thee that Thou hast revealed Thy Son as the Alpha, the pivot, the fountain, the origin of my life! May it be so with us all!

A friend of mine was staying near Mont Blanc. He had been there for a fortnight, but had not seen the "monarch of the Alps," for the thick clouds held it behind a veil. Nearly out of heart with waiting, he was preparing to leave. Going up to dress for dinner, he passed a window and saw that the monarch was still veiled in mist. Having dressed, he came downstairs, passing the window again. Every vestige of mist had now parted, and Mont Blanc stood revealed from base to snow-clad peak. So now there shall come upon you a breath of the Holy Ghost, before which the misconception of your life shall pass, and to you God will reveal His Son in you as the center of your life.

For a moment, think about Colossians 1:27, a favorite passage of mine: "To whom God would make known what is the riches of the glory of this mystery among the Gentiles; which is Christ in you, the hope of glory."

F. B. MEYER

THE WAY TO GOD

His Promises Stand

Man lost life by unbelief—by not believing God's Word; and we got life back again by believing—by taking God at His Word. In other words, we get up where Adam fell down. He stumbled and fell over the stone of unbelief; and we are lifted and stand upright by believing. As John wrote, "The Father loveth the Son, and hath given all things into his hand. He that believeth on the Son hath everlasting life: and he that believeth not the Son shall not see life; but the wrath of God abideth on him" (3:35–36).

When people say they cannot believe, show them chapter and verse, and ask them this one thing: "Has God ever broken His promise for these six thousand years?" The devil and men have been trying all the time and have not succeeded in showing that He has broken a single promise. If a man says that he cannot believe, it is well to press him on that one thing.

I can believe God better today than I can my own heart. "The heart is deceitful above all things, and desperately wicked: who can know it?" (Jeremiah 17:9). I can believe God better than I can myself. If you want to know the way of life, believe that Jesus Christ is a personal Savior; cut away from all doctrines and creeds, and come right to the heart of the Son of God. If you have been feeding on dry doctrine, there is not much growth on that kind of food. Doctrines are to the soul what the streets that lead to the house of a dinner host are to the body. They will lead me there if I take the right one; but if I remain in the streets my hunger will never be satisfied. Feeding on doctrines is like trying to live on dry husks; and lean indeed must the soul remain that partakes not of the bread sent down from heaven.

Some ask, "How am I to get my heart warmed?" It is by believing. You will not have power to love and serve God until you believe.

D. L. MOODY

TEN REASONS THE BIBLE IS THE WORD OF GOD

Thirty Writers, One Theme

This is an old argument, but a very satisfactory one. The Bible consists of sixty-six books, written by more than thirty different men, extending in the period of its composition over more than fifteen hundred years; written in three different languages, in many different countries, and by men on every plane of social life, from the herdman and fisherman and cheap politician up to the king upon his throne. Nevertheless, in all this wonderful conglomeration we find an absolute unity of thought.

A wonderful thing about it is that this unity does not lie on the surface. On the surface apparent contradiction often appears, and the unity only comes out after deep and protracted study.

More wonderful yet is the organic character of this unity, beginning in the first book and growing till you come to its culmination in the last book of the Bible. We have first the seed, then the plant, then the bud, then the blossom, then the ripened fruit.

Suppose a vast building were to be erected, the stones for which were brought from the quarries in Rutland, Vermont; Berea, Ohio; Kasota, Minnesota; and Middletown, Connecticut. Each stone was hewn into final shape in the quarry from which it was brought. These stones were of all varieties of shape and size, cubical, rectangular, cylindrical, etc., but when they were brought together every stone fitted into its place, and when put together there rose before you a temple absolutely perfect on every outline, with its dome, sidewalls, buttresses, arches, transepts—not a gap or a flaw anywhere. How would you account for it? You would say: "Back of these individual workers in the quarries was the master-mind of the architect who planned it all and gave to each individual worker his specifications for the work."

So in this marvelous temple of God's truth that we call the Bible, whose stones have been quarried at periods of time and in places so remote from one another, but where every smallest part fits each other part, we are forced to say that back of the human hands that wrought was the Master-mind that thought.

R. A. TORREY

HEAVEN

The Prize

The world scoffed at Paul, but he did not heed its scoffing. He had something the world had not; burning within him he had a love and zeal the world knew nothing about. And the love that Paul had for Jesus Christ! But, oh, the greater love the Lord Jesus had for Paul!

The hour had come. The way they used to behead them in those days was for the prisoner to bend his head, when a Roman soldier took a sword and cut it off. The hour had come, and I seem to see Paul, with a joyful countenance, bending his blessed head, as the soldier's sword comes down and sets his spirit free.

If our eyes could look as Elisha's looked, we might have seen him leap into a chariot of light like Elijah; we would have seen him go sweeping through limitless space.

Look at him yonder!

See! He is entering now the Eternal City of the glorified saints, the blissful abode of the Savior's redeemed. The prize he so long has sought is at hand. See the gates yonder; how they fly wide open. And he goes sweeping through the pearly gates, along the shining way, to the very throne of God, and Christ stands there and says, "Well done, thou good and faithful servant; enter thou into the joy of the Lord."

Just think of hearing the master say it! Will that not be enough for everything?

Oh, friends, your turn and mine will come by and by, if we are but faithful. Let us see that we do not lose the crown. Let us awake and put on the whole armor of God; let us press into the conflict; it is a glorious privilege, and to us too, as to the glorified of old, will come that blessed welcome from our glorified Lord: "Well done, thou good and faithful servant."

D. L. MOODY

CALVARY'S CROSS

St. Paul and the Cross

The cross of Christ—the death of Christ on the cross to make atonement for sinners—is the central truth in the whole Bible. This is the truth we begin with when we open Genesis. The seed of the woman bruising the serpent's head is nothing else but a prophecy of Christ crucified. This is the truth that shines out, though veiled, all through the law of Moses and the history of the Jews. The daily sacrifice, the Passover lamb, the continual shedding of blood in the tabernacle and temple—all these were emblems of Christ crucified. This is the truth that we see honored in the vision of heaven before we close the book of Revelation. "In the midst of the throne and of the four beasts," we are told, "and in the midst of the elders, stood a Lamb as it had been slain" (Revelation 5:6). Even in the midst of heavenly glory we get a view of Christ crucified.

Take away the cross of Christ, and the Bible is a dark book. It is like the Egyptian hieroglyphics without the key that interprets their meaning, curious and wonderful, but of no real use.

Reader, you may know a good deal about the Bible. You may know the outlines of the histories it contains and the dates of the events described, just as a man knows the history of England. You may know the names of the men and women mentioned in it, just as a man knows Caesar, Alexander the Great, or Napoleon. You may know the several precepts of the Bible and admire them, just as a man admires Plato, Aristotle, or Seneca. But if you have not yet found out that Christ crucified is the foundation of the whole volume, you have read your Bible hitherto to very little profit. Your religion is a heaven without a sun, an arch without a keystone, a compass without a needle, a clock without spring or weights, a lamp without oil. It will not comfort you. It will not deliver your soul from hell.

You may know a great deal about Christ by a kind of head knowledge. You may know who He was and where He was born and what He did—His miracles, His sayings, His prophecies, and His ordinances, how He lived, how He suffered, and how He died. But unless you know the power of Christ's cross by experience, unless you know and feel within that the blood shed on that cross has washed away your own particular sins, and unless you are willing to confess that your salvation depends entirely upon the work that Christ did upon the cross, Christ will profit you nothing.

J. C. RYLE

THE TRUE VINE

Obey and Abide

We may find our life and strength and joy in His love all the day, but it is only by an obedience like His we can abide in it. Perfect conformity to the vine is one of the most precious of the lessons of the branch. It was by obedience that Christ as the vine honored the Father as husbandman; it is by obedience that the believer as branch honors Christ as vine.

Obey and abide. That was the law of Christ's life as much as it is to be that of ours. He was made like us in all things, that we might be like Him in all things. He opened up a path in which we may walk even as He walked. He took our human nature to teach us how to wear it, and to show us how obedience, as it is the first duty of the creature, is the only way to abide in the favor of God and enter into His glory. And now He comes to instruct and encourage us and asks us to keep His commandments, even as He kept His Father's commandments and abides in His love.

The divine fitness of this connection between obeying and abiding, between God's commandments and His love, is easily seen. God's will is the very center of His divine perfection. As revealed in His commandments, it opens up the way for the creature to grow into the likeness of the Creator. In accepting and doing His will, I rise into fellowship with Him. Therefore it was that the Son, when coming into the world, spoke, "I come to do thy will, O God"! This was the place and this would be the blessedness of the creature. This was what he had lost in the Fall. This was what Christ came to restore. This is what, as the heavenly Vine, He asks of us and imparts to us, that even as He by keeping His Father's commandments abode in His love, we should keep His commandments and abide in His love.

ANDREW MURRAY

SOVEREIGN GRACE

The Wedding Invitation

Who would not feel highly honored if they were invited to some fine residence to the wedding of one of the members of the president's family? I can imagine you would feel rather proud of having received such an invitation. You would want all your friends to know it. Probably you will never get such an invitation. But I have a far grander invitation for you here than that. I cannot speak for others; but if I know my own heart, I would rather be torn to pieces tonight, limb from limb, and die in the glorious hope of being at the marriage supper of the Lamb, than live in this world a thousand years and miss that appointment at the last.

"Blessed is he that is called to the marriage supper of the Lamb." It will be a fearful thing for any of us to see Abraham, Isaac, and Jacob taking their place in the kingdom of God and be ourselves thrust out.

This is no myth, my friend; it is a real invitation. Every man and woman is invited. All things are now ready. The feast has been prepared at great expense. You may spurn the grace, and the gift of God; but you must bear in mind that it cost God a good deal before He could provide this feast. When He gave Christ He gave the richest jewel that heaven had. And now He sends out the invitation. He commands His servants to go into the highways and hedges and lanes and compel them to come in, that His house may be full. Who will come?

You say you are not fit to come? If the president invited you to the White House, and the invitation said you were to come just as you were; and if the sentinel at the gate stopped you because you did not wear a dress suit, what would you do? Would you not show him the document signed in the name of the president? Then he would stand aside and let you pass. So, my friend, if you can prove to me that you are a sinner, I can prove to you that you are invited to this gospel feast—to this marriage supper of the Lamb.

D. L. MOODY

FIVE "MUSTS" OF THE CHRISTIAN LIFE
The "Must" of Sacrifice

J esus knew He would tread the winepress alone. He knew that though He loved the race and desired to save every individual, the majority would repudiate Him.

He knew that he would stand before unfallen worlds and ranks of beings, as identified with a world's sin. He knew that His Father's face would be hidden, as by an eclipse. He knew that the conflict would break His heart and force the sweat of blood out on His forehead. He knew that the Serpent of hell would bruise His heel and that He would appear as a Lamb that had been slain. He knew that those whom He had chosen out of the world would deny Him and flee.

Yet He slackened not His pace, but laying aside the insignia of His glory, He became obedient unto death, even the death of the cross!

Looking at this stupendous act, shall we not catch the infection of His self-giving? Shall we not follow Him so far as we can? "Christ," says the apostle, "has left us an example that we should follow His steps." It is not what we get but what we give; not our own pleasure, but the uplifting of the fallen and the extrication of those who are slipping into the pit; not ridding ourselves of burdens but bearing the burden of others. This is the path of true blessedness, the path trodden by all saints, the path that led Christ to Gethsemane and Calvary, but has ended in the throne. Follow that path, and life will become transcendently useful and blessed!

But there is an infinite chasm between our highest attainments and the divine self-giving of our Savior to redeem and save us. He trod that wine-press alone, and of all the people there were none with Him. So far as we know, Gethsemane and Calvary have no equivalents throughout God's universe. They are the wonder into which angels desire to look, and the theme of the untiring song of the redeemed.

F. B. MEYER

THE WAY HOME
The Great Question

Now, one question: What are you going to do with Christ? You have got to settle that question. You may get angry, like a man a short time ago, who marched out of a church, saying, "What right has that man to make such a statement?" But it is true; you must settle it. Pilate wanted to shirk the responsibility and sent Jesus to Herod; but he was forced to a decision. When the Jews forced him to decide, he washed his hands, and said he "was innocent of this just man's blood." But did that take away his guilt? No.

An angel may be here, hovering over this audience, and he is listening to what is said. Someone may say, "I will receive Him; I will delay no longer."

Immediately the angel will wing his way right up to the pearly gates and tell the news that another sinner has been saved. There will be a new song ringing through the courts of heaven over a sinner repenting. God will issue the command to write down his name in the book of life and to get rooms ready for him in the new Jerusalem, where we all will soon be.

A man was once being tried for a crime, the punishment of which was death. The witnesses came in one by one and testified to his guilt; but there he stood, quite calm and unmoved. The judge and the jury were quite surprised at his indifference; they could not understand how he could take such a serious matter so calmly. When the jury retired, it did not take them many minutes to decide on the verdict "guilty"; and when the judge was passing the sentence of death upon the criminal, he told him how surprised he was that he could be so unmoved in the prospect of death.

When the judge had finished, the man put his hand in his bosom, pulled out a document, and walked out of the dock a free man. It was a free pardon from his king, which he had in his pocket all the time. The king had instructed him to allow the trial to proceed, and to produce the pardon only when he was condemned. Ah, that was how he could be so calm! No wonder he was indifferent as to the result of the trial. We who believe in Christ shall not come into judgment. We have got a pardon from the Great King, and it is sealed with the blood of His Son.

D. L. MOODY

THE EMPTY TOMB
The "Stolen" Body

The story circulated by the Jews at the time was that the body had been stolen. "Some of the watch came into the city, and showed unto the chief priests all the things that were done. And when they were assembled with the elders, and had taken counsel, they gave large money unto the soldiers, saying, 'Say ye, his disciples came by night, and stole him away while we slept.' And if this comes to the governor's ears, we will persuade him and secure you. So they took the money, and did as they were taught; and this saying is commonly reported among the Jews until this day" (Matthew 28: 11–15).

Such a thing was impossible. The sepulchre was guarded by Roman soldiers, who were forewarned to be extra careful. The stone door was closed with the Roman seal. The Jews could not have done better service to Christianity than they did by taking these precautions.

Do you tell me that every true disciple of Christ would not have been exterminated if it could have been proved that His body was stolen? That the Roman seal had been broken? Should we not have heard more of the robbery if it had been a fact? Think of the stir it makes nowadays when the grave of any prominent person is robbed. There were hosts of bitter enemies around, who would have seized on this as a pretext for putting the disciples to death. If a single disciple had been seen lurking near the sepulchre, he would probably have been killed immediately by the soldiers.

If the soldiers slept, how did they know the body had been stolen?

What could have been the motive of the disciples? Had they believed that He would rise, there was no need to steal the body. If they did not look for His reappearing, is it conceivable that they would run such a risk to carry out a fraud? Why arouse the anger of the fanatical Jews for the sake of a dead body?

Do you tell me that some of those five hundred men who Paul asserted to be witnesses of the resurrection would not have turned state's evidence during the twenty-five years that elapsed, rather than have suffered contempt and poverty, persecution and martyrdom, for confessing their faith in the doctrine? These are strange motives for their persisting in their course.

CHARLES H. SPURGEON

MOODY'S LATEST SERMONS

Mary and Martha

Martha, Martha, thou art . . . troubled about many things" (Luke 10: 41). We must stop worrying and fretting if we want real power with God and with man.

Some gentlemen were discussing which one of these sisters would make the better wife, and one said that he would prefer "Martha before dinner, and Mary after dinner." I beg to differ with him; give me Mary all the time. If I had to eat a dinner that was prepared by a fretful, irritable woman, it would not taste half so sweet. I think Mary is a good deal better all around.

I can imagine that Mary was in the habit of slipping off to the temple very often to hear Christ. Whenever He came into the city, she was there. Martha would remonstrate. She would say, "Monday, this is wash day. We must have our washing done anyway."

But Mary would say, "Christ won't be here long. He will soon be gone from Jerusalem, and I am going to get all I can from Him."

And it may be one Monday that Martha stayed at home and did the work, and Mary slipped over into the temple and came back and told Martha that she had heard Christ say, "Come unto me all ye that labor and are heavy laden, and I will give you rest." Wasn't that better than attending to the washing? I would say, "Let the washing go for a little while," if I could get such a feast of fat things.

Then Tuesday, ironing day; and Martha remonstrates again, but Mary must go. She must get all that she can. She was going to drink deep because she needed it. It is a great thing to drink from Christ's fullness when you can, so that when the time comes that you need grace, you will have it, and your soul will be kept in perfect peace and perfect rest.

I do not think that Mary was a shirk. Jesus never made people lazy, and never will. Perhaps when Mary came back from the temple she may have sat up late at night to help Martha with the mending, or she may have risen early and done some of the ironing. I don't believe she made it any harder for Martha by following Christ. If you are really serving Him, you don't make it any harder for those around you; you will help them and save them work in every way you can.

D. L. MOODY

SATAN AND THE SAINT

That Blessed Hope

If we knew what God was doing—and we might know, if we studied His Word with the illumination of the Holy Spirit—we would come into harmony with Him in the doing of it, and His work would not be the burden to some of us that it is, but a delight as we saw His purposes revealed in the history of men.

Sometimes I am asked: "What is the practical value of the teaching of the second coming of Christ?" In reply, let me say that there is not a single virtue or grace revealed in the New Testament as incumbent upon Christian believers that is not in some way associated with that hope.

Is it a question of our salvation? Paul writes to the young Christians at Thessalonica, "Ye turned . . . from idols to serve the living and true God and to wait for his Son from heaven" (1 Thessalonians 1:9–10). To those heathen people one of the first doctrines he preached was the second coming of Christ, and he evidently used it to bring them to Christ.

Is it a question of sanctification? The apostle John says in 1 John 3:2–3: "Now are we the sons of God, and it doth not yet appear what we shall be, but we know that when he shall appear, we shall be like him; for we shall see him as he is. And every man that hath this hope in him purifieth himself, even as he is pure." It is the second coming of Christ, in other words, that furnishes the motive and stimulus to a holy life.

Is it a question of service? Listen to Jesus as, addressing His disciples, He says: "What shall it profit a man though he gain the whole world, and lose his own soul; or what shall a man give in exchange for his soul? For the Son of man shall come in the glory of his Father, and then shall he bring his reward with him." It is well worthwhile to serve Christ, to suffer for Him and wait for Him when we consider the meaning of that word *reward*.

Is it a question of solace? Hearken to Paul again: "The Lord himself shall descend from heaven with a shout, . . . and the dead in Christ shall rise first: then we which are alive and remain shall be caught up together with them in the clouds, to meet the Lord in the air. . . . Wherefore comfort one another with these words."

JAMES M. GRAY

PLEASURE AND PROFIT IN BIBLE STUDY

Feed Yourself

You know it is always regarded a great event in the family when a child can feed himself. The child is propped up at table, and at first perhaps he uses the spoon upside down. But by and by he handles it all right, and mother, or perhaps sister, claps her hands and says, "Just see, baby's feeding himself!" Well, what we need as Christians is to be able to feed ourselves. How many there are who sit helpless and listless, with open mouths, hungry for spiritual things, and the minister has to try to feed them, while the Bible is a feast prepared into which they never venture.

There are many who have been Christians for twenty years who have still to be fed with an ecclesiastical spoon. If they happen to have a minister who feeds them, they get on pretty well; but if they have not, they are not fed at all. This is the test as to your being a true child of God—whether you love and feed upon the Word of God. If you go out to your garden and throw down some sawdust, the birds will not take any notice; but if you throw down some crumbs, you will find they will soon sweep down and pick them up. So the true child of God can tell the difference, so to speak, between sawdust and bread. Many so-called Christians are living on the world's sawdust, instead of being nourished by the Bread that cometh down from heaven. Nothing can satisfy the longings of the soul but the Word of the living God.

The best law for Bible study is the law of perseverance. The psalmist says, "I have stuck unto thy testimonies." Application to the Word will tend to its growth within and its multiplication without. Some people are like express trains; they skim along so quickly that they see nothing.

I met a lawyer in Chicago who told me he had spent two years in study upon one subject; he was trying to smash a will. He made it his business to read everything on wills he could get. Then he went into court and he talked two days about that will; he was full of it; he could not talk about anything else but wills. That is the way with the Bible: study it and study it, one subject at a time, until you become filled with it.

Read the Bible itself; do not spend all your time on commentaries and helps. If a man spent all his time reading up the chemical constituents of bread and milk, he would soon starve.

D. L. MOODY

CALVARY'S CROSS

Man Put God on the Cross

Oh what a revelation! Man hating God, and hating most when God is loving most! Man acting as a devil and taking the devil's side against God!

You say, "What have I to do with that cross, and what right have you to identify me with the crucifiers? Pilate did it, Caiaphas did it, the Jew did it, the Roman did it; I did it not." Nay, but you did, you did. You did it in your representatives—the civilized Roman and the religious Jew—and until you come out from the crucifying crowd, disown your representatives and protest against the deed, you are truly guilty of that blood.

"But how am I to sever myself from these crucifiers and protest against their crime?" By believing in the name of the crucified one. For all unbelief is approval of the deed and identification with the murderers. Faith is man's protest against the deed, and the identification of himself, not only with the friends and disciples of the crucified one, but with the crucified one Himself.

The cross, then, was the public declaration of man's hatred of God, man's rejection of His Son, and man's avowal of his belief that he needs no Savior. If anyone denies the ungodliness of humanity and pleads for the native goodness of the race, I ask, what means the cross? Of what is it the revealer and interpreter? Of hatred or of love? Of good or of evil?

Besides, in this rejection of the Son of God, we have also man's estimate of Him. He had been for thirty years despised and rejected. He had been valued and sold for thirty pieces of silver, a robber had been preferred to Him; but at the cross, this estimate comes out more awfully, and there we see how man undervalued His person, His life, His blood, His word. His whole errand from the Father.

"What think ye of Christ?" was God's question. Man's answer was, "The cross!" Was not that as explicit as it was appalling?

As the cross reveals man's depravity, so does it exhibit his foolishness. His condemnation of Him in whom God delighted shows this. His erection of the cross shows it still more. As if he could set at naught Jehovah and clear the earth of Him who had come down as the doer of His will! Man's attempt to cast shame on the Lord of Glory is like a child's effort to blot out or discolor the sun.

HORATIUS BONAR

KEPT FOR THE MASTER'S USE

Our Wills Kept for Jesus

It is most comforting to remember that the grand promise "Thy people shall be willing in the day of thy power" (Psalm 110:3) is made by the Father to Christ Himself. The Lord Jesus holds this promise, and God will fulfill it to Him. He will make us willing because He has promised Jesus that He will do so. And what is being made willing but having our wills taken and kept?

All true surrender of the will is based upon love and knowledge of and confidence in the one to whom it is surrendered. We have the human analogy so often before our eyes, that it is the more strange we should be so slow to own even the possibility of it as to God. Is it thought anything so extraordinary and high flown when a bride deliberately prefers wearing a color that was not her own taste or choice, because her husband likes to see her in it? Is it very unnatural that it is no distress to her to do what he asks her to do, or to go with him where he asks her to come, even without question or explanation, instead of doing what or going where she would undoubtedly have preferred if she did not know and love him? Is it very surprising if this lasts beyond the wedding day, and if year after year she still finds it her greatest pleasure to please him, quite irrespective of what used to be her own ways and likings? Yet in this case she is not helped by any promise or power on his part to make her wish what he wishes.

But He who so wonderfully condescends to call Himself the bridegroom of His church, and who claims our fullest love and trust, has promised and has power to work in us to will. Shall we not claim His promise and rely on His mighty power and say, not self-confidently, but looking only unto Jesus—

> Keep my will, for it is Thine;
> It shall be no longer mine!

Only in proportion as our own will is surrendered are we able to discern the splendor of God's will.

Conversely, in proportion as we see this splendor of His will, we shall more readily or more fully surrender our own. Not until we have presented our bodies a living sacrifice can we prove what is that good and perfect and acceptable will of God.

FRANCES R. HAVERGAL

SECRET POWER

Witnessing in Power

When Peter stood up on the day of Pentecost and testified of what Christ had done, the Holy Spirit came down and bore witness to that fact, and men were convicted by hundreds and by thousands (Acts 2). So then man cannot preach effectively of himself. He must have the Spirit of God to give ability, and study God's Word in order to testify according the mind of the Spirit.

If we keep back the gospel of Christ and do not bring Christ before the people, then the Spirit has not the opportunity to work. But the moment Peter stood up on the day of Pentecost and bore testimony to this one fact, that Christ died for sin and that He had been raised again and ascended into heaven, the Spirit came down to bear witness to the person and work of Christ.

He came down to bear witness to the fact that Christ was in heaven, and if it were not for the Holy Ghost bearing witness to the preaching of the facts of the gospel, do you think that the church would have lived during these last eighteen centuries? Do you believe that Christ's death, resurrection, and ascension would not have been forgotten as soon as His birth, if it had not been for the fact that the Holy Spirit had come? Because it is very clear that when John made his appearance on the borders of the wilderness, they had forgotten all about the birth of Jesus Christ. Just thirty short years. It was all gone. They had forgotten the story of the shepherds; they had forgotten the wonderful scene that took place in the temple, when the Son of God was brought into the temple and the older prophets and prophetesses were there; they had forgotten about the wise men coming to Jerusalem to inquire where He was who was born King of the Jews.

That story of His birth seemed to have just faded away; they had forgotten all about it, and, when John made his appearance on the borders of the wilderness, it was brought back to their minds. And if it had not been for the Holy Ghost coming down to bear witness to Christ, to testify of His death and resurrection, these facts would have been forgotten as soon as His birth.

D. L. MOODY

THE CHRIST-LIFE FOR THE SELF-LIFE
Heart Rest

How can you find "rest for your soul"? One way is by *faith*. "We which have *believed* do enter into rest" (Hebrews 4:3, italics added).

The point there is that faith has two hands. With one hand faith is always handing over, and with the other she is always reaching down—ours is the up and the down life. The angels went up on the ladder carrying Jacob's worries, and they came down the ladder bringing God's help. You have the two directions in your life. Send them up, and let them come down.

Do you know what it is when you are worried to kneel down and say to God: "Father, take this," and by one definite act to hand over the worry to God and leave it there? I heard a lady say that she had been in the habit of kneeling by her bedside and handing things over to God, and then jumping into her bed and by a strong pull pulling in all the things after her. Now that is not the best way. When you really trust God, you put a thing into His hands, and then you do not worry yourself or Him.

If there is one thing that annoys me more than another, it is for a man to say to me: "Will you do this?" And I say: "Certainly," and then he keeps sending postcards or letters to me all the time to work me up. I say: "That man does not trust me." So when I have really handed a thing over to God I leave it there, and I dare not worry for fear it would seem as if I mistrusted Him. But I keep looking up to Him—I cannot help doing that—and say, "Father, I am trusting."

My dog at home has such trust. He used to worry me very much to be fed at dinner, but he never got any food that way. But lately he has adopted something that always conquers me. He sits under the table and puts one paw on my knee. He never barks, never leaps around, never worries me, but he sits under the table with that one paw on my knee, and that conquers me; I cannot resist the appeal. Although my wife says I never must do it, I keep putting little morsels under the table.

That is the way to live—with your hand on God's knee. Say: "My God, I am not going to worry; I am not going to fret but there is my hand, and I wait until the time comes, and Thou shalt give me the desire of my heart."

F. B. MEYER

THE OVERCOMING LIFE

External Foes

Who are our enemies on the outside? According to James, "the friendship of the world is enmity with God," and whoever is "a friend of the world is the enemy of God" (4:4). According to John, Christians must "love not the world, neither the things that are in the world. If any man love the world, the love of the Father is not in him" (1 John 2:15).

The enemy is the world. Now, people want to know what is the world.

Here we have the answer in the next verse: "For all that is in the world, the lust of the flesh, and the lust of the eyes, and the pride of life, is not of the Father, but is of the world. And the world passeth away, and the lust thereof; but he that doeth the will of God abideth forever."

"The world" does not mean nature around us. God nowhere tells us that the material world is an enemy to be overcome. On the contrary, we read: "The earth is the Lord's, and the fullness thereof; the world, and they that dwell therein." The psalmist also writes, "The heavens declare the glory of God; and the firmament sheweth his handiwork."

"The world" means "human life and society that is alienated from God, through being centered on material aims and objects, and thus it opposes God's Spirit and kingdom." Christ told His disciples and tells us, "If the world hate you, ye know that it hated me before it hated you. . . . The world hath hated them because they are not of the world, even as I am not of the world." Love of the world means the forgetfulness of the eternal future by reason of love for passing things.

How can the world be overcome? Not by education, not by experience; only by faith. "This is the victory that overcometh the world, even our faith. Who is he that overcometh the world, but he that believeth that Jesus is the Son of God?"

D. L. MOODY

THE SECRET OF GUIDANCE
Our Feelings and Burdens

Our feelings are as changeable as April weather. They are affected by an infinite number of subtle causes—our physical health, the state of the atmosphere, overweariness, want of sleep—as well as by those people who seem "spiritual" in comparison. No stringed instrument is more liable to be affected by minute changes than we are. And we are apt to take it sorely to heart when we see the tide of emotion running fast out.

At such times we should question ourselves, to see whether our lack of feeling is due to conscious sin or worrying; and if not, we may hand over all future anxiety in the matter to Him who knows our frame and remembers that we are dust. And as we pass down the dark staircase, let us hold fast to the handrail of His will though the dark places. May we say, "I am as much Thine own, equally devoted to Thee now in the depths of my soul, as when I felt happiest in Thy love."

Employers with unreasonable demands; unkind gossip and slanderous tales that are being circulated about you; the perplexities and adversities of business; the difficulties in making ends meet; the question of changing your residence and obtaining another; children with the ailments of childhood and waywardness of youth. Any one of these can break our rest, as one whelping dog may break our slumber in the stillest night, and as one grain of dust in the eye will render it incapable of enjoying the finest sight.

There is nothing to do, then, but to roll our burden and, indeed, ourselves onto God (1 Peter 5:7).

F. B. MEYER

DIFFICULTIES IN THE BIBLE

The "Slaying" of Isaac

God plainly forbade the actual slaughter of Isaac (Genesis 22:11–12). That the original command was not to kill Isaac but merely to offer him up is as plain as day from the fact that we are explicitly told that Abraham did exactly what God told him to do, that is, "to offer up Isaac." "Abraham offered up Isaac" is the Bible statement (Hebrews 11:17), but Abraham did not slay Isaac—that he was not told to do.

Thus the divine commandment to offer up was not a command to slay. The story as told in the Bible is not that God had first commanded Abraham to slay and burn Isaac and that when He saw that Abraham was willing to do even this He took it back and provided a lamb to take Isaac's place. The Bible story is that God commanded Abraham to make his son Isaac to ascend the altar to be presented to God as a whole offering, and that Abraham actually did what he was commanded to do. And this did not, either in God's original intention or in the execution of the command, involve the slaughter of Isaac.

This story, then, in no way justifies human sacrifice in the sense of the actual slaying of a human victim. On the contrary, the whole force of the narrative is against such sacrifice. Instead of being commanded, Isaac's death is explicitly forbidden. It does, however, justify the offering of ourselves to God wholly, as "a living sacrifice" (Romans 12:1). But this is not all that the story as it actually occurs in the Bible tells us. For when Abraham was about to go beyond what was explicitly commanded (namely, the offering of his son) and to slay his son (which was not commanded), God intervened and positively forbade it. Jehovah sent His own angel to speak in an audible voice from heaven forbidding the shedding of Isaac's blood. "Lay not thine hand upon the lad, neither do thou anything unto him," called the angel of Jehovah out of heaven (Genesis 22:12).

This story, then, so far from encouraging human sacrifice positively and explicitly forbids it, and that in the most solemn manner. So all our difficulty with this narrative disappears when we look carefully with open eyes at the record and note precisely what is said.

R. A. TORREY

MOODY'S LATEST SERMONS
"I Will Deliver"

When God called Moses to go down into Egypt to deliver the children of Israel from the hand of the Egyptians, in all the world there wasn't a man who, humanly speaking, was less qualified than Moses. He had made the attempt once before to deliver the children of Israel, and he began by delivering one man. He failed in that and killed an Egyptian, and had to run off into the desert, where he stayed forty years. He had tried to deliver the Hebrews in his own way; he was working in his own strength and doing it in the energy of the flesh. He had all the wisdom of the Egyptians, but that didn't help him. He had to be taken back into Horeb, and kept there forty years in the school of God, before God could trust him to deliver the children of Israel in God's way. Then God came to him and said, "I have come down to deliver"; and when God worked through Moses, three million were delivered as easily as I can turn my hand over. God could do it. It was no trouble when God came on the scene.

Learn the lesson. If we want to be delivered, from every inward and outward foe, we must look to a higher source than ourselves. We cannot do it in our own strength.

We all have some weak points in our character. When we would go forward, it drags us back, and when we would rise up into higher spheres of usefulness and atmosphere of heaven, something drags us down. Now I have no sympathy with the idea that God puts us behind the blood and saves us, and then leaves us in Egypt to be under the old taskmaster. I believe God brings us out of Egypt into the promised land, and that it is the privilege of every child of God to be delivered from every foe, from every besetting sin.

If there is some sin that is getting the mastery over you, you certainly cannot be useful. You certainly cannot bring forth fruit to the honor and glory of God until you get self-control. "He that ruleth his spirit is better than he that taketh a city." If we haven't got victory over jealousy, over envy, over self-seeking and covetousness and worldly amusements and worldly pleasure, if we are not delivered from all these things, we are not going to have power with God or with men, and we are not going to be as useful as we might be if we got deliverance from every evil. There isn't an evil within or without but what He will deliver us from if we will let Him.

D. L. MOODY

THE CHRIST-LIFE FOR THE SELF-LIFE
Four Conditions

There are conditions to be met for the mighty power of God to lead you. The first is: *You must be Holy Ghost-filled.* Peter was filled often; we read of his filling three times in Acts: once in the second chapter and twice in the fourth. In character he was a Holy Ghost–filled man, and therefore he could count on the cooperation of the Spirit.

You must be emptied. Peter was empty. He spent many days in a tanner's house. I can hardly imagine how he got into such an emptying place. In the first place, it was a very inhospitable spot. Of all hotels it is about the last place I would select. The odor would be anything but savory. In the next place, as a Jew, he must have felt it almost defiling to be in such close association with carcasses. And yet he spent many days as in a city alley; this apostle, this man who had preached through large regions, who had raised Aeneas and Dorcas, got down to the tanner's house. And a man will have to come to an end of himself before the Holy Ghost will work with him.

You must be a person of prayer. Peter was a man of prayer. "Peter went up upon the housetop to pray about the sixth hour" (Acts 10:9). No true experience can ever exist apart from communion with God. But instead of asking for so many things that God cannot give, ask for a few things definitely. As a man or woman of prayer, you will feel you cannot help praying for those few things, and you will have so much to do in praising and thanking God for giving you your heart's desire that your prayer times will tend to be longer rather than shorter.

You must be willing to give up prejudice. When Peter was first commanded to kill and eat of the creatures let down from heaven in the sheet, he said: "Not so, Lord: for I have never eaten anything that is common or unclean." But after thinking about the vision, he was willing to give up lifelong prejudices.

F. B. MEYER

PLEASURE AND PROFIT IN BIBLE STUDY
One Inquirer at a Time

Always use your Bible in personal dealing. Do not trust to memory, but make the person read the verse for himself. Do not use printed slips or books. Hence, if convenient, always carry a Bible or New Testament with you.

It is a good thing to get a man on his knees (if convenient), but don't get him there before he is ready. You may have to talk with him two hours before you can get him that far along. But when you think he is about ready, say, "Shall we not ask God to give us light on this point?" Sometimes a few minutes in prayer have done more for a man than two hours in talk. When the spirit of God has led him so far that he is willing to have you pray with him, he is not very far from the kingdom. Ask him to pray for himself. If he doesn't want to pray, let him use a Bible prayer; get him to repeat it; for example: "Lord help me!" Tell the man, "If the Lord helped that poor woman, He will help you if you make the same prayer. He will give you a new heart if you pray from the heart." Don't send a man home to pray. Of course he should pray at home, but I would rather get his lips open at once. It is a good thing for a man to hear his own voice in prayer. It is a good thing for him to cry out, "God be merciful to me, a sinner!"

Urge an immediate decision, but never tell a man he is converted. Never tell him he is saved. Let the Holy Spirit reveal that to him. You can shoot a man and see that he is dead, but you cannot see when a man receives eternal life. You can't afford to deceive one about this great question. But you can help his faith and trust, and lead him aright.

Always be prepared to do personal work. When war was declared between France and Germany (during the Franco-Prussian War), Count von Moltke, the German general, was prepared for it. Word was brought to him late at night, after he had gone to bed. "Very well," he said to the messenger, "the third portfolio on the left"; and he went to sleep again.

Do the work boldly. Don't take those in a position in life above your own, but as a rule, take those on the same footing. Don't deal with a person of opposite sex, if it can be otherwise arranged. Bend all your endeavors to answer for poor, struggling souls that question of all importance to them: "What must I do to be saved?"

D. L. MOODY

THE NEW LIFE IN JESUS CHRIST
The New Life Is Christ's Life

Mere endlessness of being would not be "eternal" life. *Eternal* is "from everlasting to everlasting." Only He who "was in the beginning with God . . . was God" (John 1:1) could bestow, through the eternal Spirit, eternal life.

And this imparted life is His own life. "I am the vine, ye are the branches." What a symbol of unity of life is the vine with its branches. The branch was no independent source of life. The life of the vine and the life of the branch are one. All possibility of renewal, of growth, of fruitfulness depends upon the life energy of the vine. Well might the vine say to the branch, "Because I live, ye shall live also."

It would not be possible to state more strongly than does our Lord this identity in life of Himself and those who through faith in Him crucified have been born again. "As . . . I live by the Father so he that eateth me, even he shall live by me." "As thou, Father, art in me, and I in thee, that they also may be one in us. . . . I in them, and thou in me."

The vital suggestions are, if possible, even more intense in our Lord's simile of "the corn of wheat." Just as a grain of sown wheat dies indeed, yet it dies into countless grains of wheat. It gives its own life to each. So Christ speaks of His own death.

And this testimony to oneness of life with Christ pervades the apostolic explanation of the gospel. The church is declared to be His body. The human body, composed of many members, is the figure used to express the oneness with Him of the "many members" who constitute, like the members of the natural body, one organism. This organism is called "Christ" (1 Corinthians 12:12). It is declared of Christ, not only that He gave life to the believer, but that He "is our life." And John declares the record to be "that God hath given to us eternal life, and this life is in his Son."

CHARLES H. SPURGEON

SHORT TALKS

Removed as Far as East and West

Don't cover your sins; don't hide them. You cannot dig a grave so deep but that they will have a resurrection some time. God will touch some secret spring of your conscience and say, "Son, remember"—and tramp, tramp, tramp, they will all come back, every one of them!

I have been twice in the jaws of death. Once I had gone down in the river the second time, and was going down the third time when I was rescued, and quicker than a flash everything I had said and done came before me! How a whole life can be crowded into a second of time, I do not know. Again, in Chicago, just in the jaws of death I was saved, and again my whole life came before me like a flash, from the earliest childhood up. Everything I had said, everything I had heard, and everything I had done all came back.

Some years ago I met a man, aged 32 years, in Chicago, who twelve years previously had fled from Canada because of a crime he had committed. For twelve years he had been trying to cover up his sin, but it pursued him night and day. Finally he asked me to advise him. I told him to make restitution of the money he had stolen and to make an honest confession.

You should have seen the tears of joy run down that man's face when he found that he could be forgiven and have his sin put away. What a terrible time he had been having those twelve years! He had been trying to cover his sin in man's way.

If you want your sins blotted out completely, you must make a clean breast of them all. "If we confess our sins, he is faithful and just to forgive us our sins, and to cleanse us from all unrighteousness. . . . The blood of Jesus Christ his Son cleanseth from all sin." (1 John 1:9, 7)

I read of an ex-prisoner who had secured a position as night watchman in a store. One of his prison associates came to him and attempted to persuade the man to leave the doors open, so that he could rob the store. The watchman refused, and his former companion threatened to tell his employers about his past life. The watchman laughed in his tempter's face and replied, "Go and tell them. I have nothing to fear, for they knew all of my past life before they hired me."

Oh, man, woman, confess your sins to God! Then you shall know what it is to have heaven in your soul. Blessed—happy—is the man whose transgression is forgiven, whose sin is covered.

D. L. MOODY

DIFFICULTIES IN THE BIBLE

The Action of the Unrighteous Steward

A very puzzling passage in the Bible to many is the story of the unrighteous steward recorded in Luke 16:1–14.

Why did Jesus "hold this dishonest scoundrel up for our imitation"? The answer is found in the text itself. Jesus did not hold him up for imitation. He held him up, first of all, as a warning of what would overtake unfaithful stewards, how they would be called to give account of their stewardship, and their stewardship be taken from them.

Having taught this solemn and salutary lesson, one that is much needed today, Jesus went on to show how "the sons of this world are for their own generation wiser than the sons of the light" (verse 8 RV). They are wiser because they use their utmost ingenuity and put forth their utmost effort to make present opportunities count for the hour of future need. "The sons of light" often do not do that. Indeed, how many twentieth century sons of light, who profess to believe that eternity is all and time is nothing in comparison, are using their utmost ingenuity and efforts to make the opportunity of the present count most for the needs of the great eternity that is to follow?

The average professed Christian today uses the utmost ingenuity and puts forth his utmost effort to bring things to pass in business and other affairs of this brief present world, but when it comes to matters that affect eternity he is content with the exercise of the least possible amount of ingenuity and with the putting forth of the smallest effort that will satisfy his conscience.

Jesus did not point to the steward's dishonesty to stir our emulation—He plainly rebuked his dishonesty, but He did point to his common sense in using the opportunity of the present to provide for the necessities of the future and would have us learn to use the opportunities of the present to provide for the necessities of the future, the eternal future. Even in pointing out his common sense, Jesus carefully guarded His statement by saying that the unjust steward was wiser in his own generation. He knew only the life that now is, and from that narrow and imperfect standpoint he was wiser than "the son of light" from his broad and true standpoint of knowing eternity, but an eternity for which he is not wise enough to live wholly.

There are other utterances of our Lord and Savior, where wicked and selfish men are held up by way of contrast to show how much more godly men, or even God Himself, may be expected to act in the way suggested—for instance, Luke 18:6,7; 11:5–8; Matthew 12:11–12.

R. A. TORREY

THE TRUE VINE
Except Ye Abide

If I am to be a true branch, if I am to bear fruit, if I am to be what Christ as the Vine wants me to be, my whole existence must be as exclusively devoted to abiding in Him as that of the natural branch is to abiding in its vine (see John 15).

Abiding is to be an act of the will and the whole heart. Just as there are degrees in seeking and serving God, "not with a perfect heart," or "with the whole heart," so there may be degrees in abiding. In regeneration the divine life enters us but does not all at once master and fill our whole being. This comes as a matter of command and obedience. There is unspeakable danger of our not giving ourselves with our whole heart to abide. There is unspeakable danger of our giving ourselves to work for God and to bear fruit, with but little of the true abiding, the wholehearted losing of ourselves in Christ and His life. There is unspeakable danger of much work with but little fruit, for lack of this one thing needful. We must allow the words "not of itself," "except it abide," to do their work of searching and exposing, of pruning and cleansing, all that there is of self-will and self-confidence in our life; that will deliver us from this great evil, and so prepare us for His teaching, giving the full meaning of the word in us: "Abide in me, and I in you."

Our blessed Lord desires to call us away from ourselves and our own strength to Himself and His strength. Let us accept the warning and turn with great fear and self-distrust to Him to do His work. "Our life is hid with Christ in God!" That life is a heavenly mystery, hid from the wise even among Christians, and revealed unto babes. The childlike spirit learns that life is given from heaven every day and every moment to the soul that accepts the teaching: "not of itself," "except it abide," and seeks its all in the Vine. Abiding in the Vine then comes to be nothing more nor less than the restful surrender of the soul to let Christ have all and work all, as completely as in nature the branch knows and seeks nothing but the vine.

ANDREW MURRAY

WHAT IS FAITH?

Have Faith in God

Have faith in God and not in man. That will carry us through all darkness, and storm, and affliction. If our faith is in churches and dogmas and creeds and men, in this thing and that, we will plunge into trouble and difficulties before we get through our pilgrim's journey; but for him who has faith in God, the light will shine brighter and brighter, until he comes at last into the glory of the perfect day.

We are to have faith in God and not in man. A great many people place their faith in men, and they pin their faith to other people's doctrines and creeds. Not long ago I heard of a man who was asked what he believed. He said he believed what his church believed.

"What does your church believe?"

"The church believes what I believe."

And that was all they could get out of him.

There are a great many in that same state of mind. They believe what the church believes, but they do not know what that is. If their church teaches anything, they believe it. All the churches in the world can't save a soul. It is not to have faith in this church or that church, this doctrine or that doctrine, this man or that man, but it is to have faith in the man Christ Jesus at the right hand of God. That is the only faith that will ever save a soul.

Some people say, "He is such a good man, I cannot help but believe him. It is all right because he is such a good man, and he holds that doctrine."

Paul says, "If a man preach any other gospel unto you than that ye have received, let him be accursed." If Gabriel should come right down and proclaim a different gospel, I would not listen to him.

Deceivers are going out into the world who would deceive even the very elect if they could. Let us cling to the Word of God and have faith in God.

D. L. MOODY

LIGHT ON LIFE'S DUTIES

The Common Task

There are great tasks to be fulfilled in eternity: angels to be judged; cities to be ruled; spiritual truths to absorb. For these, suitable agents will be required: those who can rule, because they have served; those who can command, because they have obeyed; those who can teach, because they have largely learned. Perhaps even now our heavenly Father is engaged in seeking those among us who can fill these posts. And He is seeking them, not amongst such as are filling high positions in the eyes of men, but in the ranks of such as are treading the trivial round and fulfilling the common task.

From the nearest fixed star the inequalities of our earth, whether of Alp or molehill, are alike insignificant. We need to look at our positions from the standpoint of eternity, and probably we shall be startled at the small differences between the lots of men. The one thing for us all is to abide in our calling with God, to count ourselves as His fellow-workers, to do what we can in His grace and for His glory, never excusing ourselves, never condoning failure or misdoing, never content unless, by the help of the blessed Spirit, we have wrought out His promptings and suggestions to the best of our power, whether in the gold of the extraordinary or the bronze of the cheaper and more ordinary achievement.

Of course there is no saving merit in what we do. Salvation is only by simple trust in our Savior, Jesus. But when we are saved it gives new zest to life to do all for Him, as Lord and Master, and to know that He is well pleased in the right doing of the most trivial duties of the home or daily business.

"For what glory is it, if, when ye be buffeted for your faults, ye shall take it patiently? but if, when ye do well, and suffer for it, ye take it patiently, this is acceptable with God" (1 Peter 2:20).

F. B. MEYER

WEIGHED AND WANTING

The Sabbath Rest

A man ought to turn aside from his ordinary employment one day in seven. There are many whose occupation will not permit them to observe Sunday, but they should observe some other day as a sabbath. Saturday is my day of rest because I generally preach on Sunday, and I look forward to it as a boy does a holiday. God knows what we need.

Ministers and missionaries often tell me that they take no rest-day; they do not need it because they are in the Lord's work. That is a mistake. When God was giving Moses instructions about the building of the tabernacle, He referred especially to the Sabbath and gave injunctions for its strict observance; and later, when Moses was conveying the words of the Lord to the children of Israel, he interpreted them by saying that not even were sticks to be gathered on the Sabbath to kindle fires for smelting or other purposes. In spite of their zeal and haste to erect the tabernacle, the workmen were to have their day of rest. The command applies to ministers and others engaged in Christian work today as much as to those Israelite workmen of old.

In judging whether any work may be lawfully done on the Sabbath, find out the reason and object for doing it. Exceptions are to be made for works of necessity and works of emergency. By *"works of necessity"* I mean those acts that Christ justified when He approved of leading one's ox or donkey to water. Watchmen, police, stokers on board steamers, and many others have engagements that necessitate their working on the Sabbath. By *works of emergency* I mean those referred to by Christ when He approved of pulling an ox or a donkey out of a pit on the Sabbath day. In case of fire or sickness a man is often called on to do things that would not otherwise be justifiable.

A Christian man was once urged by his employer to work on Sunday. "Does not your Bible say that if your ass falls into a pit on the Sabbath, you may pull him out?"

"Yes," replied the other; "but if the ass had the habit of falling into the same pit every Sabbath, I would either fill up the pit or sell the ass."

Every man must settle the question as it effects unnecessary work with his own conscience.

D. L. MOODY

FULL ASSURANCE

Full Assurance of Faith

The feeblest faith in Christ is saving faith. The strongest faith in self, or anything else but Christ, is but a delusion and a snare, and will leave the soul at last unsaved and forever forlorn.

And so when we are bidden to draw near to God with true hearts in full assurance of faith, the meaning is that we are to rest implicitly on what God has revealed concerning His Son and His glorious work for our redemption. This is set forth admirably in Hebrews 10. There we have set out in vivid contrast the difference between the many sacrifices offered under the legal dispensation and the one perfect, all-sufficient oblation of our Lord Jesus Christ. Note some of the outstanding differences:

1. They were many and often repeated. His is but one, and no other will ever be required.
2. They did not have the necessary value to settle the sin question. His is of such infinite value, it has settled that problem forevermore.
3. They could not purge the consciences of those who brought them. His purges all who believe, giving a perfect conscience because all sin has been put away from under the eye of God.
4. They could not open the way into the Holiest. His has rent the veil and inaugurated the new and living way into the very presence of God.
5. They could not perfect the one who offered them. His one sacrifice has perfected forever those who are sanctified.
6. In them there was a remembrance again of sins from year to year. His has enabled God to say, "Their sins and iniquities will I remember no more."
7. It was not possible that the blood of bulls and of goats should put away sin. But Christ has accomplished that very thing by the sacrifice of Himself.

Here then is where faith rests, on the finished work of Christ. It will help us greatly to understand this if we glance at what is revealed concerning the sin offering of the old dispensation.

HENRY A. IRONSIDE

ALL OF GRACE

God Justifieth the Ungodly

I f God justifieth the ungodly, then, dear friend, He can justify you. Is not that the very kind of person that you are? If you are unconverted at this moment, it is a very proper description of you; you have lived without God, you have been the reverse of the godly; in one word, you have been and are ungodly. Perhaps you have not even attended a place of worship on the Sabbath, but have lived in disregard of God's day and house and Word—this proves you to have been ungodly. Sadder still, it may be you have even tried to doubt God's existence and have gone the length of saying that you did so. You have lived on this fair earth, which is full of the tokens of God's presence, and all the while you have shut your eyes to the clear evidences of His power and Godhead.

You have lived as if there were no God. Indeed, you would have been very pleased if you could have demonstrated to yourself to a certainty that there was no God whatever. Possibly you have lived a great many years in this way, so that you are now pretty well settled in your ways, and yet God is not in any of them. If you were labeled ungodly, it would as well describe you as if the sea were to be labeled salt water. Would it not?

Possibly you are a person of another sort; you have regularly attended to all the outward forms of religion, and yet you have had no heart in them at all but have been really ungodly. Though meeting with the people of God, you have never met with God for yourself; you have been in the choir, and yet have not praised the Lord with your heart. You have lived without any love to God in your heart or regard to His commands in your life. Well, you are just the kind of man to whom this gospel is sent—this gospel that says that God justifieth the ungodly. It is very wonderful, but it is happily available for you. It just suits you. Does it not?

How I wish that you would accept it! If you are a sensible man, you will see the remarkable grace of God in providing for such as you are, and you will say to yourself, "Justify the ungodly! Why, then, should not I be justified, and justified at once?"

CHARLES H. SPURGEON

MOODY'S ANECDOTES
He Trusted His Father

I was standing with a friend at his garden gate one evening when two little children came by. As they approached us he said to me, "Watch the difference in these two boys."

Taking one of them in his arms he stood him on the gatepost, and stepping back a few feet he folded his arms and called to the little fellow to jump. In an instant the boy sprang toward him and was caught in his arms. Then turning to the second boy he tried the same experiment. But in the second case it was different. The child trembled and refused to move. My friend held out his arms and tried to induce the child to trust to his strength, but nothing could move him. At last my friend had to lift him down from the post and let him go.

"What makes such a difference in the two?" I asked.

My friend smiled and said, "The first is my own boy and knows me; but the other is a stranger's child whom I have never seen before."

There was all the difference. My friend was equally able to prevent both from falling, but the difference was in the boys themselves. The first had assurance in his father's ability and acted upon it, while the second, although he might have believed in the ability to save him from harm, would not put his belief into action.

So it is with us. We hesitate to trust ourselves to that loving One whose plans for us are far higher than any we have ourselves made. He, too, with outstretched arms, calls us, and would we but listen to His voice we would hear that invitation and promise of assurance as He gave it of old:

"Come unto me, all ye that labour and are heavy laden, and I will give you rest."

D. L. MOODY

KEPT FOR THE MASTER'S USE

Our Hearts Kept for Jesus

We find both the means and the result of the keeping in the 112th Psalm: "His heart is fixed." Whose heart? Of an angel? Of a saint in glory? No! Simply the heart of the man who fears the Lord and delights greatly in His commandments. Therefore yours and mine, as God would have them be; just the normal idea of a God-fearing heart, nothing extremely and hopelessly beyond attainment.

Fixed! How does that tally with the deceitfulness and waywardness and fickleness about which we really talk as if we were rather proud of them than utterly ashamed of them?

Does our heavenly Bridegroom expect nothing more of us? Does His mighty all-constraining love intend to do no more for us than to leave us in this deplorable state, when He is undoubtedly able to heal the desperately wicked heart (compare verses 9 and 14 of Jeremiah 17), to rule the wayward one with His peace, and to establish the fickle one with His grace? Are we not without excuse?

Fixed, trusting in the Lord! Here is the means of the fixing—trust. He works the trust in us by sending the Holy Spirit to reveal God in Christ to us as absolutely, infinitely, worthy of our trust. When we see Jesus by Spirit-wrought faith, we cannot but trust Him. We distrust our hearts more truly than ever before, but we trust our Lord entirely, because we trust Him only. For, entrusting our trust to Him, we know that He is able to keep that which we commit (i.e., entrust) to Him. It is His own way of winning and fixing our hearts for Himself. Is it not a beautiful one? Thus his heart is established.

But we have not quite faith enough to believe that. So what is the very first doubting, and therefore sad thought, that crops up?

"Yes, but I am afraid it will not remain fixed."

That is your thought. Now see what is God's thought about the case: "His heart is established, he shall not be afraid."

Is that not enough? What is, if such plain and yet divine words are not?

FRANCES R. HAVERGAL

PRACTICAL AND PERPLEXING QUESTIONS ANSWERED

The Institutional Church

Whatdo you think of the institutional church? Is it not detrimental to the real work of the church as set forth in the New Testament?

By an institutional church I understand a church that not only does the direct work of preaching the gospel and building Christians up by teaching the Bible, but a church that also looks after the physical and mental welfare of its members and congregation by various institutions. Such work is not necessarily detrimental to the real work of the church as set forth in the New Testament. It may be a valuable auxiliary, provided that the physical and intellectual are kept in thorough subordination to the spiritual.

The apostolic church was in a measure an institutional church. It looked out for the physical welfare of its members, all property was held in common (Acts 2:44, 45; 4:34, 35; 6:1–4), and the Word of God increased and prospered under these circumstances (Acts 2:47; 4:4; 5:14; 6:7). Of course, the institutions were not many, nor very largely developed. In a similar way today the church can have various institutions for looking after the physical and intellectual welfare of its members. If it is located among the poor it can have savings institutions, libraries, educational classes, and so forth, and accomplish a vast amount of good. All these things can be used as means of getting hold of men, women, and children and bringing them to a saving knowledge of Jesus Christ.

But there is always a danger in an institutional church. The danger is that the institutions get to be the main thing and the gospel is put in a secondary place, or altogether lost sight of. This has been the history of more than one institutional church in this country, and it is always a danger. In such a case the institutional church becomes detrimental to the real work of the church as set forth in the New Testament. The first work of the church is seeking and saving the lost (Luke 19:10; Matthew 5:19), its second work is feeding the flock (Acts 20:28; 1 Peter 5:2), and its third work is training the membership for intelligent service (Ephesians 4:11–12). If the institutions connected with the church are allowed to put any one of these three things in the background, they do more harm than good. In contrast, if the institutions are carried on in the spirit of prayer and never lose sight of for a moment the intention of winning men for Christ, they may be very helpful. The church that is needed today is not so much the institutional church as the evangelistic church.

R. A. TORREY

TO THE WORK!

Love, the Motive Power for Service

Some years ago I read a book that did me a great deal of good. It was entitled *The Training of the Twelve*. The writer said that Christ spent most of His time during the three years He was engaged publicly about His Father's business in training twelve men. The training He gave them was very different from the training of the schools at the present day. The world teaches men that they must seek to be great; Christ taught that His disciples must be little; that in honor they must prefer one another; that they are not to be puffed up, not to harbor feelings of envy, but to be full of meekness and gentleness, and lowliness of heart.

When an eminent painter was requested to paint Alexander the Great so as to give a perfect likeness of the Macedonian conqueror, he felt a difficulty. Alexander, in his wars, had been struck by a sword, and across his forehead was an immense scar. The painter said: "If I retain the scar, it will be an offense to the admirers of the monarch, and if I omit it it will fail to be a perfect likeness. What shall I do?" He hit upon a happy expedient; he represented the Emperor leaning upon his elbow, with his forefinger upon his brow, accidentally, as it seemed, covering the scar upon his forehead. Might not we represent each other with the finger of charity upon the scar, instead of representing the scar deeper and blacker than it really is? Christians may learn even from heathendom a lesson of charity, of human kindness and of love.

This spirit of seeking to be the greatest has nearly ruined the church of God at different times in its history. If the church had not been divine it would have gone to pieces long ago. There is hardly any movement of reform today that has not been in danger of being thwarted and destroyed through this miserable spirit of ambition and self-seeking. May God enable us to get above this, to cast away our conceit and pride, and take Christ as our teacher, that He may show us in what spirit His work ought to be done.

D. L. MOODY

SALVATION FROM START TO FINISH
The Glory Covering

In these bodies "we groan," the apostle says. Ah, there is so much to make us groan, the ills that flesh is heir to, the burdens and perplexities of the mind, the sorrows and bereavements of the heart. But the special object of which the intelligent Christian groans is "the adoption, to wit, the redemption of our body" (Romans 8:23); or as 2 Corinthians 5:2 expresses it, that we may be "clothed upon with our house which is from heaven," that we may receive our resurrection body. It is then that we are delivered "from the bondage of corruption into the glorious liberty [or the glory of the liberty] of the children of God."

It is important to keep in mind that it is not *death* for which the Christian groans, but the resurrection from the dead. Death is a "naked" and "unclothed"—a disembodied—state, but resurrection is just the opposite. In resurrection we are "clothed upon," and "mortality is swallowed up of life." This is the significance of the Word: "If so be that being clothed, we shall not be found naked" (2 Corinthians 5:3) . There is no doubt that we shall be clothed, the apostle says: the reception of the resurrection body is a certainty; but what we desire is that we may not receive it after we have passed into the naked or disembodied state, but even now while we are alive in this state and occupying our present bodily frame!

Verse four of 2 Corinthians 5 is very beautiful. We give Murdock's translation from the Syriac: "For while we are here in this house we groan under its burden; yet ye desire, not to throw it off, but to be clothed over it, so that its mortality may be absorbed in life."

At death the Christian "throws off" this body, but at the translation when the Lord comes, he does not throw it off, but the resurrection body clothes him "over it." That which is mortal, "in a moment, in the twinkling of the eye" becomes "absorbed" in that which is immortal.

Therefore the hope of the Christian is the coming of Christ.

JAMES M. GRAY

THE WAY OF LIFE

Eternal Salvation

If you want eternal salvation you can have it now. The terms are right here. What are they? Obedience. "This is his commandment, That we should believe on the name of his Son, Jesus Christ" (1 John 3:23)

"He that believeth on him is not condemned: but he that believeth not is condemned already, because he hath not believed on the name of the only begotten Son of God" (John 3:18). If you disobey, you shut the only door of hope. You may make a profession of Christianity, you may join the church, you may know the doctrine, but unless you hearken unto God's commandments, it will all be of no avail.

Will you obey? You have got to settle this thing in your mind. Just make up your mind that you are going to obey. Nothing very mysterious about it. You needn't go to any old musty library to read up on obedience, need you? If God tells you to repent, then repent. This will be the grandest day you have ever seen if you make up your mind to obey Him. Will you do it?

Reader, decide now. In olden times, when a Roman ambassador came to a king who was not allied to the Empire, he said, "Will you have peace with Rome or not?" If the king asked for time to think it over, the ambassador used, with his rod, to draw a ring around the man, and say, "You must decide before you step out of that circle; for if you do not say 'peace' before you cross the line, Rome will crush you with her armies." Do not trespass any longer on God's mercy. "Choose you this day whom ye will serve."

This life will not last forever. The trumpet will one day sound and call you forth from your narrow bed. The graves will be opened, and you will be summoned forth to meet your God. The proud heart that scoffs at religion down here will be compelled to listen to the judgment sentence of God. The ears that will not obey the sound of the churchgoing bell will be compelled to obey the sound of the last trumpet. The eyes that behold evil here shall one day gaze upon the spotless throne of God. Do not forever disobey. May God help you to submit without delay your proud will in loving, childlike obedience to Himself.

D. L. MOODY

THE SECOND COMING OF CHRIST

Watch

A re we also doing our part to hasten on His coming? And is it habitually our prayer that the Lord will be pleased to hasten the fulfillment of events yet to be fulfilled before that day comes?

One thing remains to be considered, namely, the practical effect this truth should have upon our hearts. If it be really received and entered into, the child of God will say, "What can I do for my blessed Savior before He comes again? How can I most glorify Him? His will concerning me is that I should occupy 'until He comes.' How then can I best use for Him the talents with which I am entrusted, my physical strength, my mental powers? How can my sight, my tongue, all my faculties of mind and body, be best devoted to His praise? How should my time, my money, all that I am and have, be used for Him? How can my whole spirit, soul, and body be best consecrated to His service?"

These are deeply important, practical questions that all believers in the Lord Jesus should ask themselves, seeing that we are not our own, but are bought with a price, even with His precious blood. Instead of indulging in inactivity and listlessness on account of the evil state of things around us, we should pray and work, and work and pray, as if it were in our power to stem the torrent of abounding iniquity. Who can say how much good one single child of God, who is thoroughly in earnest, may accomplish, and how greatly he may glorify God by walking in entire separation from all that is hateful to Him? We must especially also guard against the temptation of slackening our efforts for the conversion of sinners, because the world will not be converted before Jesus comes. Rather should we say, "The time that He shall delay His coming may be short; what therefore can I do to warn sinners and to win souls for Him?"

GEORGE MUELLER

SELECT SERMONS

Christ Seeking Sinners

Oh that we would wake up to the thought of what it is to be lost! The world has been rocked to sleep by Satan, who is going up and down and telling people that it doesn't mean anything. I believe in the old-fashioned heaven and hell. Christ came down to save us from a terrible hell, and any man who is cast down to hell from here must go in the full blaze of the gospel and over the mangled body of the Son of God.

We hear of a man who has lost his health, and we sympathize with him, and we say it is very sad. Our hearts are drawn out in sympathy. Here is another man who has lost his wealth, and we say, "That is very sad." Here is another man who has lost his reputation, his standing among men. "That is sadder still," you say. We know what it is to lose health and wealth and reputation, but what is the loss of all these things compared with the loss of the soul?

I was in an eye-infirmary in Chicago some time before the great fire. A mother brought a beautiful little babe to the doctor—the babe was only a few months old—and wanted the doctor to look at the child's eyes. He did so, and pronounced it blind—blind for life—it would never see again. The moment he said that, the mother seized it, pressed it to her bosom, and gave a terrible scream. It pierced my heart, and I could not but weep. The doctor wept, too; we could not help it.

"Oh, my darling," she said, "are you never to see the mother that gave you birth? Oh, doctor, I cannot stand it. My child, my child!" It was a sight to move any heart. But what is the loss of eyesight to the loss of a soul? I had a thousand times rather have these eyes taken out of my head and go to the grave blind, than lose my soul. I have two sons and no one but God knows how I love them; but I would see their eyes dug out of their heads rather than see them grow up to manhood and go down to the grave without Christ and without hope. The loss of a soul! Christ knew what it meant. That is what brought Him from the bosom of the Father; that is what brought Him from the throne; that is what brought Him to Calvary. The Son of God was in earnest. When he died on Calvary it was to save a lost world; it was to save your soul and mine.

D. L. MOODY

THE TRUE VINE

Whatsoever Ye Will

Ask what ye will, and it shall be done unto you" (John 15:7).

The promise is given in direct connection with fruit-bearing. Limit it to yourself and your own needs and you rob it of its power; you rob yourself of the power of appropriating it. Christ was sending out His disciples, and they were ready to give their life for the world; to them He gave the disposal of the treasures of heaven. Their prayers would bring the Spirit and the power they needed for their work.

Let us realize that we can only fulfill our calling to bear much fruit by praying much. In Christ are hid all the treasures men around us need; in Him all God's children are blessed with all spiritual blessings; He is full of grace and truth. But it needs prayer, much prayer, strong believing prayer, to bring these blessings down. And let us equally remember that we cannot appropriate the promise without a life given up for men. Many try to take the promise and then look round for what they can ask. This is not the way; but the very opposite. Get the heart burdened with the need of souls and the command to save them, and the power will come to claim the promise.

Let us claim it as one of the revelations of our wonderful life in the Vine: He tells us that if we ask in His name, in virtue of our union with Him, whatsoever it be, it will be done to us. Souls are perishing because there is too little prayer. God's children are feeble because there is so little prayer. The faith of this promise would make us strong to pray; let us not rest till it has entered into our very heart and drawn us in the power of Christ to continue and labor and strive in prayer until the blessing comes in power. To be a branch means not only bearing fruit on earth, but power in prayer to bring down blessing from heaven. Abiding fully means praying much.

ANDREW MURRAY

ALL OF GRACE
It Is God Who Justifies

Do you not see—for I want to bring this out clearly, what a splendid thing it is—that none but God would think of justifying the ungodly, and none but God could do it? See how the apostle puts the challenge: "Who shall lay anything to the charge of God's elect? It is God that justifieth" (Romans 8:33). If God has justified a man it is well done, it is rightly done, it is justly done, it is everlastingly done. I read the other day in a print that is full of venom against the gospel and those who preach it that we hold some kind of theory by which we imagine that sin can be removed from men. We hold no theory, we publish a fact. The grandest fact under heaven is this—that Christ by His precious blood does actually put away sin and that God, for Christ's sake, deals with men on terms of divine mercy, forgives the guilty and justifies them, not according to anything that He sees in them, or foresees will be in them, but according to the riches of His own mercy. This we have preached, do preach, and will preach as long as we live. "It is God that justifieth"—that justifieth the ungodly; He is not ashamed of doing it, nor are we of preaching it.

The justification that comes from God Himself must be beyond question. If the Judge acquits me, who can condemn me? If the highest court in the universe has pronounced me just, who shall lay anything to my charge? Justification from God is a sufficient answer to an awakened conscience. The Holy Spirit by His means breathes peace over our entire nature, and we are no longer afraid. With this justification we can answer all the roarings and railings of Satan and ungodly men. With this we shall be able to die: with this we shall bodily rise again and face the last great judgment.

Friend, the Lord can blot out all your sins. I make no shot in the dark when I say this. "All manner of sin and of blasphemy shall be forgiven unto men." Though you are steeped up to your throat in crime, He can with a word remove the defilement and say, "I will, be thou clean." The Lord is a great forgiver.

"I believe in the forgiveness of sins." Do you?

CHARLES H. SPURGEON

THE SECOND COMING OF CHRIST
Christ's Second Coming

To my mind this precious doctrine—for such I must call it—of the return of the Lord to this earth is taught in the New Testament as clearly as any other doctrine in it. If you read Matthew 26:64, you will find that His own proclamation of His future return caused His death.

When the high priests asked Him who He was and if He was the true Messiah, He replied, "I say unto you, Hereafter shall ye see the Son of man sitting on the right hand of power, and coming in the clouds of heaven." That was enough. The moment they heard that, they accused Him of blasphemy and condemned Him to death, just because He said He was coming again.

Whoever neglects this has only a mutilated gospel, for the Bible teaches us not only of the death and sufferings of Christ, but also of His return to reign in honor and glory. His second coming is mentioned and referred to over three hundred times, yet I was in the church fifteen or sixteen years before I ever heard a sermon on it. There is hardly any church that does not make a great deal of baptism, but in all of Paul's epistles I believe baptism is spoken of only thirteen times, while he speaks about the return of our Lord fifty times; and yet the church has had very little to say about it. Now, I can see a reason for this; *the devil does not want us to see this truth*, for nothing would wake up the church so much. The moment a man realizes that Jesus Christ is coming back again to receive His followers to Himself, this world loses its hold upon him. Gas stocks and water stocks and stocks in banks and railroads are of very much less consequence to him then.

When we know and recall that Jesus Christ is coming again, our hearts are free, and we look for the blessed appearing of our Lord, who, at His coming, will take us into His blessed Kingdom.

D. L. MOODY

LIGHT ON LIFE'S DUTIES

Beware

Beware of anything the world itself would deem inconsistent. Though the world is not religious in our sense, yet it has a very keen appreciation of true Christianity and a very high ideal of what Christians should be. And we may well arrest our steps when we are met with a surprised interrogation—"What! are you here? We didn't expect to see you!" The very fuss that is made over us when we step over the line may well make us pause and ask whether we have not done something to forfeit the smile and "Well done" of Jesus.

Beware of anything that would injure some weaker conscience. This is one of the most important considerations in Christian living. "All things are lawful to me, but all things are not expedient." And why are they not expedient? It is inexpedient to do things that may be harmless enough in themselves and that you may feel able to do with impunity, if in doing them you lead others to do them also, not because they feel at ease, but simply because they are emboldened by your example, regarding you as further advanced than themselves in the Christian life and therefore a trustworthy guide. Estimate every action, not only as it is in itself, but as it is likely to be in its influence on others, lest you break down wholesome barriers and place them in scenes of temptation that, however harmless to you, are perilous in the extreme to them.

Beware of scenes and companionships that dull your spiritual life. Who is there who does not long for a life on fire? But how can we possibly look for such a thing if we are persistently exposing ourselves to influences which choke and repress it and damp it down? Some scenes seem incompatible with earnest prayer and Bible study before we retire to rest; they lower the inner temperature; they leave an ill-flavor in the mouth; they poison the spiritual life, as the noxious gas-fumes poison the life of flowers and plants. From all such scenes we do well to refrain our feet.

F. B. MEYER

ANSWERS TO PRAYER

Staying Stayed on God

Sometimes all has been dark, exceedingly dark, with reference to my service among the saints, judging from natural appearance. Indeed, at those times I should have been overwhelmed in grief and despair had I looked at things after the outward appearance. At such times I have sought to encourage myself in God, by laying hold in faith on His mighty power, His unchangeable love, and His infinite wisdom. During those times I have said to myself: *God is able and willing to deliver me, if it be good for me*; for it is written: "He that spared not his own Son, but delivered him up for us all, how shall he not with him also freely give us all things?" (Romans 8:32).

When, through His grace, I believed this, my soul kept in peace. Further, when in connection with the orphan houses, day schools, etc., trials have come upon me that were far heavier than the means; when lying reports were spread that the orphans had not enough to eat, or that they were cruelly treated in other respects, and the like; or when other trials, still greater, but which I cannot mention, have befallen me in connection with this work—at such times my soul was stayed upon God.

Even at times when I was almost a thousand miles absent from Bristol and had to remain absent week after week, I believed His word of promise was applicable to such cases. I poured out my soul before God and arose from my knees in peace, because the trouble that was in the soul was cast upon God in believing prayer.

Thus I was kept in peace, though I saw it to be the will of God to remain far away from work. Further, when I needed houses, fellow laborers, masters, and mistresses for the orphans or for the day schools, I have been able to look for all to the Lord and trust in Him for help. Dear reader, I may seem to boast; but, by the grace of God, I do not boast in this speaking. From my inmost soul I do ascribe it to God alone that He has enabled me to trust in Him and that hitherto He has not suffered my confidence in Him to fail.

GEORGE MUELLER

WEIGHED AND WANTING

Misusing God's Name

Even if you swear without meaning it, it is forbidden by God. Christ said, "Every idle word that men shall speak, they shall give account thereof in the day of judgment. For by thy words thou shalt be justified, and by thy words thou shalt be condemned" (Matthew 12:36–37). You will be held accountable whether your words are idle or blasphemous.

The habit of swearing is condemned by all sensible persons. It has been called "the most gratuitous of all sins," because no one gains by it; it is "not only sinful, but useless." An old writer said that when the accusing angel, who records men's words, flies up to heaven with an oath, he blushes as he hands it in.

When a man blasphemes, he shows an utter contempt for God. I was in the army during the war and heard men cursing and swearing. Some godly woman would pass along the ranks looking for her wounded son, and not an oath would be heard. They would not swear before their mothers or their wives or their sisters; they had more respect for them than they had for God!

There will be no swearing men in the kingdom of God. They will have to drop that sin and repent of it before they see the kingdom of God.

Men often ask: "How can I keep from swearing?" I will tell you. If God puts His love into your heart, you will have no desire to curse Him. If you have much regard for God, you will no more think of cursing Him than you would think of speaking lightly or disparagingly of a mother whom you love. But the natural man is at enmity with God and has utter contempt for His law. When that law is written on his heart, there will be no trouble in obeying it.

D. L. MOODY

THE SCHOOL OF OBEDIENCE

Obedience: Its Place in Holy Scripture

In the Sermon on the Mount Christ began with the call to obedience. No one could enter the kingdom "but he that doeth the will of my Father who is in heaven." And in the farewell discourse, how wonderfully He reveals the spiritual character of true obedience as it is born of love and inspired by it, and as it also opens the way into the love of God. Take into your heart the wonderful words, "If ye love me, ye will keep my commandments. And the Father will send forth the Spirit. He that hath my commandments and keepeth them, he it is that loveth me; and he shall be loved of My Father, and I will love him, and will manifest myself unto him. If a man love me, he will keep my words; and my Father will love him, and we will come unto him, and make our abode with him" (John 14:15–16, 21, 23).

No words could express more simply or more powerfully the inconceivably glorious place Christ gives to obedience, with its twofold possibility: (1) as only possible to a loving heart, (2) as making possible all that God has to give of His Holy Spirit, of His wonderful love, of His indwelling in Christ Jesus. I know of no passage in Scripture that gives a higher revelation of the spiritual life or the power of loving obedience as its one condition. Let us pray God very earnestly that by His Holy Spirit His light may transfigure our daily obedience with His heavenly glory.

How well we know the parable of the vine. How often and how earnestly we have asked how to be able to abide continually in Christ. We have thought of more study of the Word, more faith, more prayer, more communion with God, and we have overlooked the simple truth that Jesus teaches so clearly: "If ye keep my commandments, ye shall abide in my love," with its divine sanction, "Even as I kept my Father's commandments, and abide in his love."

For Him as for us, the only way under heaven to abide in divine love is to keep the commandments.

ANDREW MURRAY

WHAT IS FAITH

Scriptural Salvation

The Scripture saith, "Whosoever believeth on him shall not be ashamed." We have before us in these words a simple statement of the way of salvation. The way of salvation is to believe on Christ.

What is believing on Him? It is trusting in Him.

The language is not "believe Him"—such belief is a part of faith, but not the whole. We believe everything the Lord Jesus has taught, but we must go a step further and trust Him. It is not even enough to believe in Him, as being the Son of God and the anointed of the Lord; but we must believe on Him, just as in the building the builder takes his stone and lays it on the foundation. There it rests with all its weight, and there it abides. The faith that saves is not believing certain truths, nor even believing that Jesus is a Savior; but it is resting on Him, depending on Him, lying with all your weight on Christ, as the foundation of your hope. Believe that He can save you. Believe that He *will* save you. Leave the whole matter of your salvation with Him in unquestioning confidence. Depend upon Him without fear as to your present and eternal salvation. This is the faith that saves the soul.

This faith is believing on a person: "Whosoever believeth on"—it? No! On "him."

Our faith is not based on a doctrine or a ceremony or an experience, but on Him. Our Lord Jesus Christ is God; He is also man: He is the appointed and anointed Savior. In His death He is the propitiation for sin, in His resurrection He is the justification of His people, and in His intercession He is the eternal guarantee of their preservation. Believe "on him." Our faith fixes itself upon the person of the Lord Jesus as seen in His sufferings, His offices, and His achievements. "Whosoever believeth on him shall not be ashamed."

The text refers to the truth of the trusting. The apostle does not say, "Whosoever believeth on Him with full assurance, or with a high degree of confidence, shall not be ashamed." No; it is not the measure of our faith, but the sincerity of our faith that is the great question. If we believe on Him at all, we shall not be ashamed.

CHARLES H. SPURGEON

MOODY'S ANECDOTES
A Perfect Farce

Professor Drummond once described a man going into one of our after-meetings and saying he wanted to become a Christian.

"Well, my friend, what is the trouble?"

He doesn't like to tell and is greatly agitated. Finally he says, "The fact is, I have overdrawn my account"—a polite way of saying he has been stealing.

"Did you take your employer's money?"

"Yes."

"How much?"

"I don't know. I never kept account of it."

"Well, you have an idea you stole $1,500 last year?"

"I am afraid it is that much."

"Now, look here, sir. I don't believe in sudden work; don't steal more than a thousand dollars this next year, and the next year not more than five hundred, and in the course of the next few years you will get so that you won't steal any. If your employer catches you, tell him you are being converted; and you will get so that you won't steal any by and by."

My friends, the thing is a perfect farce! "Let him that stole steal no more." That is what the Bible says. It is a complete turnaround in the way we live.

Take another illustration. Here comes a man, and he admits that he gets drunk every week. That man comes to a meeting, and wants to be converted. Shall I say, "Don't you be in a hurry. I believe in doing the work gradually. Don't you get drunk and knock your wife down more than once a month"? Once a month, only twelve times in a year! Wouldn't his wife be glad to have him converted in this new way! After a few years he would only get drunk on the anniversary of his wedding, and at Christmas, and then it will be effective because it is gradual.

Oh! I detest all that kind of teaching. Let us go to the Bible and see what that old Book teaches. Let us believe it, and go and act as if we believed it, too. Salvation is instantaneous. I admit that a man may be converted so that he cannot tell when he crossed the line between death and life, but I also believe a man may be a thief one moment and a saint the next. I believe a man may be as vile as hell itself one moment and be saved the next.

Christian growth is gradual, just as physical growth is; but a man passes from death unto everlasting life quick as an act of the will—"He that believeth on the Son hath everlasting life."

D. L. MOODY

PRACTICAL AND PERPLEXING QUESTIONS ANSWERED

Prayer

How do you know God answers prayer? I know it first of all because the Bible says so, and I have conclusive proof that the Bible is the inerrant Word of God. The Bible abounds in statements that God answers prayer. For example, Jesus says in Matthew 7:11: "If ye, then, being evil know how to give good gifts unto your children, how much more shall your Father which is in heaven give good things to them that ask him?" And He says again to His disciples who were united to Him by a living faith and obedient love: "Whatsoever ye shall ask in my name, that will I do, that the Father may be glorified in the Son. If ye shall ask anything in my name, I will do it" (John 14:13–14).

But I also know that God answers prayer because He has answered mine. Throughout the years I have asked God for things He alone could give, for things that there was no probability whatever of my getting. I even asked praying, "If you will give me this thing I will never doubt you again as long as I live," and God has given me the very thing I asked. On one occasion God gave $6,000 within two hours in answer to prayer. On another occasion, when another person and I prayed for $5,000 for the Moody Bible Institute in Chicago, word was received by telegram that $5,000 had been given for the work by a man who was almost 1,000 miles from the place where the prayer was made, a man whom I had not known and had never given a penny to the Moody Bible Institute before—and has never given a penny since. I could multiply instances of this sort.

Now it may be said that this is merely coincidence, but the "coincidence" has occurred so often and there has been such an evident connection between prayer (the cause) and the answer (the effect), that to say it is coincidence is to be unscientific.

The history of George Mueller's Orphan Homes at Bristol, England, where about 2,000 children have been housed and clothed and fed in answer to prayer through a long period of years, where no money has ever been solicited, no debt ever incurred, and no meal ever failed though often it seemed as if it might fail up to the very last moment, is to a fair-minded investigator of facts clear proof that God answers prayer. For anyone to study the facts in connection with George Mueller's Orphan Homes and still doubt that God answers prayer is for that person not only to be willfully obstinate in his unbelief but thoroughly unscientific in his treatment of demonstrated facts.

R. A. TORREY

TO THE WORK!

Faith and Courage

In Hebrews 11 the writer brings up one person after another, and each was a man or a woman of faith; they made the world better by living in it. Listen to this description of what was accomplished by these men and women of faith: "Who through faith subdued kingdoms, wrought righteousness, obtained promises, stopped the mouths of lions, quenched the violence of fire, escaped the edge of the sword, out of weakness were made strong, waxed valiant in fight, turned to flight the armies of the aliens. Women received their dead raised to life again: and others were tortured, not accepting deliverance; that they might obtain a better resurrection: And others had trial of cruel mockings and scourgings, yea, moreover of bonds and imprisonment: They were stoned, they were sawn asunder, were tempted, were slain with the sword: they wandered about in sheepskins and goatskins; being destitute, afflicted, tormented; (of whom the world was not worthy:) they wandered in deserts, and in mountains, and in dens and caves of the earth. And these all, having obtained a good report through faith, received not the promise: God having provided some better thing for us, that they without us should not be made perfect."

Surely no child of God can read these words without being stirred. It is said that "women received their dead raised to life again." Many of you have children who have gone far astray and have been taken captive by strong drink, or led away by their lusts and passions; and you have become greatly discouraged about them. But if you have faith in God they may be raised up as from the dead, and brought back again. The wanderers may be reclaimed; the drunkards and the harlots may be reached and saved. There is no man or woman, however low he or she may have sunk, but can be reached.

We ought in these days to have far more faith than Abel or Enoch or Abraham had. They lived away on the other side of the cross. We talk about the faith of Elijah and the patriarchs and prophets; but they lived in the dim light of the past, while we are in the full blaze of Calvary and the resurrection.

D. L. MOODY

FULL ASSURANCE
The Unhappy Backslider

Peter speaks of some who through waywardness have gotten so far out of fellowship with God that they have forgotten that they were purged from their old sins. This is a sad state to be in. It is what is commonly called in the Old Testament "backsliding." "The backslider in heart shall be filled with his own ways" (Proverbs 14:14). An old preacher I knew as a boy used to say, "Backsliding always begins in the knee." And this is very true indeed. Neglect of prayer will soon dull the keen edge of one's spiritual sensibilities and make it easy for a believer to drift into worldliness and carnalities, as a result of which his soul's eyesight will become dimmed and he will lose the heavenly vision.

The backslider is short-sighted. He sees the things of this poor world very vividly, but he cannot see afar off, as he could in the days of his former, happy state. To such comes the exhortation, "Anoint thine eyes with eyesalve, that thou mayest see." Get back to your Bible and back to your knees. Let the Holy Spirit reveal to your penitent heart the point of departure where you left your first love, and judge it definitely before God. Acknowledge the sins and failures that have caused eternal things to lose their preciousness. Cry with David, as you confess your wanderings, "Restore unto me the joy of thy salvation." And He who is married to the backslider will give you again to know the blessedness of fellowship with Himself, and once more your peace will flow as a river and the full assurance of hope be yours.

As you walk with God your faith will grow exceedingly, your love unto all saints will be greatly enlarged, and the hope laid up for you in heaven will fill the vision of your opened eyes, as your heart is occupied with the Lord Himself who has restored your soul.

For it is well to remember that He Himself is our hope. He has gone back to the Father's house to prepare a place for us, and He has promised to come again and receive us unto Himself, that where He is we may be also.

HENRY A. IRONSIDE

THE SECOND COMING OF CHRIST

Occupy Till I Come

The words of the angels shall have a complete fulfillment: "This same Jesus, which is taken up from you into heaven, shall so come in like manner as ye have seen him go into heaven" (Acts 1:11). As His going away was a literal going away, so His return shall be a literal return. As He came personally the first time with a body, so He shall come personally the second time with a body. As He came visibly to this earth and visibly went away, so when He comes the second time He shall visibly return. And then, and not till then, the complete kingdom of Christ shall begin. He left His servants as "a nobleman"; He returns to His servants as "a king."

Then He intends to cast out that old usurper the devil, to bind him for a thousand years, and to strip him of his power.

Then He intends to make a restitution of the face of creation. It shall be the world's jubilee day. Our earth shall at last bring forth her increase. The King shall at length have His own again. At last the ninety-seventh psalm shall be fulfilled, and men shall say, "The Lord reigneth: let the earth rejoice!"

Then He intends to fulfill the prophecies of Enoch, John the Baptist, and St. Paul, "To execute judgment upon all the ungodly" inhabitants of Christendom—"to burn up the chaff with unquenchable fire"—and "in flaming fire to take vengeance on them that know not God, and obey not the gospel."

Then He intends to raise His dead saints and gather His living ones, to gather together the scattered tribes of Israel, and to set up an empire on earth in which every knee shall bow to Him and every tongue confess that Christ is Lord.

When, how, where, in what manner, all these things shall be, we cannot say particularly. Enough for us to know that they shall be.

J. C. RYLE

THE WAY OF LIFE

A Blessing or a Curse

In the book of Deuteronomy, we read, "Behold, I set before you this day a blessing and a curse; a blessing, if ye obey the commandments of the Lord your God which I command you this day: and a curse, if ye will not obey the commandments of the Lord your God, but turn aside out of the way which I command you this day, to go after other gods, which ye have not known" (11:26–28). Isn't that enforced? A man who serves God, isn't the blessing of God resting upon him? There is great reward in keeping God's laws and statutes, but a great curse upon them that disobey God.

A lawyer once gave a client instructions, but the latter did not follow them and lost his case. When he complained to his lawyer, "Well," said he, "you did not do what I told you." Look at the wives and mothers who have gone against the law of God and married ungodly men and drunkards. See what hells they are living in today! Just one act of disobedience. They are suffering tortures day by day, dying by inches. The whole country is more or less cursed by this disobedience.

A mother told me up in Minnesota that she had a little child who took a book and threw it out the window. She told him to go and pick it up. The little boy said, "I won't." She said, "What?" He said again, "I won't." She said, "You will. You go and pick up that book." He said he couldn't do it. She took him out, and she held him right to it. Dinner time came, and he hadn't picked up the book. She took him to dinner, and after it was over she took him out again. They sat there until tea time. When tea time came she took him in and gave him his supper, and then took him out and kept him there until bedtime. The next morning she went out again and kept him there until dinner time. He found he was in for a life job, and he picked the book up. She said she never had any trouble with the child afterwards. Mothers, if you don't make your boy obey when he is young, he will break your heart.

You say, "Cannot God make a man obey?" I suppose He could, but He does not work on those lines. He isn't going to force you against your will. He is going to draw you by the cords of love, but, if you are not going to obey Him, then you are going to suffer. God made man neither obedient nor disobedient; and a man must choose for himself.

D. L. MOODY

SATAN AND SAINT
Bringing Back the King

You remember the story of David, king of Israel, when his ungrateful son, Absalom, whom he loved best, rebelled against him and drove him from his throne. The rebellion was soon quashed and Absalom himself slain, but David was in exile beyond the Jordan still. And one day the men of Judah, David's tribe, came together and began to talk about it. Their consciences were smiting them, and they said one to another, "Why say ye never a word about bringing back the king?" And when they began to think and talk about it they began to act, and they crossed the Jordan and brought him back.

I ask you,

> Why say ye not a word of bringing back the King?
> Why speak ye not of Jesus and His reign?
> Why tell ye of His glory and of His praises sing,
> But not a word about His coming back again?

How many in our churches today are testifying to the second coming of Christ? What are we doing to hasten His return? When we become conscience-smitten upon this matter and begin to talk about it, we will begin to act, and to live and witness for Him in such a way that the day shall be hastened. God give us the grace to do it, and the love and the power!

That dear old Scottish saint Andrew Bonar visited this country once—sad for us he could not have visited it oftener. On that occasion, as he was about returning home, New York friends gave him a farewell meeting. One of them, in closing an address, applied the words of Paul to Timothy to him, saying: "There is a crown of righteousness laid up for him which the Lord, the righteous judge, shall give him in that day." But Mr. Bonar, coming forward and holding up his hand for silence, concluded the quotation, adding: "And not to me only, but also to all them that love his appearing."

Ah! there is no respect of persons with God! Do you love His appearing? Are you longing for His coming? Are you ready should He come today?

JAMES M. GRAY

WEIGHED AND WANTING

The Indwelling Christ

Behold, I stand at the door, and knock: if any man hear my voice, and open the door, I will come in to him, and will sup with him, and he with me." If Christ is in our hearts, why need we set Him before our eyes? "Where two or three are gathered together in my name, there am I in the midst of them." If we take hold of that promise by faith, what need is there of outward symbols and reminders? If the King Himself is present, why need we bow down before statues supposed to represent Him? To fill His place with an image (someone has said) is like blotting the sun out of the heavens and substituting some other light in its place. You cannot see Him through chinks of ceremonialism; or through the blind eyes of erring man; or by images graven with art and man's device; or in cunningly devised fables of artificial and perverted theology. Nay, seek Him in His own Word, in the revelation of Himself which He gives to all who walk in His ways. So you will be able to keep that admonition of the last word of all the New Testament revelation: "Little children, keep yourselves from idols."

I believe many an earnest Christian would be found wanting if put in the balances against this commandment. "Tekel" is the sentence that would be written against them, because their worship of God and of Christ is not pure. May God open our eyes to the danger that is creeping more and more into public worship throughout Christendom! Let us ever bear in mind Christ's words in the fourth chapter of John's gospel, which show that true spiritual worship is not a matter of special times and special places because it is of all times and all places:

"Believe me, the hour cometh, when ye shall neither in this mountain, nor yet at Jerusalem, worship the Father. . . . But the hour cometh, and now is, when the true worshippers shall worship the Father in spirit and in truth: for the Father seeketh such to worship him. God is a Spirit: and they that worship him must worship him in spirit and truth."

D. L. MOODY

THE TRUE VINE
The Wonderful Love

Our life must have its breath and being in a heavenly love as much as Christ's. What the Father's love was to Him, His love will be to us. If that love made Him the true Vine, His love can make us true branches. "Even as the Father hath loved me, so have I loved you."

Even as the Father hath loved me. And how did the Father love Him? The infinite desire and delight of God to communicate to the Son all He had Himself, to take the Son into the most complete equality with Himself, to live in the Son and have the Son live in Him—this was the love of God to Christ. It is a mystery of glory of which we can form no conception; we can only bow and worship as we try to think of it. And with such a love, with this very same love, Christ longs in an infinite desire and delight to communicate to us all He is and has, to make us partakers of His own nature and blessedness, to live in us and have us live in Himself.

And now, if Christ loves us with such an intense, such an infinite divine love, what is it that hinders it triumphing over every obstacle and getting full possession of us? The answer is simple. Even as the love of the Father to Christ, so His love to us is a divine mystery, too high for us to comprehend or attain to by any effort of our own. It is only the Holy Spirit who can shed abroad and reveal in His all-conquering power without intermission this wonderful love of God in Christ. It is the vine itself that must give the branch its growth and fruit by sending up its sap. It is Christ Himself who must by His Holy Spirit dwell in the heart; then shall we know and have in us the love that passes knowledge.

As the Father hath loved me, so have I loved you. Shall we not draw near to the personal living Christ and trust Him, and yield all to Him, that He may love this love into us? Just as He knew and rejoiced every hour—the Father loveth Me—we too may live in the unceasing consciousness—as the Father loved Him, so He loves me.

ANDREW MURRAY

ALL OF GRACE

Concerning Deliverance from Sinning

Salvation would be a sadly incomplete affair if it did not deal with this part of our ruined estate. We want to be purified as well as pardoned. Justification without sanctification would not be salvation at all. It would call the leper clean and leave him to die of his disease; it would forgive the rebellion and allow the rebel to remain an enemy to his king. It should remove the consequences but overlook the cause, and this would leave an endless and hopeless task before us. It would stop the stream for a time, but leave an open fountain of defilement, which would sooner or later break forth with increased power. Remember that the Lord Jesus came to take away sin in three ways: He came to remove the penalty of sin, the power of sin, and, at last, the presence of sin. At once you may reach to the second part—the power of sin may immediately be broken; and so you will be on the road to the third, namely, the removal of the presence of sin. "We know that he was manifested to take away our sins."

The angel said of our Lord, "Thou shalt call his name Jesus, for he shall save his people from their sins." Our Lord Jesus came to destroy in us the works of the devil. That which was said at our Lord's birth was also declared in His death; for when the soldier pierced His side forthwith came there out blood and water, to set forth the double cure by which we are delivered from the guilt and the defilement of sin.

If, however, you are troubled about the power of sin and about the tendencies of your nature, as you well may be, here is a promise for you. Have faith in it, for it stands in that covenant of grace that is ordered in all things and sure. God, who cannot lie, has said in Ezekiel 36:26: "A new heart also will I give you, and a new spirit will I put within you: and I will take away the stony heart out of your flesh, and I will give you a heart of flesh."

CHARLES H. SPURGEON

THE WAY OF LIFE

Obedience

As Dr. Parker says, "A child can treat God with sulkiness and silence. The tiniest knee can stiffen and refuse to bow before Him." "Strive to enter in at the strait gate." "I will not." "Look unto me and be ye saved." "I will not." "Come unto me, and I will give you rest." "I will not." "Seek ye first the kingdom of God." "I will not." "Repent." "I will not." "Turn ye, turn ye, why will ye die?" "I will not." "Believe in the Lord Jesus Christ." "I will not." "Give me thine heart." "I will not." "Go work in my vineyard." "I will not." "Remember the Sabbath day to keep it holy." "I will not." "Lay up for yourself treasures in heaven." "I will not."

So we might go through the Bible, and we would find that rebellious man refuses to obey His commandments and follows the devices and desires of his own heart. God made man for His glory, but man joined the devil and became a rebel.

Now this is the question to be settled. The battle is fought on that one word of the will; the door hangs on that one hinge of the will. Will you obey? That is the question! Will you obey the voice of God and do as He commands you? No man can obey for you any more than he can eat and drink for you. You must eat and drink for yourself, and you must obey God for yourself.

God requires literal, prompt, cheerful obedience. Nothing less will do. If you changed the doctor's prescription only a little, you might turn it into rank poison. A Sunday school teacher once asked her class, "How is the will of God done in heaven?"

One child answered, "Cheerfully."

Another, "By everybody."

A third, "All the time."

But the best answer was, "It is done without asking any questions."

D. L. MOODY

SALVATION FROM START TO FINISH

Fellowship with God

We are walking in the light as we love the brethren.

"Brethren, I write no new commandment unto you, but an old commandment which ye had from the beginning. The old commandment is the word which ye have heard from the beginning. Again, a new commandment I write unto you, which thing is true in him and in you: because the darkness is past, and the true light now shineth. He that saith he is in the light, and hateth his brother, is in darkness even until now. He that loveth his brother abideth in the light, and there is none occasion of stumbling in him. But he that hateth his brother is in darkness, and walketh in darkness, and knoweth not whither he goeth, because that darkness hath blinded his eyes" (1 John 2:7–11).

Verse seven perhaps alludes to the commandment that sums up the second table of the law—"Thou shalt love thy neighbor as thyself," while the eighth, it may be, alludes to the special commandment to love one another as brethren in Christ. There is a difference between these two loves—the love for our neighbor as such, and love for our brethren in Christ.

We cannot say that we are walking in the light and holding fellowship with God except as we are manifesting this love toward the brethren. "He that saith he is in the light, and hateth his brother, is in darkness even until now."

Some Christians think this commandment the hardest ever laid upon them but the reason is that they do not consider the real meaning of it. They think of the natural passion or emotion that we call love—between brother and sister, between husband and wife, between parent and child—and naturally ask, How can we have that love for one just because he is a Christian, one that we do not know well and who may not be very lovable in his character?

But that is not the kind of love meant. It is not natural, but supernatural love. The love born in the heart of the believer in the Lord Jesus Christ because he has been born again and is a new creation in Jesus Christ.

JAMES M. GRAY

SELECT SERMONS

Where Do You Stand with Christ?

Some time ago a little story that made a great impression upon me as a father went the round of the secular press. A father took his little child out into the field one Sabbath, and, it being a hot day, he lay down under a beautiful shady tree. The little child ran about gathering wild flowers and little blades of grass, and coming to its father and saying, "Pretty! Pretty!"

At last the father fell asleep, and while he was sleeping the little child wandered away. When he awoke, his first thought was, "Where is my child?" He looked all around but he could not see him. He shouted at the top of his voice, but all he heard was the echo of his own voice. Running to a little hill, he looked around and shouted again. No response! Then going to a precipice at some distance, he looked down, and there upon the rocks and briars he saw the mangled form of his loved child. He rushed to the spot, took up the lifeless corpse, and hugged it to his bosom, and accused himself of being the murderer of his child. While he was sleeping his child had wandered over the precipice.

I thought as I read that, what a picture of the church of God! How many fathers and mothers, how many Christian men, are now sleeping while their children wander over the terrible precipice right into the bottomless pit of hell! Father, where is your boy tonight? It may be in some saloon; it may be reeling through the streets; it may be pressing onwards to a drunkard's grave. Mother, where is your son? Is he spending his evening drinking away his soul—everything that is dear and sacred to him? Do you know where your boy is?

Father, you have been a professed Christian for forty years; where are your children tonight? Have you lived so godly and so Christlike a life that you can say, "Follow me as I follow Christ?" Are your children walking in wisdom? Are they on their way to glory? Are their names written in the Lamb's Book of Life? How many fathers and mothers today would be able to answer yes? We must pray for them; their soul's destiny must be on our hearts. Depend upon it, as long as the church is living so much like the world, we cannot expect our children to be brought into the fold.

D. L. MOODY

KEPT FOR THE MASTER'S USE

Ourselves Kept for Jesus

W e talk sometimes as if, whatever else could be subdued unto Him, self could never be. Did St. Paul forget to mention this important exception to the "all things" in Philippians 3:21? David said: "Bless the Lord, O my soul: and all that is within me, bless his holy name." Did he, too, unaccountably forget to mention that he only meant all that was within him, except self? If not, then self must be among the "all things" which the Lord Jesus Christ is able to subdue unto Himself and which are to bless His holy Name. It is self which, once His most treacherous foe, is now, by full and glad surrender, His own soldier—coming over from the rebel camp into the royal army. It is not someone else, some temporarily possessing spirit, which says within us, "Lord, Thou knowest that I love Thee," but our true and very self, only changed and renewed by the power of the Holy Ghost. And when we do that we would not, we know that "it is no more I that do it, but sin that dwelleth in me." Our true self is the new self, taken and won by the love of God and kept by the power of God.

Yes, "kept"! There is the promise on which we ground our prayer; or, rather, one of the promises. Search and look for your own strengthening and comfort, and you will find it repeated in every part of the Bible—from "I am with thee, and will keep thee," in Genesis, to "I also will keep thee from the hour of temptation," in Revelation.

And kept for Him! Why should it be thought a thing incredible with you, when it is only the fulfilling of His own eternal purpose in creating us? "This people have I formed for myself." Not ultimately only, but presently and continually; for He says, "Thou shalt abide for me"; and, "He that remaineth, even he shall be for our God." Are you one of His people by faith in Jesus Christ? Then see what you are to Him. You, personally and individually, are part of the Lord's portion (Deuteronomy 32:9) and of His inheritance (1 Kings 8:53 and Ephesians 1:18). His portion and inheritance would not be complete without you.

FRANCES R. HAVERGAL

TO THE WORK!

Enthusiasm

D r. Duff had been out in India as a missionary. He had spent twenty-five years there preaching the gospel and establishing schools. He came back with a broken-down constitution. He was permitted to address the General Assembly in order to make an appeal for men to go into the mission field. After he had spoken for a considerable time, he became exhausted and fainted away. They carried him out of the hall into another room. The doctors worked over him for some time, and at last he began to recover. When he realized where he was, he roused himself and said: "I did not finish my speech; carry me back and let me finish it." They told him he could do it only at the peril of his life. Said he, "I will do it if I die." So they took him back to the hall. My friend said it was one of the most solemn scenes he ever witnessed in his life.

They brought the white-haired man into the Assembly Hall, and as he appeared at the door every person sprang to his feet; the tears flowed freely as they looked upon the grand old veteran. With a trembling voice, he said: "Fathers and mothers of Scotland, is it true that you have no more sons to send to India to work for the Lord Jesus Christ? The call for help is growing louder and louder, but there are few coming forward to answer it. You have the money put away in the bank, but where are the laborers who shall go into the field? When Queen Victoria wants men to volunteer for her army in India, you freely give your sons. You do not talk about their losing their health, and about the trying climate. But when the Lord Jesus is calling for laborers, Scotland is saying: 'We have no more sons to give.'"

Turning to the president of the Assembly, he said: "Mr. Moderator, if it is true that Scotland has no more sons to give to the service of the Lord Jesus Christ in India, although I have lost my health in that land, if there are none who will go and tell those heathens of Christ, then I will be off tomorrow, to let them know that there is one old Scotsman who is ready to die for them. I will go back to the shores of the Ganges, and there lay down my life as a witness for the Son of God." Thank God for such a man as that!

D. L. MOODY

PRACTICAL AND PERPLEXING QUESTIONS ANSWERED

Justification

Some have asked, "What does the word *justification* mean? Is faith the only means of salvation?"

"To justify" in biblical usage signifies not "to make righteous" but "to reckon, declare, or show to be righteous." A person is justified before God when God reckons him righteous, that is, when God not only forgives his sins but puts all positive righteousness to his account.

There is one condition upon which people are justified before God: simple faith in Jesus Christ (Romans 3:36; 4:5; 5:1; and Acts 13:39). The atoning death of Jesus Christ on the cross in our place secures justification for us (Romans 5:9; Galatians 3:13; 2 Corinthians 5:21). His shed blood is the basis for our justification, and simple faith in Him applies that shed blood to us. We are actually justified when we believe in Him who shed His blood.

Faith is the only means of appropriating to ourselves the atoning virtue that exists in the blood of Jesus Christ. If one will not believe, there is nothing he can do that will bring him justification.

If one does believe, he is regarded as justified at the moment of belief (Acts 13:38–39). Not only are all his sins put out of God's sight, but in God's reckoning all of God's own righteousness in Jesus Christ is put to his account.

The moment we believe on Him we step into His place and are just as pleasing to God as Jesus Christ Himself is.

In his gospel, the apostle John says "These things are written [that is, the things contained in the gospel of John] that ye might believe that Jesus is the Christ, the Son of God, and that believing ye might have life through his name" (20:31). Here we see that life comes through believing that Jesus is the Christ, the Son of God.

R. A. TORREY

SHORT TALKS
The Gift of Power

What the church needs today is more members with power. "Herein is my Father glorified, that ye bear much fruit." I have no sympathy with the idea of toiling all night and catching nothing. And yet nine-tenths of Christian workers, not to speak of church members in general, never think of looking to the Holy Ghost for this power.

There is a difference between *strength* and *power*. Goliath had strength; David had power.

There is a difference between *influence* and *power*. The high priests and the Pharisees had influence; Peter and the apostles after Pentecost had power.

There is a difference between *the indwelling* of the Holy Ghost and His *filling one with power*. Every true child of God, who has been cleansed by the blood of Christ, is a temple or dwelling-place of the Holy Ghost. But yet he may not have fullness of power.

In the third chapter of John, Nicodemus went to Jesus by night to get light, and I have no doubt he got it; but he did not receive it in abundance, or he would not have stayed in the Sanhedrin three years, listening to all the mean, cutting things they said of Jesus. It took the death of Christ to bring him out manfully and boldly.

In the seventh chapter of John we find a different character. That last day of the feast Christ stood in the temple crying, "If any man thirst, let him come unto me, and drink, [and] . . . out of his belly shall flow rivers of living water."

A man like that would not have stayed in the Sanhedrin three years; he would have smashed up every Sanhedrin on earth. Four walls cannot contain the influence of a man who is full of the Holy Ghost and power. "Rivers of living water!" Think of the rivers that flowed from Charles H. Spurgeon and George Mueller!

Let us pray for this power. The disciples were told to wait because the Spirit was not yet given, but we do not have to wait now, because the Holy Spirit is here.

The power of the Holy Ghost is one thing that can save the church and save our country.

D. L. MOODY

WHAT IS FAITH?

Scriptural Salvation

Whosever believeth on him shall not be ashamed." If you have one foot in the grave, faith may put both feet on the Rock of Ages. You are yet on praying ground and pleading terms with God, therefore come to Jesus; for He hath said, "Him that cometh unto me I will in no wise cast out." Come with your little faith, and your trembling hope, and believe on the Lord Jesus and you shall not be ashamed.

In that day when the earth and heaven shall melt, and nothing shall be seen but Christ upon the throne, judging all the earth, those who have not believed in Him shall be ashamed. They will have no excuse to offer: they have none even now. They will then be ashamed that they did not take the counsel of their godly friends and heed the pleadings of their minister. They will be ashamed to think how they put off thoughts of Christ and lingered until they found themselves in hell. The face of the Lord Jesus will be terrible to unbelievers to the last degree.

One young person, in great trouble of soul, said to me once, "When I am lost, I shall always see your face; it will accuse and condemn me."

It will be terrible to those who refuse the gospel even to remember the preacher of it, but infinitely more so to see the face of Him who bled and died and loved unto the uttermost. Oh, to think, "I would not have Him! I would not be saved by Him! I preferred to trust to myself, or not to think at all, and now here I am!" Assuredly the flames of hell will be more tolerable than the sight of His face. The bitterest wail of Tophet is this—"Hide us from the face of him that sitteth upon the throne!"

Ye sinners, seek His face, whose wrath ye cannot bear. God help you to seek it now. He says, "Seek ye my face." May God the Holy Spirit lead you to obey the call! Amen.

CHARLES H. SPURGEON

LIGHT ON LIFE'S DUTIES
Turn from the Printed Page to Prayer

If a cluster of heavenly fruit hangs within reach, gather it. If a promise lies upon the page as a blank check, cash it. If a prayer is recorded, appropriate it, and launch it as a feathered arrow from the bow of your desire. If an example of holiness gleams before you, ask God to do as much for you. If a truth is revealed in all its intrinsic splendor, entreat that its brilliance may ever irradiate the hemisphere of your life like a star. Entwine the climbing creepers of holy desire about the latticework of Scripture. So shall you come to say with the psalmist, "Oh, how I love thy law! it is my meditation all the day."

It is sometimes well to read over, on our knees, Psalm 119, so full of devout love for the Bible. And if any should chide us for spending so much time upon the Old Testament or the New, let us remind them of the words of Christ, "Man shall not live by bread alone, but by every word that proceedeth out of the mouth of God." The Old Testament must be worth our study since it was our Savior's Bible, deeply pondered and often quoted. And the New demands it, since it is so full of what He said and did, not only in His earthly life but through the medium of His holy apostles and prophets.

The advantages of a deep knowledge of the Bible are more than can be numbered here. It is the Storehouse of the Promises. It is the Sword of the Spirit, before which temptation flees. It is the all-sufficient Equipment of Christian usefulness. It is the believer's Guidebook and Directory in all possible circumstances. Words fail to tell how glad, how strong, how useful shall be the daily life of those who can say with the prophet: "Thy words were found, and I did eat them; and thy word was unto me the joy and rejoicing of mine heart."

But there is one thing, which may be said last, because it is most important and should linger in the memory and heart, though all the other exhortations of this chapter should pass away as a summer brook. It is this. It is useless to dream of making headway in the knowledge of Scripture unless we are prepared to practice each new and clearly-defined duty which looms out before our view.

F. B. MEYER

WHAT IS FAITH?

Whom You Are to Trust

We must guard against trusting in anything but the Word of God and the Lord Himself. If you pass by all obstacles, and come right to Him, and put your trust in Him, you will have rest and peace of mind; and you need not doubt your salvation from this day until you go to your grave.

Again, God has warned us not to put trust in man. Jeremiah 17:5–9 says, "Thus saith the Lord: Cursed be the man that trusteth in man, and maketh flesh his arm, and whose heart departeth from the Lord. For he shall be like the heath in the desert, and shall not see when good cometh; but shall inhabit the parched places in the wilderness, in a salt land and not inhabited.

"Blessed is the man that trusteth in the Lord, and whose hope the Lord is. For he shall be as a tree planted by the waters, and that spreadeth out her roots by the river, and shall not see when heat cometh, but her leaf shall be green; and shall not be careful in the year of drought, neither shall cease from yielding fruit.

"The heart is deceitful above all things, and desperately wicked: who can know it?"

The same thought is brought out in Isaiah 30: "Woe to the rebellious children, saith the Lord, that take counsel, but not of me; and that cover with a covering, but not of my spirit, that they may add sin to sin: That walk to go down into Egypt, and have not asked at my mouth; to strengthen themselves in the strength of Pharaoh, and to trust in the shadow of Egypt! Therefore shall the strength of Pharaoh be your shame, and the trust in the shadow of Egypt your confusion."

In one place He says, "Woe," and in another place He says, "Cursed be the man." It is a terrible thing for a man to put faith in man.

Then Psalm 146:3–5: "Put not your trust in princes, nor in the son of man, in whom there is no help. His breath goeth forth, he returneth to his earth; in that very day his thoughts perish. Happy is he that hath the God of Jacob for his help, whose hope is in the Lord his God."

Here we are told very plainly by God that we are not to put our trust in this man or that man—not to lean upon an arm of flesh.

D. L. MOODY

DIFFICULTIES IN THE BIBLE

The Imprecatory Psalms

God oftentimes simply records what others said—bad men, good men, inspired men, and uninspired men. In the Psalms we have sometimes what God said to man, and that is always true; and on the other hand we often have what men said to God, and that may or may not be true. All of the passages cited are what men said to God. They are the inspired record of men's prayers to God. To God they breathed out the agony of their hearts. And to God they cried for vengeance upon their enemies.

Judged even by Christian standards, this was far better than taking vengeance into their own hands. Indeed, this is exactly what the New Testament commands us to do regarding those who wrong us. Vengeance belongs to God, and He will repay (Romans 12:19), and instead of taking vengeance into our own hands we should put it in His hands.

There is certainly nothing wrong in asking God to break the teeth of wicked men who are using those teeth to tear the upright. This prayer is taken from a psalm that there is every good reason to suppose is Davidic. . . . But it is a well-known fact that David in his personal dealings with his enemies was most generous, for when he had his bitterest and most dangerous enemy in his hand, an enemy who persistently sought his life, he not only refused to kill him, but refused to let another kill him (1 Samuel 26:5–9). And even when he did so small a thing to Saul as to cut off the skirt of his robe, his heart smote him even for that slight indignity offered to his bitterest and most implacable enemy (1 Samuel 24:5).

How much better we would be if instead of taking vengeance into our own hands we would breathe out the bitterness of our hearts to God and then treat our enemies in actual fact as generously as David did! While David prayed to Jehovah in Psalm 109:10: "Let his children be continually vagabonds, and beg: let them seek their bread also out of their desolate places," in point of fact, when he was in a place of power, he asked: "Is there yet any that is left of the house of Saul, that I may shew him kindness?" He found a grandson of Saul's and had him eat at the king's table as one of his own sons (2 Samuel 9:1–2, 11).

R. A. TORREY

SELECT SERMONS
We Are All Sinners Alike

It's a truth that men do not at all like, but I have noticed that the medicine that we do not like is the medicine that will do us good. If we do not think we are as bad as the description, we must just take a closer look at ourselves.

Here is a man who thinks he is not just so bad as the law makes him out to be. He is sure he is a little better than his neighbor next door; he goes to church regularly and his neighbor never goes to church at all! "Of course," he congratulates himself, "I'll certainly get saved easier." But there is no use trying to evade it. God has given us the law to measure ourselves by, and by this most perfect rule we have all sinned and come short, and "there is no difference."

In the third chapter of Romans, Paul brings in the law to show man that he is lost and ruined. God, being a perfect God, had to give a perfect law, and the law was given not to save men, but to measure them. I want you to understand this clearly, because I believe hundreds and thousands stumble at this point. They try to save themselves by trying to keep the law; but it was never meant for men to save themselves by it. The law has never saved a single man since the world began. Men have been trying to keep it, but they have never succeeded and never will. Ask Paul what it was given for. Here is his answer. "That every mouth might be stopped, and the whole world become guilty before God." In this third chapter of Romans the world has been put on trial and found guilty. The verdict has been brought in against us all—ministers and elders and church members, just as much as prodigals and drunkards—"ALL have sinned and come short."

The law stops every man's mouth. God will have a man humble himself down on his face before Him, with not a word to say for himself. Then God will speak to him, when he owns that he is a sinner and gets rid of his own righteousness. I can always tell a man who has got near the kingdom of God; his mouth is stopped. If you will allow me the expression, God always shuts up a man's lips before He saves him. Job was not saved until he stopped talking about himself.

D. L. MOODY

THE TRUE VINE

Much Fruit

H e that abideth in me, and I in him, the same bringeth forth much fruit" (John 15:5).

There is in the Vine such fullness, the care of the divine Husbandman is so sure of success, that the much fruit is not a demand but the simple promise of what must come to the branch that lives in the double abiding—he in Christ, and Christ in him. "The same bringeth forth much fruit." It is certain.

Have you ever noticed the difference in the Christian life between work and fruit? A machine can do work: only life can bear more fruit. A law can compel work: only love can spontaneously bring forth fruit. Work implies effort and labor: the essential idea of fruit is that it is the silent natural restful produce of our inner life. The gardener may labor to give his apple tree the digging and manuring, the watering and the pruning it needs; he can do nothing to produce the apple: the tree bears its own fruit. So in the Christian life: "The fruit of the Spirit is love, joy, peace." The healthy life bears much fruit. The connection between work and fruit is perhaps best seen in the expression "fruitful in every good work" (Colossians 1:10). It is only when good works come as the fruit of the indwelling Spirit that they are acceptable to God. Under the compulsion of law and conscience, or the influence of inclination and zeal, men may be most diligent in good works, and yet find that they have but little spiritual result. There can be no reason but this—their works are man's effort, instead of being the fruit of the Spirit, the restful, natural outcome of the spirit's operation within us.

Let all workers come and listen to our holy Vine as He reveals the law of sure and abundant fruitfulness: "He that abideth in me, and I in him, the same bringeth forth much fruit." The gardener cares for one thing—the strength and healthy life of his tree: the fruit follows of itself. If you would bear fruit, see that the inner life is perfectly right, that your relation to Christ Jesus is clear and close.

ANDREW MURRAY

SELECT SERMONS
His Yoke Is Easy

Do you mean to say that God is a hard master? Do you say it is a hard thing to serve God, and do you say that Satan is an easy master, and that it is easier to serve him than God? Is it honest—is it true? God a hard master! If I read my Bible right, I read that the way of the transgressor is hard. Let me tell you, it is the devil who is the hard master. Yes, "the way of the transgressor is hard." The Word of God cannot be changed.

If you doubt it, young man, look at the convict in prison, right in the bloom of manhood, right in the prime of life. He has been there for ten years and must remain for ten years more—twenty years taken out of his life, and when he comes out of that miserable cell, he comes out a branded felon! Do you think that man will tell you, "The way of the transgressor has been easy?" Go ask the poor drunkard, this man who is bound hand and foot, the slave of the infernal cup, who is hastening onward to a drunkard's hell. Ask him if he has found the way of the transgressor easy. "Easy?" he will cry—"Easy? The way of the transgressor is hard and gets harder and harder every day!" Go ask the libertine and the worldling, go ask the gambler and the blasphemer—with one voice they will tell you that the service has been hard. Take the most faithful follower of the devil and put questions to him.

The best way to settle this matter is to find out by the testimony of those that have served both masters. I do not think a man has any right to judge until he has served both. If I heard a man condemn a master, I should be very apt to ask if he had served him; and if he had not, he could not very well testify. Now, if you have served two masters, then you are very good judges.

I want to stand as a witness for Christ. I have been in this school for forty years, and I want to testify that I have found Him an easy master. I used to say, as you do, "It is a hard thing to be a Christian," and I thought it was; but now I tell you that the yoke is easy and the burden light.

D. L. MOODY

SALVATION FROM START TO FINISH

The Significance of Christ's Words

Jesus is the Very God, or else He is the greatest blasphemer and impostor who ever lived. This invitation on His part proves Him to be either the one or the other. Who has power to pour out the Holy Spirit, save God only? Is this not His prerogative alone? And yet Jesus in this instance claims it as His own. Are not His countrymen here professing to be thirsty? Are they not apparently seeking the Holy Spirit? And does He not say: "I am He who is able and willing to supply your need?" What other application can be given to the words: "If any man thirst, let him come unto me and drink?"

But how can a man "drink" of Jesus? What is the meaning of that word "drink?" Let Jesus Himself explain, when in the next sentence He says: "He that believeth on me, as the scripture hath said, out of his belly shall flow rivers of living water."

To come to Jesus and to drink is to believe on Jesus. And if one ask what it is to "believe" on Jesus, the answer is, to commit yourself to Jesus, to commit yourself to Him as your Savior to be saved and as your Lord you would serve.

On one occasion in Jesus' ministry, earlier than this, there were many who believed on Him when they saw the miracles He did. But it is added that "Jesus did not commit himself unto them, because he knew all men." We know what "commit" means in this case. We know that He did not trust Himself to these men, that He did not put Himself in their hands or "give Himself away" to them. But this word "commit" is in the Greek the same as our word "believe," and it might be rendered, "Jesus did not *believe* Himself unto them, for He knew what was in man." If, then, to commit is to believe, to believe is to commit; and the man who commits himself to Jesus, who gives himself away to Jesus as his Savior and his Lord, that man "comes" to Jesus and "drinks" of Jesus and is blessed.

JAMES M. GRAY

THE STORY OF THE PRODIGAL

The Prodigal Son

F ather, I've sinned," begins the prodigal. But the old man won't hear a word.

"Run quickly and get the best robe. You run and bring a new ring. You fetch the best pair of shoes. You go and kill the fatted calf. Send for the musicians. We are going to have music and rejoice."

The whole house is in excitement.

What a picture that is of the love of God and His joy over the return of a sinner! Come, reader, are you not ashamed to stay away from such a Father? Will you not say "I will" this moment, and turn your face homeward? God is waiting to welcome you.

I see the old man weeping tears of joy. In that home there is gladness. The boy is eating that sumptuous meal; he has not had as good a meal for many a year. It seems almost too good to be true. Picture the scene. While he is there he begins to weep; and his old father, who is weeping for joy, looks over to him and says: "What are you weeping for?"

The boy says, "Well, Father, I was thinking it would be an awful thing if I should have to leave you again and go into a foreign country."

But if you sit down at God's feast, you will not want to go back into the devil's country again. He go back? He will never go back to the swine and the husks.

Oh, my friends, come home! God wants you. His heart is aching for you. I do not care what your past life has been. Upon the authority of God's Word I proclaim salvation to every sinner. "This man receiveth sinners, and eateth with them." Every sinner has a false idea of God; he thinks God is not ready and willing to forgive him. He says it is not justice. But God wants to deal in mercy. If the old father had dealt in justice, he would have barred the door and said to his son: "You cannot come into my house."

That is not what fathers are doing. Their doors are not barred against their own children. Their doors are wide open, and they bid you come home. There is no father on earth who has as much love in his heart as God has for you. You may be as sinful as hell; yet God stands ready and willing to receive you to His bosom and to forgive you freely.

D. L. MOODY

ALL OF GRACE
Faith, What Is It?

Only one ingredient is needed to complete faith, and that is trust. Commit yourself to the merciful God; rest your hope on the gracious gospel; trust your soul on the dying and living Savior; wash away your sins in the atoning blood; accept His perfect righteousness, and all is well. Trust is the lifeblood of faith; there is no saving faith without it.

The Puritans were accustomed to explain faith by the word "recumbency." It means leaning upon a thing. Lean with all your weight upon Christ. It would be a better illustration still if I said, fall at full length and lie on the Rock of Ages. Cast yourself upon Jesus; rest in Him, commit yourself to Him. That done, you have exercised saving faith. Faith is not a blind thing; for faith begins with knowledge. It is not a speculative thing; for faith believes facts of which it is sure. It is not an unpractical, dreamy thing; for faith trusts and stakes its destiny upon the truth of revelation. That is one way of describing what faith is; I wonder whether I have "confounded" it already.

Let me try again. Faith is believing that Christ is what He is said to be and that He will do what He has promised to do, and then to expect this of Him. The Scripture speaks of Jesus Christ as being God, God in human flesh; as being perfect in His character; as being made a sin-offering on our behalf; as bearing our sins in His own body on the tree. The Scripture speaks of Him as having finished transgression, made an end of sin, and brought in everlasting righteousness.

The sacred records further tell us that He "rose again from the dead," that He "ever liveth to make intercession for [us]," that He has gone up into the glory and has taken possession of heaven on the behalf of His people, and that He will shortly come again "to judge the world in righteousness, and his people with equity." We are most firmly to believe that it is even so; for this is the testimony of God the Father when He said, "This is my beloved Son; hear him." This also is testified by God the Holy Spirit; for the Spirit has borne witness to Christ, both in the inspired Word and by many miracles and by His working in the hearts of men. We are to believe this testimony to be true.

CHARLES H. SPURGEON

THE CHRIST-LIFE FOR THE SELF-LIFE

Deliverance from the Power of Sin

Up to the limit of our light God can keep us from known sin. I will say that again: up to the limit of our light—twilight, morning, noon—God is able to keep us from all conscious and known sin. But He will not keep us from temptation. You cannot help the devil knocking at the door, but you can help inviting him in to supper. You cannot help the foul vulture flying over your head, but you can help letting him make a nest in your hair.

When you live near God you will be most tempted of the devil. Some men seem to think they are not holy because they are tempted. I should not believe in a man's holiness if he were not tempted. When I was at school, the boys used to avoid certain orchards, because they were full of crab apples; and you might know that the apples in those orchards were sour, or the boys would go for them. And if you are not tempted, it shows that your heart is empty and wicked and not worth the devil's while to spend his time over. When the Spirit of God descended upon Christ He was led by the Spirit into the wilderness to be tempted of the devil. He was Spirit-filled yet devil-tempted.

You ask, why does God let us be tempted? I think it is to show where we are weak; that upon the temptation, as our stepping-stone, we may reach out for some of God's help. I would not know how much I needed Christ unless the devil were constantly tempting me.

God is working in you. The compunction you feel when you sin, the yearning you feel for a better life, your desire to go to a religious meeting—all are proofs that God is working in you to deliver you. Many a woman of fashion or society is, perhaps, living in the very whirl of it, and yet, poor thing, in it she really wants something better. My sister, do not be disheartened—that is God working in you! I believe you are a real child of His, but you are so weak, and you do not like to stand alone, you do what other women do, and yet you hate it all the time, and you want the better life. Understand that God is working in you; you are the workshop of God.

F. B. MEYER

THE SCHOOL OF OBEDIENCE

The Obedience of Christ

The object of Christ's life of obedience was threefold: (1) As an example, to show us what true obedience was; (2) as our surety, by His obedience to fulfill all righteousness for us; (3) as our head, to prepare a new and obedient nature to impart to us.

So He died, too, to show us that His obedience means a readiness to obey to the uttermost, to die for God; that it means the vicarious endurance and atonement of the guilt of our disobedience; that it means a death to sin as an entrance to the life of God for Him and for us.

The disobedience of Adam, in all its possible bearings, was to be put away and replaced by the obedience of Christ. Judicially, by that obedience we are made righteous. Just as we were made sinners by Adam's disobedience, we are at once and completely justified and delivered from the power of sin and death; we stand before God as righteous men. Vitally—for the judicial and the vital are as inseparable as in the case of Adam—we are made one plant with Christ in His death and resurrection, so that we are truly dead to sin and alive to God, as He is. And the life we receive in Him is no other than a life of obedience.

Let every one of us who would know what obedience is, consider well: It is the obedience of Christ that is the secret of the righteousness and salvation I find in Him. The obedience is the very essence of that righteousness: obedience is salvation. His obedience, first of all to be accepted and trusted to and rejoiced in, as covering and swallowing up and making an end of my disobedience, is the one unchanging, never-to-be-forsaken ground of my acceptance. And then, His obedience—just as Adam's disobedience was the power that ruled my life, the power of death in me—becomes the life power of the new nature in me. Then I understand why Paul in this passage so closely links the righteousness and the life. "If by the trespass of one, death reigned through the one, much more shall they who receive the abundance of grace and the gift of righteousness reign in life through one," even here on earth. "The gift came unto all men unto justification of life."

ANDREW MURRAY

SELECT SERMONS
Good News

There is that terrible enemy mentioned in 1 Corinthians 15—the last enemy, death. The gospel has taken it out of the way. My mind very often runs back many years, before I was converted, and I think how dark it used to seem as I thought of the future. I well remember how I used to look on death as a terrible monster, how he used to throw his dark shadow across my path; how I trembled as I thought of the terrible hour when he should come for me; how I thought I should like to die of some lingering disease such as consumption, so that I might know when he was coming.

It was the custom in our village to toll from the old church bell the age of anyone who died. Death never entered that village and tore away one of the inhabitants but I counted the tolling of the bell. Sometimes it was seventy, sometimes eighty; sometimes it would be down among the teens, sometimes it would toll out the death of some one of my own age. It made a solemn impression upon me. I felt a coward then. I thought of the cold hand of death feeling for the cords of life. I thought of being launched forth to spend my eternity in an unknown land.

As I looked into the grave and saw the sexton throw the earth on the coffin-lid, "Earth to earth—ashes to ashes—dust to dust," it seemed like the death-knell to my soul.

But that is all changed now. The grave has lost its terror. As I go on toward heaven I can shout—"O death! Where is thy sting?" and I hear the answer rolling down from Calvary—"buried in the bosom of the Son of God." He took the sting right out of death for me and received it into His own bosom. Take a hornet and pluck the sting out; you are not afraid of it after that any more than of a fly. So death has lost its sting. That last enemy has been overcome, and I can look on death as a crushed victim. All that death can get now is this old Adam, and I do not care how quickly I get rid of it. I shall get a glorified body, a resurrection body, a body much better than this.

D. L. MOODY

THE CHRIST-LIFE FOR THE SELF-LIFE

Resurrection, Ascension, and Eternity

If you go back and live a worldly life, you have to go back through the grave to it, because the grave lies between the body of Christ, of which you are a part, and the world that cast Him out. The world cast Him out, and when they cast Him out they cast us out also, and we were buried in Christ by the world that hates the church.

But just as Eve was taken out of Adam as he slept, the church was taken out of Christ in His sleep, and when He rose we streamed out a great procession from the grave. And on Easter morning I celebrate not only the resurrection of Christ but my own, for I too was raised in Him.

Oh, it was a good thing when, as I crossed the Atlantic, we got through that storm. It was such a storm that I could hardly preach to the people in the saloon, the ship was rocking so; but after a while we got through the disturbance and left the storm behind us. And in Christ, when He died, the ark of God carried you and me through the storm of death into clear water, and above us is the blue sky of God's love.

On ascension day I celebrate my ascension also, and in God's purpose all of us who believe are seated in Christ, and we must live day by day as those who in God's purpose have passed into the heavenly life.

You tell me that when I die my eternity will begin. No such thing. My eternity began when I was born in Christ. Eternal life is in my heart today, and the only difference that will come to me when I pass through what men call death, but which to me is not death—it is only the shadow of death, for I died in Christ, and I can never pass again through the agony of death, but I will pass through the shadow of death, and no one was ever hurt by a shadow yet—the only difference that will come to me is that I shall get rid of, for a time at least, a rather crazy body, which will lie to wait until my spirit rejoins it in perfect beauty. But God will never love me more than He does today, and I shall never be nearer God than I am today and already I hunger no more, nor thirst any more, neither does the sun smite me nor any heat, because already the Lamb is leading me day by day to living fountains of waters, and God is wiping all tears from my eyes. Eternity is begun.

F. B. MEYER

LIGHT ON LIFE'S DUTIES

The Chamber of a Surrendered Will

Fxrom henceforth let no man trouble me: for I bear branded on my body the marks of Jesus" (Galatians 6:17 RV). Consecration is giving Jesus His own. We are His by right, because He bought us with His blood. But, alas! He has not had His money's worth! He paid for all, and He has had but a fragment of our energy, time, and earnings. By an act of consecration, let us ask Him to forgive the robbery of the past, and let us profess our desire to be henceforth utterly and only for Him; His slaves, His chattels, owning no master other than Himself.

As soon as we say this, He will test our sincerity, as He did the young ruler's, by asking something of us. He will lay His finger on something within us which He wants us to alter, obeying some command, or abstaining from some indulgence.

If we instantly give up our will and way to Him, we pass the narrow doorway into the Chamber of Surrender, which has a southern aspect and is ever warm and radiant with His presence because obedience is the condition of manifested love (John 14:23).

This doorway is very narrow, and the entrance is only possible for those who will lay aside weights as well as sins. A weight is anything which, without being essentially wrong or hurtful to others, is yet a hindrance to ourselves.

We may always know a weight by three signs: first, we are uneasy about it; second, we argue for it against our conscience; third, we go about asking people's advice, whether we may not keep it without harm. All these things must be laid aside in the strength Jesus waits to give. Ask Him to deal with them for you, that you may be set in joint in every good work to do His will (Hebrews 13:21).

F. B. MEYER

THE STORY OF THE PRODIGAL

The Prodigal's Climax

O reader, let your very needs, your cravings, your misery, drive you to your God! The prodigal son's fears whipped him back. He said, "I perish with hunger." He had not perished yet, but he was afraid that he soon would do so; he feared that he really would die, for he felt so faint.

O, reader, see what will become of you if you do die in your sins! What awaits you but an endless future of limitless misery? Sin will follow you into eternity and will increase upon you there, and as you shall go on to sin, so shall you go on to sorrow ever-increasing. A deeper degradation and a more tremendous penalty will accompany your sin in the world to come; therefore let your fears drive you home, as they drove home the poor prodigal.

Meanwhile, his hope drew him. This gentle cord was as powerful as the heavy whip: "In my father's house there is bread enough and to spare; I need not perish with hunger, I may yet be filled."

Oh, think of what you may yet be! Poor sinner, think of what God can do and is ready to do for you, to do for you even now! How happy He can make you! How peaceful and how blessed! So let your hope draw you to Him.

Then his resolve moved him. He said, "I will arise and go to my father." All else drove him or drew him, and now he is resolved to return home. He rose up from the earth on which he had been sitting amidst his filthiness, and he said, "I will."

Then the man became a man. He had come to himself; the manhood had come back to him, and he said, "I will, I will."

Lastly, there was the real act of going to his father; it was that which brought him home. Nay, let me correct myself; it is said, "He came to his father," but there is a higher truth at the back of that, for his father came to him.

So, when you are moved to return, and the resolution becomes an action, and you arise and go to God, salvation is yours almost before you could have expected it; for, once turn your face that way, and while you are yet a great way off, your Father will outstrip the wind and come and meet you, and fall upon your neck and kiss you with the kisses of reconciliation.

This shall be your portion if you will but trust the Lord Jesus Christ.

D. L. MOODY

FULL ASSURANCE

Discouraged Christians

Many uninstructed believers become discouraged because of their own failures, and Satan takes advantage of these to inject into their minds doubts as to whether they are not deceiving themselves after all in supposing they are Christians. But a knowledge of the truth as to the believer's two natures will often help here. It is important to understand that sin in the flesh, inherent in the old nature, is not destroyed when one is born again. On the contrary, that old sin-principle remains in the believer as long as he is in the body. What takes place at new birth is that a new and divine nature is communicated. These two natures are in conflict with each other.

But the Christian who walks in the spirit will not fulfill the desires of the flesh, even though at times those desires may be manifested. In order to so walk, one must take sides with God against this principle of evil which belongs to the old Adamic nature. God reckons it as executed at the cross of Christ; for the Lord Jesus died, not only for what we have done but for what we are by nature. Now faith accepts this as true, and the believer can exclaim, "I am crucified with Christ: nevertheless I live; yet not I, but Christ liveth in me: and the life that I now live in the flesh (that is, in the body), I live by the faith of the Son of God who loved me and gave himself for me" (Galatians 2:20).

Carefully consider what is taught here: I, the responsible I, the old man, all that I was as a man in the flesh, including my entire sinful nature—"I have been crucified with Christ." When was that? It was when Jesus died on Calvary's tree nineteen hundred years ago. He was there for me. I was there in Him. He was my representative, my substitute. He died the death I deserved to die. Therefore in God's eyes His death was my death. So I have died with Him.

Now I am called upon to make this real in my personal experience. I am to reckon myself as dead indeed unto sin but alive unto God (Romans 6:11). The old nature has no claim upon me. If it asserts itself and endeavors to bring me into bondage, I am to take sides with God against it. He has condemned sin in the flesh. I must condemn it too. Instead of yielding to it, I am to yield myself unto God as one alive from the dead, for I have been crucified in Christ's crucifixion, but I live anew in His resurrection.

HENRY A. IRONSIDE

THE WAY OF LIFE
All Things Are Ready: Come

Jesus, my Lord and Master, is the Great Physician of souls, and He heals them on just such terms as I have mentioned. Are you a far-gone sinner? Are you a deeply sinsick soul? Are you a man or woman who is bad altogether? Come along, my friend, you are just in a right condition to come to Jesus Christ. Come just as you are; that is the best style of "coming."

"What," said one, "can you mean it, that I, an unfeeling, unpenitent wretch, am bidden to come at once and believe in Jesus Christ for everlasting life?" I mean just that. I do not mean to send you round to that shop for repentance and to the other shop for feeling and to a third store for a tender heart, and then direct you to call on Christ at last for a few odds and ends. No, no, but come to Christ for everything.

> "Come, ye needy, come and welcome,
>   God's free bounty glorify;
> True belief and true repentance,
> Every grace that brings you nigh,
>   Without money
> Come to Jesus Christ and buy."

I heard of a shop some time ago in a country town where they sold everything, and the man said that he did not believe there was anything a human being wanted but what he could rig him out from top to toe. Well, I do not know whether that promise would have been carried out to the letter if it had been tried, but I know it is so with Jesus Christ; He can supply you with all you need, for "Christ is all." There is not a need your soul can possibly have but the Lord Jesus Christ can supply it, and the very best way to come is to come to Him for everything.

Trust Jesus Christ, that is all, just as you are, with all your unfitness and unreadiness. Take what God has made ready for you, the precious blood to cleanse you, a robe of righteousness to cover you, eternal joy to be your portion. Receive the grace of God in Christ Jesus, oh! receive it now. God grant you may, for Jesus Christ's sake. Amen.

CHARLES H. SPURGEON

WEIGHED AND WANTING

An Evil Harvest

Even in this life adultery and uncleanness bring their awful results, both physical and mental. The pleasure and excitement that lead so many astray at the beginning soon pass away, and only the evil remains. Vice carries a sting in its tail, like the scorpion. The body is sinned against, and the body sooner or later suffers. "Every sin that a man doeth is without the body: but he that committeth fornication sinneth against his own body," said Paul. Nature herself punishes with nameless diseases, and the man goes down to the grave rotten, leaving the effects of his sin to blight his posterity. There are nations whose manhood has been eaten out by this awful scourge.

It drags a man lower than the beasts. It stains the memory. I believe that memory is "the worm that never dies," and the memory is never cleansed of obscene stories and unclean acts. Even if a man repents and reforms he often has to fight the past.

Lust gave Samson into the power of Delilah, who robbed him of his strength. It led David to commit murder and called down upon him the wrath of God. I believe that if Joseph had responded to the enticement of Potiphar's wife, the light of his witness would have gone out in darkness.

It ends in one or other of two ways: either in remorse and shame because of the realization of the loss of purity, with a terrible struggle against a hard task-master; or in hardness of heart, brutalizing of the finer senses, which is a more dreadful condition.

We hear a good deal about intemperance nowadays. That sin advertises it-self; it shows its marks upon the face and in the conduct. But this hides itself away under the shadow of the night. A man who tampers with this evil goes on step by step until his character is blasted, his reputation ruined, his health gone, and his life made as dark as hell. May God wake up the nation to see how this awful sin is spreading!

Will anyone deny that the house of the strange woman is "the way to hell, going down to the chambers of death," as the Bible says? Are there not men whose characters have been utterly ruined for this life through this accursed sin? Are there not wives who would rather sink into their graves than live? Many a man went with a pure woman to the altar a few years ago and promised to love and cherish her. Now he has given his affections to some vile harlot and brought ruin on his wife and children!

D. L. MOODY

PRACTICAL AND PERPLEXING QUESTIONS ANSWERED

The Heathen

How is God going to judge the heathen? Can the heathen be saved by following the best light they have?

God will judge the heathen in righteousness, according to the light they have had. Those who have sinned without knowing the law revealed to Moses will also perish without the law, and as many as have sinned under the law shall be judged by the law (Romans 2:12).

The heathen are not without light. The fact that they do by nature the things required in the law shows that they have a law, though not the law revealed to Moses (Romans 2:14). If any heathen should live perfectly up to the light he has he would doubtless be saved by doing so, but no heathen has ever done this. Romans 2:12–16 is often taken as teaching that the heathen are to be saved by the light of nature, but anyone who will read the passage carefully in its connection will see that Paul's whole purpose is not to show how the heathen are saved by keeping the law written in their hearts but to show that all are under condemnation—the Jew because he has not lived up to the law given by revelation, and the Gentile because he has not lived up to the law written in his heart.

The conclusion of the matter is given in Romans 3:22–23: "For there is no distinction; for all have sinned, and fall short of the glory of God" (RV). In the verses that follow the only way of salvation is pointed out, namely, free justification by God's grace through the redemption that is in Christ Jesus on the ground of His propitiatory death, the value of which each one appropriates to himself by faith in Him. No one will be saved except through personal acceptance of Jesus Christ as his personal Savior. There is not a line of Scripture that holds out a ray of hope to any one who dies without accepting Jesus Christ.

There are those who hold that those who die without hearing of Jesus Christ in this world will have an opportunity of hearing of Him and accepting Him or rejecting Him in some future state, but the Bible does not say so, and this is pure speculation without a word of Scripture to support it.

There are also those who hold that those heathen who would have accepted Christ if He had been presented to them will be treated as if He had been presented to them and they had accepted Him, but this is all pure speculation. All the Bible teaches is that no one can be saved without personal acceptance of Christ, and the part of wisdom on our part is to do everything in our power to see that the heathen have the opportunity of accepting Christ in the life that now is.

R. A. TORREY

SHORT TALKS

Besetting Sins

The Israelites failed to drive out their enemies. I believe the reason so many Christians have such a stormy passage, and the Christian life is not what they expected it to be when they became Christians, is that they don't drive out every foe and every enemy. In other words, they are not more than half converted. They don't get control of their temper. The god of pleasure seems to have a grip upon them. Lust and covetousness and selfishness come in, and they don't get victory. Nine-tenths of the battle is won, it seems to me, if we start right.

In Psalm 41:11 are these words: "By this I know that thou favorest me, because mine enemy doth not triumph over me." Now I believe that we all have some besetting sin, and what we want is to get victory over that besetting sin, whatever it is. "By this we know that God favors us, that our enemy doth not triumph over us."

Is there some habit marring your Christian life, hindering your usefulness, checking your progression in divine life? Then make up your mind that you are going to get victory over it. It may look like a small enemy, but it will become stronger and stronger if not checked. You remember God told Saul to go and utterly destroy Amalek. He did not fully obey but spared some, and in the thirty-first chapter of Samuel we read that it was an Amalekite who boasted that he had slain Saul and stripped him of his crown. Someone has said that it would be easier to find a man that had not done any one sin than to find a man who had done it only once. Sin multiplies. The tendency to sin gathers force with every new commission. So the battle goes on in every one of us. We must either overcome sin, or it will overcome us; we must decide.

Have you completely forsaken your sins, or is there some enemy that you allow to remain alive?

D. L. MOODY

WHAT IS FAITH?

A Warning to Unbelievers

W ell," says one, "I cannot see how simply trusting in Christ and believing God's witness of Him would save my soul." My dear man, are you never to believe anything but what you can see, and how are you to see this thing till you have tried it?

"That medicine will heal you," a physician says.

"I want to see that it does heal me before I take it," the patient replies.

That man is a fool, and so are you if that is how you trifle with God. You must believe the gospel on the evidence of God, and not otherwise, or your faith is not faith in God at all. The faith that is commanded in the gospel is faith in the record God has given concerning His Son, a faith that takes God at His word. Believe, then, on the Lord Jesus Christ and you have believed God to be true; refuse to trust in Jesus Christ, unless you get some other evidence beyond the witness of God, and you have practically said that God's testimony is not enough—that is to say, you have made God a liar.

Another cries out: "That is too good to be true."

Ah, poor soul, but have you never read, "As high as the heavens are above the earth, so are my ways above your ways, and my thoughts above your thoughts"? A less salvation would not avail for you, nor glorify God. Some feel that the gospel is too simple. They want a more complicated system than— "believe and live." How can it be too simple for finite minds like ours?

Then I have heard them turn round and say, "It is too mysterious," and yet after all where is this mystery? "Believe on the Lord Jesus Christ and thou shalt be saved." What can be more plain than that? Anyhow, dear friend, let me say to you, whether it is a mystery or not, God bears witness to it, and if you do not believe it you make God a liar. Whether you think it too simple, or too good, or too wonderful, or too anything, you must either believe God or make Him a liar, there is no third course; for, be it simple or mysterious, wonderful or commonplace, the Lord asserts it to be true, and if you refuse His witness you make Him a liar and must take the consequences.

To disbelieve God is a sin indeed!

CHARLES H. SPURGEON

THE STORY OF THE PRODIGAL

The Prodigal Son

Now, just for a moment, think what the prodigal son lost in all these years. He lost his home. His friends, when he had money, might have invited him around to their homes; but it was not home for him. There is not a prodigal upon the face of the earth but has lost his home. You may live in a gilded palace; but if God is not there, it is not home. If your conscience is lashing you, it is not home.

He lost his food. His father's table did not go to that country. He would have fed on the husks that the swine did not eat. This world cannot satisfy the soul.

Then he lost his testimony. I can imagine that some of the young men of that country saw him among the swine, feeding them, and they said, "Look at that poor wretched young man, with no shoes on his feet, and with such shabby garments." They looked at him and called him a beggar and pointed the finger of scorn at him.

He said: "You need not call me a beggar. My father is a wealthy man."

"Your father, a wealthy man?"

"Yes."

"You look like a wealthy man's son!"

Not a man believed him when he said he was a wealthy man's son. His testimony was gone. So when a man goes into the service of the devil he sinks lower and lower; and it is not long before everyone loses confidence in him. One sin leads on to another. His testimony is gone.

He lost his health, his good name, his time. And he did not gain much to compensate him for these losses. He got a good many things, however. He got the jeers of his former companions. He got rags and filth. He got a gnawing hunger and a depraved appetite. He got a sad experience of the unsatisfying nature of worldly pleasures.

But there is one thing he did not lose, and if there is a poor backslider reading this, there is one thing you have not lost. That young man never lost his father's love.

D. L. MOODY

THE SCHOOL OF OBEDIENCE

The Secret of True Obedience

He learned obedience." And now that He teaches it, He does so first and most by unfolding the secret of His own obedience to the Father.

The power of true obedience is to be found in the clear personal relationship to God. It was so with our Lord Jesus. Of all His teaching He said, "I have not spoken of myself, but the Father which sent me gave me a commandment, what I should say and what I should speak. And I know that his commandment is life everlasting; whatever I speak therefore, even as the Father said unto me, so I speak."

This does not mean that Christ received God's commandment in eternity as part of the Father's commission to Him on entering the world. No. Day by day, each moment as He taught and worked, He lived, as man, in continual communication with the Father and received the Father's instructions just as He needed them. Does He not say, "The Son can do nothing of himself but what he seeth the Father do; for the Father showeth the Son all things that himself doeth; and he will show him greater things"? In other Scriptures Christ says, "As I hear, I judge"; "I am not alone, but I and the Father that sent me"; "the words that I speak, I speak not of myself, but the Father that dwelleth in me." It is everywhere a dependence upon a present fellowship and operation of God, a hearing and a seeing of what God speaks and does and shows.

Our Lord ever spoke of His relation to the Father as the type and the promises of our relation to Him, and to the Father through Him. With us as with Him, the life of continual obedience is impossible without continual fellowship and continual teaching. It is only when God comes into our lives, in a degree and a power which many never consider possible, when His presence as the eternal and ever-present one is believed and received, even as the Son believed and received it, that there can be any hope of a life in which every thought is brought into captivity to the obedience of Christ.

ANDREW MURRAY

SELECT SERMONS
Sinners Seeking Christ

If I read my Bible correctly, the man who preaches the gospel is not the man who tells me to seek Christ tomorrow or an hour hence, but now. He is near to every one of us this minute to save. If the world would just come to God for salvation, and be in earnest about it, they would find the Son of God right at the door of their heart.

Suppose I should say I have lost a very valuable diamond here—worth $1,000,000. I had it in my pocket when I came into the hall, and when I had done preaching I found it was not in my pocket, but was in the hall somewhere. Suppose I should say that anyone who finds it could have it. How earnest you would all become! You would not get very much of my sermon; you would all be thinking of the diamond. I do not believe the police could get you out of this hall. The idea of finding a diamond worth $1,000,000! If you could only find it, it would lift you out of poverty at once, and you would be independent for the rest of your days. Oh, how soon everybody would become terribly in earnest then!

I would to God I could get men to seek for Christ in the same way. I have got something worth more than a diamond to offer you. Is not salvation—eternal life—worth more than all the diamonds in the world?

People seem to sleep and to forget that there is no door out of hell. If they enter there they must remain, age after age. Millions on millions of years will roll on, but there will be no door, no escape out of hell. May God wake you up and make you anxious about your soul. People talk about our being earnest and fanatical—about our being on fire. Would to God the church was on fire! This world would soon shake to its foundation. May God wake up a slumbering church! What we want men to do is not to shout, "Amen," and clasp their hands. The deepest and quickest waters very often run swiftest. We want men to go right to work; there will be a chance for them to shout by-and-by. Go and speak to your neighbor and tell him of Christ and heaven. You need not go far before you will find someone who is passing down to the darkness of eternal death. Let us haste to the rescue!

D. L. MOODY

ALL OF GRACE

How May Faith Be Illustrated?

Faith is the hand that grasps. When our hand takes hold of anything for itself, it does precisely what faith does when it appropriates Christ and the blessings of His redemption. Faith says, "Jesus is mine." Faith hears of the pardoning blood and cries, "I accept it to pardon me." Faith calls the legacies of the dying Jesus her own; and they are her own, for faith is Christ's heir; He has given himself and all that He has to faith. Take, O friend, that which grace has provided for thee. You will not be a thief, for you have a divine permit: "Whosoever will, let him take the water of life freely." He who may have a treasure simply by his grasping it will be foolish indeed if he remains poor.

Faith is the mouth that feeds upon Christ. Before food can nourish us, it must be received into us. This is a simple matter—this eating and drinking. We willingly receive into the mouth that which is our food, and then we consent that it should pass down into our inward parts, wherein it is taken up and absorbed into our bodily frame. Paul says in his epistle to the Romans, in the tenth chapter, "The word is nigh thee, even in thy mouth." Now then, all that is to be done is to swallow it, to suffer it to go down into the soul.

Oh that men had an appetite! For he who is hungry and sees meat before him does not need to be taught how to eat. "Give me," said one, "a knife and a fork and a chance." He was fully prepared to do the rest. Truly, a heart which hungers and thirsts after Christ has but to know that He is freely given, and at once it will receive Him. If my reader is in such a case, let him not hesitate to receive Jesus; for he may be sure that he will never be blamed for doing so; for unto "as many as received him, to them gave he power to become the sons of God" (John 1:12). He never repulses one, but He authorizes all who come to remain sons forever.

CHARLES H. SPURGEON

PRACTICAL AND PERPLEXING QUESTIONS ANSWERED

More than a Father

Would an earthly father consign his child to everlasting suffering? And if he would not, can we believe that God is not as good as we are and that He would treat His children in a way that we would not treat ours?

This question takes it for granted that all men are God's children. The Bible teaches that this is not true. All men are God's creatures and were created originally in His likeness, and in this sense they are all His offspring (Acts 17:26–29), but men become God's children in the fullest sense by being born again of the Holy Spirit (John 3:3–6) through the personal acceptance of Jesus Christ as their Savior (John 1:12; Galatians 3:26).

Second, God is something besides the Father even of believers. He is the moral governor of this universe. As a righteous moral governor of the universe He must punish sin, and if sin is eternally persisted in He must eternally punish it. Even a wise earthly father would separate one of his own children who persisted in sin from contact with his other children. If a man had a dearly beloved son who was a moral monster he certainly would not allow him to associate with his daughters. If one whom you greatly loved should commit a gross wrong against someone you loved more, and should persist in it eternally, would you not consent to his eternal punishment?

Third, it is never safe to measure what an infinitely holy God would do by what we would do. As we look about us in the world today do we not see men and women suffering agonies that we would not allow our children to suffer if we could prevent it? What one of us could endure to see our children suffering some of the things that the men and women in the slums of the great city are suffering today? Why a God of love permits this to go on may be difficult for us to explain, but that it does go on we know. What men and women suffer even in the life that now is as a result of their disobedience to God and their persistence in sin and their rejection of Jesus Christ ought to be a hint of what men will suffer in the eternal world if they go on in sin as the result of their having rejected the Savior in the life that now is. It may sound well to say, "I believe in a God of love, and I do not believe that He will permit any of His creatures to go to an eternal hell," but if we open our eyes to the facts as they exist about us on every hand we will see how empty our speculations on this point are, for we do see even now this same God of love permitting many of His creatures to endure awful and ever-increasing agonies in the life that now is.

R. A. TORREY

TO THE WORK!

The Power of Little Things

John Bunyan, the poor Bedford tinker, was worth much more than all the nobility of his day. God took him in hand, and he became mighty. He wrote that wonderful book that has gone marching through the nations, lifting up many a weary heart, cheering many a discouraged and disheartened one. Let us remember that if we are willing to be used, God is willing and waiting to use us.

I once heard an Englishman speak about Christ feeding the five thousand with the five barley loaves and the two small fishes. He said that Christ may have taken one of the loaves and broken off a piece and given it to one of the disciples to divide. When the disciple began to pass it round he only gave a very small piece to the first, because he was afraid it would not hold out. But after he had given the first piece it did not seem to grow any less; so the next time he gave a larger piece, and still the bread was not exhausted. The more he gave, the more the bread increased, until all had plenty.

At the first all could be carried in one basket; but when the whole multitude had been satisfied the disciples gathered up twelve baskets full of fragments. They had a good deal more when they stopped than when they began. Let us bring our little barley loaves to the master that He may multiply them.

You say you have not got much; well, you can use what you have. The longer I work in Christ's vineyard the more convinced I am that a good many are kept out of the service of Christ, deprived of the luxury of working for God, because they are trying to do some great thing. Let us be willing to do little things. And let us remember that nothing is small in which God is. Elijah's servant came to him and told him he saw a cloud not larger than a man's hand. That was enough for Elijah. He said to his servant, "Go, tell Ahab to make haste; there is the sound of abundance of rain." Elijah knew that the small cloud would bring rain. Nothing that we do for God is small.

D. L. MOODY

LIGHT ON LIFE'S DUTIES
The Cleansing Blood of Jesus

I t is sweet to notice the present tenses of Scripture. He forgives, heals, redeems, crowns, satisfies, executes judgment; but the sweetest of all is "the blood of Jesus cleanseth from all sin." It cleansed us when first we knelt at His cross. It will cleanse away the last remnant of sin as we cross the golden threshold. But it does cleanse us every hour; as the brook flows over the stones in its bed till they glisten with lustrous beauty; and as tears pouring constantly over the eye, keep it bright and clean, in spite of all the smuts that darken the air.

The possession of a sinful nature is an evil that ever needs an antidote. The risings and stirrings of that nature beneath the appeals of temptation ever need cleansing. The permission of things in our life, which we now count harmless, but which we shall some day, amid increasing light, condemn and put away—all these need forgiveness. But for all these needs there is ample provision for us in the blood of Jesus, which is always crying to God for us. Even when we do not plead it, or remember it, or realize our need of it, it fulfills for us and in us its unceasing ministry of blessing.

Reckon yourself dead to the appeals of sin. Sin has no power over a dead man. Dress it in its most bewitching guise, yet it stirs him not. Tears and smiles and words and blows alike fail to awaken a response from that cold corpse. No appeal will stir it until it hears the voice of the Son of God.

This is our position in respect to the appeals of sin. God looks on us as having been crucified with Christ and being dead with Him. In Him we have passed out of the world of sin and death into the world of resurrection glory. This is our position in the mind of God; it is for us to take it up and make it real by faith. We may not feel any great difference, but we must believe that there is; we must act as if there were. Our children sometimes play at make believe; we, too, are to make believe, and we shall soon come to feel as we believe. When, then, a temptation solicits you, say, "I am dead to you."

F. B. MEYER

SELECT SERMONS
Where Do You Stand with Christ?

Not long ago the only daughter of a wealthy friend of mine sickened and died. The father and mother stood by her dying bed. He had spent all his time in accumulating wealth for her. She had been introduced into fashionable society; but she had been taught nothing of Christ. As she came to the brink of the river of death, she said, "Won't you help me? It is very dark, and the stream is bitterly cold." They wrung their hands in grief but could do nothing for her; and the poor girl died in darkness and despair. What was their wealth to them then? And yet, mothers and fathers are doing the very same thing today by ignoring the work God has given you to do. I beseech you, each one of you, begin to labor now for the souls of your children!

Some time ago a young man lay dying, and his mother thought he was a Christian. One day, passing the door of his room, she heard him say, "Lost! Lost! Lost!" The mother ran into the room and cried, "My boy, is it possible you have lost your hope in Christ, now you are dying?"

"No, mother, it is not that. I have a hope beyond the grave, but I have lost my life. I have lived twenty-four years and have done nothing for the Son of God, and now I am dying. My life has been spent for myself. I have lived for this world, and now, while I am dying, I have given myself to Christ; but my life is lost."

Would it not be said of many of us, if we should be cut down, that our lives have been almost a failure—perhaps entirely a failure as far as leading anyone else to Christ is concerned? Young lady! Are you working for the Son of God? Are you trying to win some soul to Christ? Have you tried to get some friend or companion to have her name written in the Book of Life? Or would you say, "Lost! Lost! Long years have rolled away since I became a child of God, and I have never had the privilege of leading one soul to Christ"? If there is one professed child of God who has never had the joy of leading even one soul into the kingdom of God, oh! let him begin at once. There is no greater privilege on earth.

Oh, may God wake up the church! Let us trim our lights and go forth and work for the kingdom of His Son.

D. L. MOODY

THE WAY OF LIFE
The Feast Is Ready

The perfect readiness of the feast of divine mercy is evidently intended to be a strong argument with sinners as to why they should come at once. To the sinner, then, do I address myself.

Do you desire eternal life? Is there within your spirit a hungering and a thirsting after such things as may satisfy your spirit and make you live forever? Then hearken while the master's servant gives you the invitation. "Come, for all things are ready"—all, not some, but *all*. There is nothing that you can need between here and heaven but what is provided in Jesus Christ, in His person and in His work. All things are ready, life for your death, forgiveness for your sin, cleansing for your filth, clothing for your nakedness, joy for your sorrow, strength for your weakness, yea, more than all that ever you can want is stored up in the boundless nature and work of Christ.

You must not say, "I cannot come because I have not this or have not that." Are you to prepare the feast? Are you to provide anything? Are you the purveyor of even so much as the salt or the water? You know not your true condition, or you would not dream of such a thing. The great householder Himself has provided the whole of the feast; you have nothing to do with the provision but to partake of it. If you lack, come and take what you lack; the greater your need the greater reason why you should come where all things that your need can possibly want will be at once supplied. If you are so needy that you have nothing good at all about you, all things are ready. What would you provide more when God has provided all things?

Great wickedness would it be if you were to think of adding to His "all things." It would be but a presumptuous competing with the provisions of the great King, and this He will not endure. All that you want—I can but repeat the words—between the gates of hell, where you now liest, and the gates of heaven, to which grace will bring you if you believe—all is provided and prepared in Jesus Christ the Savior.

CHARLES H. SPURGEON

WHAT IS FAITH?

Enough Faith

Then people say: "I don't know that I have enough faith." Christ said that if you have faith "as a grain of mustard seed," you will be able to move mountains.

Then there is another impression that faith is indicated by feelings. Now, faith is not feeling. Your feelings may change forty times before sundown, but your faith may be the same right along. What made the slaves free? Was it their feelings or Lincoln's proclamation? Suppose that a slave said he "felt free" six months before the proclamation, I think he would have felt the lash on his back.

We are living in very strange days. Some people tell us it does not make any difference what a man believes if he is only "sincere." One church is just as good as another if you are only sincere. I do not believe any greater delusion ever came out of the pit of hell than that. It is ruining more souls at the present time than anything else.

I never read of any men more sincere or more earnest than those men at Mount Carmel, those false prophets. They were terribly in earnest. Some people say, "Why, if these men are holding, as you say, error, why should they be so in earnest?" Those prophets of Baal were the most earnest men I ever read of. You do not read of men getting so in earnest now that they take knives and cut themselves. Look at them leaping upon their altars; hear their cry, "O Baal! O Baal!" We never hear that kind of prayer nowadays. They acted like mad men. They were terribly in earnest, yet did God hear their cry? They were all slain. "I believe one religion is just as good as another, if you are only sincere in what you believe"—it is one of the devil's lies.

Some men seem to think it is a great misfortune that they do not have faith. Bear in mind it is not a misfortune, but it is the damning sin of the world. The greatest enemy God and man have got is unbelief. Christ found it on both sides of the cross. It was the very thing that put Him to death.

D. L. MOODY

THE TRUE VINE

True Disciples

Herein is my Father glorified, that ye bear much fruit: so shall ye be my disciples, " Jesus declared (John 15:8). And are those who do not bear much fruit not disciples? They may be, but in a backward and immature stage. Of those who bear much fruit, Christ says: "These are my disciples, such as I would have them be—these are true disciples." Just as we say of someone in whom the idea of manliness is realized, "That is a man!" so our Lord tells who are disciples after His heart: Those who bear much fruit.

We find this double sense of the word *disciple* in the gospel. Sometimes it is applied to all who accepted Christ's teaching. At other times it includes only the inner circle of those who followed Christ wholly and gave themselves to His training for service. The difference has existed throughout all ages. There have always been a smaller number of God's people who have sought to serve Him with their whole heart, while the majority have been content with a very small measure of the knowledge of His grace and will.

And what is the difference between this smaller inner circle and the many who do not seek admission to it? We find it in the words *much fruit.* With many Christians the thought of personal safety, which at their first awakening was a legitimate one, remains to the end the one aim of their religion. The idea of service and fruit is always a secondary and very subordinate one. The honest longing for much fruit does not trouble them. Souls that have heard the call to live wholly for their Lord, to give their life for Him as He gave His for them, can never be satisfied with this. Their cry is to bear as much fruit as they possibly can, as much as their Lord ever can desire or give them.

Bear much fruit; so shall you be His disciples. Consider His command most seriously. Be not content with the thought of gradually doing a little more, or better, work. In this way it may never come. Take the words *much fruit* as the revelation of your heavenly Vine of what you must be, of what you can be. Accept fully the impossibility, the utter folly of attempting it in your strength. Let the words call you to look anew upon the Vine, an undertaking to live out its heavenly fullness in you.

ANDREW MURRAY

WEIGHED AND WANTING

A Temptation and a Snare

Think of Balaam. He is generally regarded as a false prophet, but I do not find that any of his prophecies that are recorded are not true; they have been literally fulfilled. Up to a certain point his character shone magnificently, but the devil finally overcame him by the bait of covetousness. He stepped over a heavenly crown for the riches and honors that Balak promised him. He went to perdition backwards. His face was set toward God, but he backed into hell. He wanted to die the death of the righteous, but he did not live the life of the righteous. It is sad to see so many who know God miss everything for riches.

Then consider the case of Gehazi. There is another man who was drowned in destruction and perdition by covetousness. He got more out of Naaman than he asked for, but he also got Naaman's leprosy. Think how he forfeited the friendship of his master, Elisha, the man of God! So today lifelong friends are separated by this accursed desire. Homes are broken up. Men are willing to sell out peace and happiness for the sake of a few dollars.

Didn't David fall into foolish and hurtful lusts? He saw Bathsheba, Uriah's wife, who was "very beautiful to look upon," and David became a murderer and an adulterer. The guilty longing hurled him into the deepest pit of sin. He had to reap bitterly as he had sowed.

I heard of a wealthy German out west who owned a lumber mill. He was worth nearly two million dollars, but his covetousness was so great that he once worked as a common laborer carrying railroad ties all day. It was the cause of his death.

Achan was no different. "Indeed I have sinned against the Lord God of Israel, and thus and thus have I done: When I saw among the spoils a goodly Babylonish garment, and two hundred shekels of silver, and a wedge of gold of fifty shekels weight, then I coveted them, and took them; and, behold, they are hid in the earth in the midst of my tent, and the silver under it" (Joshua 7:20–21).

He saw, he coveted, he took, and he hid! The covetous eye was what led Achan up to the wicked deed that brought sorrow and defeat upon the camp of Israel.

D. L. MOODY

FULL ASSURANCE
The Witness

When our Savior had made purification for sins He was taken up into heaven and seated on God's right hand. The Holy Spirit then came down to earth to give power to the testimony of the work so blessedly accomplished when the Roman spear pierced the side of the dead Christ and "forthwith came there out blood and water." That blood and water bore mute witness to His holy life given up for sinners. To this the Spirit adds His divine record. And so, as we are informed in 1 John 5:8, "There are three who bear witness, the Spirit, the water, and the blood: and the three agree in one" (RV).

Thus God has given abundant testimony to the perfection of the redemptive work of His Son. And now He calls on man to receive that testimony in faith and thus be eternally saved. We credit the testimony of men in whom we have confidence, even though they speak of matters beyond our knowledge or our ability to verify. Surely, then, we should accept unquestioningly the witness that God has given concerning His Son! To do otherwise, to refuse to trust His record, is to make Him a liar. To believe the record is to receive this divinely-given message into the very heart and soul. Therefore John tells us, "He that believeth on the Son of God hath the witness in himself." John also says, "These things have I written unto you that believe on the name of the Son of God; that ye may know that ye have eternal life" (1 John 5:13).

It becomes evident, then, that the term "these things" embraces all that the venerable apostle has been setting before us in this epistle of light and love. Go over it again. Take it up point by point. Follow the Spirit's presentation of "the message" from verse to verse and theme to theme. Receive it as it is in truth the very Word of the living God and know beyond any doubt that you are born from above and have everlasting life as a present possession. And so your heart shall be assured before Him.

HENRY A. IRONSIDE

KEPT FOR THE MASTER'S USE

Christ for Us

Creation and providence are but the whisper of its power, but redemption is its music, and praise is the echo which shall yet fill His temple. The whisper and the music, yes, and the thunder of His power, are all for thee. For what is the good pleasure of His will? (Ephesians 1:5). Oh, what a grand list of blessings purposed, provided, purchased, and possessed, all flowing to us out of it! And nothing but blessings, nothing but privileges, which we never should have imagined, and which, even when revealed, we are slow of heart to believe—nothing but what should even now fill us with joy unspeakable and full of glory!

Think of this will as always and altogether on our side—always working for us and in us and with us, if we will only let it. Think of it as always and only synonymous with infinitely wise and almighty love. Think of it as undertaking all for us, from the great work of our eternal salvation down to the momentary details of guidance and supply. As we think of those things, do we not feel utter shame and self-abhorrence at ever having hesitated for an instant to give up our tiny, feeble, blind will to be—not crushed, not even bent—but blended with His glorious and perfect will?

His heart for thee. "Behold, God is mighty . . . in [heart]," said Job (Job 36:5, margin). And this mighty and tender heart is for you! If He had only stretched forth His hand to save us from bare destruction and said, "My hand for thee!" how could we have praised Him enough? But what shall we say of the unspeakably marvelous condescension which says, "Thou hast ravished my heart, my sister, my spouse!" The very fountain of His divine life, light, and love, the very center of His being, is given to His beloved ones, who are not only set as a seal upon His heart but taken into His heart, so that our life is hid there. We dwell there in the very center of all safety and power and love and glory.

What will be the revelation of that day, when the Lord Jesus promises, "Ye shall know that I am in my Father, and ye in me?" For He implies that we do not yet know it and that our present knowledge of this dwelling in Him is not knowledge at all compared with what He is going to show us about it.

Now shall we, can we, reserve any corner of our hearts from Him?

FRANCES R. HAVERGAL

HEAVEN

Loving God

The more we know God, the more we love Him. A great many of us would love God more if we only became better acquainted with Him. While on earth it gives Christians great pleasure to think of the perfection of Jesus Christ, but how will it be when we see Him as He is? We shall be like Christ.

Someone once asked a Christian what he expected to do when he got to heaven. He said he expected to spend the first thousand years looking at Jesus Christ, and after that he would look for Peter, and then for James, and for John, and all the time he could conceive of would be joyfully filled with looking upon these great persons. But it seems to me that one look at Jesus Christ will more than reward us for all we have ever done for Him down here; for all the sacrifices we can possibly make for Him, just to see Him; only to see Him. But we shall become like Him when we once have seen Him, because we shall have His Spirit. Jesus, the Savior of the world, will be there, and we shall see Him face to face.

It will not be the pearly gates, nor the jasper walls, or the streets paved with transparent gold, that will make it heaven to us. These would not satisfy us. If these were all, we would not want to stay there forever. I heard of a child whose mother was very sick; and while she lay very low, one of the neighbors took the child away to stay with her until the mother should be well again. But instead of getting better, the mother died; and they thought they would not take the child home until the funeral was over, and would never tell her about her mother being dead. So a while afterward they brought the little girl home. First she went into the sitting-room to find her mother; then she went into the parlor to find her mother there; and she went from one end of the house to the other and could not find her. At last she said, "Where is my mamma?" And when they told her her mamma was gone, the little thing wanted to go back to the neighbor's house again. Home had lost its attraction to her since her mother was not here any longer.

No; it will not be the jasper walls and the pearly gates that will make heaven attractive. It is our being with God. We shall be in the presence of the Redeemer; we shall be forever with the Lord.

D. L. MOODY

LIGHT ON LIFE'S DUTIES
Giving Him All

He does not wait for us to free ourselves from evil habits, or to make ourselves good, or to feel glad and happy. His one desire is that we should put our will on His side in everything. When this is done, He instantly enters the surrendered heart and begins His blessed work of renovation and renewal. From the very moment of consecration, though it be done in much feebleness and with slender appreciation of its meaning, the spirit may begin to say with emphasis, "I am His! I am His! Glory to God, I am His!" Directly the gift is laid on the altar, the fire falls on it.

Sometimes there is a rush of holy feeling. It was so with James Brainerd Taylor: "I felt that I needed something I did not possess. I desired it, not for my benefit only, but for that of the Church and the world. I lifted up my heart that the blessing might descend. At this juncture I was delightfully conscious of giving up all to God. I was enabled in my heart to say: 'Here, Lord, take me, take my whole soul, and seal me Thine now, and Thine for ever. If Thou wilt, Thou canst make me clean.' Then there ensued such emotions as I never before experienced. All was calm and tranquil, and a heaven of love pervaded my soul. I had the witness of God's love to me, and of mine to Him. Shortly after I was dissolved in tears of love and gratitude to our blessed Lord, who came as King, and took possession of my heart."

It is very delightful when such emotions are given to us; but we must not look for them or depend on them. Our consecration may be accepted and may excite the liveliest joy in our Savior's heart, though we are filled with no answering ecstasy. We may know that the great transaction is done, without any glad outburst of song. We may even have to exercise faith, against feeling, as we say, many scores of times each day, "I am His." But the absence of feeling proves nothing. We must pillow our heads on the conviction that Jesus took what we gave, at the moment of our giving it, and that He will keep against that day that which was committed to Him.

F. B. MEYER

SELECT SERMONS
What Think Ye of Christ?

W orthy is the Lamb that was slain to receive power, and riches, and wisdom, and strength, and honour, and glory, and blessing." Yes, He is worthy of all this. Heaven cannot speak too well of Him. Oh, that earth would take up the echo and join with heaven in singing, "Worthy to receive power, and riches, and wisdom, and strength, and honor, and glory, and blessing!"

But there is yet another witness, a higher still. Some think that the Jehovah of the Old Testament is the Christ of the New. But when Jesus came out of Jordan, baptized by John, there came another voice from heaven. God the Father spoke. It was His testimony to Christ: "This is my beloved Son, in whom I am well pleased."

Ah, yes! God the Father thinks well of the Son. And if God is well pleased with Him, so ought we to be. If the sinner and God are well pleased with Christ, then the sinner and God can meet. The moment you say as the Father said, "I am well pleased with Him," and accept Him, you are wedded to God. Will you not believe this witness, this last of all, the Lord of hosts, the King of kings, Himself? Once more He repeats it, so that all may know it. To Peter and James and John, on the mount of transfiguration, He says again, "This is my beloved Son; hear him." And that voice went echoing and re-echoing through Palestine, through all the earth from sea to sea; yes, that voice is echoing still, "Hear him! Hear him!"

My friends, will you hear Him now? Hark! What is He saying to you? "Come unto me, all ye that labour and are heavy laden, and I will give you rest. Take my yoke upon you, and learn of me; for I am meek and lowly in heart: and ye shall find rest unto your souls. For my yoke is easy, and my burden is light." Will you not think well of such a Savior? Will you not believe in Him? Will you not trust in Him with all your heart and mind? Will you not live for Him? If He laid down His life for us, is it not the least we can do to lay down ours for Him? Do you think it is right and noble to lift up your voice against such a Savior? Do you think it is just to cry, "Crucify him! Crucify him!"?

Oh, may God help all of us to glorify the Father by thinking well of His only-begotten Son.

D. L. MOODY

THE CHRIST-LIFE FOR THE SELF-LIFE

Holy Spirit Power

You cannot have the power of the Holy Ghost without having the Holy Ghost Himself. That is, the Holy Ghost must come to you as a person before you can enjoy His attribute. In other words, you must be a holy man before you can wield the power of the Holy Ghost. There are plenty of men who think that if they could only get the power of the Holy Ghost they would be able to fill their churches and sell their books and get themselves name and fame. They want it, but not Him. You cannot have it without having Him. If you want the power of the Holy Ghost, open your heart today and be filled with the Holy Ghost, and then you will have His power.

You must be a cleansed vessel. Now I know that I might here amplify on many of those indulgences that men and women permit. I would much prefer not to characterize them, because you yourselves know of those things in your life that are inconsistent with the perfect majesty and purity of the Spirit who has made your body His temple. But if my body is really the temple, the residence and the throne of the Holy Ghost, I must be as careful of it as I would be if I were the custodian of a temple in the inner part of which the light of God shone. I need not say more than that.

You must live for the glory of Christ as your supreme end. Jesus Christ came into the world to glorify the Father, and the Holy Ghost came into the world to glorify the Son. If therefore you want the Holy Ghost to work with you, you must agree with the Holy Ghost to glorify Jesus, for the Spirit was not given till Jesus was glorified.

F. B. MEYER

THE SCHOOL OF OBEDIENCE

Morning Watch in Life of Obedience

I want now to say a few words on what prayer is to be in the morning watch. *First of all, see that you secure the presence of God.* Do not be content with anything less than seeing the face of God, having the assurance that He is looking on you in love and listening and working in you.

If our daily life is to be full of God, how much more the morning hour, where the life of the day alone can have God's seal stamped upon it. In our religion we want nothing so much as more of God—His love, His will, His holiness, His Spirit living in us, His power working in us for men. Under heaven there is no way of getting this but by close personal communion. And there is no time so good for securing and practicing it as the morning watch.

The superficiality and feebleness of our religion and religious work all come from having so little real contact with God. If it be true that God alone is the fountain of all love and good and happiness and that to have as much as possible of His presence and His fellowship, of His will and His service, is our truest and highest happiness, surely then to meet Him alone in the morning watch ought to be our first care.

To have God appear to them, and speak to them, was with all the Old Testament saints the secret of their obedience and their strength. Do give God time in secret so to reveal Himself, that your soul may call the name of the place Peniel—"for I have seen him face to face."

My next thought is: *let the renewal of your surrender to absolute obedience for that day be a chief part of your morning sacrifice.* Let any confession of sin be very definite—a plucking out and cutting off of everything that has been grieving to God. Let any prayer for grace for a holy walk be as definite—an asking and accepting in faith of the very grace and strength you are specially in need of. Let your outlook on the day you are entering on be a very determined resolve that obedience to God shall be its controlling principle.

ANDREW MURRAY

LIGHT ON LIFE'S DUTIES

Walk in the Spirit

The Holy Spirit is in the heart of every believer (Romans 8:9); but alas, too often He is shut up in some mere attic in the back of the house, while the world fills the rest. As long as it is so, there is one long weary story of defeat and unrest. But He is not content. The Spirit, which God has made to dwell in us, yearns even with a jealous envy (see James 4:5). Happy are they who yield to Him. Then He will fill them, as the tide fills the harbor and lifts the barges off the banks of mud. He will dwell in them, shedding abroad the perfume of the love of Jesus, and He will reveal the deep things of God.

We can always tell when we are wrong with the Spirit of God; our conscience darkens in a moment when we have grieved Him. If we are aware of such a darkness, we do well never to rest until, beneath His electric light, we have discovered the cause and confessed it and put it away. Besides this, if we live and walk in the Spirit, we shall find that He will work against the risings of our old nature, counteracting them as disinfecting power counteracts the germs of disease floating in an infected house, so that we may do the things that we would (see Galatians 5:17). This is one of the most precious words in the New Testament. If you have never tried it, I entreat you to begin to test it in daily experience. "Walk in the Spirit," hour by hour, by watchful obedience to His slightest promptings, and you will find that "you will not fulfill the lust of the flesh."

As soon as you are aware of temptation, look instantly to Jesus. Flee to Him quicker than a chicken runs beneath the shelter of its mother's wing when the falcon is in the air. In the morning, before you leave your room, put yourself definitely into His hands, persuaded He is able to keep that which you commit unto Him. Go from your home with the assurance that He will cover you with His feathers, and under His wings shall you trust. And when the tempter comes, look instantly up and say, "Jesus, I am trusting Thee to keep me."

F. B. MEYER

SOVEREIGN GRACE

Restraining Grace

Out of the knottiest timber," says Rutherford, "He can make vessels of mercy for service in the high place of glory."

"'I came, I saw, I conquered,' says Toplady, "may be inscribed by the Savior on every monument of grace. I came to the sinner; I looked upon him; and with a look of omnipotent love, I conquered."

My friend, we would have been this day wandering stars, to whom is reserved the blackness of darkness—Christless, hopeless, portionless—had not grace invited us and grace constrained us.

Restraining grace is grace that, at this moment, keeps us. We have often been a Peter—forsaking our Lord but brought back to Him again. Why not a Demas or a Judas? "I have prayed for thee that thy faith fail not." Is not this our own comment and reflection on life's retrospect? "Yet not I, but the grace of God which was with me."

Oh, let us seek to realize our continual dependence on this grace every moment! "More grace! more grace!" should be our continual cry. But the infinite supply is commensurate with the infinite need. The treasury of grace, though always emptying is always full: the key of prayer that opens it is always at hand. The recorded promise never can be canceled or reversed—"My grace is sufficient for thee."

Let us seek to dwell much on this inexhaustible theme. The grace of God is the source of minor temporal, as well as of higher spiritual, blessings.

It accounts for the crumb of daily bread as well as for the crown of eternal glory. But even in regard to earthly mercies, never forget the channel of grace through Christ Jesus. It is sweet thus to connect every (even the the smallest and humblest) token of providential bounty with Calvary's cross—to have the common blessings of life stamped with the print of the nails; it makes them doubly precious to think this flows from Jesus. Let others be contented with the uncovenanted mercies of God. Be it ours to say as the children of grace and heirs of glory, "Our Father which art in heaven . . . give us this day our daily bread," reposing in the all-sufficiency in all things, promised by "the God of all grace."

D. L. MOODY

PRACTICAL AND PERPLEXING QUESTIONS ANSWERED
The Devil

Do you believe in a personal devil? Most assuredly I do. I could not believe in the Bible without believing in a personal devil. I have conclusive proof that the Bible is the Word of God, therefore I believe what it teaches about the existence of a personal devil.

In the account of the temptation of our Lord recorded in the gospels of Matthew and Luke, we are distinctly told that the devil (and the whole account evidently means a personal devil) was the author of the temptations that came to our Lord (see Matthew 4:1–11; Luke 4:1–13). These accounts have no meaning if we try to make the devil of the passage a mere figure of speech.

Furthermore, our Lord in the parable of the sower (in Matthew 13:1–23) distinctly teaches that there is a personal devil. The devil does not appear in the parable, where it might be explained as being figurative, but in the interpretation of the parable: "Then cometh the wicked one . . ." Now in parables we have figures, and in the interpretation of parables we have the literal facts for which the figures stand, so we have a literal devil in the interpretation of this parable. It is only one of the numerous instances in which Jesus teaches the existence of a personal devil.

Paul teaches the same, as (for example) in Ephesians 6:11–12: "Put on the whole armor of God, that ye may be able to stand against the wiles of the Devil. For our wrestling is not against flesh and blood, but against the principalities, against the powers, against the world-rulers of this darkness, against the spiritual hosts of wickedness in the heavenly places" (RV).

No rational interpretation of the Bible can interpret the devil out of it. Any system of interpretation that does away with the devil would do away with any doctrine a man does not wish to believe.

But I also believe that there is a personal devil because my own experience and observation teach me the existence of an unseen, very subtle, very cunning spirit of evil, who has domination over men throughout human society wherever found. The more I come in contact with men, the more I study history, and the more men open their hearts to me, the more firmly convinced I become that there is such a devil as the Bible teaches that there is.

It is not pleasant to believe that there is a personal devil, but the question is not what is pleasant to believe but what is true.

R. A. TORREY

SHORT TALKS
Walking Differently

W alk not as other Gentiles walk" (Ephesians 4:17). God expects a difference when we become His. The world expects a difference, and the church of God expects a difference between one who professes to be a child of light and one who is a child of darkness; and if there is not a difference in your life since you have become a Christian, then I am afraid that you have not become a real one.

The course of this world is away from God; therefore I must go against the current of the world, if I'm a child of God. What we want today is separation. The church will have a convincing testimony and will become a power in the world when it is separated from the world; but as long as it is hand and glove with the world, it cannot have power. I believe that when we are told not to be unequally yoked together with unbelievers it means just what it says: and if I live just as the Gentiles, the ungodly, live, I shall have trouble.

It was said of Lot that his righteous soul was vexed. Of course it was. Righteousness can never be at peace with unrighteousness. And if I walk as other Gentiles walk, as the world walks, I will be constantly getting into trouble, because I will go in the course of the world.

You say, "I will walk as I please."

You can do it. You can take a course away from God, but it will bring you into bondage and darkness.

"Walk as children of light" (Ephesians 5:8). Put off the ways of darkness. Put off the works of darkness.

Now the question arises, "How am I going to get light?"

"God is light, and in him is no darkness at all"; "The entrance of thy words giveth light.' Are you in the dark? Let the Word of God into your heart, and it will dispel the darkness. "Thy word is a lamp unto my feet"; if you want light, just take the Word. It is the privilege of every one of us to walk in an unclouded sun all our days, if we will. I don't believe that it is the will of God that any child of His shall be in the dark. We are children of the day, children of the light; we have been born of His Spirit, and He brings light and peace.

D. L. MOODY

ALL OF GRACE
Why Are We Saved by Faith?

Faith, again, *has the power of working by love;* it influences the affections toward God, and draws the heart after the best things. He that believes in God will beyond all question love God. Faith is an act of the understanding; but it also proceeds from the heart. "With the heart man believeth unto righteousness"; and hence God gives salvation to faith because it resides next door to the affections and is near akin to love; and love is the parent and the nurse of every holy feeling and act. Love to God is obedience, love to God is holiness. To love God and to love man is to be conformed to the image of Christ; and this is salvation.

Moreover, *faith creates peace and joy;* he that has it rests and is tranquil, is glad and joyous, and this is a preparation for heaven. God gives all heavenly gifts to faith; for this reason among others, that faith develops in us the life and spirit that one day shall be manifested eternally in heaven. Faith furnishes us with armor for this life and education for the life to come. It enables a man both to live and to die without fear; it prepares both for action and for suffering; and hence the Lord selects it as a most convenient medium for conveying grace to us and thereby securing us for glory.

Certainly faith does for us what nothing else can do; it gives us joy and peace and causes us to enter into rest. Why do men attempt to gain salvation by other means? An old divine says, "A silly servant who is bidden to open a door, sets his shoulder to it and pushes with all his might; but the door stirs not, and he cannot enter, use what strength he may. Another comes with a key and easily unlocks the door and enters right readily. Those who would be saved by works are pushing at heaven's gate without result; but faith is the key which opens the gate at once."

Reader, will you not use that key? The Lord commands you to believe in His dear Son, therefore you may do so; and doing so you shall live. Is not this the promise of the gospel, "He that believeth and is baptized shall be saved" (Mark 16:16)? What can be your objection to a way of salvation which commends itself to the mercy and the wisdom of our gracious God?

CHARLES H. SPURGEON

TO THE WORK!

She Has Done What She Could

Thank God, every one of us can love Christ, and we can all do something for Him. It may be a small thing; but whatever it is shall be lasting; it will outlive all the monuments on earth. The iron and the granite will rust and crumble and fade away, but anything done for Christ will never fade. It will be more lasting than time itself. Christ says: "Heaven and earth shall pass away, but My word shall not pass away."

Look again and see that woman in the temple. Christ stood there as the people passed by and cast their offerings into the treasury. The widow had but two mites, and she cast it all in. The Lord saw that her heart was in it, and so He commended her. If some nobleman had cast in a thousand dollars Christ would probably not have noticed it, unless his heart had gone with it. Gold is of little value in heaven. It is so plentiful there that they use it to pave the streets with; and it is transparent gold, much better gold than we have in this world. It is when the heart goes with the offering that it is accepted of Christ. So He said of this woman: "She hath cast in more than they all." She had done all she could.

I think this is the lesson we are to learn from these Scripture incidents. The Lord expects us to do what we can. We can all do something. In one of our Southern cities a few Christian people gathered together at the beginning of the war to see what could be done about building a church in a part of the city where the poor were very much neglected. After they had discussed the matter they wanted to see how much could be raised out of the congregation.

One said he would give so much; others said they would give so much. They only got about half the amount that was needed, and it was thought they would have to abandon the project. Away back in the meeting there sat a washerwoman. She rose and said her little boy had died a week before. All he had was a gold dollar. She said: "It is all I have, but I will give the dollar to the cause." Her words touched the hearts of many of those who heard them. Rich men were ashamed at what they had given. The whole sum was raised within a very short time.

D. L. MOODY

THE TRUE VINE
You Can Do Nothing

A part from me ye can do nothing," Jesus reminds us (John 15:5). In everything the life of the branch is to be the exact counterpart of that of the vine. Of Himself Jesus had said: "The Son can do nothing of himself." As the outcome of that entire dependence, He could add: "All that the Father doeth, doeth the Son also likewise." As Son He did not receive His life from the Father once for all, but moment by moment. His life was a continual waiting on the Father for all He was to do. And so Christ says of His disciples: "Ye can do nothing apart from me." He means it literally. To everyone who wants to live the true disciple life, to bring forth fruit and glorify God, the message comes: You can do nothing. What had been said, "He that abideth in me, and I in him, the same beareth much fruit," is here enforced by the simplest and strongest of arguments: "Abiding in Me is indispensable, for, you know it, of yourselves you can do nothing to maintain or act out the heavenly life."

A deep conviction of the truth of this word lies at the very root of a strong spiritual life. As little as I created myself, as little as I could raise a man from the dead, can I give myself the divine life. As little as I can give it myself, can I maintain or increase it: every motion is the work of God through Christ and His Spirit. It is as a man believes this, that he will take up that position of entire and continual dependence that is the very essence of the life of faith. With the spiritual eye he sees Christ every moment supplying grace for every breathing and every deepening of the spiritual life. His whole heart says Amen to the word: "You can do nothing." And just because he does so, he can also say: "I can do all things through Christ who strengtheneth me." The sense of helplessness, and the abiding to which it compels, leads to true fruitfulness and diligence in good works.

"Apart from me ye can do nothing." What a plea and what a call every moment to abide in Christ! We have only to go back to the vine to see how true it is. Look again at that little branch, utterly helpless and fruitless except as it receives sap from the vine, and learn that the full conviction of not being able to do anything apart from Christ is just what you need to teach you to abide in your heavenly Vine.

ANDREW MURRAY

WHAT IS FAITH?

How to Trust

God is my Savior and my Redeemer; not prayers or feelings or works or tears or anything in or of myself. "God is my salvation; I will trust, and not be afraid: for the Lord Jehovah is my strength and my song; he also is become my salvation." There is salvation in front of you and salvation behind you; salvation to begin with and salvation to end with. So now, just pray to the Lord to help you to trust Him from this hour—from this minute—trust Him with your body and with your soul.

There is a grand proverb teaching us how to trust: "Trust in the Lord with all thine heart; and lean not unto thine own understanding. In all thy ways acknowledge him, and he shall direct thy paths" (Proverbs 3:5–6). I never knew a man who was willing to trust the Lord with all his heart but the Lord saved him, and delivered him from all his doubts. The great trouble is that we do not trust Him with all our heart. God says, "Ye shall seek me, and find me, when you search for me with all your heart." God says, "Trust me with all your heart." Is there anything to hinder you from putting your whole trust in Him?

If Satan comes to you and wants to hear you explain some mysterious sayings in the Bible, do not lean on your own understanding; tell him you are going to trust the Lord and not yourself. If God cannot be trusted, who can? Trust Him without any doubts. There cannot be true faith where there is doubt; the very fact that you doubt should show you that you do not trust with all your heart.

It is said that Alexander the Great had a favorite physician who followed him through all his battles. This favorite doctor had an enemy who wanted to get him out of the way. The latter wrote a letter to Alexander, stating that the favorite physician intended to give him a poison cup on the following morning. The man thought the Emperor would order the physician to be put to death. Next morning, however, the Emperor took the message and read it out loud; and, before the physician had time to reply, he drank what was in the cup before his eyes to show his friend that he did not believe one word that his enemy had said.

That is believing with all the heart; and when Satan comes with some insinuation about God not being love, tell him that you believe God with all your heart.

D. L. MOODY

FULL ASSURANCE
Christ's Bodily Resurrection

Only the personal appearances of the risen Christ convinced the disciples of the realities of His resurrection. The forty days during which He appeared to them on many occasions, instructing them concerning the kingdom of God, furnished ample proof that He had really triumphed over death, and this glorious fact gave them that confidence which enabled them to stand against all opposition, witnessing to every man that God had raised His body from the grave. They beheld Him as He was taken up from them into heaven in that same body, and after receiving the Pentecostal enduement, they went about bearing witness to the resurrection of their Lord with great power.

This is the outstanding message of the church. He who died for our sins lives again for our justification. The resurrection of the material body of flesh and bones is the proof that God is satisfied with the redemptive work of His Son. It declares that God can now be just and the justifier of him who believes on the Lord Jesus. To say that, though Christ is dead as to the body, He is alive as to the spirit will not do. That might be true of any man. It would be no evidence of divine satisfaction in His work.

Some years ago an eloquent New York preacher, who denies the physical resurrection of the Savior, declared, "The body of Jesus still sleeps in an unknown Syrian tomb, but His soul goes marching on!" Many applauded this as a wonderful explanation of the influence of Jesus down through the ages. But it is utterly false and fallacious. If the body of Jesus still rests in the grave, He was not what He professed to be and is powerless to save.

This heresy (for heresy it is) is not new. It became prevalent in certain circles even in apostolic days, as 1 Corinthians 15 proves. In the Corinthian church there were some who accepted the teaching of the Sadducees and denied the reality of a literal resurrection. Sternly, Paul challenges them in the well-known words: "Now if Christ be preached that he rose from the dead, how say some among you that there is no resurrection of the dead? But if there be no resurrection of the dead, then is Christ not risen: and if Christ be not risen, then is our preaching vain, and your faith is also vain."

HENRY A. IRONSIDE

WEIGHED AND WANTING

Less than the Truth

False rumor—exaggeration—misrepresentation—insinuation—gossip—equivocation—holding back of the truth when it is due and right to tell it—disparagement—perversion of meaning: these are common transgressions of the ninth commandment, differing in form and degree of guilt according to the motive or manner of their expression. They bear false witness against a man before the tribunal of public opinion—a court whose judgment none of us can escape. As so much of our life is passed in public view, any untruth that leads to a false judgment is a grievous wrong.

Government of the tongue is made the test of true religion by James. "If any man among you seem to be religious, and bridleth not his tongue, but deceiveth his own heart, this man's religion is vain. . . . For in many things we offend all. If any man offend not in word, the same is a perfect man, and able also to bridle the whole body." Just as a doctor looks at the tongue and can tell the condition of the bodily health, so a man's words are an index of what is within. Truth will spring from a good heart: falsehood and deceit from a corrupt heart. When Ananias kept back part of the price of the land, Peter asked him, "Why hath Satan filled thine heart to lie to the Holy Ghost?" Satan is the father of lies and the prompter of lies.

The tongue can be an instrument of untold good or incalculable evil. Someone has said that a sharp tongue is the only edged tool that grows keener with constant use. "Thy tongue deviseth mischiefs; like a sharp razor, working deceitfully. . . . They have sharpened their tongues like a serpent; adders' poison is under their lips. . . . The mouth of a righteous man is a well of life: but violence covereth the mouth of the wicked. . . . A wholesome tongue is a tree of life: but perverseness therein is a breach in the spirit." Bishop Hall said that the tongues of busybodies are like the tails of Samson's foxes—they carry firebrands and are enough to set the whole field of the world in a flame.

D. L. MOODY

FIT FOR THE MASTER'S USE
Touch No Unclean Thing

We are so fussy, so eager to serve God after our own style, so prone to take up anything that another has done successfully, without staying to ask whether it is God's will for ourselves. We work so much for God, instead of waiting for Him to work through us. We do not wait for the pattern to be shown us from the Mount. One of God's most honored teachers tells us that we ought perpetually to sink into Christ's grave, to claim the silence of Christ's grave, to die to the activities of our own nature, even when they are exerted in a right direction and for a holy purpose, to allow God to winnow away the chaff before we attempt to sow the wheat.

From all such things we must cleanse ourselves. There is a defilement of the spirit as well as of the flesh. There are weights as well as sins. There are things that are not expedient, as well as those that are positively unlawful and wrong. From all we must be separate and clean.

You may say that you have tried to separate yourself, but in vain; the evil clings to you like a shadow. Then fall back on the philosophy of the will. Be willing to be clean. Be willing to be made willing. Then say to Christ: "I am eager to have my leprosy cleansed; if Thou wilt, Thou canst make me clean"; and immediately He will stretch forth His hand and touch you, saying, "I will, be thou clean." And you will be delivered.

But do not suppose that you are always to be looking on this side of your life, on the renunciations, the excisions, the amputations. Present yourself to Jesus, as those who are alive from the dead and constrained by His mercies.

You are His because He made you. "It is He that hath made us, and His we are." Surely the builder of a house has a right to the product of His own labor.

You are His because He redeemed you. You were redeemed with precious blood, and are not your own, but His by purchase.

You are His because God the Father has given Him all who come to Him. And if you have come to Him, you are assuredly His, though you have not avowed yourself so (John 6:37).

Will you not, therefore, present yourself to Him, that He may forgive all your sins and cleanse you from all that is unholy and inconsistent and fill you with His sacred fullness?

F. B. MEYER

MOODY'S LATEST SERMONS
Adoption, Sonship, and Heirship

L ook a moment at this verse: "That the righteousness of the law might be fulfilled in us, who walk not after the flesh, but after the Spirit" (Romans 8:4). If we have been born of the Spirit, and have the divine life within us, we are not to follow after the flesh, but after the Spirit. Do you know that the flesh and the Spirit divide all men, and there is no third state? Either we are in the flesh and following after the flesh, or we are in the Spirit and following after the Spirit.

Note the fourfold description: first, their nature, after the flesh; second, they mind the things of the flesh; third, their state is death, dead to spiritual things; fourth, they are carnal-minded and cannot please God.

The flesh has its religion. You will find hardly a man today on the face of the earth that hasn't some sort of religion. You will find people living in the blackest, vilest kinds of sin, and you begin to talk with them, and they tell you: "I won't give up my religion for yours."

That woman who Christ met at the well of Sychar was looking for the Messiah; she was a disciple of Jacob; she was all right. Yet she was living in the vilest kind of sin. We find the same state of things now. What is your creed good for if it hasn't got grace in it, and if there is no regeneration? A man told me the other day that he wanted a religion that was beautiful. There are a good many of that kind now; they want a dead, cold formalism; they don't want anything that has life in it. A man got quite angry some time ago because I said religion had something to do with his moral character. He had divorced the two. That is human; that is man's religion.

Now people say, "Well, how can you tell?"

Paul, in his letter to the Galatians, has drawn the picture so vividly that no one need be deceived. Let me read to you a few words from the fifth chapter of Galatians, starting with the nineteenth verse: "Now the works of the flesh are manifest, which are these; adultery, fornication, uncleanness, lasciviousness, idolatry, witchcraft, hatred, variance, emulations, wrath, strife, seditions, heresies, envyings, murders, drunkenness, revellings, and such like: of the which I tell you before, as I have also told you in time past, that they which do such things shall not inherit the kingdom of God."

D. L. MOODY

ANSWERS TO PRAYER

The Daily Bread

Augustus 3, 1844. Saturday—With the twelve shillings we began the day. My soul said: "I will now look out for the way in which the Lord will deliver us this day again; for He will surely deliver. Many Saturdays, when we were in need, He helped us, and so He will do this day also." Between nine and ten o'clock this morning I gave myself to prayer for means, with three of my fellow-laborers, in my house. While we were in prayer, there was a knock at my room door, and I was informed that a gentleman had come to see me. When we had finished prayer, it was found to be a brother from Tetbury, who had brought from Barnstaple one pound, two shilling, six pence for the orphans. Thus we have one pound, fourteen shilling, six pence, with which I must return the letter-bag to the orphan houses, looking to the Lord for more.

Aug. 6—Without one single penny in my hands the day began. The post brought nothing, nor had I yet received anything, when ten minutes after ten this morning the letter bag was brought from the orphan houses for the supplies of today. Now see the Lord's deliverance! In the bag I found a note from one of the laborers in the orphan houses, enclosing two sovereigns, which she sent for the orphans, stating that it was part of a present she had just received unexpectedly, for herself. Thus we are supplied for today.

Sept. 4—Only one farthing was in my hand this morning. Pause a moment, dear reader! Only one farthing in hand when the day commenced. Think of this, and think of nearly 140 persons to be provided for. You poor brothers, who have six or eight children and small wages, think of this; and you, my brothers, who do not belong to the working classes, but have, as it is called, very limited means, think of this! May you not do what we do under your trials? Does the Lord love you less than He loves us? Does He not love all His children with no less love than that with which He loves His only begotten Son, according to John 17:20–23? Or are we better than you?

GEORGE MUELLER

THE WAY HOME
Good Tidings

Behold, I bring you good tidings of great joy, which shall be to all people. For unto you is born this day in the city of David a Saviour."

Now if those shepherds had been like a good many people today, they would have said, "We don't believe it is good news. It is all excitement. Those angels want to get up a revival. Don't believe them!"

That is what Satan is saying now. "Don't believe that the gospel is good news." Because he knows that the moment a man believes good news, he just receives it. I never saw a man in all my life who did not like good news. And every man and woman who is under the power of the devil does not believe the gospel is good news. The moment you are out from under his power and influence, then you believe it. May God grant that the gospel may sink deep into your hearts, and that you may believe it and be saved!

It is the best news that ever came to this sin-cursed earth. It means "Good spell," or in other words, "God's spell." We are dead in trespasses and sins, and God wants us to be reconciled. It is a gospel of reconciliation, and God is calling from the heights of glory.

"Oh, men, I am reconciled, now be ye reconciled!"

The great apostle says, "We beseech you in Christ's stead, be ye reconciled to God." The moment a man believes the gospel, down goes his arm of rebellion, and the unequal controversy is over. A light from Calvary crosses his path, and he can walk in unclouded sunshine, if he will. It is the privilege of every man and woman to walk in unclouded sunshine if they will. What brought darkness into the world? Darkness came because of sin, and the man who does not believe the gospel is blinded by the god of this world.

I like the gospel, because it is the very best news I have ever heard. The reason I like to preach it is because it has done me so much good. A man cannot preach the gospel until he believes it himself. He must know it down deep in his own heart before he can tell it out; and then he tells it out but very poorly at the best. We are very poor ambassadors and messengers; but never mind the messenger, take hold of the message—that is what you want. If a boy brought me good news tonight, I would not care about the look of the boy; I would not care whether he was black or white, learned or unlearned. The message is what would do me good. A great many look at the messenger! My friends, get hold of the message tonight. The gospel is what saves, and what I want is that you may believe the gospel now.

D. L. MOODY

CHARGE THAT TO MY ACCOUNT

Standing in for a Stranger

There was One who knew to the full what all the consequences of His act would be, and yet, in grace, deigned to become "surety for a stranger." Meditate upon these wonderful words: "For ye know the grace of our Lord Jesus Christ, that, though he was rich, yet for your sakes he became poor, that ye through his poverty might be rich" (2 Corinthians 8:9). He was the stranger's surety.

A surety is one who stands good for another. Many a man will do this for a friend, long known and trusted; but no wise man will so act for a stranger, unless he is prepared to lose. But it was when we were strangers and foreigners and enemies and alienated in our minds by wicked works, that Jesus in grace became our surety. "Christ also hath once suffered for sins, the just for the unjust, that he might bring us to God."

All we owed was exacted from Him when He suffered upon the tree for sins not His own. He could then say, "I restored that which I took not away" (Psalm 69:4). Bishop Lowth's beautiful rendering of Isaiah 53:7 reads: "It was exacted and He became answerable." This is the very essence of the gospel message. He died in my place; He paid my debt.

How fully He proved the truth of the words quoted from Proverbs, when He suffered on that cross of shame! How He had to "smart for it" when God's awful judgment against sin fell upon Him. But He wavered not! In love to God and to the strangers whose surety He had become, "he endured the cross, despising the shame."

His sorrows are now forever past. He has paid the debt, met every claim in perfect righteousness. The believing sinner is cleared of every charge, and God is fully glorified.

"He bore on the tree the sentence for me, and now both the Surety and sinner are free."

None other could have met the claims of God's holiness against the sinner and have come out triumphant at last. He alone could atone for sin. Because He has settled every claim, God has raised Him from the dead and seated Him at His own right hand in highest glory.

Have you trusted "the stranger's surety?" If not, turn to Him now while grace is free.

HENRY A. IRONSIDE

ACCORDING TO PROMISE

The Two Seeds

I t is written that Abraham had two sons, the one by a bondmaid, the other by a freewoman. But he who was of the bondwoman was born after the flesh; but he of the freewoman was by promise" (Galatians 4:22–23).

Abraham had two sons. Ishmael and Isaac were beyond all dispute veritable sons of Abraham. Yet one of them inherited the covenant blessing, and the other was simply a prosperous man of the world. See how close these two were together! They were born in the same society, called the same great patriarch "father," and sojourned in the same encampment with him. Yet Ishmael was a stranger to the covenant, while Isaac was the heir of the promise. How little is there in blood and birth!

A more remarkable instance than this happened a little afterward; for Esau and Jacob were born of the same mother, at the same birth, yet is it written, "Jacob have I loved, and Esau have I hated." One became gracious and the other profane. So closely may two come together and yet so widely may they be separated! Verily, it is not only that two shall be in one bed, and the one shall be taken, and the other left; but two shall come into the world at the same moment and yet one of them will take up his inheritance with God, and the other will for a morsel of meat sell his birthright. We may be in the same church, baptized in the same water, seated at the same Communion table, singing the same psalm, and offering the same prayer; and yet we may be of two races as opposed as the seed of the woman and the seed of the serpent.

Abraham's two sons are declared by Paul to be the types of two races of men, who are much alike and yet widely differ. They are unlike in their origin. They were both sons of Abraham; but Ishmael, the child of Hagar, was the offspring of Abraham upon ordinary conditions: he was born after the flesh. Isaac, the son of Sarah, was not born by the strength of nature; for his father was more than a hundred years old, and his mother was long past age. He was given to his parents by the Lord and was born according to the promise through faith. This is a grave distinction, and it marks off the true child of God from him who is only so by profession. The promise lies at the bottom of the distinction, and the power that goes to accomplish the promise creates and maintains the difference. Hence the promise, which is our inheritance, is also our test and touchstone.

CHARLES H. SPURGEON

SECRET POWER
The Reservoir of Love

We read that the fruit of the Spirit is love. God is love, Christ is love, and we should not be surprised to read about the love of the Spirit. What a blessed attribute is this. May I call it the dome of the temple of the graces. Better still, it is the crown of crowns worn by the Triune God. Human love is a natural emotion that flows forth toward the object of our affections. But divine love is as high above human love as the heaven is above the earth. The natural man is of the earth, earthy and however pure his love may be, it is weak and imperfect at best. But the love of God is perfect and entire, wanting nothing. It is as a mighty ocean in its greatness, dwelling with and flowing from the eternal Spirit.

In Romans 5:5 we read: "And hope maketh not ashamed, because the love of God is shed abroad in our hearts by the Holy Ghost which is given to us." Now if we are co-workers with God, there is one thing we must possess and that is love. A man may be a very successful lawyer and have no love for his clients, and yet get on very well. A man may be a very successful physician and have no love for his patients, and yet be a very good physician; a man may be a very successful merchant and have no love for his customers, and yet he may do a good business and succeed; but no man can be a co-worker with God without love. If our service is mere profession on our part, the quicker we renounce it, the better. If a man takes up God's work as he would take up any profession, the sooner he gets out of it, the better.

We cannot work for God without love. It is the only tree that can produce fruit on this sin-cursed earth, that is acceptable to God. If I have no love for God nor for my fellow man, then I cannot work acceptably. I am like sounding brass and a tinkling cymbal. We are told that "the love of God is shed abroad in our hearts by the Holy Ghost." Now if we have had that love shed abroad in our hearts, we are ready for God's service; if we have not, we are not ready.

It is so easy to reach a man when you love him; all barriers are broken down and swept away. Paul, when writing to Titus (2:2), tells him to be sound in faith, in charity, and in patience.

D. L. MOODY

THE TRUE VINE

The Pruning Knife

The Word is God's pruning knife. Jesus says in John 15, "Ye are already clean, because of the word I have spoken unto you." How searchingly that word had been spoken by Him, out of whose mouth there went a sharp two-edged sword, as He had taught them! "Except a man deny himself, lose his life, forsake all, hate father and mother, he cannot be my disciple, he is not worthy of me"; or as He humbled their pride, or reproved their lack of love, or foretold their all forsaking Him. From the opening of His ministry in the Sermon on the Mount to His words of warning in the last night, His Word had tried and cleansed them. He had discovered and condemned all there was of self; they were now emptied and cleansed, ready for the incoming of the Holy Spirit.

It is as the soul gives up its own thoughts, and men's thoughts of what is religion, and yields itself heartily, humbly, patiently to the teaching of the Word by the Spirit, that the Father will do His blessed work of pruning and cleansing away all of nature and self that mixes with our work and hinders His Spirit. Let those who would know all the Husbandman can do for them, all the Vine can bring forth through them, seek earnestly to yield themselves heartily to the blessed cleansing through the Word. Let them, in their study of the Word, receive it as a hammer that breaks and opens up, as a fire that melts and refines, as a sword that lays bare and slays all that is of the flesh. The word of conviction will prepare for the word of comfort and of hope, and the Father will cleanse them through the Word.

All you who are branches of the true Vine, each time you read or hear the Word, wait first of all on Him to use it for His cleansing of the branch. Set your heart upon His desire for more fruit. Trust Him as the Husbandman to work it. Yield yourselves in simple childlike surrender to the cleansing work of His Word and Spirit, and you may count upon it that His purpose will be fulfilled in you.

ANDREW MURRAY

THE WAY TO GOD
The Divinity of Christ

When I was a boy I thought that Jesus was a good man like Moses, Joseph, or Abraham. I even thought that He was the best man who had ever lived on the earth. But I found that Christ had a higher claim. He claimed to be God-Man, to be divine, to have come from heaven. He said: "Before Abraham was I am" (John 8:58). I could not understand this; and I was driven to the conclusion—and I challenge any candid man to deny the inference or meet the argument—that Jesus Christ is either an impostor or deceiver, or He is the God-Man—God manifest in the flesh. And for these reasons.

The First Commandment is, "Thou shalt have no other gods before me" (Exodus 20:2). Look at the millions throughout Christendom who worship Jesus Christ as God. If Christ be not God, this is idolatry. We are all guilty of breaking the First Commandment, if Jesus Christ were mere man—if He were a created being and not what He claims to be.

Some people who do not admit His divinity say that He was the best man who ever lived; but if He were not divine, for that very reason He ought not to be reckoned a good man, for He laid claim to an honor and dignity to which these very people declare He had no right or title. That would rank Him as a deceiver.

Others say that He thought He was divine but really was deceived. As if Jesus Christ were carried away by a delusion and deception, and thought that He was more than He was! I could not conceive of a lower idea of Jesus Christ than that. This would not only make Him out an impostor, but that He was out of His mind and that He did not know who He was or where He came from. Now if Jesus Christ was not what He claims to be, the Savior of the world, and if He did not come from heaven, He was a gross deceiver.

But how can any one read the life of Christ and make Him out a deceiver? A man has generally some motive for being an impostor. What was Christ's motive? He knew that the course He was pursuing would conduct Him to the cross, that His name would be cast out as vile, and that many of His followers would be called upon to lay down their lives for His sake. Nearly every one of the apostles was a martyr; and they were considered as off-scouring and refuse in the midst of the people. If a man is an impostor, he has a motive at the back of his hypocrisy. But what was Christ's object? The record is that "He went about doing good." This is not the work of an impostor. Do not let the enemy of your soul deceive you.

D. L. MOODY

GOD'S WAY OF HOLINESS
The New Life

The tendency of the present day is to underestimate sin and to misunderstand its nature. From the cross of Christ men strike out the very elements that intimate the divine opinion of its evil; and that accursed tree is not recognized as a condemnation of sin but simply as an exhibition of self-surrender in a noble sufferer. It is admitted to be an evil, greater or less according to circumstances; a hereditary poison, which time and earnestness will work out of the constitution; an unruly but inevitable appetite, which is to be corrected gradually by moral discipline and wholesome intellectual diet, rendered medicinal by a moderate infusion of the "religious element"; a sickening pain, sometimes in the conscience, sometimes in the heart, which is to be soothed by the dreamy mysticism, which, acting like spiritual chloroform, dulls the uneasiness without touching its seat; this is all!

Why a loving God should, for so slight and curable an evil, have given over our world for six thousand years to such sorrow, pain, tears, weariness, disease and death, as have overflowed it with so terrible a deluge, is a question which such a theory of evil leaves unanswered. Yet such are the representations of sin with which we find a large amount of the literature and the religion of our day penetrated. Humanity is struggling upward, nobly self-reliant! The race is elevating itself (for the Darwinian theory has found its way into religion); and Christianity is a useful help in this process of self-regeneration, this development of individual constitutions, by which perfection is to be reached at last and the kingdom won! Thus does many a prophet speak peace when there is none; bent on "healing the hurt" by the denial of its deadlines. Of what avail this calling evil good and good evil is now, or will be in the great day of reckoning, a coming hour will show.

"Awake to righteousness and sin not" is God's message to us (1 Corinthians 15:34). "Be ye holy; for I am holy" (1 Peter 1:16). "Present your bodies a living sacrifice, holy, acceptable unto God" (Romans 12:1).

HORATIUS BONAR

ALL OF GRACE
Confirmation from God

A ll who are in Christ will be confirmed in Him till that illustrious day. Has He not said, "Because I live ye shall live also"? He also said, "I give unto my sheep eternal life; and they shall never perish, neither shall any man pluck them out of my hand." He that hath begun a good work in you will confirm it unto the day of Christ.

The work of grace in the soul is not a superficial reformation; the life implanted at the new birth comes of a living and incorruptible seed, which lives and abides forever; and the promises of God made to believers are not of a transient character, but involve for their fulfillment the believer's holding on his way till he comes to endless glory. We are kept by the power of God, through faith unto salvation. "The righteous shall hold on his way." Not as the result of our own merit or strength, but as a gift of free and undeserved favor those who believe are "preserved in Christ Jesus."

Of the sheep of His fold Jesus will lose none; no member of His body shall die; no gem of His treasure shall be missing in the day when He makes up His jewels. Dear reader, the salvation that is received by faith is not a thing of months and years; for our Lord Jesus hath "obtained eternal salvation for us," and that which is eternal cannot come to an end.

Paul also declares his expectation that the Corinthian saints would be "confirmed to the end blameless." This blamelessness is a precious part of our keeping. To be kept holy is better than merely to be kept safe. It is a dreadful thing when you see religious people blundering out of one dishonor into another; they have not believed in the power of our Lord to make them blameless. The lives of some professing Christians are a series of stumbles; they are never quite down, and yet they are seldom well on their feet. This is not a fit thing for a believer; he is invited to walk with God, and by faith he can attain to steady perseverance in holiness; and he ought to do so. The Lord is able not only to save us from hell but to keep us from falling.

CHARLES H. SPURGEON

THE WAY HOME

On the Cross

A t last He cried, "I thirst!" Instead of giving Him a draught of water from one of His own springs, they gave Him a draught of gall mixed with vinegar. It was about the only thing He ever asked of the world, and you see how they treated His request.

There He hung! You can see those soldiers casting lots for His garments, as they crowd around the foot of the cross. While they were casting lots, the crowd would mock and deride Him and make all manner of sport of Him. He only cried, "Father, forgive them; for they know not what they do!"

But now He cries, "My God, my God, why hast thou forsaken me?" Though He greatly suffered physically, His mental sufferings were too deep for any mortal man to understand. He was dying in the sinner's stead, with the sins of the world upon His head. A righteous God could not look upon sin, even when borne by the eternal substitute; and He hid His face from Him. Men had mocked and rejected Him; His own disciples had forsaken Him and fled; and now that God would not look upon Him, it well nigh broke our Savior's heart. In anguish of soul He cried, "My God, my God, why hast thou forsaken me?"

Right in the midst of the darkness and gloom there came a voice from one of those thieves. It flashed into His soul as He hung there. "This must be more than man; this must be the true Messiah!" He cried out, "Lord, remember me when thou comest into thy Kingdom!" We are anxious to get the last word or act of our dying friends. Here was the last act of Jesus. He snatched the thief from the jaws of death, saying, "This day shalt thou be with me in Paradise."

Again He spoke. What was it? "It is finished!" was His cry. Salvation was wrought out, atonement was made. His blood had been shed; His life had been given. Undoubtedly, if we could, we would have seen legions of devils hovering around the cross. The dark clouds of death and hell came surging up against the bosom of the Son of God, and He drove them back, as you have seen the waves come gathering up and surging against the rock, then receding, and then returning. The billows went over Him. He was conquering death and Satan and the world in those last moments. He was treading the wine-press alone.

"It is finished!" Perhaps no one who heard it knew what it meant. But the angels in heaven knew. I can imagine the bells of heaven ringing out and angels singing, "The God-man is dead! Full restitution has opened the way back to Paradise, and all man has to do is to look and live!"

D. L. MOODY

FIT FOR THE MASTER'S USE

The Last Conviction Is the One Need of a Penitent Sinner

We read in Isaiah 6 that when Isaiah cried, one of the seraphim immediately went for the live coal. Now, mark this: the angel was not told to go, but he knew just what to do. The fact is, the angels have gone so often for the live coal that whenever they hear a sinner crying that he is undone, they go for it; they do not need to be told. It is as if a druggist's boy were so in the habit of getting the same medicine for the same symptoms that when the patient comes to the door, he knows just what medicine to seek without going to the doctor to get advice.

The seraph took the live coal from off the altar, and that stood for blood and fire, the two things we want today. We want blood and fire.

Blood! Can you not hear the hiss of the blood of the lamb as it flows gurgling around that coal? As he takes it up with his tongs of gold and bears it to the prophet's lips, it takes the atoning blood with it. We want that first. I call upon all of you to claim that first—the blood. Nothing else will do. "This is he that came by water and blood; not by water only, but by water and blood." You and I need blood first. Let us then betake ourselves to our compassionate Lord and seek from Him that forgiveness which He purchased on the cross. Do you want it? Are you quite satisfied? Do you look upon your past with perfect complacency? Is there nothing to regret? Are there no sins to put away?

It is natural to respond that you are undone. Then let us begin by opening our whole nature to Christ and believe that His blood now cleanses from all sin. Let us dare to believe that as soon as we turn to that blood, and claim the forgiveness that is based on it, the whole of our past sin is gone, blotted out, lost to view; and if we remind God about it, He will say: "My child, you need not tell me about it. I have forgotten it. It is as though it had never been."

Next we need the fire, the live coal. God grant that the live coal, which has never lost its glow since the day of Pentecost, may come to every heart, to every mouth, to every life; and that this day a fire shall begin to burn in every mission, in every Sunday school, in every church.

F. B. MEYER

CALVARY'S CROSS

Remission of Sins

See, my brothers, to what the blood of your Lord destines you. Oh, my soul, bless God for that one cup, which reminds you of the great sacrifice and prophesies to you—your glory at the right hand of God forever!

We are told in Matthew 26:28 that this blood is shed "for many for the remission of sins." In that large word "many" let us exceedingly rejoice. Christ's blood was not shed for the handful of apostles alone. There were but eleven of them who really partook of the blood symbolized by the cup. The Savior does not say, "This is My blood which is shed for you, the favored eleven"; but "shed for many." Jesus did not die for the ministers alone. I recollect in Martin Luther's life that he saw, in one of the churches, a picture of the pope and the cardinals and bishops and priests and monks and friars, all on board a ship. They were all safe, every one of them. As for the laity, poor wretches, they were struggling in the sea, and many of them drowning. Only those were saved to whom the good men in the ship were so kind as to hand out a rope or a plank. That is not our Lord's teaching. His blood is shed "for many," and not for the few. He is not the Christ of a caste, or a class, but the Christ of all conditions of men.

Those in the upper room were all Jews, but the Lord Jesus Christ said to them: "This blood is shed for many," to let them see that He did not die alone for the seed of Abraham but for all races of men that dwell upon the face of the earth. "Shed for many!" His eye, I doubt not, glanced at these far-off islands, and at the vast lands beyond the western sea. He thought of Africa, and India, and the land of Sinim. A multitude that no man can number gladdened the far-seeing and fore-seeing eye of the Redeemer. He spoke with joyful emphasis when He said, "Shed for many for the remission of sins."

Believe in the immeasurable results of redemption. Whenever we are making arrangements for the preaching of this precious blood, let us make them on a large scale. The mansion of love should be built for a large family. The masses must be compelled to come in. A group of a half dozen converts makes us very glad, and so it should; but oh, to have half a dozen thousand at once! Why not? This blood is shed for many.

CHARLES H. SPURGEON

CALVARY'S CROSS
Peace Through the Blood

One gaze at Him will be enough to reward us for all we have had to bear. Yes, there is peace for the past, grace for the present, and glory for the future. These are three things that every child of God ought to have. When the angels came bringing the gospel, they proclaimed, "Glory to God, peace on earth, and good will towards men." That is what the blood brings—sin covered and taken away, peace for the past, grace for the present, and glory for the future.

Would you now turn to John 19:34: "But one of the soldiers with a spear pierced his side, and forthwith came there out blood and water."

You know that in Zechariah it was foretold that there should be opened in the house of David a fountain for sin and for uncleanness. Now we have it opened. The Son of God has been pierced by that Roman soldier's spear. It seems to me that that was the crowning act of earth and hell—the crowning act of sin. Look at that Roman soldier as he pushed his spear into the very heart of the God-Man. What a hellish deed! But what took place? Blood covered the spear! Oh, thank God, the blood covers sin.

A usurper has got this world now, but Christ will have it soon. The time of our redemption draws near. A little more suffering, and He returns to set up His kingdom and reign upon the earth. He will rend the heavens, and His voice will be heard again. He will descend from heaven with a shout. He will sway His scepter from the river to the ends of the earth. The thorn and the briar shall be swept away, and the wilderness shall rejoice. Let us rejoice also. We shall see better days. The dreary darkness and sin that sweep along our earth shall be done away with, the dark waves of death and hell shall be beaten back. Oh, let us pray to the Lord to hasten His coming!

Let us remember Romans 3:24: "Being justified freely by his grace, through the redemption that is in Christ Jesus."

What God does He does freely, because He loves to do it. Mark these words, "through the redemption that is in Christ Jesus." Then in the fifth chapter, ninth verse, we read, "Much more then, being now justified by his blood, we shall be saved from wrath through him." The sinner is justified with God by His matchless grace through the blood of His Son.

D. L. MOODY

THE TRUE VINE

Love One Another

This is my commandment, that ye love one another" (John 15:12).

Christ is the Son of God's love, the bearer, the revealer, the communicator of that love. His life and death were all love. Love is His life, and the life He gives. He only lives to love, to live out His life of love in us, to give Himself in all who will receive Him. The very first thought of the true Vine is love—living only to impart His life to the branches.

The Holy Spirit is the Spirit of love. He cannot impart Christ's life without imparting His love. Salvation is nothing but love conquering and entering into us; we have just as much of salvation as we have of love. Full salvation is perfect love.

No wonder that Christ said: "A new commandment I give unto you"; "This is my commandment"—the one all-inclusive commandment—"that ye love one another." The branch is not only one with the vine, but with all its other branches; they drink one spirit, they form one body, they bear one fruit. Nothing can be more unnatural than that Christians should not love one another, even as Christ loved them. The life they received from their heavenly Vine is nothing but love. This is the one thing He asks above all others. "Hereby shall all men know that ye are my disciples . . . love one another." As the special sort of vine is known by the fruit it bears, the nature of the heavenly Vine is to be judged of by the love His disciples have to one another.

See that you obey this commandment. Let your "obey and abide" be seen in this. Love your brethren as the way to abide in the love of your Lord. Let your vow of obedience begin here. Love one another. Let your conversation with the Christians in your own family be holy, tender, Christlike love. Let your thoughts of the Christians around you be, before everything, in the spirit of Christ's love. Let your life and conduct be the sacrifice of love—give yourself up to think of their sins or their needs, to intercede for them, to help and to serve them. Be in your church or circle the embodiment of Christ's love. The life Christ lives in you is love; let the life in which you live it out be all love.

ANDREW MURRAY

MOODY'S LATEST SERMONS
Temptation

I t is said that Edinburgh Castle, in all the wars of Scotland, was never taken but once. Then the enemy came up the steep rocks at a place where the garrison thought it was so safe they needn't guard it. Very often temptation comes in an unexpected form or from an unexpected quarter, when you are off your guard; hence, the necessity of watching and praying, because if you are not on the alert, you will be tripped up by the tempter.

Then Christ adds: "Let him that thinketh he standeth, take heed lest he fall." No man on earth is beyond the reach of the tempter. I used to think that when I got along a certain distance in my Christian life I would get beyond the tempter, and he would have no more influence over me. I have given that up. The tempter will follow you from the cradle to the grave, and the nearer you get to Christ, the hotter the fight will be. As someone has said, Satan aims high. When he wanted one to sell the Lord, he went to the treasurer of the company; and when he wanted one to deny Him, he went to the chief apostle. When he wanted to call down fire from heaven on those Samaritans who refused the disciples' hospitality, he went to John, who was nearest the heart of the Son of God. The angels fell, even in heaven. Adam fell in Paradise. Think of it!

Speaking of the four watches, someone has said that the time a man is most liable to fall is in the second and third watch. The first watch, he starts out, and says, "I must be on my guard; I am weak." He realizes his weakness and keeps his eye upon the Master, going to Him daily and hourly for strength; and so he is not so liable to fall. But in the second and third watches he begins to feel his manhood, and says, "I am strong now, and I can stand." So he begins to lean on the arm of flesh, and then the peril comes, and the fall. As he gets into the fourth watch, he is nearing home, and he begins to see this old world receding from his vision. He realizes how weak the flesh is, because it has failed him so often, and he is on his guard again. He is not so liable to fall if he passes through the second and third watches, though he is always liable.

D. L. MOODY

CHARGE THAT TO MY ACCOUNT

The Way to the City

In that last wonderful book of the Bible, the book of the Revelation, the description of that city is beyond anything that these poor finite minds of ours can comprehend. It is a city with a street of gold, with foundations of precious stones, with gates of pearl, and walls of diamonds; for the jasper of the book of Revelation is clear as crystal, and not the opaque jasper that we know, but evidently the diamond in all its glory. In this way we are given to understand something of what God has provided for those who love Him. What a solemn thing to miss the way to that city! We dwell in this world for some seventy years, and if, after we have passed our little life here, we find ourselves going out into a dark eternity, what a tragedy life will really be!

In Ecclesiastes 10:15, Solomon uses a striking figure. He imagines a countryman on his way to the city, desiring to go perhaps to the great capital of Palestine—Jerusalem, or to some other city upon which his heart is set. But that man starts out trying to find his way with neither guidepost to direct him nor authoritative information to tell him which route to take. He tries first one road and then another, only to be disappointed every time, until at last, utterly wearied, he throws himself down in despair as the shades of night are falling, and says, "It is no use, I cannot find my way." He is "foolish" and weary, "because he knoweth not how to go to the city."

If we think of that city as heaven, or as the glorious New Jerusalem, then indeed we may see how aptly Solomon's words apply to myriads of mankind about us. Speak to men about their hope of heaven and they will say uncertainly, "Oh, yes, I trust I shall enter heaven when earth's short day is over; I hope that some day my feet will walk the gold-paved street of the New Jerusalem." If you ask them what assurance they have that they are really on the road that leads to heaven, you will find that they are all in confusion. Many of them will not even thank you for trying to give them authoritative information from the Word of God. Instead of "Thus saith the Lord," you will find them substituting, "I think." What a common thing it is to hear men say, "I think that everything will come out all right in the end; there are many different roads to eternity, many men of many minds, but we are all going to the same place at last; every road will eventually lead to heaven, we hope." But you know that this is not logical, it is not reasonable. It is a principle that does not work in this world, and what reason have we to believe that it will work when we come to another world?

HENRY A. IRONSIDE

PLEASURE AND PROFIT IN BIBLE STUDY
Controversy

Take the return of the Lord. I know it is a controverted subject. Some say He is to come at the end of the Millennium, others say this side of the Millennium. What we want is to know what the Bible says. Why not go to the Bible and study it up for yourself; it will be worth more to you than anything you get from anyone else.

Then separation. I believe that a Christian man should lead a separated life. The line between the church and the world is almost obliterated today. I have no sympathy with the idea that you must hunt up an old musty church record in order to find out whether a man is a member of the church or not. A man ought to live so that everybody will know he is a Christian. The Bible tells us to lead a separated life. You may lose influence, but you will gain it at the same time. I suppose Daniel was the most unpopular man in Babylon at a certain time, but thank God, he has outlived all the other men of his time. Who were the chief men of Babylon? When God wanted any work done in Babylon, He knew where to find someone to do it. You can be in the world, but not of it. Christ didn't take His disciples out of the world, but He prayed that they might be kept from evil. A ship in the water is all right, but when the water gets into the ship, then look out. A worldly Christian is just like a wrecked vessel at sea.

I remember once I took up the grace of God. I didn't know the difference between law and grace. When that truth dawned upon me and I saw the difference, I studied the whole week on grace and I got so filled that I couldn't stay in the house. I said to the first man I met, "Do you know anything about the grace of God?" He thought I was a lunatic. And I just poured out for about an hour on the grace of God.

Study the subject of prayer. "For real business at the mercy seat," says Spurgeon, "give me a home-made prayer, a prayer that comes out of the depths of your heart, not because you invented it, but because the Holy Spirit put it there. Though your words are broken and your sentences disconnected, God will hear you. Perhaps you can pray better without words than with them. There are prayers that break the backs of words; they are too heavy for any human language to carry."

Some people say, "I do not believe in assurance." I never knew anybody who read their Bibles who did not believe in assurance. This book teaches nothing else. Paul says, "I know in whom I have believed." Job says, "I know that my Redeemer liveth." It is not "I hope, I trust."

D. L. MOODY

ACCORDING TO PROMISE
The Two Lives

Ishmael, who was born after the flesh, the child of the bondwoman, must always bear the servile taint. The child of a slave is not free-born. Ishmael is not, cannot be what Isaac is—the child of the freewoman. Now mark: I do not say that Ishmael ever desired to be like Isaac; I do not say that he felt himself to be a loser by differing from Isaac; but indeed, he was so. The man who is laboring for self-salvation by his own doings, feelings, and self-denials may be proudly ignorant of his servile state; he may even boast that he was born free and was never in bondage to any; and yet he spends his whole life in servitude. He never knows what liberty means, what content means, what delight in God means. He wonders when men talk about "full assurance of faith." He judges that they must be presumptuous. He has scarcely time to breathe between the cracks of the whip. He has done so much, but he must do so much more; he has suffered so much, but he must suffer so much more. He has never come into "the rest which remaineth for the people of God"; for he is born of the bondwoman, and his spirit is ever in bondage. On the other hand, he who is born of the freewoman, and understands that salvation is of the grace of God from first to last, and that where God has given His grace, He does not take it back, for "the gifts and calling of God are without repentance"—such a man accepting the finished work of Christ, and knowing his acceptance in the Beloved, rests in the Lord and rejoices exceedingly. His life and his spirit are filled with joy and peace, for he was born free, and he is free, yea, free indeed.

Does my reader understand the freedom of the child of God, or is he still in servitude under the law, afraid of punishment, afraid of being sent away into the wilderness? If you are in this latter case, you have not received the promise, or you would know that such a thing could not be. To Isaac, the child of the promise, the heritage belongs, and he abides forever, without fear of being cast out.

Those that are born as Ishmael was, according to the flesh, and whose religion is a matter of their own power and strength, mind earthly things, as Ishmael did.

CHARLES H. SPURGEON

SECRET POWER

Power In and Upon

We find the very moment that Solomon completed the temple, when all was finished, they were just praising God with one heart—the choristers and the singers and the ministers were all one; there was not any discord; they were all praising God, and the glory of God came and just filled the temple as the tabernacle. Now, as you turn over into the New Testament, you will find, instead of coming to tabernacles and temples, believers are now the temple of the Holy Ghost. When, on the day of Pentecost, before Peter preached that memorable sermon, as they were praying, the Holy Spirit came and came in mighty power. We now pray for the Spirit of God to come, and we sing: "Come, Holy Spirit, heavenly Dove, with all thy quickening power; kindle a flame of heavenly love in these cold hearts of ours."

I believe, if we understand it, it is perfectly right; but if we are praying for Him to come out of heaven down to earth again, that is wrong, because He is already here; He has not been out of this earth for 1800 years; He has been in the church, and He is with all believers; the believers in the church are the called-out ones; they are called out from the world, and every true believer is a temple for the Holy Ghost to dwell in. In John 14:17 we have the words of Jesus: "The Spirit of Truth, whom the world cannot receive, because it seeth him not, neither knoweth him; but ye know him, for he dwelleth in you."

"Greater is he that is in you than he that is in the world." If we have the Spirit dwelling in us, He gives us power over the flesh and the world and over every enemy. "He is dwelling with you, and shall be in you."

Paul's question in 1 Corinthians 3:16 reminds us of a great truth, "Know ye not that ye are the temple of God, and that the Spirit of God dwelleth in you?"

D. L. MOODY

BACK TO BETHEL

All the Keys

I knelt by my bed, with the door of my room locked, and resolved that I would not sleep until I had settled the matter and surrendered everything to Jesus. It seemed as though Jesus was by my side and that I took from my pocket a large bunch of keys. From that bunch I took one tiny key, which I kept, and then held to Jesus the bunch with the one missing.

"Here are the keys of my life," I said.

He looked at me sadly and asked, "Are all there?"

"All but one tiny one, to a small cupboard. It is so small that it cannot amount to anything."

He replied, "Child, if you cannot trust Me with everything, you cannot trust Me with anything."

Satan whispered to me: "You cannot give up that thing. Besides if you let Christ have His way, you don't know what He will ask of you next. Don't give it to Him!"

Then the thought came to me of my only child, who at that time was somewhat wayward. Supposing she were to come to me and say, "Father, I give my whole life up to you; you may choose anything you want for me." I know I would not call her mother and say, "Now here is our chance. What can we do to make her life miserable and unhappy?"

Instead I would say, "Wife, let's now take away everything that hurts her, and we will make her life one long summer day."

Christ would not be harder on me than I on my child, and at last I said, "Lord, I cannot give the key, but I am willing to have you come and take it."

It was as I expected. I seemed to hold out my hand, and He came and opened the fingers and took the key from me. Then He went straight to that cupboard, unlocked and opened it and saw there a thing that was terrible and hideous. He said: "This must go out. You must never go that way again."

And the moment He took the thing from me, He took the desire for it out of my soul, and I began to hate it. Then I yielded myself absolutely to Him and said, "From this night I want You to do as You will with my life."

The next morning I awoke expecting a sort of hallelujah feeling, but I was as calm and quiet as I am now. I only had a delightful sense that I did belong to Jesus Christ, and a hundred times that day I said to myself: "I am His! I am absolutely His!"

F. B. MEYER

THE WAY HOME

Unconditional Surrender

One interesting thought suggested to us by the history of Naaman in 2 Kings 5:15 shows what Naaman's faith led him to believe. "And he returned to the man of God, he and all his company, and came, and stood before him; and he said, 'Behold, now I know that there is no God in all the earth, but in Israel: now therefore, I pray thee, take a blessing of thy servant.'" I want particularly to call your attention to the words "I know."

There is no hesitation about it, no qualifying the expression. Naaman doesn't now say, "I think"; no, he says, "I know there is a God who has power to forgive sins and to cleanse the leprosy."

Then there is another thought. Naaman left only one thing in Samaria, and that was his sin, his leprosy. The only thing God wishes you to leave with Him is your sin; and yet it is the only thing you seem not to care about giving up.

"Oh," you say, "I love it, it is so delightful, I can't give it up; I know God wants it, that He may make me clean. But I can't give it up."

Why, what downright madness is it for you to love leprosy; and yet that is your condition!

"Ah, but," says someone, "I don't believe in sudden conversions."

Don't you? Well, how long did it take Naaman to be cured? The seventh time he went down, away went the leprosy! Read the great conversions recorded in the Bible—Saul of Tarsus, Zacchaeus, and a host of others; how long did it take the Lord to bring them about? They were effected in a minute. We are born in iniquity, shaped in it, dead in trespasses and sin; but when spiritual life comes it comes in a moment, and we are freed both from sin and death.

D. L. MOODY

GOD'S WAY OF HOLINESS

Christ for Us, the Spirit in Us

That we "believe through grace," that faith is "the gift of God," does not prove faith to be a work of ours, any more than Christ's raising of Lazarus proved resurrection to be a work of the dead man. The divine infusion of life in the one case, and the divine impartation of faith in the other, so far from showing that there must be a work in either, indicates very plainly that there could not be any such thing. The work comes after the believing, and as the fruit of it. "Faith worketh by love," that is, the believing soul shows its faith by works of love.

Yes, faith worketh; so also does love, so also does hope. These all work; and we read of "the work of faith," that is, work to which faith prompts us; the "labor of love," that is, the toil to which love impels us; the "patience of hope," that is, the patience that hope enables us to exercise. But is faith a work because it works? Is love a toil because it toils? Is hope patience because it makes us patient? Israel's looking to the brazen serpent was a ceasing from all remedies and letting health pour itself into the body by the eye. Was the opening of the eye a work? The gospel does not command us to do anything in order to obtain life, but it bids us live by that which another has done: and the knowledge of its life-giving truth is not labor but rest, rest of soul, rest that is the root of all true labor; for in receiving Christ we do not work in order to rest, but we rest in order to work. In believing, we cease to work for pardon, in order that we may work from it; and what incentive to work, or source of joy in working, can be greater than an ascertained and realized forgiveness?

That there are works done before faith we know; but we are assured that they profit nothing, "for without faith it is impossible to please God." That there are works done after faith we also know; and they are all well-pleasing to God, for they are the works of believing men. But, as to any work intermediate between these two, Scripture is silent; and against transforming faith into a work the whole theology of the Reformation protested, as either a worthless verbal quibble or as the subtlest dregs of Roman Catholicism.

Truly faith comes from God. The revelation we believe and the power by which we believe it are both divine.

HORATIUS BONAR

THE WAY TO GOD
Christ Is Our Keeper

A great many young disciples are afraid they will not hold out. "He that keepeth Israel shall neither slumber nor sleep" (Psalm 121:4). It is the work of Christ to keep us; and if He keeps us there will be no danger of our falling. I suppose if Queen Victoria had to take care of the Crown of England, some thief might attempt to get access to it; but it is put away in the Tower of London and guarded night and day by soldiers. The whole English army would, if necessary, be called out to protect it.

We have no strength in ourselves. We are no match for Satan; he has had six thousand years' experience. But then we remember that the One who neither slumbers nor sleeps is our keeper. In Isaiah 41:10, we read, "Fear thou not; for I am with thee: be not dismayed; for I am thy God: I will strengthen thee, yea, I will help thee; yea, I will uphold thee with the right hand of my righteousness." In Jude also, verse 24, we are told that He is "able to keep us from falling."

But Christ is something more. He is our shepherd. It is the work of the shepherd to care for the sheep, to feed them and protect them. "I am the Good Shepherd." "My sheep hear my voice." "I lay down my life for the sheep." In that wonderful tenth chapter of John, Christ uses the personal pronoun no less than twenty-eight times, in declaring what He is and what He will do. In verse 28 he says, "They shall never perish; neither shall any [man] pluck them out of my hand." But notice the word man is in italics. See how the verse really reads: "Neither shall ANY pluck them out of my hand"—no devil or man shall be able to do it. In another place the Scripture declares, "Your life is hid with Christ in God" (Colossians 3:3). How safe and how secure!

Christ says, "My sheep hear my voice . . . and they follow me" (John 10:27). A gentleman in the East heard of a shepherd who could call all of his sheep to him by name. He went and asked if this were true. The shepherd took him to the pasture where they were and called one of them by some name. One sheep looked up and answered the call, while the others went on feeding and paid no attention. In the same way he called about a dozen of the sheep around him. The stranger said, "How do you know one from the other? They all look perfectly alike."

"Well," said he, "you see that sheep toes in a little, that other one has a squint, one has a little piece of wool off, another has a black spot, and another has a piece out of its ear."

The man knew all his sheep by their failings, for he had not a perfect one in the whole flock. I suppose our shepherd knows us in the same way.

D. L. MOODY

TEN REASONS THE BIBLE IS THE WORD OF GOD

Growing Toward the Bible

The nearer and nearer we get to God's standpoint the less and less becomes the disagreement between us and the Bible. What is the inevitable mathematical conclusion? When we get where God is, we and the Bible will meet. In other words, the Bible was written from God's standpoint.

Suppose you are traveling through a forest under the conduct of an experienced and highly recommended guide. You come to a place where two roads diverge. The guide says the road to the left is the one to take, but your own judgment passing upon the facts before it sees clear evidence that the road to the right is the one to take. You turn and say to the guide, "I know that you have had large experience in this forest, and you have come to me highly recommended, but my own judgment tells me clearly that the road to the right is the one we should take, and I must follow my own judgment. I know my reason is not infallible, but it is the best guide I have."

But after you have followed that path for some distance you are obligated to stop, turn around, and go back and take the path that the guide said was the right one.

After a while you come to another place where two roads diverge. Now the guide says the road to the right is the one to take, but your judgment clearly says the one to the left is the one to take, and again you follow your own judgment with the same result as before.

After you had this experience forty or fifty times and found yourself wrong every time, I think you would have enough sense the next time to follow the guide.

That is just my experience with the Bible. I received it at first on the authority of others. Like almost all other young men, my confidence became shaken, and I came to the fork in the road more than forty times, and I followed my own reason, and in the outcome found myself wrong and the Bible right every time, and I trust that from this time on I shall have sense enough to follow the teachings of the Bible whatever my own judgment may say.

R. A. TORREY

CALVARY'S CROSS

Two Cries

The blood has two cries: it cries either for my condemnation (or if you will allow me to use a stronger word, for my damnation), or for my salvation. If I reject the blood of Christ, it cries out for my condemnation; if I accept it, it cries out for pardon and peace. The blood of Abel cried out against his brother Cain. So it was in the days of Christ.

When Pilate had Christ on his hands, he said to the Jews, "What shall I do with Him?"

"Away with Him! Crucify Him!" they cried out.

And when he asked which one he should release, Barabbas or Christ, they cried out, "Barabbas!"

Then when he asked again, "What shall I then do with Him?" A universal shout went up from Jerusalem, "Let Him be crucified! Away with Him! We do not want Him."

Pilate turned and washed his hands, and said, "I am innocent of this just Man's blood," and they cried, "His blood be on us and on our children. We shall take the responsibility of it. We endorse the act. Crucify Him, and let His blood be on us and on our children."

Would to God that there might be a cry going up, "Let His blood be on us to save, not to condemn."

Turn now to Colossians 1:20: "Having made peace through the blood of his cross." I can tell you there is no peace in the world. There are many rich men, many great men in the world, who have got no peace. No, I have never seen a man who knew what peace was until he got it at Calvary. "Being justified by faith, we have peace with God through our Lord Jesus Christ" (Romans 5:1). Sin covered—that brings peace. There is no peace for the wicked; they are like the troubled sea that cannot rest. Calvary is the place to find peace—peace for the past and grace for the present.

But there is something better still: "And rejoice in hope of the glory of God." Some people think that when they get to Calvary they have got the best; but there is something better in store—glory! I do not know how near it may be to us; it may be that some of us will be ushered very soon into the presence of the King.

D. L. MOODY

THE TRUE VINE

Election

Ye did not choose me, but I chose you" (John 15:16). And with what view does Christ say this? That they may know what the object is for which He chose them, and find, in their faith in His election, the certainty of fulfilling their destiny. Throughout Scripture this is the great object of the teaching of election. "Predestinated to be conformed to the image of his son" (to be branches in the image and likeness of the Vine). "Chosen that we should be holy." "Chosen to salvation, through sanctification of the Spirit." "Elect in sanctification of the Spirit unto obedience." Some have abused the doctrine of election, and others, for fear of its abuse, have rejected it, because they have overlooked this teaching. They have occupied themselves with its hidden origin in eternity, with the inscrutable mysteries of the counsels of God, instead of accepting the revelation of its purpose in time and the blessings it brings into our Christian life.

Just think what these blessings are. In our verse Christ reveals His twofold purpose in choosing us to be His branches: that we may bear fruit on earth, and that we may have power in prayer in heaven. What confidence the thought that He has chosen us for this gives, that He will not fail to fit us for carrying out His purpose! What assurance that we can bear fruit that will abide and can pray so as to obtain! What a continual call to the deepest humility and praise, to the most entire dependence and expectancy! He would not choose us for what we are not fit for or what He could not fit us for. He has chosen us; this is the pledge, He will do all in us.

Let us listen in silence of soul to our holy Vine speaking to each of us: "You did not choose Me!" And let us say, "Yea, Lord, but I chose You! Amen, Lord!" Ask Him to show what this means. In Him, the true Vine, your life as branch has its divine origin, its eternal security, and the power to fulfill His purpose.

ANDREW MURRAY

MOODY'S LATEST SERMONS

Four Questions from God

I want to call your attention to four questions that God has put: the first question ever put to man, "Where art thou?" the first question ever put to woman, "What is this that thou hast done?" the question put to Cain, "Where is thy brother?" and the question put to Elijah, "What doest thou here?"

"Where art thou?" A man said to me, "How do you know that God put that question to Adam?"

The best answer I can give is, because He has put it to me many a time. I doubt whether there ever has been a son or a daughter of Adam who has not heard that voice ringing through his soul many a time. Who am I? What am I? Where am I going? So let us put the question to ourselves personally, "Where am I?"—not in the sight of man; that is of very little account; but where am I in the sight of God?—that is the question.

Adam ought to have been the first seeker. Adam ought to have gone up and down Eden crying: "My God, my God, where art Thou? I have sinned. I have fallen."

But God, then as now, took the place of the seeker. No man, from the time that Adam fell down to the present hour, ever thought of seeking God until God first sought for him. "The Son of Man is come to seek and to save that which was lost." I believe that the Son of Man who uttered those words is the same whose voice was heard back there in Eden, "Adam, where art thou?" For six thousand years God has been seeking for man.

In the fifteenth chapter of Luke there are three parables just to teach us that God is the seeker. It was not the sheep that was seeking the shepherd; it was the shepherd going out into the desert to hunt until he found the lost sheep. It was not that piece of silver seeking the woman; it was the woman seeking for the lost piece of silver. Those parables are given to teach us that God is the great Seeker. If you can discover yourself and find out who you are, and what you are, that will be the greatest discovery you can ever make. That is what the prodigal did when he came to himself—he found out who he was.

D. L. MOODY

BACK TO BETHEL
Wrestling for a Blessing

The stars shining above, the brook rushing down to the Jordan, the trees and shrubs overhanging it! Rachel the beloved, Leah and the children, the flocks and herds had all gone forward, and Jacob was left alone. And the angel of God met him (Genesis 32:24). Too often that wonderful scene has been used as a symbol of wrestling prayer, but it is not meant to be taken only in that sense. It seems to me that it was not Jacob who wrestled with the angel, but the angel who wrestled with Jacob. It was as though God knew it was his only chance. He wanted to lift Jacob up to a new royal life, and so He actually wrestled with him as though to compel him to yield to Him. Jacob was a proud man. He stood his ground and resisted the effort of the angel to humble him. He struggled. He antagonized the angel of God's love. It was only when the angel put forth his hand and touched the sinew of his thigh, which shriveled as a cord in the flame, and the man was no longer able to resist, that he cast his arms around the angel and said:

"I yield, I yield! But I will not let thee go until thou bless me!"

The angel blessed him and said: "What is thy name?" He answered: "Jacob—supplanter, cheat, mean, crafty."

The angel said, "No more Jacob, but Israel! God wants you to leave all that behind and step up into a royal life."

Did you ever have that experience in your life? I had it twenty years ago, and I think many another can point back to some secret hour when God's angel came to lift him back into princeliness and make him the servant of God. Perhaps when your wife lay at the point of death the angel came, and you vowed if God would spare her you would live a worthy, godly life. You remember, woman, that time when your first babe was dangerously ill. You sat at the bedside and lifted up your heart to God and said: "If you will spare my child I will renounce my worldliness, my low living, and I will live a true Christian life." That was your Jabbok, and you left it resolved that God and you would be forever in close and blessed fellowship.

F. B. MEYER

PLEASURE AND PROFIT IN BIBLE STUDY

Conversion

Christian growth is gradual, just as physical growth is; but a man passes from death unto everlasting life quick as an act of the mind—"He that believeth on the Son hath everlasting life."

People say they want to become heavenly-minded. Well, read about heaven and talk about it. I once preached on heaven, and after the meeting a lady came to me and said, "Why, Mr. Moody, I didn't know there were so many verses in the Bible about heaven." And I hadn't taken one out of a hundred.

When you are away from home, how you look for news! You skip everything in the daily paper until your eye catches the name of your own town or country. Now, the Christian's home is in heaven. The Scriptures contain our title-deeds to everything we shall be worth when we die. If a will has your name in it, it is no longer a dry document. Why, then, do not Christians take more interest in the Bible?

Then, again, people say they don't believe in revivals. There's not a denomination in the world that didn't spring from a revival. There are the Catholic and Episcopal churches claiming to be the apostolic churches and to have sprung from Pentecost; the Lutheran from Martin Luther, and so on. They all sprung out of revivals, and yet people talk against revivals! I'd as soon talk against my mother as against a revival. Wasn't the country revived under John the Baptist? Wasn't it under Christ's teachings? People think that because a number of superficial cases of conversion occur at revivals that therefore revivals ought to be avoided. They forget the parable of the sower, where Jesus Himself warns us of emotional hearers, who receive the word with joy, but soon fall away. If only one out of every four hearers is truly converted, as in the parable, the revival has done good.

Suppose you spend a month on regeneration, or the kingdom of God, or the church in the New Testament, or the divinity of Christ or the attributes of God. It will help you in your own spiritual life, and you will become a workman who need not be ashamed, rightly dividing the word of truth.

D. L. MOODY

HEAVEN

A City Without Sorrow

The idea that heaven is everywhere and nowhere is not according to Scripture. Heaven is God's habitation, and when Christ came on earth He taught us to pray: "Our Father, which art in heaven." This habitation is spoken of as "the city of eternal life." Think of a city without a cemetery—they have no dying there. If there could be such a city as that found on this earth what a rush there would be to it! How men would try to reach that city! You cannot find one of the face of this earth. A city without tears—God wipes away all the tears up yonder. This is a time of weeping, but by-and-by there will be a time when God shall call us, where there will be no tears. A city without pain, a city without sorrow, without sickness, without death. There is no darkness there. "The Lamb is the light thereof." It needs no sun, it needs no moon.

The paradise of Eden was as nothing compared with this one. The tempter came into Eden and triumphed, but in that city nothing that defiles shall enter. There will be no tempter there. Think of a place where temptation cannot come. Think of a place where we shall be free from sin; where pollution cannot enter and where the righteous shall reign forever. Think of a city that is not built with hands, where the buildings do not grow old with time; a city whose inhabitants are numbered by no census except the Book of Life, which is the heavenly directory. Think of a city through whose streets run no tide of business, where no hearses with their nodding plumes creep slowly with their sad burdens to the cemetery; a city without griefs or graves, without sins or sorrows, without marriages or mournings, without births or burials; a city that glories in having Jesus for its King, angels for its guards, and whose citizens are saints!

We believe this is just as much a place and just as much a city as is New York, London, or Paris. We believe in it a good deal more, because earthly cities will pass away, but this city will remain forever. It has foundations whose builder and maker is God.

D. L. MOODY

ABSOLUTE SURRENDER

The Fruit of the Spirit Is Love

The fruit of the Spirit is love." Why? Because nothing but love can expel and conquer our selfishness.

Self is the great curse, whether in its relation to God, to our fellow men in general, or to fellow Christians—thinking of ourselves and seeking our own. Self is our greatest curse. But, praise God, Christ came to redeem us from self. We sometimes talk about deliverance from the self-life—and thank God for every word that can be said about it to help us—but I am afraid some people think deliverance from the self-life means that now they are going to have no longer any trouble in serving God; and they forget that deliverance from self-life means to be a vessel overflowing with love to everybody all the day.

And there you have the reason why many people pray for the power of the Holy Spirit, and they get something, but oh, so little! Because they prayed for power for work and power for blessing, but they have not prayed for power for full deliverance from self. That means not only the righteous self in intercourse with God, but the unloving self in intercourse with men. And there is deliverance. "The fruit of the Spirit is love." I bring you the glorious promise of Christ that He is able to fill our hearts with love.

A great many of us try hard at times to love. We try to force ourselves to love, and I do not say that is wrong; it is better than nothing. But the end of it is always very sad. "I fail continually," such a one must confess. And what is the reason? The reason is simply this: They have never learned to believe and accept the truth that the Holy Spirit can pour God's love into their hearts. That blessed text; often it has been limited! "The love of God is shed abroad in our hearts." It has often been understood in this sense: It means the love of God to me. Oh, what a limitation! That is only the beginning. The love of God is always the love of God in its entirety, in its fullness as in indwelling power, a love of God to me that leaps back to Him in love and overflows to my fellow men in love—God's love to me, and my love to God, and my love to my fellow men.

ANDREW MURRAY

THE WAY HOME

A Guilty Memory

I f Cain is in that lost world tonight, no doubt he can remember the pleading look of his brother Abel. He can remember how he looked when he smote him—he can hear that piercing cry tonight; he has not forgotten it. All these long years Cain remembers what he might have been, how he despised the God of grace and how he lost his soul.

I have no doubt but that Judas remembers how Christ preached that sermon he heard on the mountain, how Christ looked when He wept over Jerusalem, and he can see those tears tonight, he can hear that voice as He cried over Jerusalem: "O Jerusalem, Jerusalem, thou that killest the prophets, and stonest them that are sent unto thee, how often would I have gathered thy children together, even as a hen gathereth her chickens under her wings, and ye would not!" He hears that cry; he can see that kind, mild, gentle look of the Son of God. He can hear that voice as Christ said to him in Gethsemane, "Betrayest thou the Son of Man with a kiss?"

Yes, memory is at work. His memory woke up before he died, when he went out and destroyed himself, taking his remorse and despair with him into the lost world.

Do you think those antediluvians have forgotten how Noah pleaded with them? They laughed at the ark. I have no doubt, if you had gone and preached to them a week before the flood, and told them that there was a hell, not one would have believed it. If you had told them that there was to be a deluge, and that God was going to sweep them away from the earth, they would not have believed it.

So with Jerusalem. Christ told how destruction would come upon it, and they mocked at Him and crucified Him. But look down the stream of time! In forty short years Titus came up against that city and besieged it, and there were a million that perished within it. Yes, those Jerusalem sinners can remember in the lost world tonight how Christ wept over Jerusalem, how He walked their streets, how He went into the temple and preached, and how He pleaded with them to escape for their lives and to flee the damnation of hell. But they mocked on, they laughed on, they made light until it was too late, and they are gone now.

Oh, may God wake up this audience, and may every man and woman here before it is too late escape for their lives! "How shall we escape," says the apostle, "if we neglect so great salvation?"

D. L. MOODY

ALL OF GRACE
The Increase of Faith

Think over what it is that you have to believe, that the Lord Jesus Christ suffered in the room and place and stead of sinners and is able to save all who trust Him. Why, this is the most blessed fact that ever men were told to believe; the most suitable, the most comforting, the most divine truth that was ever set before mortal minds. I advise you to think much upon it and to search out the grace and love that it contains. Study the four evangelists, study Paul's epistles, and then see if the message is not such a credible one that you are forced to believe it.

If that does not do, then think upon the person of Jesus Christ—think of who He is, and what He did, and where He is, and what He is. How can you doubt Him? It is cruelty to distrust the ever truthful Jesus. He has done nothing to deserve distrust; on the contrary, it should be easy to rely upon Him. Why crucify Him anew by unbelief? Is not this crowning Him with thorns again, and spitting upon Him again? What! Is He not to be trusted? What worse insult did the soldiers pour upon Him than this? They made Him a martyr; but you make Him a liar—this is worse by far. Do not ask, How can I believe? But answer another question—How can you disbelieve?

If none of these things avail, then there is something wrong about you altogether, and my last word is, submit yourself to God! Prejudice or pride is at the bottom of this unbelief. May the Spirit of God take away your enmity and make you yield. You are a rebel, a proud rebel, and that is why you do not believe your God. Give up your rebellion; throw down your weapons; yield at discretion, surrender to your King. I believe that never did a soul throw up its hands in self-despair, and cry, "Lord, I yield," but what faith became easy to it before long. It is because you still have a quarrel with God and resolve to have your own will and your own way that therefore you cannot believe. "How can ye believe," said Christ, "that have honor one of another?" Proud self creates unbelief. Submit, O man. Yield to your God, and then shall you sweetly believe in your Savior.

CHARLES H. SPURGEON

THE WAY HOME

Heaven and How to Get There

Heaven is the dwelling place of God, whose glory fills the whole earth. He is there. His peculiar dwelling place, His throne, His habitation is there. King Solomon's prayer when the temple had been consecrated, and he sought God's blessing on his people, was, "Hear thou from thy dwelling-place, even from heaven" (2 Chronicles 6:21). God says through the prophet Isaiah (66:1), "The heaven is my throne." And the martyr Stephen reminds us of God, "Heaven is my throne" (Acts 7:49). Again in Psalm 123:1: "Unto thee lift I up mine eyes, O thou that dwellest in the heavens." Again, Psalm 33:13 and Psalm 11:4: "The Lord's throne is in heaven."

Surely that is a sweet thought. If I am to spend my eternity in heaven, I like to know and to be assured that my Father is there and to feel that He is there ruler over all—that He is the first, the chief, the holiest, the highest in all high heaven, "King of kings, and Lord of lords." "I dwell in the heavens," says the Almighty God; and yet, "If my people shall humble themselves and pray, and seek my face, and turn from their wicked ways; then will I hear from heaven, and will forgive their sin, and will heal their land" (2 Chronicles 7:14). Though He is high and mighty, yet "He dwells also with him who is of a humble and a contrite spirit."

Yes, that is one of His greatest and most wonderful characteristics—He is the hearer and answerer of prayer. As an instance of this, see Daniel 2:18, where there is a prayer that God would reveal to His servants, not only the interpretation of a dream, but even the dream itself. "Is there anything too hard for the Lord?" No. In the very next verse we have the answer right back, as it were, by telegraph from heaven: "Then was the secret revealed unto Daniel in a night vision."

The Scripture is full of such answers; every page of it encourages prayer. God will have us pray, and He will answer prayer. Surely we have all found that out in our experience; if not, it is our own fault. "The arm of the Lord is not shortened that it cannot save." It is our own prayers that are shortened and that are weak and faithless. Oh, let us "ask in faith, nothing wavering!" Some people are like the disciples in Jerusalem praying for the release of Peter; their prayers were answered, and Peter stood at the door, but they could not believe it; they said it must be his spirit. Oh, let us take God at His word! He says, "While they are yet speaking, I will answer." Is not that encouraging? He delights to hear our prayers; He will not weary with our often coming.

D. L. MOODY

THE SECRET OF GUIDANCE
Lifting the Burdens

The one cure for burden-bearing is to cast all burdens on the Lord. The margin of the Revised Version of Psalm 25:22 reads thus: "Cast that He hath given thee upon the Lord." Whatever burden the Lord hath given thee, give it back to Him. Treat the burden of care as once the burden of sin; kneel down and deliberately hand it over to Jesus. Say to Him, "Lord, I entrust to You this, and this, and this. I cannot carry them, they are crushing me; but I definitely commit them all to You to manage and adjust and arrange. You have taken my sins. Take my sorrows, and in exchange give me Your peace, Your rest." As George Herbert says, "We must put them all into Christ's bag."

Will not our Lord Jesus be at least as true and faithful as the best earthly friend we have ever known? And have there not been times in all our lives when we have been too weary or helpless to help ourselves and have thankfully handed some wearing anxiety to a good, strong man, sure that when once it was entrusted to him, he would not rest until he had finished it to his satisfaction?

And surely He who loved us enough to die for us may be trusted to arrange all the smaller matters of our daily lives!

Of course, there are one or two conditions we must fulfill, before we shall be able to hand over our burdens to the Lord Jesus and leave them with Him in perfect confidence. We must have cast our sins on Him before we can cast our cares. We must be at peace with God through the work of our Savior before we can have the peace of God through faith in His gracious interposition on our behalf. We must also be living on God's plan, tarrying under the cloud, obeying His laws and executing His plans so far as we know them. We must also feed faith with promise, for this food is essential to make it thrive. And when we have done all this we shall not find it so difficult.

Some earnest people carry another great burden. They go from convention to convention, from one speaker to another, notebook in hand, so eager to get the blessing (as they term it). And because they hear of others having experiences that they know not, they carry heavy burdens of disappointment and self-reproach.

Equally well might a student in the beginning class fret because he has not entered the higher classes of the school. But why should he worry about his future progress? His one business is to learn the lessons set by his teacher. And it is for us to learn the lessons that the Lord Jesus sets before us day by day, leaving Him to lead us into the fuller knowledge and love of God.

F. B. MEYER

MOODY'S STORIES

Too Late!

At our church in Chicago I was closing the meeting one day when a young soldier got up and entreated the people to decide for Christ at once. He said he had just come from a dark scene. A comrade of his, who had enlisted with him, had a father who was always entreating him to become a Christian, and in reply he always said he would when the war was over. At last he was wounded and was put into the hospital, but he got worse and was gradually sinking. One day, a few hours before he died, a letter came from his sister, but he was too far gone to read it. It was such an earnest letter! The comrade read it to him, but he did not seem to understand it, he was so weak, till it came to the last sentence, which said:

"Oh, my dear brother, when you get this letter, will you not accept your sister's Savior?"

The dying man sprang up from his cot, and said, "What do you say? What do you say?" And then, falling back on his pillow, feebly exclaimed, "It is too late! It is too late!"

My dear friends, thank God it is not too late for you today. The master is still calling you. Let every one of us, young and old, rich and poor, come to Christ at once, and He will put all our sins away. Don't wait any longer for feeling, but obey at once. You can believe, you can trust, you can lay hold on eternal life, if you will. Will you not do it now?

D. L. MOODY

ABSOLUTE SURRENDER

Separated unto the Holy Spirit

What is now the will of God as the Holy Spirit reveals it? It is contained in one word: *separation* unto the Holy Spirit. That is the keynote of the message from heaven.

"Separate unto me Barnabas and Saul for the work whereunto I have called them. The work is mine, and I care for it, and I have chosen these men and called them, and I want you who represent the church of Christ upon earth to set them apart unto me."

Look at this heavenly message in its twofold aspect. The men were to be set apart to the Holy Spirit, and the church was to do this separating work. The Holy Spirit could trust these men to do it in a right spirit. There they were abiding in fellowship with the heavenly, and the Holy Spirit could say to them, "Do the work of separating these men." And these were the men the Holy Spirit had prepared, and He could say of them, "Let them be separated unto me."

Here we come to the very root, to the very life of the need of Christian workers. The question is: What is needed that the power of God should rest upon us more mightily, that the blessing of God should be poured out more abundantly among those poor wretched people and perishing sinners among whom we labor? And the answer from heaven is: "I want men separated unto the Holy Spirit."

What does that imply? You know that there are two spirits on earth. Christ said, when He spoke about the Holy Spirit: "The world cannot receive Him." Paul said: "We have received not the spirit of the world, but the Spirit that is of God." That is the great want in every worker—the spirit of the world going out, and the Spirit of God coming in to take possession of the inner life and of the whole being.

I am sure there are workers who often cry to God for the Holy Spirit to come upon them as a Spirit of power for their work, and when they feel that measure of power, and get blessing, they thank God for it. But God wants something more and something higher. God wants us to seek for the Holy Spirit as a Spirit of power in our own heart and life, to conquer self and cast out sin, and work the blessed and beautiful image of Jesus into us.

ANDREW MURRAY

CALVARY'S CROSS

Bearing the Cross

What He bore for us is done; it cannot be borne over again; it is not for any but Himself to carry. But as He had a cross to bear for us, so have we a cross to bear for Him; and "for his body's sake, which is the church."

In entering Christ's service, let us count the cost. In following Him, let us not shrink from the cross. It was His badge of serve for us; let us accept it as ours for Him.

To the world the cross is an offense and a stumblingblock in two ways: it makes those who have taken it up objects of dislike to others, and it is itself an object of dislike to these others. Thus, while it unites the saints, it divides them from the world. It is the banner round which the former rally and gather; it is the mark against which the arrows of the latter are turned.

For there are "enemies of the cross of Christ" and enemies of Christ Himself. Of them the apostle says, "Their end is destruction." Thus the cross is both life and death, salvation and destruction. It is the golden scepter; it is the iron rod. It is the Shepherd's staff of love; it is the Avenger's sword of fire. It is the tree of life and cup of blessing; it is the cup of the wine of the wrath of God.

Oh, enemy of the cross of Christ, know your awful doom! Do not take refuge in fancied neutrality, reasoning with yourself that because you are not a scoffer or a profligate, you are not an enemy. Remember that it is written, "He that is not for me is against me," and, "The friendship of the world is enmity with God." That cross shall be a witness against you in the day when the Crucified One returns as Judge and King.

The early Christians had a tradition among themselves that the cross was to be a sign of His coming, appearing in the heavens as the herald of His advent. Whether this is to be the case or not, the cross in that day will be the object of terror to its enemies. They would not be saved by it; they shall perish by it. They would not take its pardon; they must bear its condemnation. The love that it so long proclaimed shall be turned into wrath. Their night shall begin—the long eternal night that has no dawn in prospect and no star to break its gloom.

HORATIUS BONAR

SOWING AND REAPING

A Dreadful Place

A converted Chinese once said: "I was down in a deep pit, half sunk in the mire, crying for someone to help me out. As I looked up I saw a venerable, gray-haired man looking down at me.

"'My son,' he said, 'this is a dreadful place.'

"'Yes,' I answered, 'I fell into it; can't you help me out?'

"'My son,' was his reply, 'I am Confucius. If you had read my books and followed what they taught, you would never have been here.'

"'Yes, father,' I said, 'but can't you help me out?'

"As I looked he was gone. Soon I saw another form approaching, and another man bent over me, this time with closed eyes and folded arms. He seemed to be looking to some far-off place.

"'My son,' Buddha said, 'just close your eyes and fold your arms, and forget all about yourself. Get into a state of rest. Don't think about anything that can disturb. Get so still that nothing can move you. Then, my child, you will be in such delicious rest as I am.'

"'Yes, father,' I answered, 'I will when I am above ground. Can't you help me out?' But Buddha, too, was gone.

"I was just beginning to sink into despair when I saw another figure above me, different from the others. There were marks of suffering on His face. I cried out to Him, 'O, Father, can you help me?'

"'My child,' He said, 'what is the matter?'

"Before I could answer Him, He was down in the mire by my side. He folded His arms about me and lifted me up; then He fed me and rested me. When I was well He did not say, 'Now don't do that again,' but He said, 'We will walk on together now'; and we have been walking together until this day."

D. L. MOODY

ACCORDING TO PROMISE

The Promise: A Free Gift

Pride is not becoming among dependents. He who lives upon gifts should be humble and grateful. We are beggars at the door of mercy. At the beautiful gate of the temple we sit down every day to ask an alms, not of the worshipers, but of Him whom angels worship. As often as our Lord passes by, we ask and He gives; and we are not surprised that we receive from His love, for He has promised to bestow great mercies. He taught us to say, "Give us this day our daily bread," and therefore we are neither ashamed nor afraid to ask all things from Him.

Ours is a life of dependence, and we delight to have it so. It is sweet to take all things from the hands of our crucified Lord. Happy is the poverty that leads us to be rich in Christ. We earn nothing and yet receive everything, thrice blest in being hourly partakers of the gift of God. "Whereby are given unto us exceeding great and precious promises."

Beloved, this teaching as to the promise coming of pure gift should be exceedingly encouraging to all who feel their lost estate and own that they are spiritually bankrupt. To such it is a word of good cheer, that everything is freely given to us of God; why should He not give to them as well as to other needy ones? Those of us who rejoice in God have received all things as a free gift; why should not others receive the like? They say, "There is nothing freer than a gift"; why should not my reader receive as well as myself? To one who is willing to give, poverty on the part of the receiver is a recommendation instead of an obstacle.

Come, then, you who are without merit, Christ will be your merit. Come, you that have no righteousness, He will be your righteousness. Come, you who are as full of sin as an egg is full of meat, and the pardoning Lord will put away your sin. Come, you who are utterly forlorn, and be made rich in Jesus.

CHARLES H. SPURGEON

ABSOLUTE SURRENDER

Splendid Peter, Selfish Peter

Peter was a man of absolute surrender; he gave up all to follow Jesus. Peter was also a man of ready obedience. You remember Christ said to him: "Launch out into the deep, and let down the net." Peter the fisherman knew there were no fish there, for they had been toiling all night and had caught nothing; but he said: "At thy word I will let down the net." He submitted to the word of Jesus. Further, he was a man of great faith. When he saw Christ walking on the sea, he said: "Lord, if it be thou, bid me come unto thee"; and at the voice of Christ he stepped out of the boat and walked upon the water. And Peter was a man of spiritual insight. When Christ asked the disciples: "Whom do ye say that I am?" Peter was able to answer: "Thou art the Christ, the Son of the living God."

To that statement, Christ said: "Blessed art thou, Simon Bar-jona; for flesh and blood hath not revealed it unto thee, but my Father which is in heaven." And Christ spoke of him as the rock man and of his having the keys of the kingdom. Peter was a splendid man, a devoted disciple of Jesus, and, if he was living nowadays, everybody would say that he was an advanced Christian. And yet how much there was wanting in Peter!

Look next at Peter living the life of self, pleasing self, and trusting self, and seeking the honor of self.

You recollect that just after Christ had said to him: "Flesh and blood hath not revealed it unto thee, but my Father which is in heaven," Christ began to speak about His sufferings, and Peter dared to say: "Be it far from thee, Lord; this shall not be unto thee." Then Christ had to say, "Get thee behind me, Satan; for thou savorest not the things that be of God, but those that be of men."

There was Peter in his self-will, trusting his own wisdom, and actually forbidding Christ to go and die. Whence did that come? Peter trusted in himself and his own thoughts about divine things. We see later on, more than once, that among the disciples there was a questioning who should be the greatest, and Peter was one of them, and he thought he had a right to the very first place. He sought his own honor even above the others. It was the life of self strong in Peter. He had left his boats and his nets, but not his old self.

ANDREW MURRAY

MOODY'S STORIES

Napoleon and the Conscript

There is a well-known story told of Napoleon's time. In one of the conscriptions, during one of his many wars, a man was balloted as a conscript who did not want to go, but he had a friend who offered to go in his place. His friend joined the regiment in his name and was sent off to the war. By and by a battle came on, in which case he was killed, and they buried him on the battlefield. Some time after, the emperor wanted more men, and by mistake the first man was balloted a second time. They went to take him, but he remonstrated.

"You cannot take me."

"Why not?"

"I am dead."

"You are not dead; you are alive and well."

"But I *am* dead," he said.

"Why, man, you must be mad. Where did you die?"

"At such a battle, and you left me buried on such a battlefield."

"You talk like a madman," they cried; but the man stuck to his point that he had been dead and buried some months.

"Look it up in your books," he said, "and see if it is not so."

They looked and found that he was right. They found the man's name entered as drafted, sent to the war, and marked off as killed.

"Look here," they said, "you didn't die; you must have got someone to go for you; it must have been your substitute."

"I know that," he said; "he died in my stead. You cannot touch me; I died in that man, and I go free. The law has no claim against me."

They would not recognize the doctrine of substitution, and the case was carried to the emperor. He said that the man was right, that he was dead and buried in the eyes of the law, and that France had no claim against him.

This story may or may not be true, but one thing I know is true; Jesus Christ suffered death for the sinner, and those who accept Him are free from the law.

D. L. MOODY

THE SECRET OF GUIDANCE
How to Bear Sorrow

In sorrow the Comforter is very near, "Very present in time of trouble." He sits by the crucible, as a refiner of silver, regulating the heat, marking every change, waiting patiently for the scum to float away, and His own face to be mirrowed in clear, translucent metal. No earthly friend may tread the winepress with you, but the Savior is there, His garments stained with the blood of the grapes of your sorrow. Dare to repeat it often, though you do not feel it, and though Satan insists that God has left you, "Thou art with me." Mention His name again and again, "Jesus, *Jesus*, You are with me." So you will become conscious that He is there.

When friends come to console you they talk of time's healing touch, as though the best balm for sorrow were to forget; or in their well-meant kindness they suggest travel, diversion, amusement, and show their inability to appreciate the black night that hangs over your soul. So you turn from them sick at heart and prepared to say, as Job of his, "Miserable comforters are ye all." But all the while Jesus is nearer than they are, understanding how they wear you, knowing each throb of pain, touched by a similar feeling, silent in a love too full to speak, waiting to comfort from hour to hour as a mother her weary and suffering baby.

Be sure to study the art of this divine comfort, that you may be able to comfort them who are in any affliction with the comfort with which you yourself have been comforted of God (2 Corinthians 1:4). There can be no doubt that some trials are permitted to come to us, as to our Lord, for no other reason than that by means of them we should become able to give sympathy and comfort to others. And we should watch with all care each symptom of the pain, and each prescription of the Great Physician, since in all probability at some future time we shall be called to minister to those passing through similar experiences.

F. B. MEYER

SALVATION FROM START TO FINISH

A New Work in Us

Take the analogy of our physical life. A child is just born into the world. He has life, but it must be maintained and continued from day to day, week to week, month to month, and year to year, if he shall live; and his Creator has made provision for it. But what is true in the physical is true as well in the spiritual sense. When God begins this new work in us, He perfects it unto the day of Jesus Christ. He not only regenerated but renews from day to day, week to week, month to month, and year to year. Ah, no unsaved man need hesitate to commit himself to Jesus Christ for salvation! God not only regenerates the believer, makes him entirely over, creating within him a new heart and renewing within him a right spirit, but continually gives him a supply of the Spirit of Christ Jesus, that he may be able to please Him in all things.

This regeneration and renewing of the Holy Ghost is what God has shed upon us abundantly through Jesus Christ our Savior. You remember that John the Baptist, in witnessing to Jesus as "the Lamb of God, which taketh away the sin of the world," said that He was the one who baptized with the Holy Ghost. "Therefore being by the right hand of God exalted, and having received of the Father the promise of the Holy Ghost, he had shed forth this, which ye now see and hear." Those words were spoken by Peter on the Day of Pentecost—and from that day until this God has been pouring out the Holy Ghost as the result of the finished work of Jesus on the cross, regenerating and renewing his people.

Notice, therefore, how our change from nature to grace is the work of the triune God. There is God the Father, loving us and expressing His mercy toward us; there is God the Son, dying for us upon the cross and purchasing us with His own blood; and there is God the Holy Spirit, taking of the things of Christ and showing them to us, regenerating and renewing us in the strength of God from day to day. What a God and Savior we have! What a salvation is this that God has given us in Christ!

JAMES M. GRAY

ACCORDING TO PROMISE

Counting on God's Promises

Our duty to God demands that we accept His promise and act upon it. Every honest man has a right to our trust, and much more does the God of truth deserve it. We ought to treat the promise as in itself the substance of the thing promised, just as we look upon a man's check or note of hand as an actual payment. Promises to pay are passed from hand to hand in daily business, as if they were current money of the merchant; and God's promises should be regarded in the same light. Let us believe that we have the petitions that we have asked of Him. He warrants our so doing and promises to reward such faith.

Let us regard the promise as a thing so sure and certain that we act upon it and make it to be a chief figure in all our calculations. The Lord promises eternal life to those who believe in Jesus; therefore, if we really believe in Jesus, let us conclude that we have eternal life and rejoice in the great privilege. The promise of God is our best ground of assurance; it is far more sure than dreams and visions and fancied revelations; and it is far more to be trusted than feelings, either of joy or sorrow. It is written, "He that believeth in him is not condemned." I believe in Jesus, therefore I am not condemned. This is good reasoning, and the conclusion is certain. If God has said so, it is so, beyond all doubt. Nothing can be more certain than that which is declared by God Himself; nothing more sure to happen than that which He has guaranteed by His own hand and seal.

When a soul is under conviction, it perceives the threatenings of the Lord with an intensity of belief that is very noticeable, since its awe-stricken faith breeds within the heart overwhelming terror and dismay. Why should not the promises be accepted with a similar realization? Why not accepted with the same certainty? If it be made true in the conscience that he who believeth not shall be damned, it may be accepted with equal assurance that he that believeth and is baptized shall be saved, since the latter is as much the Word of God as the former.

CHARLES H. SPURGEON

MOODY'S STORIES
The Father Knew Best

Dr. Arnot, one of the greatest Scottish divines, was in this country before he died. His mother died when he was a little boy only three weeks old, and there was a large family of Arnots. I suppose they missed the tenderness and love of the mother. They got the impression that their father was very stern and rigid and that he had a great many laws and rules.

One rule was that the children should never climb trees. When the neighbors found out that the Arnot children could not climb trees, they began to tell them about the wonderful things they could see from the tops of the trees. Well, tell a boy of twelve years that he mustn't climb a tree, and he will get up that tree some way. And so the Arnot children were all the time teasing their father to let them climb the tree; but the old sire said, "No."

One day he was busy reading his paper, and the boys said, "Father is reading his paper. Let's slip down into the lot and climb a tree."

One of the little fellows stood on the top of the fence to see that father did not catch them. When his brother got up on the first branch, he asked, "What do you see?"

"Why, I don't see anything!"

"Then go higher; you haven't got high enough." So he went higher, and again the little boy asked, "Well, what do you see now?"

"I don't see anything."

"You aren't high enough; go higher."

And the little fellow went up as high as he could go, but he slipped, and down he came, and broke his leg. Willie said he tried to get him into the house, but he couldn't do it. He had to tell his father all about it. He said he was scared nearly out of his wits. He thought his father would be very angry. But his father just threw aside the paper and started for the lot. When he got there, he picked the boy up in his arms and brought him up to the house. Then he sent for the doctor. And Willie said he got a new view of that father. He found out the reason why that father was so stern. He said the moment that boy got hurt, no mother could have been more loving and gentle.

My dear friends, there is not one commandment that has been given us that has not been for our highest and best interest. There isn't a commandment that hasn't come from the loving heart of God, and what He wants is to have us give up that which is going to mar our happiness in this life and in the life to come.

D. L. MOODY

CHARGE THAT TO MY ACCOUNT
Scotland's Great King

My heart was stirred as I heard A. H. Stewart tell a story of Scotland's great king Robert Bruce. On one occasion he was fleeing from the English soldiers of King Edward. They were almost upon him, and he realized he was not maintaining the speed he should, so he left the path and started through the thick forest, hoping to escape. He ran mile after mile thinking that perhaps, at last, he had eluded the vengeance of his foes, when suddenly he heard a sound that caused his heart almost to stand still. It was the baying of his own bloodhounds. He knew the English had let loose his hounds and put them on their master's track, and the animals that might be supposed to be doing Robert Bruce a favor in running him down were leading his foes to the place where he was hidden. He knew now that all was over with him, unless he was able to put something between himself and the dogs to throw off the scent.

Spent and worn, he toiled on several more weary miles until he came to a clear rapid mountain stream. He plunged in and then hastened down the stream a mile or so and came out on the other side of the forest. There he hid from the sight of his pursuers and listened as the hounds came to the water and ran up and down, baying and crying out for the scent. The water had washed it away. They were unable to follow their master, and Robert Bruce escaped from the vengeance of the enemy.

Oh, my friends, there is only one stream that will wash out the scent of sin, and that is the precious blood of Christ that cleanses from all sin. All who come to Jesus, all who trust in Him, are forever free from the judgment their sins deserve. So David tells us that the time came when it was impossible for him to hide his own sin, impossible to cover his own transgression, and he says, "I acknowledged my sin unto thee, and mine iniquity have I not hid. I said, I will confess my transgressions unto the Lord; and thou forgavest the iniquity of my sin" (Psalm 32:5). We read that "If we confess our sins, he is faithful and just to forgive us our sins, and to cleanse us from all unrighteousness" (1 John 1:9).

HENRY A. IRONSIDE

CALVARY'S CROSS

The Cross and the Church

B rethren," said a North American Indian after his conversion, "I have been a heathen and know how heathens think. Once a preacher came and began to explain to us that there was a God; but we told him to return to the place from whence he came. Another preacher came and told us not to lie, steal, or drink; but we did not heed him. At last another came into my hut one day and said, 'I have come to you in the name of the Lord of heaven and earth. He sends to let you know that He will make you happy and deliver you from misery. For this end He became a man, gave His life a ransom, His blood for sinners.' I could not forget his words. I told them to the other Indians, and an awakening began among us."

I say, therefore, preach the sufferings and death of Christ our Savior if you wish your words to gain entrance among the heathen.

The cross is the foundation of a church's prosperity. No church will ever be honored in which Christ crucified is not continually lifted up. Nothing whatever can make up for the want of the cross. Without it all things may be done decently and in order. Without it there may be splendid ceremonies, beautiful music, learned ministers, crowded Communion tables, and large collections for the poor; but without the cross no good will be done. Dark hearts will not be enlightened, proud hearts will not be humbled, mourning hearts will not be comforted, fainting hearts will not be cheered.

A gorgeous banqueting room and splendid gold plate on the table will never make up to a hungry man for the want of food. Christ crucified is God's grand ordinance for doing good to men. Whenever a church keeps back Christ crucified, or puts anything whatever in that foremost place which Christ crucified should always have, from that moment the church ceases to be useful.

Without Christ crucified in her pulpits, a church is little better than a cumberer of the ground, a dead carcass, a well without water, a barren fig tree, a sleeping watchman, a silent trumpet, a speechless witness, an ambassador without terms of peace, a messenger without tidings, a lighthouse without fire, a stumbling block to weak believers, a comfort to infidels, a hot-bed for formalism, a joy to the devil, and an offense to God.

J. C. RYLE

MOODY'S LATEST SERMONS
Denominations Born in Revivals

Now I cannot for the life of me see how any man or woman who knows the Bible can throw his influence against a revival. I am amazed to find, in the history of the church, denomination after denomination setting their faces against what I call the work of God.

The Roman Catholic church claims to be apostolic. How then can they be opposed to revivals, when the Christian church was born at Pentecost? That was the mightiest revival this world has ever seen, and yet the Catholic church does not like that word "revival," although the priests hold "missions," which are the same thing.

If the Episcopal church can trace their line back to Pentecost, they too are a child of a revival. I don't see how any Episcopalian can set his face against a revival. The older the church is, the more it needs to be revived, because the tendency is into formalism.

Then where did the Lutheran church come from, if it wasn't born of a revival in the days of Martin Luther? How any Lutheran can set his face against revivals is a mystery to me. And God have mercy on a Methodist who doesn't believe in revivals, because that church sprang straight out of a revival almost in our own day. Where did Methodism come from, if not from the revival under Charles and John Wesley and George Whitefield? Wasn't the nation stirred mightily under the preaching of these men? Where did the Quakers come from if not from a revival under Fox? Is not our Young Men's Christian Association a result of the revival of '57? All our best institutions have sprung out of revivals; and yet many people are afraid of them and bring up objection after objection against them.

One popular objection is: So many converts do not hold out. That is quite true. If all the people who have professed conversion had been faithful, we would have had this world brought to Christ long before now. But, you know, I find that some ministers and elders and deacons do not hold out. If all held out, it would be contrary to scriptural experience. This argument against revivals does not bear looking into. The professed converts did not hold out in Christ's day. In John 6 we read: "Many of his disciples went back and walked no more with him."

D. L. MOODY

THE SECRET OF GUIDANCE
Realizing His Nearness

I will commune with thee from off the mercy seat." That golden slab on which Aaron sprinkled blood whenever he entered the Most Holy Place was a type of Jesus. He is the true mercy seat. And it is when you enter into deepest fellowship with Him in His death and live most constantly in the spirit of His memorial supper that you shall realize most deeply His nearness. Now, as at Emmaus, He loves to make Himself known in the breaking of bread.

"And is this all? For I have heard this many times, and still fail to live in the secret place as I would."

Exactly so; and therefore, to do for us what no effort of ours could do, our Lord has received of His Father the promise of the Holy Spirit, that He should bring into our hearts the very presence of God. Understand that since you are Christ's, the blessed Comforter is yours. He is within you as He was within your Lord, and in proportion as you live in the Spirit and walk in the Spirit and open your entire nature to Him, you will find yourself becoming His Presence-chamber, irradiated with the light of His glory. And as you realize that He is in you, you will realize that you are ever in Him. Thus John the apostle wrote, "Hereby know we that we dwell in him, and he in us, because he hath given us of his Spirit."

"All this I know, and yet I fail to realize this marvelous fact of the indwelling of the Spirit in me; how then can I ever realize my indwelling in Him?"

It is because your life is so hurried. You do not take time enough for meditation and prayer. The Spirit of God within you and the presence of God without you cannot be discerned while the senses are occupied with pleasure, or the pulse beats quickly, or the brain is filled with the tread of many hurrying thoughts. It is when water stands that it becomes transparent and reveals the pebbly beach below. Be still and know that God is within you and around! In the hush of the soul the unseen becomes visible, and the eternal becomes real. The eye dazzled by the sun cannot detect the beauties of its pavilion till it has had time to rid itself of the glare. Let no day pass without its season of silent waiting before God.

F. B. MEYER

SECRET POWER
Greater Work

The Jewish law required that there should be two witnesses, and so we find that when Peter preached there was a second witness. Peter testified of Christ, and Christ says that when the Holy Spirit comes, "He will testify of me." And they both bore witness to the truths of our Lord's incarnation, ministry, death, and resurrection, and the result was that a multitude turned as with one heart unto the Lord.

Our failure now is that preachers ignore the cross and veil Christ with sapless sermons and superfine language. They don't just present Him to the people plainly, and that is why I believe that the Spirit of God doesn't work with power in our churches. What we need is to preach Christ and present Him to a perishing world. The world can get on very well without you and me, but the world cannot get on without Christ, and therefore we must testify of Him, and the world, I believe, today is just hungering and thirsting for this divine, satisfying portion. Thousands and thousands are sitting in darkness, knowing not of this great light, but when we begin to preach Christ honestly, faithfully, sincerely and truthfully—holding Him up and not ourselves, presenting Christ and not our opinions—then the Holy Spirit will come and bear witness. He will testify that what we say is true.

The Spirit's presence is one of the strongest proofs that our gospel is divine, that it is of divine origin. Remember, when Christ was preparing to leave the world He said, "He shall glorify me," and "He will testify of me." And so the Spirit is here now, as in the days of Pentecost, when Christ was preached clearly. The message Peter preached should be the same: "Therefore let all the house of Israel know assuredly, that God hath made that same Jesus, whom ye have crucified, both Lord and Christ" (Acts 2:36). When Peter said this, the Holy Spirit descended upon the people and testified of Christ—bore witness in signal demonstration that all this was true.

D. L. MOODY

CHARGE THAT TO MY ACCOUNT
A Girl's Horror of God

A little girl who lived in Luther's day had been brought up with a perfect horror of God. She thought of Him as always watching her, taking note of every wrong thing she did, and just waiting to visit judgment upon her. Her parents could not get that fear out of her mind. Her father was a printer, and he was working on Luther's first German Bible. One day she was in his shop, when just a corner of one of the sheets of the Bible caught her eye. She looked at it, and as she read it, her whole attitude toward God changed, and she said, "Mother, I am not afraid of God anymore."

"Well, my dear," said the mother, "I am glad of that, but why are you not afraid of God?"

"Oh," she replied, "look what I found, a piece of the Bible, and it says, 'God so loved, that he gave.'" It was just a part of two lines.

"Well," her mother said, "how does that take away your fear of God? It doesn't say what He gave."

"Oh, but if He loved us enough to give anything, I am not afraid," said the child. And then her mother sat down and opened up the whole truth to her.

People are stumbling over the simplest things. Take, for instance, that word *believes*. You would think that was plain enough for anybody, but all my life I have heard people say, "I have always believed, and yet I am not saved." It does not say, "Whosoever believes the Bible or creeds or even the gospel story," but it does say, "Whosoever believes in him."

What is it to believe in Him? It means to put your soul's confidence in Him, to trust in Him, God's blessed Son. When in Toronto, I picked up a copy of a broad Scotch translation of the New Testament, and the first thing I noticed was that this word *believes* is not found there at all. Instead of *believes* there is the Scotch word, *lippen*, and it means to throw your whole weight upon. This is the way it reads, "Whosoever *lippens* to Jesus should not perish, but have the life of the ages"—the life that runs on through all the ages.

HENRY A. IRONSIDE

ABSOLUTE SURRENDER
How to Abide

What has the branch to do? You know that precious inexhaustible word that Christ used in John 10: Abide. Your life is to be an abiding life. And how is the abiding to be? It is to be just like the branch in the vine, abiding every minute of the day. There are the branches, in close communion, in unbroken communion, with the vine, from January to December. And cannot I live every day—it is to me an almost terrible thing that we should ask the question—cannot I live in abiding communion with the heavenly vine?

You say, "But I am so much occupied with other things."

You may have ten hours' hard work daily, during which your brain has to be occupied with temporal things: God orders it so. But the *abiding* work is the work of the heart, not of the brain or the muscle, the work of the heart clinging to and resting in Jesus, a work in which the Holy Spirit links us to Christ Jesus. Oh, do believe that deeper down than the brain, deep down in the inner life, you can abide in Christ, so that every moment you are free the consciousness will come: "Blessed Jesus, I am still in Thee." If you will learn for a time to put aside other work and to get into this abiding contact with the heavenly vine, you will find that fruit will come.

What is the application to our life of this abiding communion? What does it mean? It means close fellowship with Christ in secret prayer. I am sure there are Christians who do long for the higher life and who sometimes have got a great blessing and have at times found a great inflow of heavenly joy and a great outflow of heavenly gladness; and yet after a time it has passed away. They have not understood that close personal actual communion with Christ is an absolute necessity for daily life. Take time to be alone with Christ. Nothing in heaven or earth can free you from the necessity for that, if you are to be happy and holy Christians.

Many Christians look upon it as a burden and a tax and a duty and a difficulty to get much alone with God. That is the great hindrance to our Christian life everywhere. We need more quiet fellowship with God, and I tell you in the name of the heavenly vine that you cannot be healthy branches, branches into which the heavenly sap can flow, unless you take plenty of time for communion with God.

ANDREW MURRAY

GOD'S WAY OF HOLINESS

A Full Pardon

A forgiven man is the true worker, the true lawkeeper. He can, he will, he must work for God. He has come into contact with that part of God's character that warms his cold heart. Forgiving love constrains him. He cannot but work for Him who has removed his sins from him as far as the east is from the west. Forgiveness has made him a free man and given him a new and most loving master.

Forgiveness, received freely from the God and Father of our Lord Jesus Christ, acts as a spring, an impulse, a stimulus of divine potency. It is more irresistible than law or terror or threat. A half forgiveness, an uncertain justification, a changeable peace, may lead to careless living and more careless working; it may slacken the energy and freeze up the springs of action (for it shuts out that aspect of God's character that gladdens and quickens); but a complete and assured pardon can have no such effect. This is "the truth which is after godliness" (Titus 1:1). Its tendencies toward holiness and consistency of life are marvelous in their power and certainty.

Forgiveness gives a momentum thus to the soul, a momentum that owes its intensity to the entireness and sureness of the pardon. Some, in their ignorance of Scripture, as well as of the true deep springs of human action, doubt such forgiveness can occur for certain sins, and miss this freeing momentum. They think a pardon, doled out in crumbs or drops, requires that they be fruitful in good works. But the pardon is given at once, and given in such a way as to be sure even to the chief of sinners. This is a pardon worthy, both in its greatness and its freeness, of the boundless generosity of God.

HORATIUS BONAR

CALVARY'S CROSS
The Blood of the Lamb

A s I have traveled up and down Christendom, I have found out that a minister who gives a clear sound upon this doctrine is successful. A man who covers up the cross, though he may be an intellectual man and draw large crowds, will have no life there, and his church will be but a gilded sepulchre. Those who preach the doctrine of the cross and hold up Christ as the sinner's only hope of heaven and as the sinner's only substitute, God honors. Souls are always saved in the church where the blood of Christ is preached.

May God help us to make much of the blood of His Son. It cost God so much to give us His Son, and shall we try to keep Him from the world that is perishing from the want of Him? The world can get along without us, but not without Christ. Let us preach Christ in season and out of season. Let us go to the sick and dying, and hold up the Savior who came to seek and save them— who died to redeem them. "They overcame by the blood of the Lamb and the word of their testimony."

Once more, in Revelation 7:14, "These are they which came out of great tribulation, and have washed their robes and made them white in the blood of the Lamb." Sinner, how are you going to get your robes clean if you do not get them washed in the blood of the Lamb? How are you going to wash them? Can you make them clean?

I pray that at last we may all get back to the paradise above. There they are singing the sweet song of redemption. May it be the happy lot of each of us to join them. It will be a few years at the longest before we shall be there to sing the sweet song of Moses and the Lamb. But if you die without Christ, without hope and without God, where will you be? Oh, sinner, be wise, do not make light of the blood.

An aged minister of the gospel, on his dying bed, said, "Bring me the Bible." Putting his finger upon the verse, "The blood of Jesus Christ his Son cleanseth us from all sin," he said. "I die in the hope of this verse."

It was not his fifty years' preaching but the blood of Christ. May God grant that when we come at last to stand before His throne, our robes may be washed in the cleansing blood of Christ!

D. L. MOODY

GOD'S WAY OF HOLINESS

The Power of the Cross

God's description of a Christian is clear and well-defined. It has so little of the vague and wide that one wonders how so many dubious, so many false claims have appeared about what is a Christian.

A Christian is one who "has tasted the Lord is gracious" (1 Peter 2:3), who has been "begotten again unto a lively hope" (1 Peter 1:3) and "has been quickened together with Christ" (Ephesians 2:5). He has been "made partaker of Christ" (Hebrews 3:14) and a "partaker of the divine nature" (2 Peter 1:4); he "has been delivered from this present evil world" (Galatian 1:4).

Such is God's description of one who has found his way to the cross and is warranted in taking to himself the Antiochian name of "Christian," or the apostolic name of "saint." Of good about himself, previous to his receiving the record of the free forgiveness, he cannot speak. He remembers nothing lovable that could have recommended him to God; nothing fit that could have qualified him for the divine favor, save that he needed life. All that he can say for himself is that he "has known and believed the love that God hath to us" (1 John 4:16) and, in believing, has found that which makes him not merely a happy, but a holy man. He has discovered the fountain-head of a holy life.

Have I then found my way to the cross? If so, I am safe. I have the everlasting life. The first true touch of that cross has secured for me the eternal blessing. I am in the hands of Christ, and none shall pluck me from that spot (John 10:28).

The cross makes us whole; not all at once indeed, but it does the work effectually. Before we reached it we were not "whole," but broken and scattered, without a center toward which to gravitate. The cross forms that center, and in doing so, it draws together the disordered fragments of our being; it "unites our heart" (Psalm 86:11), producing a wholeness or unity that no object of less powerful attractiveness could accomplish: a wholeness or unity that, beginning with the individual, reproduces itself on a larger scale in God's holy church.

Of spiritual health, the cross is the source. From it there goes forth the "virtue" (*dunamis*, the power; Luke 6:19) that heals all maladies, be they slight or deadly. For "by his stripes we are healed" (Isaiah 53:5), and in Him we find "the tree of life," with its healing leaves (Revelation 22:2). Golgotha has become Gilead, with its skillful physician and its "bruised" balm (Jeremiah 8:22; Isaiah 53:5).

HORATIUS BONAR

SECRET POWER

Love, Peace, and Joy

When a man who has been living in sin turns from his sins and turns to God with all his heart, he is met on the threshold of the divine life by these sister graces. The love of God is shed abroad in his heart by the Holy Spirit. The peace of God comes at the same time and also the joy of the Lord. We can all put the test to ourselves, if we have them. It is not anything that we can make. The great trouble with many is that they are trying to make these graces. They are trying to make love; they are trying to make peace; they are trying to make joy. But they are not creatures of human planting. To produce them of ourselves is impossible. That is an act of God. They come from above. It is God who speaks the word and gives the love; it is God who gives the peace; it is God who gives the joy, and we possess all by receiving Jesus Christ by faith into the heart; for when Christ comes by faith into the heart, then the Spirit is there, and if we have the Spirit, we will have the fruit.

If the whole church of God could live as the Lord would have them live, why Christianity would be the mightiest power this world has ever seen. It is the low standard of Christian life that is causing so much trouble. There are a great many stunted Christians in the church; their lives are stunted; they are like a tree planted in poor soil—the soil is hard and stony, and the roots cannot find the rich loamy soil needed. Such believers have not grown in these sweet graces. Peter, in his second epistle, first chapter and fifth verse, writes:

"And besides this, giving all diligence, add to your faith, virtue; and to virtue, knowledge; and to knowledge, temperance; and to temperance, patience; and to patience, godliness; and to godliness, brotherly kindness; and to brotherly kindness, charity. For if these things be in you and abound, they make you that ye shall neither be barren nor unfruitful in the knowledge of our Lord Jesus Christ."

Now, if we have these things in us, I believe that we will be constantly bringing forth fruit that will be acceptable with God.

D. L. MOODY

ACCORDING TO PROMISE

The Peculiar Treasure of Believers

The time for the fulfillment of many a promise is not by-and-by; but by faith we realize the promise, and the foreshadowing of the expected blessing fills our souls with the benefit long before it actually comes. We have an instance of this upon a large scale in Old Testament saints. The great promise of the seed in whom the nations should be blessed was the cause of salvation to thousands of believers before the Son of God actually appeared among men. Did not our Lord say, "Abraham saw my day: he saw it and was glad?" The great father of the faithful saw the day of Christ through the telescope of God's promise, by the eye of faith; and though Abraham did not obtain the fulfillment of that promise, but fell asleep before the coming of the Lord, as did Isaac and Jacob and many others of the saints, yet he had Christ to trust in, Christ to rejoice in, and Christ to love and serve. Before He was born in Bethlehem or offered upon Calvary, Jesus was so seen of the faithful as to make them glad. The promise gave them a Savior before the Savior actually appeared.

So is it with us at this time: by means of the promise we enter into possession of things not seen as yet. By anticipation we make the coming blessing present to us. Faith obliterates time, annihilates distance, and brings future things at once into its possession. The Lord has not as yet given us to join the hallelujahs of heaven; we have not yet passed through the gates of pearl, nor have we trodden the streets of transparent gold. But the promise of such happiness lights up the gloom of our affliction and yields us immediate foretastes of glory. We triumph by faith before our hands actually grasp the palm. We reign with Christ by faith before our heads are encircled with our unfading coronets.

We have seen enough by means of the promise to make us quite sure of the glory that the Lord hath prepared for them that love Him.

CHARLES H. SPURGEON

THE SECRET OF GUIDANCE
The Fullness of the Spirit

B e prepared to let the Holy Spirit do as He will with you. The Holy Spirit is in us, and by this means Christ is in us; for He dwells in us by the Spirit, as the sun dwells in the world by means of the atmosphere vibrating with waves of light. But we must perpetually yield to Him, as water to the containing vessel. This is not easy; indeed, it can only be accomplished by incessant self-judgment, and the perpetual mortification of our own self-life.

What is our position before God in this respect? We have chosen Jesus as our substitute; but have we also chosen Him by the Holy Spirit as our life? Can we say, like the apostle Paul: "Not I, but Christ liveth in me"? If so, we must be prepared for all that it involves. We must be willing for the principle of the new life to grow at the expense of the self-life. We must consent for the one to increase, while the other decreases, through processes that are painful enough to the flesh. Nay, we must ourselves be ever on the alert, hastening the processes of judgment, condemnation, and crucifixion. We must keep true in our allegiance to the least behest of the Holy Spirit, though it cost tears of blood.

The perpetual filling of the Holy Spirit is only possible to those who obey Him and who obey Him in all things. There is nothing trivial in this life. By the neglect of slight commands, a soul may speedily get out of the sunlit circle and lose the gracious plentitude of Spirit-power. A look, a word, a refusal, may suffice to grieve Him in ourselves and to quench Him in others. Count the cost; yet do not shrink back afraid of what He may demand. He is the Spirit of love; and He loves us too well to cause grief, unless there is a reason, which we should approve if we knew as much as He.

F. B. MEYER

TEN REASONS THE BIBLE IS THE WORD OF GOD
The Authority of the Whole Bible

Many people accept the authority of Christ who do not accept that of the Bible as a whole. We all must accept His authority. He is accredited to us by five divine testimonies: by the testimony of the divine life He lived; by the testimony of the divine words He spoke; by the testimony of the divine works He wrought; by the divine proof of the resurrection from the dead; and by the testimony of His divine influence upon the history of mankind. But if we accept the authority of Christ we must accept the authority of the Bible as a whole. He testifies definitely and specifically to the divine authorship of the whole Bible.

We find His testimony as to the Old Testament in Mark 7:13. Here He calls the law of Moses the "Word of God." That, of course, covers only the first five books of the Old Testament, but in Luke 24:27 we read, "And beginning at Moses and all the prophets, he expounded unto them in *all the Scriptures* the things concerning himself," and in verse 44 He said, "All things must be fulfilled which were written in the law of Moses and in the prophets and the psalms."

The Jews divided the Old Testament into three parts—the Law, the Prophets, and the Psalms—and Christ takes up each of these parts and sets the stamp of His authority upon it. In John 10:35 Christ says, "The Scripture cannot be broken," thereby teaching the absolute accuracy and inviolability of the Old Testament. More specifically still, if possible, in Matthew 5:18, Jesus says, "One jot or one tittle shall in no wise pass from the law till all be fulfilled." A jot is the smallest letter of the Hebrew alphabet—less than half the size of any other letter, and a tittle is the merest point of a consonant—less than the cross we put on a "t"—and Christ here declares that the Scripture is absolutely true, down to the smallest letter or point of a letter. So if we accept the authority of Christ we must accept the divine authority of the entire Old Testament.

R. A. TORREY

SOWING AND REAPING

Forgiveness and Retribution

It was to Christian men that Paul said, "Be not deceived, God is not mocked; whatsoever a man soweth, that shall he also reap" (Galatians 6:7). God loves us too well not to punish His children when they sin, and He loves us too well to annihilate (were it possible) the secondary consequences of our transgressions. The two sides of the truth must be recognized—that the deeper and (as we call them) the primary penalties of our evil, which are separation from God and the painful consciousness of guilt, are swept away; and also that other results are allowed to remain, which, being allowed, may be blessed and salutary for the transgressors.

MacLaren says, "If you waste your youth, no repentance will send the shadow back upon the dial, or recover the ground lost by idleness, or restore the constitution shattered by dissipation, or give back the resources wasted upon vice, or bring back the fleeting opportunities. The wounds can all be healed, for the Good Physician . . . has lancets and bandages, and balm and anodynes for the deadliest; but scars remain even when the gash is closed."

God forgave Moses and Aaron for their sins, but both suffered the penalty. Neither one was permitted to enter the promised land. Jacob became a "prince of God" at the ford of Jabbok, but to the end of his days he carried in his body the mark of the struggle. Paul's thorn in the flesh was not removed, even after most earnest and repeated prayer. It lost its sting, however, and became a means of grace.

Perhaps that is one reason God does not remove these penalties of sin. He may intend them to be used as tokens of His chastening. "Whom the Lord loveth he chasteneth." And if the temporal consequences were completely removed we would be liable to fall back again into sin. The penalty is a continual reminder of our weakness and of the need of caution and dependence upon God.

D. L. MOODY

ACCORDING TO PROMISE

Persecution and the Promise

The envy of Ishmael displayed itself most at the great feast that had been made at his brother's weaning; and even thus do formalists, like the elder brother in the parable, become most provoked when there is most occasion for rejoicing in connection with the Father's beloved child. The music and dancing of the true family are gall and wormwood to proud base-born professors. The carnal religionist puts on a sneer and calls the godly mad, or fanatical, or murmurs with sudden sarcasm, "Poor fools! Let them alone; they are a sadly deluded crew." People who are religious but not truly regenerated, who are working and hoping to be saved by their own merits, usually exhibit a bitter hatred toward those who are born of the promise.

Sometimes they mock their feebleness. Maybe Ishmael called Isaac a mere baby, just weaned. So are believers a feeble folk and exceedingly likely to excite the derision of those who think themselves strong-minded. Isaac could not deny that he was weak, neither can believers deny that they are faulty and are subject to infirmities that may put them under just censure: but the world makes more of this than justice will allow and mocks at saints for weaknesses that in others would be overlooked. We must not think it a strange thing if our insignificance and imperfection should set proud and self-righteous Pharisees jeering at us and our gospel.

Frequently the sport is raised by the believer's pretensions. Isaac was called "the heir," and Ishmael could not bear to hear it. "Look," says the legalist, "yonder man was not long ago a known sinner; now he says he has believed in Jesus Christ, and therefore he declares that he knows himself to be saved and accepted and sure of heaven. Did you ever hear of such presumption?" He who hugs his chains hates the presence of a free man. He who refuses the mercy of God because he proudly trusts his own merits is angry with the man who rejoices to be saved by grace.

CHARLES H. SPURGEON

CHARGE THAT TO MY ACCOUNT

The Way to Eternal Life

He that believeth on the Son hath everlasting life: and he that believeth not the Son, shall not see life; but the wrath of God abideth on him" (John 3:36).

People say, "Oh, Paul or John or Peter may have believed this doctrine of eternal judgment for sin, but give me the words of Jesus, Jesus, the loving, gentle, tender, gracious Galilean teacher, let me hear what Jesus says; His Word will be enough for me." Listen, my dear friends, no one ever spoke as seriously and as solemnly of the eternal consequences of sin as Jesus did. It is He who said, "If thine eye offend thee, pluck it out, and cast it from thee: it is better for thee to enter into life with one eye, rather than having two eyes to be cast into hell fire" (Matthew 18:9). It is Jesus who speaks so solemnly over and over again of that awful pit of woe, "where their worm dieth not, and the fire is not quenched" (Mark 9:48).

Moreover, of Judas Christ said, "It had been good for that man if he had not been born." If there is any possibility of Judas ever being saved, even after the lapse of countless ages of misery, I submit that it would be good for him that he had been born. But Jesus said, "Good for that man if he had not been born." That man sold his Savior! He companied with Jesus for three and one-half years, and yet he sinned against the Holy Ghost in rejecting Christ. You have heard the gospel over and over again, and if you should reject Him too, could it not be said of you, "Good for that man if he had not been born"?

But now it is Jesus again who utters these words, "He that believeth on the Son hath everlasting life." You cannot find fault with the love of God, for it gave Christ and thereby provided a way of salvation. God is not holding you responsible because you are a sinner; you were born a sinner. You are not responsible because you have a sinful nature; you cannot help that. God is not going to cast you away from His presence simply because that corrupt nature has manifested itself in sin, for Christ has put away sin, and any man who will may be saved from his sin through the atoning work of the Lord Jesus Christ and receive a new nature. Why are men lost? The answer is clear: "He that believeth not the Son shall not see life; but the wrath of God abideth on him."

HENRY A. IRONSIDE

SOWING AND REAPING

A Warning

No matter how painful it may be, break with sin at once. Severe operations are often necessary, for the skillful surgeon knows that the disease cannot be cured by surface applications. The farmer takes his hoe and his spade and his axe, and he cuts away the obnoxious growths and burns the roots out of the ground with fire.

If your right eye offend you, pluck it out, as Christ says, and cast it away, for it is better for you that one of your members should perish, rather than your whole body should be cast into hell. And if your right hand offend thee, cut it off and cast it from you rather than that your whole body should be cast into hell.

Remember that the tares and the wheat will be separated at the judgment day, if not before. Sowing to the flesh and sowing to the spirit inevitably lead in diverging paths. The axe will be laid at the root of the trees, and every tree that brings not forth good fruit will be hewn down and cast into the fire. The threshing-floor will be thoroughly purged, and the wheat will be gathered into the garner, while the chaff will be burned with unquenchable fire.

Beware of your habits. A recent writer has said: "Could the young but realize how soon they will become mere walking bundles of habits, they would give more heed to their conduct while in the plastic state. We are spinning our own fates, good or evil, and never to be undone. Every smallest stroke of virtue or of vice leaves its ever-so-little scar. The drunken Rip Van Winkle, in Jefferson's play, excuses himself for every fresh dereliction by saying, "I won't count this time." Well, he may not count it, and a kind heaven may not count it, but it is being counted nonetheless. Down among his nerve cells and fibers the molecules are counting it, registering and storing it up, to be used against him when the next temptation comes.

D. L. MOODY

GOD'S WAY OF HOLINESS
The Study of God's Word

The Word must be studied in all its fullness. Over its whole length and breadth we must spread ourselves. Above all theologies, and creeds, and catechisms, and books, and hymns, must the Word be meditated on, that we may grow in the knowledge of all its parts and in assimilation to its models. Our souls must be steeped in it; not in certain favorite parts of it, but in the whole. We must know it, not from the report of others but from our own experience and vision, else will our life be but an imitation, our religion second-hand and therefore second-rate. Another cannot breathe the air for us, nor eat for us, nor drink for us. We must do these for ourselves. So no one can do our religion for us, nor infuse into us the life or truth he may possess. These are not things of proxy or merchandise or human impartation.

Out of the book of God and by the Spirit of God must each one of us be taught, else we learn in vain. Hence the exceeding danger of human influence or authority. A place of influence in such a case becomes perilous alike to the possessor of the influence and to those over whom that sway is wielded. Even when altogether on the side of truth, its issue may be but an unfruitful formalism, a correct petrifaction, an intelligent orthodoxy.

Thus both they who possess the influence or are under its power ought to be greatly on their guard lest the human supplant the divine, and the "fear of God be taught by the precept of men" (Isaiah 29:13), lest an artificial piety be the result, a mere facsimile religion, without vitality, without comfort, and without influence.

HORATIUS BONAR

THE TRUE VINE
Proof of Friendship

O ur Lord has said what He gave as proof of His friendship: He gave His life for us. He now tells us what our part is to be—to do the things He commands. "Ye are my friends, if ye do the things which I command you" (John 15:14). He gave His life to secure a place for His love in our hearts to rule us; the response His love calls us to, and empowers us for, is that we do what He commands us. As we know the dying love, we shall joyfully obey its commands. As we obey the commands, we shall know the love more fully. Christ had already said: "If ye keep my commandments, ye shall abide in my love." He counts it needful to repeat the truth again: the one proof of our faith in His love, the one way to abide in it, the one mark of being true branches is to do the things He commands us.

He began with absolute surrender of His life for us. He can ask nothing less from us. This alone is a life in His friendship.

This truth of the imperative necessity of obedience, doing all that Christ commands us, has not the place in our Christian teaching and living that Christ meant it to have. We have given a far higher place to privilege than to duty. We have not considered implicit obedience as a condition of true discipleship. The secret thought that it is impossible to do the things He commands us, and that therefore it cannot be expected of us, and a subtle and unconscious feeling that sinning is a necessity have frequently robbed both precepts and promises of their power. The whole relation to Christ has become clouded and lowered, the waiting on His teaching, the power to hear and obey His voice, and through obedience to enjoy His love and friendship, have been enfeebled by the terrible mistake.

Do let us try to return to the true position, take Christ's words as most literally true, and make nothing less of the law of our life: "Ye are my friends, if ye do the things that I command you." Surely our Lord asks nothing less than that we heartily and truthfully say, "Yea, Lord, what You command, that will I do."

These commands are to be done as a proof of friendship. The power to do them rests entirely in the personal relationship to Jesus.

ANDREW MURRAY

CHARGE THAT TO MY ACCOUNT

Dreams That Will Never Come True

Another dream that will never come true is the dream that if you do the best you can, if you live a respectable life, if you join the church, if you give your money for the cause of Christ, then when you die you will go to heaven on your own merit. That is the worst dream of all, and in eternity men who have died trusting in something of that character will be "even as when an hungry man dreameth, and behold, he eateth: but he awaketh, and his soul is empty."

Mark this! God has provided the bread of life whereby, if a man eat thereof, he shall live forever. The Lord Jesus Christ said, "I am the living bread which came down from heaven: if any man eat of this bread, he shall live forever: and the bread that I will give is my flesh, which I will give for the life of the world" (John 6:51). What is it to eat Christ? It is this, to receive Him into your inmost being. Just as you take food and receive it into your physical body, so take Christ. When by faith you receive Him into your own life and heart, you are eating the living bread and will never waken to find out that this is all a dream.

People of the world think that Christians are dreamers. Thirty years ago when I was a Salvation Army officer, they were having a street meeting, and a poor fellow who had been deep in sin, but wonderfully converted, was standing out on the street telling what the Lord had done for him. A great big burly man in the crowd suddenly shouted out: "Wake up, old man, wake up; you're dreaming!"

At that a little girl stepped up to him and said, "Oh, please sir, please don't wake him up. That is my daddy, and he is such a good daddy now. But he used to be so different before he began to 'dream,' as you call it. He was always beating mother, he spent all his money for drink, and we were so miserable; but when he began to 'dream' like this, everything was different. He brings his money home now and provides for us all. He is so kind to mother and to all of us, and we want him just like he is now."

Oh yes, the world thinks it is the Christian, the believer, who is the dreamer, but we know that it is the Christ-rejecter who is dreaming. The un-saved man who hopes that everything is going to come out all right, when in reality it is all wrong and will be so for all eternity, unless he turns to Christ, is the real dreamer. Be persuaded that there is no other Savior but Jesus; there is no other way but His way. May it be today that God is awakening you out of your dreams. You have never found peace in the world, and you never will, for that is the dream. Why not come to Christ?

HENRY A. IRONSIDE

ACCORDING TO PROMISE

The Parting

Ishmael and Isaac represent deliverance by work versus by promise. As the two men ultimately parted, so the principles they represent must never be mingled, for they can by no means be made to agree. We cannot be saved in part by self and in part by the promise of God. The principle and notion of earning salvation must be expelled from the mind. Every degree and form of it must be "cast out." If we are so unwise as to place our dependence partly on grace and partly on merit, we shall be resting one foot on a rock and the other on the sea, and our fall will be certain.

There can be no dividing of the work or of the glory of salvation. It must be all of grace or all of works, all of God or all of man; but it cannot be half of one and half of the other. Cease from the vain attempt to unite two principles that are as adverse as fire and water. The promise, and the promise alone, must be the foundation of our hope, and all legal notions must be sternly dismissed as irreconcilable with salvation by grace.

We must not begin in the spirit and hope to be made perfect in the flesh. Our religion must be all of a piece. To sow with mingled seed, or to wear a garment of linen and woolen mixed, was forbidden to the Lord's ancient people; and to us it is unlawful to mingle mercy and merit, grace and debt. Whenever the notion of salvation by merit or feeling or ceremonies comes in, we must cast it out without delay, though it be as dear to us as Ishmael was to Abraham. Faith is not sight, the spirit is not the flesh, and grace is not merit; and we must never forget the distinction, lest we fall into grievous error and miss the heritage that belongs only to the heirs according to promise.

Here is our confession of faith: "Knowing that a man is not justified by the works of the law, but by the faith of Jesus Christ, even we have believed in Jesus Christ, that we might be justified by the faith of Christ, and not by the works of the law: for by the works of the law shall no flesh be justified" (Galatians 2:16).

CHARLES H. SPURGEON

SECRET POWER
The Secret of Joy

It is the privilege, I believe, of every Christian to walk in the light, as God is in the light, and to have that peace that will be flowing unceasingly as we keep busy about His work. And it is our privilege to be full of the joy of the Lord. We read that when Philip went down to Samaria and preached, there was great joy in the city. Why? Because they believed the glad tidings. And that is the natural order, joy in believing. When we believe the glad tidings, there comes a joy into our souls. Also we are told that our Lord sent the seventy out and that they went forth preaching salvation in the name of Jesus Christ, and the result was that there were a great many who were blessed; and the seventy returned, it says, with great joy, even making the very devils subject to them through His name. The Lord seemed to just correct them in this one thing when He said, "Rejoice not that the devils are subject to you, but rejoice that your names are written in heaven." There is assurance for you. They had something to rejoice in now.

God doesn't ask us to rejoice over nothing, but He gives us some ground for our joy. What would you think of a man or woman who seemed very happy today and full of joy and couldn't tell you what made him or her so? Suppose I should meet a man on the street and he was so full of joy that he should get hold of both my hands and say, "Bless the Lord, I am so full of joy!"

"What makes you so full of joy?"

"Well, I don't know."

"You don't know?"

"No, I don't; but I am so joyful that I just want to get out of the flesh."

Despite my attempts to find out why he feels so joyful, his answer still remains, "I don't know." Would we not think such a person unreasonable? But there are a great many people who feel—who want to feel—that they are Christians before they are Christians; they want the Christian's experience before they become Christians; they want to have the joy of the Lord before they receive Jesus Christ. But this is not the gospel order. He brings joy when He comes, and we cannot have joy apart from Him; there is no joy away from Him; He is the author of it, and we find our joy in Him.

D. L. MOODY

FIT FOR THE MASTER'S USE
A Time of Temptation

This is a life in which we are kept in time of temptation. You will be tempted to the end of your life, and the nearer you live to Christ the more you will be tempted. After Jesus had seen the open heaven He was led into the wilderness to be tempted of the devil; the man who sees the heavenly vision is the man whom the devil will tempt to the uttermost. God will permit it because temptation does for us what the storms do for the oaks—it roots us—and what the fire does for the painting on porcelain—it makes us permanent. You never know that you have a grip on Christ, or that He has a grip on you so well as when the devil is using all his force to attract you from Him; then you feel the pull of Christ's right hand.

As long as the soldier slinks outside the battle, he faces little danger, but let him plunge in and follow the captain and he will soon have the bullets flying about him. Some of us have had a good time because there was no use in the devil wasting powder and shot upon us; we haven't been doing him any harm. But once we begin to wake up and set to work for God, the devil will set a thousand evils to worrying us.

Children never break into an orchard when the apples are sour, but always when they are ripe and juicy; one can know that a certain orchard contains good fruit by the raids the boys make on it. Similarly, if you are acrid and sour, the devil will not worry you; there is nothing in you worth his attack. But just as soon as you have been in the summering of Christ's love and got ripe, you will suffer being tempted day and night, for there will be something worth the stealing.

The nearer you get to Christ the more you will have to do with temptation. The closer you get into the heart of the fight the more the devil will torment you. People are sometimes heard to say, "I think I must be retreating in the Christian life, I am so tempted." But the virulence of the temptation means not that you are declining into sin, but that you are advancing in holiness; that the devil is afraid of you and hopes only to wound Christ by hurting you.

F. B. MEYER

ABSOLUTE SURRENDER

Impossible with Man, Possible with God

Your religious life is every day to be a proof that God works impossibilities; your religious life is to be a series of impossibilities made possible and actual by God's almighty power. That is what the Christian needs. He has an almighty God that he worships, and he must learn to understand that he does not need a little of God's power, but he needs—with reverence be it said— the whole of God's omnipotence to keep him right and to live like a Christian.

The whole of Christianity is a work of God's omnipotence. Look at the birth of Christ Jesus. That was a miracle of divine power, and it was said to Mary: "With God nothing shall be impossible." It was the omnipotence of God. Look at Christ's resurrection. We are taught that it was according to the exceeding greatness of His mighty power that God raised Christ from the dead.

Every tree must grow on the root from which it springs. An oak tree three hundred years old grows all the time on the one root from which it had its beginning. Christianity had its beginning in the omnipotence of God, and in every soul it must have its continuance in that omnipotence. All the possibilities of the higher Christian life have their origin in a new apprehension of Christ's power to work all God's will in us.

I want to call upon you now to come and worship an almighty God. Have you learned to do it? Have you learned to deal so closely with an almighty God that you know omnipotence is working in you? In outward appearance there is often little sign of it. The apostle Paul said: "I was with you in weakness and in fear and in much trembling, and . . . my preaching was . . . in demonstration of the Spirit and of power." From the human side there was feebleness, from the divine side there was divine omnipotence. And that is true of every godly life; and if we would only learn that lesson better, and give a whole-hearted, undivided surrender to it, we should learn what blessedness there is in dwelling every hour and every moment with an almighty God.

ANDREW MURRAY

CHARGE THAT TO MY ACCOUNT

The Chains of Sin

There was no resistance on Peter's part. The message came, "Get up!" and Peter obeyed immediately. Only a little while before that word would have meant nothing to him, but now he is awake. When men and women are awakened, the message comes: "Believe the Word; arise, He calleth thee."

Then his chains fell off. Do you want to be delivered from your chains? Believe the Word! I have a friend who years ago was a victim of that dreadful habit of smoking and eating opium. He had fallen into that vice when very young, and the thing had gotten such a grip on him that he could not break it. At last, at twenty-two years of age, he was such a wreck that he had made up his mind that he might as well end it all by suicide, for there was no hope for him. But one night in Fresno, California, he was going down the street, crying out, "What a fool I have been to form a habit like this that I cannot free myself from," when he heard a little group of Salvation Army folk singing, "He breaks the power of canceled sin, he sets the prisoner free; His blood can make the foulest clean, His blood availed for me."

He said, "What's that?" They sang it again. That poor young fellow stood there trembling, for he had hardly strength enough to stand erect. "I wonder if it is true—'the foulest'—that's me!" and he followed them into their hall. When they invited sinners to come to Christ, he went forward and knelt at the penitent bench, but he was so loathsome that they said, "Oh, he is too far gone." However, they were faithful and knelt with him and pointed him to Christ. By and by, as he arose, he said, "I will trust Him," and went away. One of them said to another, "You better go and see if he has any lodging tonight; he has no will power, there is no hope for him, if he gets away." Somebody did take an interest in him; he got him a lodging and helped him in other ways.

When he put his trust in Christ, he was delivered, and he has often testified since, "I am free; Christ has delivered me; I never even had a struggle to get rid of that habit." In two weeks you would not have known him. He was a new creature, physically, mentally, and every way. Whatever your sins are, come to Christ, trust in Him, and find deliverance. Peter's bonds fell off; he was freed from his chains—you too may be free.

HENRY A. IRONSIDE

GOD'S WAY OF HOLINESS
The True Creed and True Life

When the body's nervous system falls into disorder, often Satan (through this inlet) enters the soul and perplexes the conscience; magnifying fancied sin, making men mistake a disease for a tender conscience. But this ought not to lead to the disparagement of thorough conscientiousness in little things as well as great, in business, in the ordering of our households, in the laying out of our time and our money, in keeping promises, in bearing witness for Christ, in nonconformity to the world.

The man who knows that he is risen with Christ and has set his affection on things above will be a just, trustworthy, unselfish, truthful man. He will "add to his faith virtue, and to virtue knowledge, and to knowledge temperance, and to temperance patience, and to patience godliness, and to godliness brotherly kindness, and to brotherly kindness charity" (2 Peter 1:5-7). He will seek not to be "barren nor unfruitful." "Whatsoever things are true, whatsoever things are honest, whatsoever things are just, whatsoever things are pure, whatsoever things are lovely, whatsoever things are of good report," these he will think upon and do.

For there is some danger of falling into a soft Christianity, under the plea of a lofty and ethereal theology. Christianity was born for endurance; it is not an exotic, but a hardy plant, braced by the keen wind; not languid, nor childish, nor cowardly. It walks with strong step and erect frame; it is kindly, but firm; it is gentle, but honest; it is calm, but not facile; decided, but not churlish. It does not fear to speak the stern word of condemnation against error, nor to raise its voice against surrounding evils, knowing that it is not of this world. It does not shrink from giving honest reproof, lest it come under the charge of displaying an unchristian spirit. It calls sin *sin*, on whomsoever it is found, and would rather risk the accusation of being motivated by a bad spirit than not discharge an explicit duty. Let us not misjudge strong words used in honest controversy. The religion of both Old and New Testament is marked by fervent outspoken testimonies against evil. To speak smooth things in such a case may be sentimentalism, but it is not Christianity. It is a betrayal of the cause of truth and righteousness.

If anyone should be frank, manly, honest, cheerful (I do not say blunt or rude, for a Christian must be courteous and polite), it is he who has tasted that the Lord is gracious and is looking for and hasting unto the coming of the day of God.

HORATIUS BONAR

ALL OF GRACE

Kept by the Power of God

In some there is a painful fear that they shall not persevere in grace because they know their own fickleness. Certain persons are constitutionally unstable. Some men are by nature conservative, not to say obstinate; but others are as naturally variable and volatile. Like butterflies, they flit from flower to flower, till they visit all the beauties of the garden and settle upon none of them. They are never long enough in one stay to do any good, not even in their business nor in their intellectual pursuits. Such persons may well be afraid that ten, twenty, thirty, forty, perhaps fifty years of continuous religious watchfulness will be a great deal too much for them. We see men joining first one church and then another, till they box the compass. They are everything by turns and nothing long. Such have double need to be made not only steadfast but unmovable, or otherwise they will not be found "always abounding in the work of the Lord."

All of us, even if we have no constitutional temptation to fickleness, must feel our own weakness if we are really made alive by God. Dear reader, do you not find enough in any one single day to make you stumble? You that desire to walk in perfect holiness, as I trust you do; you that have set before you a high standard of what a Christian should be—do you not find that before the breakfast things are cleared away from the table, you have displayed enough folly to make you ashamed of yourselves? If we were to shut ourselves up in the lone cell of a hermit, temptation would follow us; for as long as we cannot escape from ourselves we cannot escape from incitements to sin. There is that within our hearts which should make us watchful and humble before God. If He does not confirm us, we are so weak that we shall stumble and fall, not overturned by an enemy but by our own carelessness. Lord, be our strength. We are weakness itself.

Besides that, there is the weariness that comes of a long life. When we begin our Christian profession, we mount up with wings as eagles, further on we run without weariness; but in our best and truest days we walk without fainting. Our pace seems slower, but it is more serviceable and better sustained. I pray God that the energy of our youth may continue with us so far as it is the energy of the Spirit and not the mere fermentation of proud flesh.

CHARLES H. SPURGEON

FIT FOR THE MASTER'S USE
New Clothing

There must be the removal of the filthy garments. I am not sure that Joshua saw how filthy they were until he came near the angel. The light from the angel's face fell on his garments and revealed their stains. The garment always stands for habit or dress. We are dealing now with our daily habits.

It is remarkable how people change their dress when the sun begins to shine in March and April. We wear shabby things in the winter. We say it does not matter much what we wear; who sees? The light is so obscure. But as the spring breaks, we put off the shabby dress and put on the spring attire. So it is when we stand beneath the light that streams from the Sun of Righteousness; we see a great many shabby things in our lives, and God calls upon us to drop them without discussion or delay.

We do not grow out of them, but we drop them. We do not gradually recede from them, but we put them off. It is remarkable that in Peter's epistle and in Colossians and Ephesians, the apostles tell us to put off suddenly the habit of sin. You will not grow out of your anger, you must put it off. You will not grow out of your envy and jealousy, you must put them off. You will not grow out of your impurity, you must put it off. As when a prisoner comes forth to freedom he puts off the prison clothes, so you must not wait to grow out of evil things but must put them off by a distinct and instantaneous act of your will.

I trust that, by the grace and Spirit of God, you will take step by step with me as I proceed. I am not trying merely to explain a thing to you. I am giving you an opportunity of taking up a position; and I want you to ask, in the light of God's Spirit, if there is any habit of thought or life or any habitual indulgence in which you are condemned, which always arises before you at a holy time, such as the Lord's Supper, in private prayer or in the chamber of sickness; and if at this minute any such thing is revealed to you, I bid you, put it off.

Have you ever studied the life of the evergreen? All through the dark winter it retains its dead, dull leaves; they are better than nothing. But just so soon as the new shoot of spring comes, it presses off the old leaves, and they drop away to be replaced by the new.

So in your heart today there is a shoot of new Christ-life which is pressing against the old leaves, the old habits, the old methods of life.

F. B. MEYER

FULL ASSURANCE

What if You Don't "Feel" Different?

It is a remarkable fact that the word "feel" is found only once in the King James Version of the New Testament, and that is in Paul's sermon to the Athenians (Acts 17). There he rebukes the Greeks for imagining the Godhead to be like unto silver and gold and shows that the true God is the Creator of all things, "and hath made of one blood all nations of men for to dwell on all the face of the earth, and hath determined the times before appointed, and the bounds of their habitation; that they should seek the Lord, if haply they might feel after him, and find him, though he be not far from every one of us: for in him we live, and move, and have our being; as certain also of your own poets have said, For we are also his offspring" (verses 26–28).

The word *feel* appears in the very midst of this passage, but it has nothing to do with the gospel, but rather with the heathen groping in the dark: "if haply they might feel after God." We, however, are not in their ignorant condition. We have heard the gospel. We know of the one living and true God. We are not told to feel anything but to believe His record.

Then it may interest you to know that the word *feeling* is only found twice in the New Testament and never has anything to do with the message of salvation. In Ephesians 4:19 the Spirit of God describes the state of certain unbelieving Gentiles in these words: "Who being past feeling have given themselves over unto lasciviousness, to work all uncleanness with greediness." This is what continual indulgence in sin does for people. They become insensate—"past feeling"—and so conscience ceases to register, as they plunge into one excess and enormity after another.

The only other place where we read of *feeling* is in a very different connection. In Hebrews 4:15 our blessed Lord Himself is described as having empathy for our infirmities: "For we have not an high priest which cannot be touched with the feeling of our infirmities; but was in all points tempted like as we are, yet without sin."

Nowhere else do we read of feeling in all the New Testament! But oh, how many times we read of believing, of faith, of trust, of confidence! Yes, these are the words for us. Ignore your feelings altogether, and tell the Lord Jesus now that you will trust Him and confess Him before men.

HENRY A. IRONSIDE

TEN REASONS THE BIBLE IS THE WORD OF GOD

The Superior Teachings of the Bible

I t is quite fashionable in some quarters to compare the teachings of the Bible with the teachings of Zoroaster, and Buddha, and Confucius, and Epictetus, and Socrates, and Marcus Aurelius Antoninus, and a number of other heathen authors. The difference between the teachings of the Bible and those of these men is found in three points—

First, the Bible has in it nothing but truth, while all others have truth mixed with error. It is true that Socrates taught how a philosopher ought to die; he also taught how a woman of the town ought to conduct her business. Jewels there are in the teachings of these men, but (as Joseph Cook once said) they are "jewels picked out of the mud."

Second, the Bible contains *all* truth. There is not a truth to be found anywhere on moral or spiritual subjects that you cannot find in substance within the covers of that old Book. I have often, when speaking upon this subject, asked anyone to bring me a single truth on moral or spiritual subjects, which, upon reflection, I could not find within the covers of this book, and no one has ever been able to do it. I have taken pains to compare some of the better teachings of infidels with those of the Bible. They indeed have jewels of thought, but they are, whether they knew it or not, stolen jewels, and stolen from the very book they ridicule.

The *third* point of superiority is this: the Bible contains more truth than all other books put together. Get together from all literature of ancient and modern times all the beautiful thoughts you can; put away all the rubbish; put all these truths that you have culled from the literature of all ages into one book, and even then you will not have a book that will take the place of this one book.

This is not a large book. I hold in my hand a copy that I carry in my vest pocket, and yet in this one little book there is more of truth than in all the books that man has produced in all the ages of his history. How will you account for it? There is only one rational way. This is not man's book, but God's book.

R. A. TORREY

PRACTICAL AND PERPLEXING QUESTIONS ANSWERED

Heaven

Some question whether heaven is a place or a state of the soul. Jesus Christ plainly declares that heaven is a place. In John 14:2 He says: "I go to prepare a *place* for you," and to make it even more plain He adds in the next verse that when the place is prepared He will come again and receive us unto Himself, that *where* He is we may be also.

Let's consider how the Scriptures describe heaven. Heaven is a place more beautiful than any of us can conceive. In our present state every sense and faculty of perception is blunted by sin and the disease that results from sin. In our redeemed bodies every sense and faculty will receive enlargement and exist in perfection. There may be new senses, but what they may be we cannot now imagine. The fairest sights that we have ever beheld on earth are nothing in beauty to what will greet us in that fair "city that hath no foundations."

Heaven will be free from everything that curses or mars our lives here. There will be no servile grinding toil, no sickness or pain (Revelation 21:4), no death, no funerals, and no separations. Above all, there will be no sin. It will be a place of universal and perfect knowledge (1 Corinthians 13:12), of universal and perfect love (1 John 3:2; 4:8), and of perpetual praise (Revelation 7:9–12). It will be a land of melody and song.

There is just one thing that anyone needs to do to get to heaven, that is, to accept Jesus Christ as his personal Savior, surrender to Him as his Lord and Master, and openly confess Him before the world. Jesus Christ says: "I am the way, the truth, and the life. No man cometh unto the Father but by me" (John 14:6). Again He says: "I am the door. By me if any man enter in he shall be saved" (John 10:9). Any one who receives Jesus becomes at once a child of God, an heir of God, a joint-heir with Jesus Christ (John 1:12; Romans 8:16, 17).

Anyone can know whether he is already on the way to heaven or not by simply asking himself the questions:

"Have I received Jesus Christ? Have I taken Him as my Sin-bearer, the One who bore my sins in His own body on the cross (Isaiah 53:6; 1 Peter 2:24; Galatians 3:13)? Am I trusting God to forgive my sins because Jesus bore them for me?" If any one can answer yes to these simple questions he may know he is on the way to heaven.

R. A. TORREY

ABSOLUTE SURRENDER

O Wretched Man That I Am

He is utterly unhappy and miserable; and what is it that makes him so utterly miserable? It is because God has given him a nature that loves Himself. He is deeply wretched because he feels he is not obeying his God. He says, with brokenness of heart, "It is not I that do it, but I am under the awful power of sin, which is holding me down. It is I, and yet not I: alas! it is myself; so closely am I bound up with it, and so closely is it intertwined with my very nature." Blessed be God when a man learns to say: "O wretched man that I am!" from the depth of his heart. He is on the way to the eighth chapter of Romans.

There are many who make this confession a pillow for sin. They say that Paul had to confess his weakness and helplessness in this way; what are they that they should try to do better? So the call to holiness is quietly set aside. Would God that every one of us has learned to say these words in the very spirit in which they are written here! When we hear sin spoken of as the abominable thing that God hates, do not many of us wince before the word? Would that all Christians who go on sinning and sinning would take this verse to heart. If ever you utter a sharp word say: "O wretched man that I am!" And every time you lose your temper, kneel down and understand that it was never meant by God that this was to be the state in which His child should remain. Instead, we are to take this word into our daily life and say it every time we are touched about our own honor, and every time we say sharp things, and every time we sin against the Lord God and against His self-sacrifice. Forget everything else and cry out: "O wretched man that I am! Who shall deliver me from the body of this death?"

Why should you say this whenever you commit sin? Because it is when a man is brought to this confession that deliverance is at hand.

And remember it was not only the sense of being impotent and taken captive that made him wretched, but it was above all the sense of sinning against his God. The law was doing its work, making sin exceedingly sinful in his sight. The thought of continually grieving God became utterly unbearable—it was this that brought forth the piercing cry: "O wretched man!"

ANDREW MURRAY

ANSWERS TO PRAYER

He Has Never Failed

October 21, 1868—As the days come, we make known our requests to Him, for our outgoings have now been for several years at the rate of more than one hundred pounds each day; but though the expenses have been so great, He has never failed us. We have been, as to the outward appearance, like the "Burning Bush in the Wilderness"; yet we have not been consumed. Moreover, we are full of trust in the Lord, and therefore of good courage, though we have before us the prospect, that, year by year, our expenses will increase more and more.

If all my beloved fellow disciples, who seek to work for God, knew the blessedness of looking truly to God alone, and trusting in Him alone, they would soon see how soul refreshing this way is, and how entirely beyond disappointment, so far as He is concerned. Earthly friends may alter their minds regarding the work in which we are engaged; but if indeed we work for God, whoever may alter his mind regarding our service, He will not. Earthly friends may lose their ability to help us, however much they may desire so to do; but He remains throughout eternity the infinitely rich one. Earthly friends may have their minds after a time diverted to other objects, and, as they cannot help everywhere, much as they may desire it, they may have to discontinue to help us; but He is able, in all directions, though the requirements were multiplied a million times, to supply all that can possibly be needed. And He does it with delight, where His work is carried on and where He is confided in. Earthly friends may be removed by death, and thus we may lose their help, but He lives for ever; He cannot die.

In this latter point of view I have especially, during the past forty years, in connection with this institution, seen the blessedness of trusting in the living God alone. Not one nor two, nor even five or ten, but many more, who once helped me much with their means, have been removed by death; but have the operations of the institution been stopped on that account? No. And how came this? Because I trusted in God, and in Him alone.

GEORGE MUELLER

THE SCHOOL OF OBEDIENCE

A Note on the Morning Watch

Christ asked great sacrifices of His disciples; He has perhaps asked little of you as yet. But now He allows, He invites, He longs for you to make some. Sacrifices make strong men. Sacrifices help wonderfully to wrench us away from earth and self-pleasing and lift us heavenward. Do not try to pare down the time limit of the morning watch to less than the half-hour. There can be no question about the possibility of finding the time. Ten minutes from sleep, ten from company or amusement, ten from lessons. How easy where the heart is right, hungering to know God and His will perfectly!

If you feel that you do not need so much time and know not how to wait, we are content you should speak of your quiet time or your hour of prayer. God may graciously, later on, draw you out to the morning watch. But do not undertake it unless you feel your heart stirred with the determination to make a sacrifice and have full time for intimate intercourse with God. But if you are ready to do this, we urge you to join. The very fact of setting apart such a period helps to awaken the feeling: I have a great work to do, and I need time for it. It strengthens in your heart the conviction: "If I am to be kept all this day without sin I must have time to get near to God." It will give your Bible study new point, as you find time, between the reading, to be still and bow in humility for the Holy Spirit's hidden working, and wait till you get some real apprehension of God's will for you through the Word. And, by the grace of God, it may help you to begin that habit of specific intercession of which the church so surely stands in need.

Students! You know not whether in your future life your time may be more limited, your circumstances more unfavorable, your Christian earnestness feebler. Now is the accepted time. Today, as the Holy Ghost says. Listen to the invitation of your brothers in all lands, and fear not to form an undiscouragable resolution to spend at least half an hour each morning with God alone.

ANDREW MURRAY

ACCORDING TO PROMISE

Whose Are the Promises?

He has chosen to make His promises to elect persons, who in process of time are discovered by their exercising faith in Him. Those whom God has chosen are led by the Holy Spirit to choose God and His way of salvation by faith in Christ Jesus. Those of the elect who come to years of discretion are led to faith in Jesus; and all who have faith in Him may conclude beyond doubt that they are of the chosen number to whom the promises are given. To those who live and die in unbelief there is no absolute and personal promise of God: they are not under grace but under law, and to them belong the threatenings and not the promises. These prefer another method of dealing to that of gracious promise, and in the end they perish as the result of their foolish preference. The chosen of the Lord are led to relinquish the proud way of self and merit; they take to the road of faith, and so find rest unto their souls. To believe the Word of God and to trust in Him whom God has sent to be our Savior may seem a small thing; but indeed it is not so. It is the sign of election, the token of regeneration, the mark of coming glory. So to believe that God is true as to rest one's eternal interests upon His promise bespeaks a heart reconciled to God, a spirit in which the germ of perfect holiness is present.

When we believe God as He is revealed in Christ Jesus, we believe all His promises. Confidence in the person of Christ involves confidence in all that He speaks: hence we accept all the promises of God as being sure and certain. We do not trust one promise and doubt another, but we rely upon each one as true, and we believe it to be true to us so far as it has respect to our condition and circumstances. We argue from general statements to particular applications. He who has said that He will save those who believe in Him will save me since I believe in Him; and every blessing which He has engaged to bestow upon believers He will bestow upon me as a believer.

This is sound reasoning, and by it we justify the faith by which we live and are comforted. Not because I deserve anything, but because God has freely promised it to me in Christ Jesus, therefore I shall receive it: this is the reason and ground of our hope.

CHARLES H. SPURGEON

FIT FOR THE MASTER'S USE
The Veil That Separates

What is the veil that hangs between you and the presence of the Holy Spirit? It is probably some misunderstanding between yourself and another. What veils man from man also veils man from God. He who does not love his brother whom he has seen cannot love God whom he has not seen. Perhaps you are unwilling to forgive someone who has wronged you; or you will not ask forgiveness from one whom you have wronged. Perhaps you owe restitution money on a debt or a theft of twenty years ago. The conviction that you ought to make it good forms a thickly-woven veil between your Lord and you. Or perhaps there is some duty, some obedience to a positive command that you ought to perform but that you have evaded and shirked. Any of these things is enough to curtain off the filling of the Holy Spirit and make it a dim uncertainty.

Oh, let God reveal to you the cause of your shadowed experience! Then dare to obey Him at whatever cost. Make right what is wrong, repay what is owing, obey what is incumbent. Do it though it cost you an earthquake and a crucifixion. The peace of God will immediately settle upon you, and the light within will break forth speedily.

This kind of teaching should be as good for businessmen as a revival of trade, for if people acted up to it they would pay their bills. Women would pay for their last dresses. The men would go and pay for their last coats. People who have been owing money for the last two or three years would write a check for it. Relatives who have not spoken to one another for the last ten or twelve years would contrive to make up their quarrel. There would be a dragging and tearing down of the veil between man and woman, woman and woman, and then the life of Christ would be seen in you.

The Holy Spirit is in you, but waits to fill you. Away with every hindrance, and let Him sanctify you wholly! As He fills, He will drive your sin before Him, as the steam in the radiator drives the cold before it when you turn the valve.

F. B. MEYER

CHARGE THAT TO MY ACCOUNT

No Confession to Make

Notice the prayer life of our blessed Lord. Because He became man, He prayed to the Father. He took the place of a dependent. He trod the path of faith and drew His strength from above. He was often found at night on a hillside, or in a garden, pouring out His heart in prayer. But His prayer never took the character of confession. Hence He always prayed alone. He never prayed in fellowship with anyone else. He prayed for others. He did not pray with them. We never find Him kneeling with Peter, James, and John, His intimate disciples, and joining together with them in intercession, nor with anyone else. We who serve Christ today have some of our most blessed experiences as we mingle our prayers and supplications with those of our fellow believers and bow together before God in acknowledgment of our common sinfulness and our common need. He never did this with anyone. He taught His disciples to pray, "Forgive us our trespasses, as we forgive those who trespass against us," but He could not, in the very nature of things, pray that prayer with them. He stood altogether apart. They were sinners; He was sinless, the Savior of sinners. "He knew no sin."

The Word of God teaches that He not only never made the acquaintance of sin by actual failure, by transgression, by disobedience in thought, word, or deed, but He knew no sin in the sense that His humanity was never contaminated by an inward tendency to sin. He was absolutely, from the moment of His incarnation, the holy One. The angel said to the blessed virgin mother: "That holy thing which shall be born of thee shall be called the Son of God." In Adam, unfallen, we see humanity innocent; in all his children since, we see humanity fallen; but in Christ Jesus we see humanity holy.

We are told that He was tempted in all points like as we are, yet without sin. Some people have taken this last expression to mean, "Yet without sinning." That was true as we have seen, but it is not all of the truth. That verse really means this: He was tempted in all points like as we are, apart from sin. He was never emptied by inbred sin. He could say, "The prince of this world cometh, and hath nothing in me." You cannot say that; I cannot. When the enemy comes at me from without, there is a traitor inside who would gladly surrender the citadel, if he could; but with my Lord it was quite otherwise.

HENRY A. IRONSIDE

GOD'S WAY OF HOLINESS

The Rod, the Serpent, and Holiness

He who would be like Christ must study Him. We cannot make ourselves holy by merely trying to be so, any more than we can make ourselves believe and love by simple energy of endeavor. No force can effect this. Men try to be holy, and they fail. They cannot by direct effort work themselves into holiness. They must gaze upon a holy object; and so be changed into its likeness "from glory to glory" (2 Corinthians 3:18). They must have a holy being for their bosom friend. Companionship with Jesus, like that of John, can alone make us to resemble either the disciple or the Master.

He who would be holy must steep himself in the Word, must bask in the sunshine which radiates from each page of revelation. It is through *the truth* that we are sanctified (John 17:17). Exposing our souls constantly to this light, we become more thoroughly "children of the light," and, like the stained web that whitens in the sun, grow pure by being purely shone upon.

For against evil, divine truth is quick and powerful. It acts like some chemical ingredient that precipitates all impurities and leaves the water clear. It works like a spell of disenchantment against the evil one, casting him out, and casting him down. It is "the sword of the Spirit," with whose keen edge we cut our way through hostile thousands. It is the rod of Moses, by which we divide the Red Sea, and defeat Amalek, and bring water from the desert rock. What evil, what enemy, within or without, is there that can withstand this unconquered and unconquerable Word? Satan's object at present is to undermine that Word and to disparage its perfection. Let us the more magnify it, and the more make constant use of it. It is indeed only a fragment of man's language, made up of human letters and syllables; but it is furnished with superhuman virtue.

That rod in the hand of Moses, what was it? A piece of common wood. Yet it cut the Red Sea in two. That serpent on the pole, what was it? A bit of brass. Yet it healed thousands. Why all this? Because that wood and that brass were connected with omnipotence, conductors of the heavenly electricity. So let the Bible be to us the book of all books, for wounding, healing, quickening, strengthening, comforting, and purifying.

HORATIUS BONAR

FIT FOR THE MASTER'S USE
Take, Take, Take

Now consider the daily life. You get up in the morning, and when you are living like this, you forecast the day. You say: "I am going to have breakfast with people I dread, and I am so afraid I may lose my temper. Lord, I take grace for the breakfast hour. At ten o'clock I have to meet two or three men to discuss a very difficult problem. Lord, I claim and take wisdom for ten o'clock. At twelve o'clock I may be thrown into society and greatly tempted to exaggerate, or to backbite, or to libel other people's character. Lord, for twelve o'clock I take the spirit of perfect love." And so you forecast the whole day and take things from God; moreover you believe that you have what you take. Then you count on God. You do not keep on praying, but you rise from your knees, saying, "I thank You, Father. Give me also what You see I need," and you go along your way reckoning on God.

A man said to me, "If you pray like that, don't you pray very short?"

I replied, "Perhaps it does make one more short and businesslike in the supplication part of prayer, but there is so much to thank for, so many answers received that it more than makes up for what is lost in direct supplication."

You may be weak, sinful, full of failure. You may be at the end of yourself, but you are very near God. Lame Mephibosheth sat at the king's table. And the poor, paralyzed man at the Beautiful Gate of the temple was made perfectly whole.

Now, lame soul, take. What do you want from Jesus? Take Him to be that. Take the glorious Lord to be what you want most. Go home, and as you walk along say: "Yes, yes, I do take Jesus, my glorious Lord, to be to me a place of broad rivers for protection and streams to supply my thirst and irrigate my plot. Then I shall have a habitation quiet from anxiety, quiet from restlessness, quiet from fear. The stakes will never be taken down. Sennacherib will never get inside. My heart will lie on the very heart of God, satisfied and safe."

F. B. MEYER

ACCORDING TO PROMISE

Searching Out the Promise

You pray, but have not the liberty in prayer that you desire. A definite promise is what you want. You try one and another of the inspired words, but they do not fit. The troubled heart sees reasons to suspect that they are not strictly applicable to the case in hand, and so they are left in the old Book for use another day; for they are not available in the present emergency. You try again, and in due season a promise presents itself which seems to have been made for the occasion; it fits as exactly as a well-made key fits the wards of the lock for which it was originally prepared. Having found the identical word of the living God, you hasten to plead it at the throne of grace, saying, "Oh, my Lord, you have promised this good thing unto Thy servant; be pleased to grant it!" The matter is ended; sorrow is turned to joy; prayer is heard.

Frequently the Holy Spirit brings to our remembrance with life and power words of the Lord that otherwise we might have forgotten. He also sheds a new light upon well-remembered passages and so reveals a fullness in them that we had little suspected. In cases known to me, the texts have been singular, and for a while the person upon whose mind they were impressed could hardly see their bearing.

For years one heart was comforted with the words "His soul shall dwell at ease; and his seed shall inherit the earth." This passage was seldom out of his mind; indeed, it seemed to him to be perpetually whispered in his ear. The special relation of the promise to his experience was made known by the event. A child of God who mourned his years of barrenness was lifted at once into joy and peace by that seldom-quoted word "I will restore to you the years that the locust hath eaten." The bitter experiences of David as to slander and malice led to the utterance of consoling promises, which have been a thousand times appropriated by obscure and broken-hearted Christians when afflicted with "trials of cruel mockings."

CHARLES H. SPURGEON

ABSOLUTE SURRENDER

Having Begun in the Spirit

I have often been asked by young Christians: "Why is it that I fail so? I did so solemnly vow with my whole heart, and did desire to serve God; why have I failed?"

To such I always give the one answer: "My dear friend, you are trying to do in your own strength what Christ alone can do in you."

And when they tell me: "I am sure I knew Christ alone could do it, I was not trusting in myself," my answer always is:

"You were trusting in yourself or you could not have failed. If you had trusted Christ, He could not have failed."

Oh, this perfecting in the flesh what was begun in the Spirit runs far deeper through us than we knew. Let us ask God to reveal to us that it is only when we are brought to utter shame and emptiness that we shall be prepared to receive the blessing that comes from on high.

And so I come with these two questions. Are you living, beloved brother-minister, under the power of the Holy Ghost? Are you living as an anointed, Spirit-filled man in your ministry and your life before God? Oh brothers, our place is an awful one. We have to show people what God will do for us, not in our words and teaching, but in our life. God help us to do it!

I ask it of every member of Christ's church and of every believer: Are you living a life under the power of the Holy Spirit day by day, or are you attempting to live without that? Remember you cannot. Are you consecrated, given up to the Spirit to work in you and to live in you? Oh, come and confess every failure of temper, every failure of tongue however small, every failure owing to the absence of the Holy Spirit and the presence of the power of self. Are you consecrated, are you given up to the Holy Spirit?

If your answer be no, then I come with a second question—Are you willing to be consecrated? Are you willing to give up yourself to the power of the Holy Spirit?

ANDREW MURRAY

ACCORDING TO PROMISE
Like Abraham and Jacob

In the life of Abraham we perceive that his faith had to do with all the events of his earthly pilgrimage; it was connected with his removals from one country to another, with the separation of a nephew from his camp, with fighting against invaders, and especially with the birth of the long-promised son. No part of the patriarch's life was outside of the circle of his faith in God. Toward the close of his life it is said, "And the Lord had blessed Abraham in all things," which includes temporal as well as spiritual. In Jacob's case the Lord promised him bread to eat and raiment to put on, and the bringing of him to his father's house in peace; and all these things are of a temporal and earthly character.

Assuredly these first believers did not spirit away the present blessings of the covenant or regard it as an airy, mystical matter to believe in God. One is struck with the want of any line of demarcation between secular and sacred in their lives; they journeyed as pilgrims, fought like crusaders, ate and drank like saints, lived as priests, and spoke as prophets. Their life was their religion, and their religion was their life. They trusted God not merely about certain things of higher import but about everything, and, hence, even a servant from one of their houses, when he was sent on an errand, prayed, "Oh Lord God of my master, prosper the way which I go!"

This was genuine faith, and it is ours to imitate it, and no longer to allow the substance of the promise and the life of faith to evaporate in mere sentimental and visionary fancies. If trust in God is good for anything, it is good for everything within the line of the promise, and it is certain that the life which now is lies within that region.

CHARLES H. SPURGEON

FIT FOR THE MASTER'S USE

A Life of Altruism

Two painters were set to paint a picture of rest, and one painted a placid pool in which the mountains were reflected, an utter solitude. The other depicted a living cataract, and over it the bough of a tree on which a nest was securely fixed, and a bird was brooding over her young. That picture of the bird at rest in the midst of the foam and rushing of the cataract is the truest conception of rest. There is a life in the will of God, so quiet, so at peace with Him, so at rest in His joy, so perfectly content that He is doing best, that the lines are wiped out of the face, the fever is gone from the restless eye, and the whole nature is still. "Rest in the Lord and wait patiently for him," and then spend the strength that other men waste in fussy anxiety in helping your fellow men.

The life of which I speak is a life of taking in. Many think it is only a giving up. I do not deny that there is a giving up in it, but it is not without the hope of taking; you see something better, and in reaching for that you drop the worse.

Upon the placid waters of a lake everything that is highest in reality is lowest in the reflection. The higher the trees, the lower their shadow. That is a picture of this world: what is highest in this world is lowest in the other, and what is highest in that world is lowest in this. Gold is on top here; they pave the streets with it there. To serve is looked upon as ignoble here; there those who serve reign, and the last are first.

I never saw a girl unwilling to fling away paste diamonds when she could have real stones, and when a man understands what God can be to the soul, he is independent of things he used to care for most.

Oh friends, no words can tell what eye has not seen, nor ear heard, nor the heart of man conceived of the things that God has prepared for them that love Him. I cannot do it; I do not believe any man can. But there beckons you a life of deliverance from self, of freedom from known sin, of deliverance from the power of the devil, of influence over thousands of men, of rest and peace in the heart, of conscious rightness with God, independent of mood and feeling, in which the will is one with the will of God. That is a life so blessed, so transcendent, so radiant, that it is like the life of paradise.

F. B. MEYER

ACCORDING TO PROMISE

The Valuation of the Promises

How precious are the promises when we lie sick, gazing into an empty month, sorely tried and tempted through pain and weariness! All depressing circumstances lose their power for evil when our faith takes firm hold upon the promises of God. How sweet to feel I have my head on the promise and my heart on the promise; at that point I can rest on the truth of the Most High. Not on earthly vanity, but on heavenly truth do I repose. There is nothing to be found elsewhere comparable to this perfect rest.

The pearl of peace is found among the precious promises. That is precious indeed which can support dying men and cause them to pass into eternity with as much delight as if they were going to a marriage feast. That which lasts forever, and lasts good forever, is most treasured. That which brings all things with it and has all things in it—that is precious indeed; and such is the promise of God.

If such be the greatness and value of the promises, let us joyfully accept and believe them. Shall I urge the child of God to do this? No, I will not so dishonor Him; surely He will believe his own Father! Surely, surely, it ought to be the easiest thing in the world for the sons and daughters of the Most High to believe in Him who has given them power to become the children of God! My brethren, let us not stagger at the promise through unbelief, but believe up to the hilt!

Furthermore, let us know the promises. Should we not carry them at our fingers' ends? Should we not know them better than anything else? The promises should be the classics of believers. Though you have not read the last new book and have not heard the last act of the government, yet know right well what God the Lord has said, and look to see His Word made good. We ought to be so versed in Scripture as always to have at the tip of our tongue the promise that most exactly meets our case. We ought to be transcripts of Scripture; the divine promise should be as much written upon our hearts as upon the pages of the Book.

CHARLES H. SPURGEON

FIT FOR THE MASTER'S USE
The Living Shepherd

Now the God of peace, that brought again from the dead our Lord Jesus, that great Shepherd of the sheep, through the blood of the everlasting covenant, make you perfect in every good work to do His will, working in you that which is well pleasing in His sight, through Jesus Christ" (Hebrews 13:20–21).

God who raised the Shepherd can raise the sheep; He who raised the head can raise the member; He who lifted Jesus to the heavenlies can lift you. He will do it as the God of Peace.

How peaceful was the resurrection! I know there was an earthquake and the rolling away of the stone, but the resurrection of Christ itself was a noiseless act. He quietly arose, and he put on the vesture of light as a garment. He came forth with footsteps so gentle that the flowerets and blades of grass did not bend beneath His tread, and He passed out with no noise or footfall ringing in the dawn. Thus He began His beneficent ministry among men like the gentlest and therefore the strongest forces of nature. At last He glided upwards from the Ascension Mount without blare of trumpet or sound of opening heavens.

So our buried life and power shall rise today at the call of the God of peace. Do not be afraid. God will not hurt you. He does not work through wild change, but gradually and quietly. He raised Christ in spite of all the devil could do to keep you down. Rise and live in resurrection glory and power!

We have been thinking much of the great God, and it is all true; but when you are nearest God and most conscious of His power, when you look into His face, you will see it is your Shepherd's. God works through Jesus. He deals with the flock and each member of it through the Shepherd. Occupy yourself, then, with the Shepherd. Keep Him in view, follow Him closely, dwell on His words, follow His steps, and absorb yourself with Him.

Do you doubt this; does it all seems too wonderful? Take heart! You are one with Jesus in the eternal covenant that He ratified with His blood. God has entered into covenant relations that He cannot break with your soul. Be of good cheer. What He has done for the Great Shepherd He will do for all who are included in His flock.

F. B. MEYER

TO THE WORK
Love for Your Neighbor

D
o you want to know how you can reach the masses? Go to their homes and enter into sympathy with them. Tell them you have come to do them good, and let them see that you have a heart to feel for them. When they find out that you really love them, all those things that are in their hearts against God and against Christianity will be swept out of the way. Atheists may tell them that you only want to get their money and that you do not really care for their happiness. We have to contradict that lie by our lives and send it back to the pit where it came from.

We are not going to do it unless we go personally to them and prove that we really love them. There are thousands of families that could easily be reached if we had thousands of Christians going to them and entering into sympathy with their sorrows. That is what they want. This poor world is groaning and sighing for sympathy—human sympathy. I am quite sure it was that in Christ's life that touched the hearts of the common people. He made Himself one with them. He who was rich for our sakes became poor. He was born in the manger so that He might put Himself on a level with the lowest of the low.

I think that in this manner He teaches His disciples a lesson. He wants us to convince the world that He is their friend. They do not believe it. If once the world were to grasp this thought, that Jesus Christ is the friend of the sinner, they would soon flock to Him.

D. L. MOODY

THE TRUE VINE

More Fruit

As churches and individuals we are in danger of nothing so much as self-contentment. The secret spirit of Laodicea—we are rich and increased in goods, and have need of nothing—may prevail where it is not suspected. The divine warning—poor and wretched and miserable—finds little response just where it is most needed. Revelation 3:17 is a very searching Scripture.

Let us not rest content with the thought that we are taking an equal share with others in the work that is being done, or that men are satisfied with our efforts in Christ's service, or even point to us as examples. Let our only desire be to know whether we are bearing all the fruit Christ is willing to give through us as living branches, in close and living union with Himself. We need to determine whether we are satisfying the loving heart of the great husbandman, our Father in heaven, in His desire for more fruit.

The Word comes with divine authority to search and test our life; the true disciple will heartily surrender himself to its holy light and will earnestly ask that God Himself may show what may be lacking in the measure or the character of the fruit he bears. Let us believe that the Word is meant to lead us on to a fuller experience of the Father's purpose of love, of Christ's fullness, and of the wonderful privilege of bearing much fruit in the salvation of men.

The Word is most encouraging. Let us listen to it. It is just to the branch that is bearing fruit that the message comes: more fruit.

ANDREW MURRAY

BACK TO BETHEL

Two Mountains

There are two mountains in our Savior's life, the mount of temptation and the mount of ascension. On the mount of temptation Christ saw the kingdoms of the world, and the devil said: "I will give Thee these if Thou wilt worship me." But the Lord refused and went down that mountain poor, lonely, to suffering and to death; but at last through the cross and the grave He came out on the other side more than a conqueror and said: "All power is given to me in heaven and on earth. Go and preach." He refused the devil's crown and got God's crown; and one day we shall hear the anthem float over the redeemed world, "The kingdoms of this world have become the kingdoms of our Lord and of his Christ."

But it would not help us if Jesus had done this for Himself only. We must remember that on the cross Jesus Christ became the representative man, and again He met the world, the flesh, and the devil in the hour of His weakness.

If He could overcome them then, what can He not do now that He is strong in resurrection glory? He said distinctly in John 14:30, "The prince of this world cometh, and hath nothing in me"; and again, "I have overcome the world." When our Savior died He put His foot on the devil; He bruised the serpent's head. When He rose as the representative man, He was raised above the power of the devil and got back the dominion that God gave Adam and Adam lost. We see not yet all things put under man, but we see Jesus crowned with glory and honor (Hebrews 2:8–9). In the ascended Lord, man rose above the devil and resumed the honor and glory, the power and authority, with which God had endowed him in the first moments of his creation. When Satan saw that God was lifting our race, in the person of a perfect man, to sit in glory, he knew that the work of six thousand years was in vain and that in spite of everything God's purpose would stand, that man should have dominion and power.

F. B. MEYER

MOODY'S STORIES

His Promises

God is always true to what He promises to do. He made promises to Abraham, Jacob, Moses, Joshua, and the others, and did He not fulfill them? He will fulfill every word of what He has promised; yet how few take Him at His word.

When I was a young man I was clerk in the establishment of a man in Chicago, whom I observed frequently occupied sorting and marking bills. He explained to me what he had been doing; on some notes he had marked B, on some D, and on others G. Those marked B, he told me, were bad, those marked D meant they were doubtful, and those with G on them meant they were good; and, said he, you must treat all of them accordingly. And thus people endorse God's promises by marking some as bad and others as doubtful; whereas we ought to take all of them as good, for He has never once broken His word, and all that He says He will do in the fullness of time.

I heard of a woman once who thought there was no promise in the Bible for her; she thought the promises were for someone else, not for her. There are a good many of these people in the world. They think it is too good to be true that they can be saved for nothing. This woman one day got a letter, and when she opened it she found it was not for her at all; it was meant for another woman who had the same name; and she had her eyes opened to the fact that if she should find some promise in the Bible directed to her name, she would not know whether it meant her or someone else that bore her name. But you know the word "whosoever" includes everyone in the wide world.

D. L. MOODY

GOD'S WAY OF HOLINESS
"Little" Things

With many of us the Christian life has not gone on to maturity. "Ye did run well, who did hinder you?" Ours has been a work well begun, but left unfinished; a battle boldly entered on, but only half fought out. Is not thus Christ dishonored? Is not His gospel thus misrepresented, His cross denied, His words slighted, His example set at nought?

Often sunsets have become the abrupt endings of the bright dawns. Must suns go down at noon? Must Ephesus leave her first love, Laodicea grow lukewarm, and Sardis cold? Are issues such as these inevitable and universal? Or shall we not protest against them as failures, perversions, crimes—and altogether inexcusable?

If a holy life consisted of one or two noble deeds, we might account for the failure and reckon it small dishonor to turn back in such a conflict. But a holy life is made up of a multitude of small things. It is the little things of the hour, and not the great things of the age, that fill up a life like that of Paul and John, like that of Rutherford or Brainerd. Little words, not eloquent speeches or sermons; little deeds, not miracles, nor battles, nor one great heroic act or mighty martyrdom, make up the true Christian life. The true symbols of a holy life are the little constant sunbeam, not the lightning. The avoidance of little evils, little sins, little inconsistencies, little weaknesses, little follies, little indiscretions and imprudencies, little indulgences of self and of the flesh—the avoidance of such *little* things as these goes far to make up at least the negative beauty of a holy life. Add to this list other littles: little equivocations or aberrations from high integrity, little touches of shabbiness and meanness, little indifferences to the feelings or wishes of others, little outbreaks of temper, or crossness, or selfishness, or vanity.

In their place we should give attention to the little duties of the day and hour, in public transactions or private dealings, or family arrangements; to little words, and looks, and tones; little benevolences, or forbearances, or tendernesses; little self-denials and self-restraints; little plans of quiet kindness for others. These are the active developments of a holy life, the rich and divine mosaics of which it is composed. What makes yonder green hill so beautiful? Not the outstanding peak or stately elm but the bright deep green that clothes its slopes, composed of innumerable blades of slender grass.

It is of small things that a great life is made up.

HORATIUS BONAR

ACCORDING TO PROMISE

Taking Possession of the Promise

You may say, by a realizing faith, "This promise is mine," and straightway it is yours. It is by faith, therefore, that we "receive promises," and not by sight and sense.

The promises of God are not enclosures to be the private property of this saint or that, but they are an open common for all the dwellers in the parish of Holy Faith. No doubt there are persons who would, if they could, make a freehold of the stars and a personal estate out of the sun and moon. The same greed might put a fence around the promises; but this cannot be done. As well might misers hedge in the songbirds and claim the music of lark and thrush as their own sole inheritance, as propose to keep promises all to themselves. No, not the best of saints can, even if they wished to do so, put a single word of the God of grace under lock and key. The promise is not only "unto you, and to your children," but also "to all that are afar off, even as many as the Lord our God shall call." What a comfort is this! Let us take up our common rights and possess by faith what the Lord has made ours by a covenant of salt.

Words spoken to Jacob belong equally to all believers. Hosea says of him, "Yea, he had power over the angel, and prevailed: he wept, and made supplication unto him: he found him in Bethel, and there he spake with us." Thus Jehovah spoke with us when He spoke with the patriarch. The wonders that God displayed at the Red Sea were wrought for all His people, for we read, "there did we rejoice in him" (see Psalm 66:6).

It is true we were not there, and yet the joy of Israel's victory is ours. The apostle quotes the word of the Lord to Joshua as if it were spoken to any and every child of God, "He hath said, I will never leave thee nor forsake thee" (Hebrew 13:5); thus it should be clear that no word of the Lord ends with the occasion which called it forth or spends itself in blessing the individual to whom it was first addressed. All the promises are to believers who have faith enough to embrace them and plead them at the throne of grace.

CHARLES H. SPURGEON

TO THE WORK

Because We Love Him

When we get to the higher plane of love it will not be hard for us to work for the Lord. We will be glad to do anything, however small. God hates the great things in which love is not the motive power; but He delights in the little things that are prompted by a feeling of love. A cup of cold water given to a disciple in the spirit of love is of far more value in God's sight than the taking of a kingdom, done out of ambition and vain glory.

I am getting sick and tired of hearing the words *duty, duty.* You hear so many talk about it being the Christian's duty to do this and do that. My experience is that such Christians have very little success. Is there not a much higher platform than that of mere duty? Can we not engage in the service of Christ because we love Him? When that is the constraining power it is so easy to work. It is not hard for a mother to watch over a sick child. She does not look upon it as any hardship.

You never hear Paul talking about what a hard time he had in his master's service. He was constrained by love to Christ, and by the love of Christ to him. He counted it a joy to labor, and even to suffer, for his blessed master.

Perhaps you say I ought not to talk against duty; because a good deal of work would not be done at all if it were not from a sense of duty. But I want you to see what a poor, low motive that is, and how you may reach a higher plane of service.

D. L. MOODY

TO SHEW THYSELF APPROVED

To Show Yourself Approved

T he fifth great promise of God for the Bible student and soul-winner is found in Acts 1:8: "But ye shall receive power, after that the Holy Ghost is come upon you: and ye shall be witnesses unto me both in Jerusalem, and in all Judea, and in Samaria, and unto the uttermost part of the earth." The greatest need of a missionary, a minister and personal worker, or a father and a mother, when they study God's Word and when they go out to win souls, is power—power to penetrate the sacred cloisters of God's Word where such abundant treasures of truth are stored and power to present to others the truth discovered in such a way as to convict of sin and reveal Jesus Christ and to bring men to accept Jesus as their Lord and Savior.

This verse reveals the great secret of that power: "Ye shall receive power, *after that the Holy Ghost is come upon you.*" We need power, a power not from this earth, not from human culture, not the power learned in schools of oratory, nor the power that comes from the tricks of the world, not the power to draw crowds learned from Douglas Fairbanks, Mary Pickford, or Charlie Chaplin. No! No! *No!* We need "power from on high" (Luke 24:29).

This promise tells us how to get such power. It tells us how any child of God can get it. Listen again, "Ye shall receive power, *after that the Holy Ghost is come upon you:* and ye shall be witnesses unto me both in Jerusalem, and in all Judea, and in Samaria, and unto the uttermost part of the earth." The source of all power is the Holy Spirit within us. "For the promise is unto you, and to your children, and to all that are afar off, even as many as the Lord our God shall call unto him."

R. A. TORREY

MOODY'S ANECDOTES
Are You Seeking Rest?

A lady in Wales told me this little story: An English friend of hers, a mother, had a sick child. At first they considered there was no danger, until one day the doctor came in and said the the symptoms were very unfavorable. Once he had the mother out of the room, and he told her directly that her daughter could not live. It came like a thunderbolt. After the doctor had gone the mother went into the room where the girl lay and began to talk to her and tried to divert her mind.

"Darling, do you know you will soon hear the music of heaven? You will hear a sweeter song than you have ever heard on earth. You will hear them sing the song of Moses and the Lamb. You are very fond of music. Won't it be sweet, darling?"

And the tired, sick child turned its head away and said, "Oh, Momma, I am so tired and so sick that I think it would make me worse to hear all that music."

"Well," the mother said, "you will soon see Jesus. You will see the seraphim and cherubim and the streets all paved with gold"; and she went on picturing heaven as it is described in Revelation.

The little girl again turned her head away, and said, "Oh, Momma, I am so tired that I think it would make me worse to see all those beautiful things!"

At last the mother took the girl up in her arms, and pressed her to her loving heart. And the little sick one whispered:

"Oh, Momma, that is what I want. If Jesus will only take me in His arms and let me rest!"

Dear friend, are you not tired and weary of sin? Are you not weary of the turmoil of life? You can find rest on the bosom of the Son of God.

D. L. MOODY

GOD'S WAY OF HOLINESS

Redeeming the Time

If we would aim at a holy and useful life, let us learn to redeem time. "I am large about redeeming time," says Richard Baxter in the preface to his Christian Directory, "because therein the sum of a holy, obedient life is included." Yes; "let us redeem the time, because the days are evil" (Ephesians 5:16; Colossians 4:5). A wasted life is the result of unredeemed time. Desultory working, impulsive giving, fitful planning, irregular reading, ill-assorted hours, perfunctory or unpunctual execution of business, hurry and bustle, loitering and unreadiness—these, and such like, are the things that take the power from life, hinder holiness, and eat like a canker into our moral being. Misuse of time makes success and progress an impossibility, either in things temporal or spiritual.

There needs not to be routine, but there must be regularity; there ought not to be mechanical stiffness, but there must be order; there may not be haste, but there must be no trifling with our own time or that of others; "Whatsoever thy hand findeth to do, do it with thy might" (Ecclesiastes 9:10). If the thing is worth doing at all, it is worth doing well; and, in little things as well as great, we must show that we are in earnest. There must be no idling, but a girding up of the loins; a running the race with patience; the warring of a good warfare. The call is to be "steadfast and . . . always abounding in the work of the Lord."

The flowers are constant in their growing, the stars are constant in their courses; the rivers are constant in their flowing—they lose not time. So must our life be, not one of fits, or starts, or random impulses, not one of levity or inconstancy, or fickle scheming, but steady and resolute. We must be resolute men and women, those who know their earthly mission and have their eye upon the heavenly goal.

HORATIUS BONAR

BACK TO BETHEL
Sensitive Senses

Now, most of us never use our spiritual sense. God has given us a nose to smell with, eyes to see with, hands to feel with, a tongue to taste with. We are made in three parts—body, soul, and spirit. The soul has senses equivalent to those of the body, and the spirit behind that has a third set of senses that an unregenerate man has not commenced to use. But if you are a spiritual man you will use these spiritual senses to discriminate the thoughts as they come to your heart. " By reason of use" you will have your senses exercised to discern both good and evil.

I remember once going back from the United States across the ocean, and getting my lungs full of ozone. On reaching England I went to a watering place to stay with some dear friends. They said:

"Isn't this a lovely place?"

I tried to think so, but as I went out on the doorstep I detected a very noxious smell. I said:

"I am very sorry, but I am not at all sure that this place is as healthy as you think it."

"Of course it is," they said; "it is swept by the wind from the North Sea."

I inquired and found that within about a mile of their house there was what is called a sewage farm, and a whiff from those fields neutralized all the benefit of the sea breezes.

My friends asked how I came to be so keen of scent, and I replied:

"You have come from London where you live in a vitiated atmosphere, but I have come off the Atlantic and am used to pure air, so I can detect a bad smell where you cannot."

If you live in the midst of bad people, bad books, and bad things, you lose your power of detecting bad thoughts when they come teeming about you like microbes. But if every day you spend an hour on God's mountains or upon the broad sea of the Bible, and get some of God's accurate senses into you, you will be able to detect things which are wrong that other people, even Christians, pass without seeing as wrong.

F. B. MEYER

TO THE WORK

Love, the Motive for Service

I am thinking of going back to my home soon. My old, white-haired mother lives on the banks of the Connecticut River, in the same little town where she has been for the past eighty years. Suppose when I return I take her a present, and when I give it to her I say, "You have been so very kind to me in the past that I thought it was my duty to bring you a present." What would she think? But how different it would be when I give it to her because of my strong love to her. How much more she would value it. So God wants His children to serve Him for something else than mere duty. He does not want us to feel that it is a hard thing to do His will.

Take an army that fights because it is compelled to do so; they will not gain many victories. But how different when they are full of love for their country and for their commanders. Then nothing can stand before them. Do not think you can do any work for Christ and hope to succeed if you are not impelled by love.

Napoleon tried to establish a kingdom by the force of arms. So did Alexander the Great, and Caesar, and other great warriors; but they utterly failed. Jesus founded His kingdom on love, and it is going to stand. When we get on to this plane of love, then all selfish and unworthy motives will disappear, and our work will stand the fire when God shall put it to the test.

D. L. MOODY

THE SECOND COMING OF CHRIST

Living and Looking

We read in Scripture: "The grace of God that bringeth salvation hath appeared to all men; teaching us that, denying ungodliness and worldly lusts, we should live soberly, righteously, and godly in this present world; looking for that blessed hope, and the glorious appearing of the great God and our Saviour Jesus Christ; who gave himself for us, that He might redeem us from all iniquity, and purify unto himself a peculiar people, zealous of good works."

Indeed, we must be willing to deny ungodliness and worldly lusts. But ours is not merely a negative religion; we must have something positive. Thus the next word after *denying* is *living*—that "we should live soberly, righteously, and godly in this present world." Observe that the Holy Spirit expects us to live in this present world, and therefore we are not to exclude ourselves from it. This age is the battlefield in which the soldier of Christ is to fight.

Society is the place in which Christianity is to exhibit the graces of Christ. It is no use for you to scheme to escape from it. You are bound to ford across this torrent and buffet all its waves. If the grace of God is in you, that grace is meant to be displayed, not in a select and secluded retreat, but in this present world.

And there is *looking*, as well as living. One work of the grace of God is to cause us to be "looking for the blessed hope of the glorious appearing of the great God and our Saviour Jesus Christ." This hope is not of debt, but of grace; though our Lord will give us a reward, it will not be according to the law of works. The Lord will come again, and in the coming of the Lord lies the great hope of the believer, his great stimulus to overcome evil, his main incentive to perfect holiness in the fear of the Lord. Oh, to be found blameless in the day of the manifestation of our Lord! God grant us this.

CHARLES H. SPURGEON

GOD'S WAY OF HOLINESS
Counsels and Warnings

I f sin be but a common scar or wrinkle, to be erased from the soul's surface by a few simple touches; if pardon be a mere figure of speech, meaning God's wide benevolence or good-natured indifference to evil, why tell of wrath, and fire, and judgment? Does God love to torment His creatures by harsh words or fill their imaginations with images of woe that He does not intend to realize? Or why did the Son of God suffer, weep, and grieve? If error be but a trifle, a foible, a freak at worst; or if it be a display of honest purpose and the inevitable result of free thought, why is the "strong delusion" (literally, "the energy of error") spoken of so awfully: "that they all might be damned who believed not the truth" (2 Thessalonians 2:12). Even the Lord Himself has said concerning false doctrine that it is that "thing I hate."

As the strongest yet calmest thing in the world is light, so should a Christian life be the strongest and greatest, as well as the calmest and brightest. As the only perfectly straight line is a ray of light, and as the only pure substance is sunshine, so ought our course to be, and so should we seek to shine as lights in the world; reflections of Him who is its light, the one straight, pure thing on earth.

Let us then shine. Stars indeed, not suns; but still stars, not candles or meteors. Let us shine! Giving perhaps slender light, but that light certain and pure; enough to say to men, "It is night," lest they mistake. Our light should be enough to guide the seeking or the erring in the true direction, though it is not enough to illuminate the world. The sun alone can do that. It is the sun that shows us the landscape; stars show but themselves. Let us then show ourselves beyond mistake. The day when all things shall be seen in full warm light is the day of the great sun-rising.

"The night is far spent, the day is at hand." We shall not set nor be clouded; we shall simply lose ourselves in light. And we need not grudge thus losing ourselves, when we call to mind that the splendor in which our light is to be absorbed is that of the everlasting Sun.

HORATIUS BONAR

MOODY'S ANECDOTES

Proud of Their False Religions

I do not believe there is any false religion in the world that men are not proud of. The only religion of which I have ever heard that men were ashamed of is the religion of Jesus Christ. Some time ago I preached two weeks in Salt Lake City, and I did not find a Mormon that was not proud of his religion. When I came within forty miles of Salt Lake City, the engineer came into the car and wanted to know if I wouldn't like to ride on the engine. I went with him, and in the forty-mile ride he talked Mormonism to me the whole time and tried to convert me so that I would not preach against the Mormons. I never met an unconverted Chinese who wasn't proud of being a disciple of Confucius; and I never met a Muslim who wasn't proud of the fact that he was a follower of Mohammed; but how many, many times I have found men ashamed of the religion of Jesus Christ, the only religion that gives men the power over their affections and lusts and sins. If there was some backdoor by which men could slip into heaven, there would be a great many who would want to enter it, but they don't like to make public confession.

I remember reading of a blind man who was found sitting at the corner of a street in a great city with a lantern beside him. Some one went up to him and asked what he had the lantern there for, seeing that he was blind, and the light was the same to him as the darkness. The blind man replied:

"I have it so that no one may stumble over me."

Think of that. Where one man reads the Bible, a hundred read you and me. That is what Paul meant when he said we were to be "living epistles of Christ, known and read of all men." I would not give much for all that can be done by sermons, if we do not preach Christ by our lives. If we do not commend the gospel to people by our holy walk and conversation, we shall not win them to Christ.

D. L. MOODY

ACCORDING TO PROMISE

The Rule Without Exception

Nor can the promise fail because of a change in the divine promiser. We change, poor, frail things that we are! But the Lord knows no variableness, neither shadow of turning; hence His Word abides forever the same. Because He changes not, His promises stand fast like the great mountains. "Hath he said, and shall he not do it?" Our strong consolation rests upon the immutable things of God.

Nor can the Word of the Lord fall to the ground through forgetfulness on His part. With our tongues we outrun our hands: for, although we are willing, we fail in the performing because other things come in and distract our attention. We forget or we grow cold; but never is it so with the faithful promiser. His most ancient promise is still fresh in His mind, and He means it now as He did when He first uttered it. He is, in fact, always giving the promise, since there is no time with Him. The old promises of Scripture are new promises to faith; for every word still proceeds out of the mouth of the Lord, to be bread for men.

Because of all this, the Word of the Lord deserves all faith, both implicit and explicit. We can trust men too much, but we can never do so toward God. It is the surest thing that has been or that can ever be. To believe His Word is to believe what none can fairly question. Has God said it? Then so it must be. Heaven and earth will pass away, but God's Word will never pass away. The laws of nature would be suspended; fire may cease to burn and water to drown, for this would involve no unfaithfulness in God; but for His Word to fail would involve dishonoring variableness in the character and nature of the Godhead, and this can never be. Let us set our seal that God is true, and never permit a suspicion of His veracity to cross our minds.

The immutable word of promise is, and ever must be, the rule of God's giving. Against this rule no other can stand. With the rule of God's promise no other law, supposed or real, can ever come into conflict.

CHARLES H. SPURGEON

MOODY'S ANECDOTES
They Are Old Enough

I have no sympathy with the idea that our children have to grow up before they are converted. Once I saw a lady with three daughters at her side, and I stepped up to her and asked her if she was a Christian.

"Yes, sir."

Then I asked the oldest daughter if she was a Christian. The chin began to quiver, and the tears came into her eyes, and she said:

"I wish I was."

The mother looked very angrily at me and said, "I don't want you to speak to my children on that subject. They don't understand." And in great rage she took them all away from me. One daughter was fourteen years old, one twelve, and the other ten, but they were not old enough to be talked to about religion! Let them drift into the world and plunge into worldly amusements, and then see how hard it is to reach them. Many a mother is mourning today because her boy has gone beyond her reach and will not allow her to pray with him. She may pray *for* him, but he will not let her pray or talk *with* him. In those early days when his mind was tender and young, she might have led him to Christ.

Bring them in. "Suffer the little children to come unto me."

Is there a prayerless father reading this? May God let the arrow go down into your soul! Make up your mind that, God helping you, you will get the children converted. God's order is to the father first, but if he isn't true to his duty, then the mother should be true and save the children from the wreck. Now is the time to do it while you have them under your roof. Exert your parental influence over them.

D. L. MOODY

THE CHRIST-LIFE FOR THE SELF-LIFE

The Castaway

Look for a moment upon the pages of Scripture and see how they are littered with castaways.

Take the first case, that of Esau. He comes in from hunting. He is born to the birthright. The birthright includes the power of standing between God and the clan, speaking to God for men. He is famished. Yonder is the steaming bowl of pottage prepared by his brother, Jacob.

"Give me that red lentil pottage," he cries.

Jacob, crafty in heart, bargains. "Give me your spiritual birthright."

Have we not in the past had some steaming bowl of pottage appealing to the senses? Almost all of us have been tempted by some temptation to sense. If we glance back at our past, many of us must admit that we have yielded—not once or twice, but oftener—to the appeal to the senses. We have indulged some appetite and have despised our birthright.

"Give it to me. I must have it. I cannot live without it. Even though I have not quite the spiritual power that I had, give it to me." It may be some silent, beautiful form that allures you from your heart's true love. The temptations of pleasure, wealth, and fame have pulled many a man from his family and his God.

So men despise their birthright still, and they are cast away. Esau became a prince in this world, and the father of a line of dukes, and all the world flattered him and thought him a prosperous successful man, but God wrote over him the awful epitaph:

"This man is a castaway. He did eat and drink, and rose up and went his way: thus he despised his birthright." Do not despise your relationship with God to live for yourself. He offers far more than the world can give.

F. B. MEYER

THE TRUE VINE

Christ's Friendship: Its Intimacy

The highest proof of true friendship, and one great source of its blessedness, is the intimacy that holds nothing back and admits the friend to share our inmost secrets. It is a blessed thing to be Christ's servant; His redeemed ones delight to call themselves His slaves. Christ had often spoken of the disciples as His servants. In His great love our Lord now says, "No longer do I call you servants"; with the coming of the Holy Spirit a new era was to be inaugurated. "The servant knoweth not what his lord doeth." The servant has to obey without being consulted or admitted into the secret of all his master's plans. "But, I have called you friends, for all things I heard from my Father I have made known unto you."

Christ's friends share with Him in all the secrets the Father has entrusted to Him.

Let us think what this means. When Christ spoke of keeping His Father's commandments, He did not mean merely what was written in Holy Scripture but those special commandments which were communicated to Him day by day and from hour to hour. It was of these He said, "The Father loveth the Son, and showeth him all things that he doeth, and he will show him greater things." All that Christ did was God's working. God showed it to Christ, so that He carried out the Father's will and purpose, not as man often does, blindly and unintelligently, but with full understanding and approval. As one who stood in God's counsel, He knew God's plan.

ANDREW MURRAY

MOODY'S ANECDOTES
They Did Not Believe Him

Several years ago an evangelist in England prepared some great placards and posted them all over the town, declaring that if any man in that town was in debt would come to his office before twelve o'clock on a certain day with the proof of indebtedness, he would pay the debt. This news spread all over the town, but the people did not believe him.

One man said to his neighbor, "John, do you believe this man will pay our debts?"

"No, of course not, it's only a hoax."

The day came, and instead of there being a great rush, nobody came. Now it is a wonder there is not a great rush of men into the kingdom of God to have their debts paid, when a man can be saved for nothing.

About ten o'clock a man was walking in front of the office. He looked this way and that to see if anybody was looking, and by and by, satisfied that there was no one looking, he slipped in and said, "I saw a notice about town that if any one would call here at a certain hour you would pay their debts; is there any truth in it?"

"Yes," said the man. "It's quite true. Did you bring the necessary papers with you?"

"Yes."

After the man had paid the debt, he said, "Sit down, I want to talk with you," and he kept him there until twelve o'clock. Before twelve o'clock had passed two more came in and had their debts paid. At twelve o'clock he let them all out. Some other men were standing around the door.

"Well, did he pay your debts?"

"Yes," they said, "it was quite true; our debts were all paid."

"Oh, then we'll go in and get ours paid."

They went, but it was too late. Twelve o'clock had passed. To every one of you who is a bankrupt sinner—and you never saw a sinner in the world that was not a bankrupt sinner—Christ comes and He says: "I will pay your debts."

D. L. MOODY

THE EMPTY TOMB

Evidence for the Resurrection

So clear is the evidence for the resurrection that when Gilbert West, a celebrated infidel, selected this subject as a point of attack and sat down to weigh the evidence, he was startled with the abundant witness to the truth of this fact, even though he was filled with prejudice. He finally arose and soon expressed himself a convert, and he has left as a heritage to the church a most valuable treatise, entitled *Observation on the Resurrection of Christ*. He went to the subject as though he had been a lawyer examining the pros and cons of any matter in dispute. The resurrection, which is the fundamental doctrine of our faith became to him so exceedingly clear that he renounced his unbelief and became a professor of Christianity.

Does it not strike you that many events of the greatest importance recorded in history, and commonly believed, could not in the nature of things have been witnessed by one-tenth as many as the resurrection of Christ? The signing of famous treaties affecting nations, the birth of princes, and the deeds of assassins —any of these have been made turning points in history and are never questioned as facts, yet only a few were present to witness them.

If it came to a matter of dispute, it would be far easier to prove that Christ is risen than to prove that Oliver Cromwell or George Washington is dead. If it came to counting the witnesses who saw them die and could attest to the identity of the dead body they saw in the death chamber, it would turn out to be far fewer than those who saw the Lord after He had risen and were persuaded that it was Jesus of Nazareth who was crucified and had burst the bonds of death.

Oh, how we should rejoice that beyond a doubt it is established that "now is Christ risen from the dead."

CHARLES H. SPURGEON

MOODY'S ANECDOTES

Counterfeit Humility

A man can counterfeit love, he can counterfeit faith, he can counterfeit hope and all the other graces, but it is very difficult to counterfeit humility. You soon detect mock humility. They have a saying in the East among the Arabs that as the tares and the wheat grow they show which God has blessed. The ears of wheat that God has blessed bow their heads and acknowledge every grain, and the more fruitful they are the lower their heads are bowed. The tares, which God has sent as a curse, lift up their heads erect, high above the wheat, but they are only fruitful of evil.

I have a pear tree on my farm that is very beautiful; it appears to be one of the most beautiful trees on my place. Every branch seems to be reaching up to the light and stands almost like a wax candle, but I never get any fruit from it. I have another tree, which was so full of fruit last year that the branches almost touched the ground. If we only get down low enough, my friends, God will use every one of us to His glory.

"As the lark that soars the highest builds her nest the lowest; as the nightingale that sings so sweetly sings in the shade when all things rest; as the branches that are most laden with fruit bend lowest; as the ship most laden sinks deepest in the water; so the holiest Christians are the humblest."

Some years ago the *London Times* told the story of a petition that was being circulated for signatures. The petition was intended to have great influence in the House of Lords, but one word was left out. Instead of reading, "We humbly beseech thee," it read, "We beseech thee." So it was ruled out. My friends, if we want to make an appeal to the God of heaven, we must humble ourselves; and if we do humble ourselves before the Lord, we shall not be disappointed.

D. L. MOODY

THE SECOND COMING OF CHRIST

Coming Again

Little is mentioned between Christ's ascent to heaven and His descent to come. True, a rich history comes between; but it lies in a valley between two stupendous mountains: we step from Alp to Alp as we journey in meditation from the ascension to the second advent.

Both His ascension and second coming are possible because of what happened during His first coming. Had He not come a first time in humiliation, born under the law, He could not come a second time in amazing glory "without a sin offering unto salvation." Because He died once, we rejoice that He dies no more. Death has no more dominion over Him, and therefore He will come again to destroy that last enemy whom He has already conquered. It is our joy, as we think of our Redeemer as risen, to feel that in consequence of His rising, the trump of the archangel shall assuredly sound for the awaking of all His slumbering people, when the Lord Himself shall descend from heaven with a shout.

As for His ascension, He could not a second time descend if He had not first ascended; but having perfumed heaven with His presence, and prepared a place for His people, we may fitly expect that He will come again and receive us unto Himself, that where He is there we may be also.

He will come again, for *He has promised to return.* We have His own word for it. That is our first reason for expecting Him. Among the last of the words that He spoke to His servant John are these, "Surely I come quickly." You may read it. "I am coming quickly. I am even now upon the road. I am traveling as fast as wisdom allows. I am always coming, and coming quickly."

CHARLES H. SPURGEON

BACK TO BETHEL

"It Is Not I"

Augustine was swept as by a mighty current between two women: his mother, Monica, a saintly woman, and another woman, who had fascinated him almost to damnation. His life hovered between these two just as your life hovers between Christ and Satan. Sometimes Monica attracted him heavenward, and then the evil influence of this woman dragged him to the very pit of the abyss. The conflict was long and terrible, and Augustine was like a ship upon the tide, swept backward and forward.

One afternoon, he states in his memorable confessions, he and his friend were in the garden together, and he thought he heard voices as of children calling over the garden wall, saying, "Take and read!" He thought it meant he was to take up the New Testament, which Monica had left on the garden seat. He picked it up and read in Romans 13 about casting off the works of darkness and putting on the works of light.

Instantly he arose. He had made his decision. He had counted the cost. He told his friend, and they went and told Monica, and Monica was glad.

The next day he went down the main street of Carthage. As he did so, he met the woman who had been the fascination of his soul for evil. As he met her she said, "Augustine, it is I!"

He said, "It is not I," and passed her and was saved. He became, as you know, St. Augustine.

I believe that I am talking to Augustines here; men who know better, but are doing worse; men who have sweet wives and the memory of holy mothers, and when they go home and take their little children upon their knees, it is impossible to describe the rush of holy love that comes. I tell you, your heart is between Satan and Christ—Satan, who will ruin it, and Christ, who wants to inhabit it. This is the moment of your choice. If you will quit sin and give yourself to God you shall yet be "St. Augustine," one of the children of God. There is a wonderful destiny awaiting you. You must call on Jesus Christ, and if you will, He will come in and keep you.

F. B. MEYER

MOODY'S ANECDOTES
"For Charlie's Sake"

Some years ago at a convention, an old judge was telling about the mighty power Christians summon to their aid in the petitions "for Christ's sake" and "in Jesus' name," and he told a story that made a great impression on me. When the war came on, the judge said, his only son left for the army, and he became suddenly interested in soldiers. Every soldier that passed by brought his son to remembrance; he could see his son in him. He went to work for soldiers. When a sick soldier came there to Columbus one day, so weak he couldn't walk, the judge took him in a carriage and got him into the Soldier's Home.

Soon the judge became president of the Soldier's Home in Columbus, and would go down every day and spend hours in looking after those soldiers and seeing that they had every comfort. He spent on them a great deal of time and money.

One day he said to his wife, "I'm giving too much time to these soldiers. I've got to stop it. There's an important case coming on in court, and I've got to attend to my own business."

He said he went down to the office that morning, resolved in the future to let the soldiers alone. He went to his desk and then to writing. Pretty soon the door opened, and he saw a soldier hobble slowly in. He started at the sight of him. The man was fumbling at something in his breast, and pretty soon he got out an old soiled paper. The father saw it was his son's own writing.

Dear father: This young man belongs to my company. He has lost his leg and his health in defense of his country, and he is going home to his mother to die. If he calls on you, treat him kindly,
For Charlie's sake.

"For Charlie's sake." The moment he saw that, a pang went to his heart. He sent for a carriage, lifted the maimed soldier in, drove home, put him into Charlie's room, sent for the family physician, kept him in the family, and treated him like he was his own son. When the young soldier got well enough to go to the train to go home to his mother, he took him to the railway station, put him in the nicest, most comfortable place in the carriage, and sent him on his way.

"I did it," said the old judge, "for Charlie's sake."

Now, whatsoever you do, my friends, do it for the Lord Jesus' sake. Do and ask everything in the name of Him "who loved us and gave himself for us."

D. L. MOODY

THE SECOND COMING OF CHRIST

"Godly" in Form Only

In passage after passage in the New Testament we are expressly told, either by Christ or by the apostles, that at the close of the present dispensation *wickedness will abound* both among professed believers and in the world at large. For example, in 2 Timothy 3 we read "that in the last days perilous times shall come. For men shall be lovers of their own selves, covetous, boasters, proud, blasphemers, disobedient to parents, unthankful, unholy, without natural affection, truce-breakers, false accusers, inconsistent, fierce, despisers of those that are good, traitors, heady, high-minded, lovers of pleasure more than lovers of God; having a *form of godliness* but denying the power thereof." This is not a description of pagans, mind you, but of the professed disciples of the Lord Jesus; for to such a state will Christendom, or the professing church of Christ, be reduced at the end of the present dispensation.

Notice especially that of these persons it is said that they have a *form* of godliness. They wish to be considered Christians. They are not avowed unbelievers and athiests, but professed *believers*.

Are we, then, to expect that things around us will gradually improve or rather that, as we approach the end of the age, they will become darker? True it is that one day, "the earth will be filled with the knowledge of the Lord, as the waters cover the sea," but this will never be until Jesus Himself comes.

GEORGE MUELLER

THE EMPTY TOMB

Eternal Adoration

Our body may be taken down as the tabernacle was in the wilderness, but it will be taken down to be put up again. "We know that if this earthly house of our tabernacle were dissolved, we have a building of God, a house not made with hands, eternal in the heavens."

My brothers, it would not be a complete victory over sin and Satan if the Savior left a part of His people in the grave; it would not look as if He had destroyed all the works of the devil if He only emancipated their spirits. There shall not be a bone, nor a piece of bone, of any of Christ's people left in the charnel house at last. Death shall not have a solitary trophy to show; the prison house shall be utterly rifed of all the spoil that he has gathered from our humanity. The Lord Jesus shall vanquish death and the grave, leading our captivity captive.

As Christ has redeemed the entire man, and sanctified the entire man, so our complete manhood shall have its power to glorify Him. The hands with which we sinned shall be lifted in eternal adoration; the eyes which have gazed on evil shall behold the king in his beauty. The spirit which contemplates him will delight forever in Him, but this very body which has been a clog and hindrance to the spirit, and an arch-rebel against the sovereignty of Christ, shall yield Him homage with voice and hand and brain and ear and eye.

We look to the time of the resurrection for the accomplishment of our adoption, specifically the redemption of our body.

CHARLES H. SPURGEON

MOODY'S ANECDOTES

"He Is My Brother!"

A fearful storm was raging, when the cry was heard: "Man overboard!" A human form bravely churned the furious elements toward the ship, but the raging waves carried the struggler rapidly in the direction of the shore. Before the boats could be lowered, a fearful space separated the victim from help. Above the shriek of the storm and roar of the waters rose his rending cry. It was an agonizing moment. With bated breath and blanched cheek, every eye was strained to the struggling man. Manfully did the brave rowers strain every nerve in that race of mercy; but all their efforts were in vain. One wild shriek of despair, and the victim went down.

A piercing cry, "Save him, save him!" rang through the hushed crowd; and into their midst darted an agitated man, throwing his arms wildly in the air, shouting, "A thousand pounds for the man who saves his life!" But his staring eyes rested only on the spot where the waves rolled remorselessly over the perished. He whose strong cry broke the stillness of the crowd was captain of the ship from whence the drowned man fell—and the man was *his brother*.

This is the feeling we should have in the various ranks of those bearing commission under the great captain of our salvation. "Save him! he is my brother."

The fact is, men do not believe in Christianity because they think we are not in earnest about it. When the people see that we are in earnest in all that we undertake for God, they will begin to tremble; men and women will be inquiring the way to Zion.

D. L. MOODY

KEPT FOR THE MASTER'S USE
Our Silver and Gold Kept for Jesus

The silver is mine, and gold is mine, saith the Lord of Hosts." Yes, every coin we have is literally our Lord's money. Simple belief of this fact is the stepping-stone to full consecration of what He has given us, whether much or little.

"Then you mean to say we are never to spend anything on ourselves?"

Not so. Another fact must be considered—our Lord has given us our bodies as a special personal charge, and we are responsible for keeping these bodies —according to the means given and the work required—in working order for Him. This is part of our "own work." A master entrusts a worker with a delicate machine for the assigned task. He also provides him with a sum of money to keep the machine in thorough repair. Is it not obvious that it is the man's distinct duty to see to this faithfully? Would not the worker be failing in duty if he chose to spend it all on something for somebody else's work or on a present for his master, fancying that would please him better, while the machine is creaking and wearing for want of a little oil or working badly for the want of a new band or screw? Just so, we are to spend what is really needful on ourselves, because it us our charge to do so; but not for ourselves, because we are not our own but our master's.

He knows our frame, knows its need of rest and medicine, food, and cloth-ing; and the securing of these for our own entrusted bodies should be done just as much "for Jesus" as the greater pleasure of obtaining them for someone else. Therefore, the assertion is true: consecration is not real and complete while we are looking upon a single cent as our own to do what we like with. Also the principle is exactly the same, whether we are spending pennies or dollars: It is our Lord's money and must not be spent without reference to Him.

FRANCES R. HAVERGAL

THE WAY TO GOD

Wooing Those Who Have Forsaken

How many once in fellowship and daily communion with the Lord now think more of their dresses and ornaments than of their precious souls! Love does not like to be forgotten. Mothers would have broken hearts if their children left them and never wrote a word or sent any memento of their affection; and God pleads over backsliders as a parent over loved ones who have gone astray. He tries to woo them back. He asks, "What have I done that they should have forsaken Me?"

The most tender and loving words to be found in the whole of the Bible are from Jehovah to those who have left Him without a cause. Hear how He argues with such: "Thine own wickedness shall correct thee, and thy backslidings shall reprove thee: know therefore and see that it is an evil thing and bitter, that thou hast forsaken the Lord thy God, and that my fear is not in thee, saith the Lord God of hosts" (Jeremiah 2:19).

I do not exaggerate when I say that I have seen hundreds of backsliders come back, and I have asked them if they have not found it an evil and a bitter thing to leave the Lord. You cannot find a real backslider who has known the Lord but will admit that it is an evil and a bitter thing to turn away from Him. I do not know of any one verse more used to bring back wanderers than that very one. May it bring you back if you have wandered into the far country.

Look at Lot. Did he not find it an evil and a bitter thing? He was twenty years in Sodom and never made a convert. He got on well in the sight of the world. Men would have told you that he was one of the most influential and worthy men in all Sodom. But alas! He ruined his family. And it is a pitiful thing to see that old backslider going through the streets of Sodom at midnight, after he has warned his children, and they have turned a deaf ear.

I have never known a man and his wife to backslide without its proving utter ruin to their children. They will make a mockery of religion and will deride their parents: "Thine own wickedness shall correct thee; and thy backsliding shall reprove thee!" Did not David find it so? Mark him, crying, "O my son Absalom, my son, my son Absalom! would God I had died for thee; O Absalom, my son, my son!" I think it was the ruin, rather than the death, of his son that caused this anguish.

D. L. MOODY

THE NEW LIFE IN JESUS CHRIST
Developing the Inner Life

The inner life is neither the entire eradication of the flesh, the death of self, nor is it sinless perfection. True, self is abhorred, distrusted, and detested. But so uniform are the characteristics of this experience, whatever the age, that it is not difficult to state both the results of and the steps to a strong inner life.

First, in developing the inner life, we have the revelation of God Himself to the soul. The revelation is not something about God—some new testimony concerning God or some lesson of sorrow or trial. It is God's own act to reveal of Himself something that the testimony of others had never communicated. Thus, there is a new and intense apprehension of Himself.

Second, the instances quoted from the Scriptures agree, too, in the effect of this unveiling of God. Before that vision of God, self is abhorred. So absolute is this effect that, as we have seen, it is constantly spoken of as the utter deprivation of strength. The self-life is not slain, but in that glory it is seen as never again to be trusted or in any way counted on in the things of God. As Paul said, "We had the sentence of death in ourselves, that we should not trust in ourselves, but in God, which raiseth the dead" (2 Corinthians 1:9), in the God of the new, undying life.

Third, the biblical instances agree that this destruction of self-confidence is followed by the infilling with the strength of Him who was dead and is alive again. Though the man at first is on his face before the awful, beautiful vision, not once is he left prostrate. "I received strength," is the unvarying testimony.

And then comes the new and higher service. This is the blessed consummation: this and the new fruitfulness. Could I covet anything better for you than that you should see God face to face? Could I desire more than that there should come to you this highest word in the epic of the inner life? May He grant it, for His name's sake.

C. I. SCOFIELD

FIT FOR THE MASTER'S USE

The Secret of Fruitfulness

I, the Almighty God, swear by myself, since I can swear by no greater, that if thou wilt fulfill the conditions of my covenant, I will make thee exceeding fruitful, and thou shalt be father to a great multitude."

"Walk before me, and be thou perfect."

This is the one prime and irreversible condition for the life that shall become fruitful. We have walked before our friends, our neighbors, our church, and the world, very eager to win their regard and approval. Each step we have taken with the consciousness that we were being watched and with the secret desires that it should be approved. All that must be changed. "Walk before me," He says, whose eyes are as a flame of fire. "Let your eye be single. Let your intention be Godward. Let it be your one aim to please Me. The eyes of the Lord run to and fro in all the earth." "My eyes are ever toward the Lord."

The word rendered "perfect" does not mean that moral blamelessness with which we are accustomed to associate it. It connotes wholeheartedness, entire surrender, absolute consecration, up to the measure of light. Be perfect: there must be no reserve. Be perfect: there must be no Babylonish garment withheld from the fire. Be perfect: there must be no gold, silver, or precious stone that are not freely exposed to the searching tongue of flame. Be perfect: there must be no lowing of the herds or bleating of the flocks that have been unsurrendered to God.

It is the prime condition of fruitfulness. Have we conformed to it? Is there a glad acquiescence to God's every command? Have we presented ourselves as a living sacrifice? Are we willing that God should have all? Do we recognize His will as the one blessed code of life? And are we prepared to walk like this, step by step, though the feet bleed as we pass over the jagged rock? Then take heart, for it is to such that God says, "I will make thee exceeding fruitful."

F. B. MEYER

ACCORDING TO PROMISE

Confidence in the Promise

When the storm was raging against the ship that was taking Paul to Rome, Paul believed that all in the ship with him would escape because God had promised it. He accepted the promise as ample security for the fact and acted accordingly. He was calm amid the storm; he gave his comrades sage and sensible advice as to breaking their fast; and, in general, he managed matters as a man would do who was sure of a happy escape from the tempest. Thus, he treated God as He should be treated, namely, with unquestioning confidence. An upright man likes to be trusted; it would grieve him if he saw that he was regarded with suspicion. Our faithful God is jealous of His honor and cannot endure that men should treat Him as if He could be false. Unbelief provokes the Lord above any other sin; it cuts Him to the quick. Far be it from us to perpetrate so infamous a wrong toward our heavenly Father. Let us believe Him up to the hilt, placing no bounds to our hearty reliance upon His Word.

Paul openly avowed his confidence in the promise. It is well that we should do the same. Bold, outspoken testimonies to the truth of God are greatly needed at this time, and they may prove to be of sevenfold value. The air is full of doubt; indeed, few really and substantially believe. Such a man as George Mueller, who believes in God for the maintenance of two thousand children, is a rare personage.

"When the Son of man cometh, shall he find faith on the earth?" Therefore let us speak out. Infidelity has defied us; let no man's heart fail him, but let us meet the giant with the sling and stone of actual experience and unflinching witness. God does keep His promise, and we know it. We dare endorse every one of His promises. We would do it with our blood if it were needful! The Word of the Lord endures forever, and of this we are undaunted witnesses, even all of us who are called by His name.

CHARLES H. SPURGEON

THE TRUE VINE

The Power of Prayer

As fruit is the great proof of the true relation to Christ, so prayer is of our relation to the Father. A fruitful abiding in the Son and prevailing prayer to the Father are the two great factors in the true Christian life.

"That whatsoever ye shall ask of the Father in my name, he may give it you." These are the closing words of the parable of the vine in John 15. The whole mystery of the vine and its branches leads up to the other mystery—that whatever we ask in His name the Father gives! See here the reason of the lack of prayer and of the lack of power in prayer. It is because we so little live the true branch life, because we so little lose ourselves in the vine, abiding in Him entirely, that we feel so little constrained to much prayer, so little confident that we shall be heard, and so do not know how to use His name as the key to God's storehouse. The vine planted on earth has reached up into heaven; it is only the soul wholly and intensely abiding in it that can reach into heaven with power to prevail much. Our faith in the teaching and the truth of the parable, in the truth and the life of the vine, must prove itself by power in prayer. The life of abiding and obedience, of love and joy, of cleansing and fruit-bearing, will surely lead to the power of prevailing prayer.

"Whatsoever ye shall ask. . . ." The promise was given to disciples who were ready to give themselves, in the likeness of the true vine, for their fellow men. This promise was all their provision for their work; they took it literally, they believed it, they used it, and they found it true. Let us give ourselves, as branches of the true vine and in His likeness, to the work of saving men, of bringing forth fruit to the glory of God, and we shall find a new urgency and power to pray and to claim the "whatsoever ye ask."

ANDREW MURRAY

PLEASURE AND PROFIT IN BIBLE STUDY
The Title Deed

I have heard some people say that it was not their privilege to know that they were saved; they had heard the minister say that no one could know whether they were saved or not; and they took what the minister said instead of what the Word of God said. Others read the Bible to make it fit in and prove their favorite creed or notions; and if it does not do so, they will not read it. It has been well said that we must not read the Bible by the blue light of Presbyterianism; nor by the red light of Methodism; nor by the violet light of Episcopalianism; but by the light of the Spirit of God. If you will take up your Bible and study about assurance for a week, you will soon see that it is your privilege to know that you are a child of God.

Then take the promises of God. Let a man feed for a month on the promises of God, and he will not talk about his poverty and how downcast he is and what trouble he has day by day. If you would only go from Genesis to Revelation and see all the promises made by God to Abraham, to Isaac, and to Jacob, to the Jews and the Gentiles, and to all His people everywhere; if you would spend a month feeding on the precious promises of God, you would not go about with your heads hanging down like bulrushes, complaining how poor you are; but you would lift up your heads with confidence and proclaim the riches of His grace, because you could not help it. After the Chicago fire a man came up to me and said in a sympathizing tone, "I understand you lost everything, Moody, in the Chicago fire."

"Well, then," said I, "someone has misinformed you."

"Indeed! Why I was certainly told you had lost all."

"No. It is a mistake," I said, "quite a mistake."

"Have you got much left, then?" asked my friend.

"Yes," I replied. "I have got much more left than I lost; though I cannot tell how much I have lost."

"Well, I am glad of it, Moody; I did not know you were that rich before the fire."

"Yes," said I. "I am a good deal richer than you could conceive; and here is my title deed: 'He that overcometh shall inherit all things.'"

They say the Rothschilds cannot tell how much they are worth; and that is just my case. All things in the world are mine; I am joint heir with Jesus the Son of God. Someone has said, "God makes a promise; faith believes it; hope anticipates it; and patience quietly awaits it."

D. L. MOODY

FIT FOR THE MASTER'S USE
The Great Shepherd of the Sheep

Deep down in the heart of man God has set eternity; that is, yearnings and desire that cannot be satisfied with mere immortality or immunity from sin and sorrow. We might have these, but if we were not righteous, if we did not do God's will, if we were not pleasing Him and fulfilling His ideal, we should be always conscious of a secret, infinite regret.

Such hunger is prophetic of its satisfaction. The seabirds do not roam the acres of sparkling wavelets in vain; nor in vain do the young lions roar after their food. The babe does not cry for sustenance that is not stored for it or the youth demand the love the maiden cannot give. It were rather a devil who should make the appetite without providing means for its satisfaction. But our God creates the desire that He may give it realization. The very desire is blessed. As we desire, we possess. "Blessed are they that hunger and thirst after righteousness, for they shall be filled."

And God wants us to realize His ideal perfectly. A lily, it has been truly said, is a very beautiful object, though in England it does not attain to the full beauty of the *Victoria Regia* of Australia. A voice may be very sweet for the drawing room, which would be altogether deficient in compass for the concert room. We may be easily able to fulfill the measure of a comparatively small and limited sphere, when we would altogether fail in the greater one. It is extremely delightful to see the swallows as they dart to and fro perfected in flight up to the measure of their requirement, though unable to attain the majestic flight of the eagle. So God wants us to be perfect up to the measure of our capacity and sphere—"perfect in every good work to do his will."

God seems to say, "I want you to be full-orbed, to fill up the circumference of your disc with light, to be as strong and sweet and gentle as possible, to please Me in all directions, to attain to a perfect balance of character, to add in your faith virtue, and in your virtue knowledge, self-control, godliness, love of the brethren."

F. B. MEYER

ABSOLUTE SURRENDER
Kept by the Power of God

Think, first of all, that God's keeping is all-inclusive.

What is kept? You are kept. How much of you? The whole being. Does God keep one part of you and not another? No. Some people have an idea that this is a sort of vague, general keeping and that God will keep them in such a way that when they die they will get to heaven. But they do not apply that word *kept* to everything in their being and nature. And yet that is what God wants.

Here I have a watch. Suppose that this watch had been borrowed from a friend and that he said to me, "When you go to Europe I will let you take it with you, but mind you keep it safely and bring it back."

And suppose I injured the watch, had the hands broken and the face defaced and some of the wheels and springs spoiled and took it back in that condition and handed it to my friend. He would say, "Ah, but I gave you that watch on condition that you would keep it."

"Have I not kept it? There is the watch."

"But I did not want you to keep it in that general way, so that you should bring me back only the shell of the watch, or the remains. I expected you to keep every part of it."

And so God does not want to keep us in this general way, so that at the last, somehow or other, we shall be saved as by fire and just get into heaven. But the keeping power and love of God applies to every particular of our being.

There are some people who think God will keep them in spiritual things but not in temporal things. This latter, they say, lies outside of His line. Now, God sends you to work in the world, but He did not say, "I must now leave you to go and earn your own money and to get your livelihood for yourself." He knows you are not able to keep yourself. But God says, "My child, there is no work you are to do, and no business in which you are engaged, and not a cent which you are to spend, but I, your Father, will take that up into My keeping."

ANDREW MURRAY

ANSWERS TO PRAYER

God Will Supply All Our Needs

My comfort was that, if it were His will, He would provide not merely the means but also suitable individuals to take care of the children. The whole of those two weeks I never asked the Lord for money or for persons to engage in the work.

On December 5, however, the subject of my prayer all at once became different. I was reading Psalm 81 and was particularly struck, more than any time before, with verse 10: "Open thy mouth wide, and I will fill it." I thought a few moments about these words, and then was led to apply them to the case of the orphan house. It struck me that I had never asked the Lord for anything concerning it, except to know His will, respecting its being established or not; and then I fell on my knees and opened my mouth wide, asking Him for much.

I asked in submission to His will, without fixing a time when He should answer my petition. I prayed that He would give me a house, either as a loan or that someone might be led to pay the rent for one or that one might be given permanently for this object; further, I asked him for 1,000 pounds; and likewise for suitable individuals to take care of the children. Besides this, I have been since led to ask the Lord to put into the hearts of His people to send me articles of furniture for the house and some clothes for the children. When I was asking the petition, I was fully aware what I was doing—that I was asking for something that I had no natural prospect of obtaining from the brothers whom I know, but which was not too much for the Lord to grant.

December 10, 1835—This morning I received a letter in which a brother and sister wrote thus: "We propose ourselves for the service of the intended orphan house, if you think us qualified for it; also to give up all the furniture, etc., which the Lord has given us, for its use; and to do this without receiving any salary whatever; believing that if it be the will of the Lord to employ us, He will supply all our needs."

GEORGE MUELLER

CHARGE THAT TO MY ACCOUNT

Not of Blood

A few years ago my wife and I and our children were on our way West. My eldest son, just a little boy at the time, was fond of going through the train pretending that he was the news agent. He said, "Father, have you any tracts I could give out?" I had some and so handed them to him. He handed everybody one of these gospel tracts, and soon most of the people were reading them. A little later I was passing through the car, and a lady occupying one of the sections stopped me and said, "I beg your pardon, sir, but I think it was your child who gave me this tract, was it not?"

"Yes, it was," I said.

"Won't you sit down a moment?" she asked.

So I introduced my wife, and we sat down.

"You cannot imagine," she said, "how pleased I am to know that there are other religious people on this train."

"You are interested in these things?" I inquired.

"Yes, indeed," she said. "I have been religious all my life."

"When were you born again?" I asked.

"Oh," she replied, "my father was a class leader, and an uncle and two brothers of mine are all clergymen."

"That is very interesting," I said. "And may I ask again, have you been converted yourself?"

"Why, you don't seem to understand; my father was a class leader, and my uncle and two brothers are earnest clergymen."

"But you don't expect to go to heaven hanging on their coattails, even if they are born again, do you? Have you been truly converted to God yourself?" I asked.

"Not at all," she replied, "but I thought if I put it that way, you would understand that religion runs in our family."

"Religion may run in your family, but religion and Christianity are two very different things," I said. "There are a great many people who are intensely religious, but they are not saved. Our blessed Lord was speaking to a very religious man when He said, 'Ye must be born again.'"

I had great difficulty getting that lady to see that salvation is not of blood. She could scarcely understand how a family such as hers needed regeneration. Perhaps you have rather prided yourself in the fact that you too came from a line of Christian progenitors and have taken it for granted that because your parents were Christians, you are. Let's remember, "which were born, not of blood."

HENRY A. IRONSIDE

THE NEW LIFE IN JESUS CHRIST

Something from Without Put Within the Heart

We find the wretched man of Romans 7 at peace and victorious in Romans 8; what is now his testimony? "The law of the Spirit of life in Christ Jesus hath made me free from the law of sin and death" (Romans 8:2). Not a new resolution, nor a new habit, nor a deeper hold on himself, nor more prayer. Do you think that a man in the agony of Romans 7 does not pray? You may be sure that the apostle Paul, when he was there, prayed day and night on his face before God. Yet neither more prayer nor more anything that you and I can do, nor that Paul could do, made the difference. It's only something that God can do.

That is what Paul means: not more from within, but something from without put within. And almost while he is saying, "Oh, wretched man that I am," out of the very agony of spiritual defeat Paul lifts up his face in triumphant testimony, for he has found the secret, and he says, "The law of the spirit of life in Christ Jesus hath made me free from the law of sin and death."

So this man can write afterward, "For me to live is Christ." He writes this to the Philippians, who knew him more intimately than you know me. And he could say to those Galatians who had seen him under trial and testing, "The life which now I live in the flesh, I live by the faith of the Son of God." He realized that Christian life proceeded not by his efforts, his resolutions, nor his vows, but by the power and the authority of the Spirit of life in Christ Jesus.

Defeated along the line of the will, he is victorious by the power of the Spirit within him; the superhuman standard achieved by superhuman power. Paul laid hold of that power, and so we have the triumphant eighth chapter of Romans, which may be the experience of every child of God—a life of continual victory, peace, and power.

C. I. SCOFIELD

GOD'S WAY OF HOLINESS

Recognizing the Truth

Our spiritual constitution must be braced, not only that we may be strong for work or fight, but that we may be proof against the infection of the times, against the poison with which the god of this world, "the prince of the power of the air," has impregnated our atmosphere. For this we need not only the "strong meat" recommended by the apostle (Hebrews 5:12–14) but the keen, fresh mountain air of trial, vicissitude, and hardship—by means of which we shall be made hardy in constitution and robust in frame, impervious to the contagion around, whether that come from ecclesiastical pictorialism or religious liberalism; impregnable against the assaults of Satan the Pharisee or Satan the Sadducee.

They who have slid into a creed (they know not how) or been swept into it by the crowd; they to whom the finding of a creed has been a matter of reading, education, or emotion—they possess not the true power of resistance; they carry no disinfecting virtue, no error-repelling power about with them. The epidemics of the age tell sorely upon them, and, even though they may have taken hold of the truth, it becomes evident that the truth has not taken hold of them. In a time of uncertainty, skepticism, speculation, false progress, we need to recognize the full meaning of the apostolic "we know" (1 John 5:19–20), "we believe" (2 Corinthians 4:13), "we are confident" (2 Corinthians 5:6), "we are persuaded" (2 Timothy 1:12). For that which is divine must be true; and that which is revealed must be certain; and that which is thus divinely true and certain must be immortal. Like the results of the exact sciences, it is fixed, not varying with men and ages. That which was true is true and shall be true forever.

It is the more needful to recognize all this, because the ground underneath us has been thoroughly mined and is very largely hollow; a process of skeptical decomposition and disintegration has been going on, the extent of which will soon be manifest when the treacherous crust gives way.

HORATIUS BONAR

MOODY'S LATEST SERMONS

The Comforting Christ

If she had thought He was going to rise, I believe Mary would have been at the grave early on the third morning. No Roman soldier, no power on earth could have kept that loving heart away from that sepulchre. But she believed He was going to die, and so she took an alabaster box of ointment and broke it over Him.

Did you ever think that there were only two gifts that were given to the Son of God when He was on earth that He could not give away? In the seventh chapter of Luke we read of a poor woman who came with an alabaster box and anointed Him with ointment, and here Mary also takes a box and breaks it and pours out the precious ointment upon Him.

The disciples were indignant and found fault. The best things I have ever done since I became a Christian, I have been blamed for. People have found fault with me, and even the religious papers attack me for the best things that I have ever done. When I am dead and gone, people will acknowledge it. Oh, it is so hard when you are working for Christ to have His disciples indignant with you and say bitter things!

When Mary broke that box and anointed Jesus, there was great indignation among the disciples. Judas, that traitor, who was already planning to sell his Lord, was the most indignant of all. He was treasurer of the company. Mary thought he had great influence and undoubtedly esteemed him more highly than herself. She thought she was the least of His disciples, but thank God, love just overflowed, and she broke that box and anointed Him.

It was a great thing when Samuel anointed David, but no king ever had such a kingly anointing as when Mary anointed Christ with that ointment that was so sweet and so precious. One of the disciples figured up the price and said that it was worth three hundred pence! A penny would hire a man all day, so that one pound of ointment had cost a year's work.

But Jesus estimated the worth differently. He rebuked the disciples, and said: "Why trouble ye the woman, for she hath wrought a good work upon me . . . For in that she hath poured this ointment on my body, she did it for my burial. Verily I say unto you, wheresoever this gospel shall be preached in the whole world, there shall also this that this woman hath done be told for a memorial."

Think of it! Wherever the gospel of the Son of God is to be preached in this wide world, that story is to be told!

There is nothing lost that we do for Christ.

D. L. MOODY

FIT FOR THE MASTER'S USE

Living the Life of Jesus

Had Jesus so chosen, He might have planned His own life and from the transfiguration mountain have stepped into paradise. He might have spoken His own words and have poured forth upon men such a flood of eloquence as would have shone on the pages of literature with dazzling brilliancy. He might have done His work by His own power, working His miracles merely to increase His own reputation. He might have sought His own glory as the supreme end of His life, so displaying His power and glory that His divinity should be apparent to all. Our Lord Jesus might have lived an independent life, and Satan was always luring Him to do it.

Straight from the river Jordan Jesus was led up of the Spirit into the wilderness to be tested of the devil. You who have been baptized for service are almost certain to be led by the Spirit into the wilderness to be tempted, just because God desires to do a mighty work in your soul. The oak, which is to live for a hundred years, must be rooted and moored to stand the storm, and God, wanting you to become a strong, sturdy oak, will most certainly lead you into testing. [The testing can bring temptation, but] temptation is not sin if the temptation is resisted. The effect of being tempted is to root us more in Christ.

In effect, the first thing the devil said to Jesus was, "Thou art the Son of God. God has just owned Thee as such, as the second person of the holy Trinity. Thou hast all power. Now use that power for Thyself, and make these stones bread."

That was the crucial point in our Lord's life, and He said, "No, I am going to be a dependent human being. Inasmuch as those whom I have come to save depend upon My Father and upon Me, I will learn what it is to depend by faith absolutely upon My Father. If My Father does not feed Me, I will die of hunger. Man shall not live by bread alone but by every word of God, and I am going to wait for My Father to speak."

F. B. MEYER

ACCORDING TO PROMISE

The Time of the Promise

The Lord is prompt to the moment in carrying out His gracious engagements. The Lord had threatened to destroy the world with a flood, but He waited the full time of respite until Noah had entered the ark; and then, on the selfsame day, the fountains of the great deep were broken up. He had declared that Israel should come out of Egypt, and it was so: "And it came to pass at the end of the four hundred and thirty years, even at the selfsame day it came to pass, that all the hosts of the Lord went out from the land of Egypt" (Exodus 12:41). According to Daniel, the Lord numbers the years of His promise and counts the weeks of His waiting. As for the greatest promise of all, namely, the sending of His Son from heaven, the Lord was not slow in that great gift, "but when the fullness of the time was come, God sent forth his Son, made of a woman." Beyond all question, the Lord our God keeps His Word to the moment.

When we are in need, we may be urgent with the Lord to come quickly to our rescue, even as David pleaded in the seventieth psalm, "Make haste, O God, to deliver me; make haste to help me, O Lord" (verse 1). "I am poor and needy; make haste unto me, O God: Thou art my help and my deliverer; O Lord, make no tarrying" (verse 5). The Lord even condescends to describe Himself as making speed to carry out His gracious engagements: "I the Lord will hasten it in his time" (Isaiah 60:22). But we must not pray in this fashion as though we had the slightest fear that the Lord could or would delay or that He needed us to quicken His diligence. No. "The Lord is not slack concerning His promise, as some men count slackness" (2 Peter 3:9). Our God is slow to anger, but in the deeds of grace "his word runneth very swiftly" (Psalm 147:15). Sometimes His speed to bless His people outstrips time and thought: as, for instance, when He fulfills that ancient declaration, "It shall come to pass, that before they call, I will answer; and while they are yet speaking, I will hear" (Isaiah 65:24).

CHARLES H. SPURGEON

THE WAY HOME
Rest Awaits Us

When men go up in a balloon, they carry with them what they call ballast, that is, small bags of sand, and when they want to rise higher they just throw out some of the sand. So must we if we want to rise nearer heaven, just throw out some of the sand and cast aside every weight. We won't rise higher till we do so. But you say, "I can't throw my money into the street; I have made it and saved it, and I am not going to waste it."

Oh no, you'll soon find a good use for it if you want to, and thus you may get rid of some of the ballast that is holding you on the way to heaven. When you are enabled thus to lend to the Lord, to put your money in His bank, the world will soon lose its power with you.

When Abraham once caught sight of the holy city with the eyes of his understanding, which were opened to see its glories, then it was that he "confessed that he was a stranger and a pilgrim on the earth, and that he looked for a city which hath foundations, whose builder and maker is God." He had no desire to stay here—heaven was his home—so much brighter, so much better than anything he could find here below. We must all feel we are but pilgrims here, our home is above. Our feet are often weary and our hearts heavy, but never mind that. Let us look forward to that "city which hath foundations." Weary we may be, and often are, but, blessed be God, there is a place of rest! There is rest for the weary there.

A great many look upon the Christian church on earth as a place of rest. Never was a greater mistake. The church is no place of rest; it is a place of work. "There remaineth therefore a rest to the people of God" (Hebrews 4:9).

"If Joshua had given them rest, then would he not afterwards have spoken of another day." Do you look for that rest here? There is none. If you are resting you are neglecting your duty, you are shirking your work, and will never enjoy heaven thoroughly. It's the weary only who know what true rest is. "Work while it is called today." Be up and doing. That which your hand finds to do in your master's vineyard, do it with all your might. "Be not weary in well-doing; for in due time ye shall reap, if ye faint not."

Blessed be God, "there remaineth a rest"! No rest here below; nothing but toil and labor. And you will enjoy your rest all the more when you come to the beautiful land above. There are always trials, and tribulations, and labors here. The rest is up yonder where Christ is. Work on, hope on, pray on!

D. L. MOODY

THE CHRIST-LIFE FOR THE SELF-LIFE

The Natural Man

When God created man, He gave all intelligent beings a self-hood, a power of self-determination. He gave it to angels. Demons have it, because they are angels. Men have self-hood. The Creator meant the self-hood to be dependent on Him, so that a Christian might turn to the Creator and say: "May Your will live through me."

When Jesus Christ, the perfect man, came among men, during all His earthly life He said nothing and willed nothing from Himself; He lived a truly dependent life.

The vegetable creation, the flowers, the trees—they depend on God absolutely, and that makes them so beautiful. And the angels who have kept their first estate live on God. Satan was once an archangel dependent on God, but something passed over him and he caught the fever of independence, and began to make himself his own pivot. As a result, Satan earned himself hell; because hell is the assertion of self to the exclusion of God, and heaven is the assertion of God to the exclusion of self. The devil fell, and all his crew that leaned on him, instead of on God, fell also. Then when man was made, Satan whispered to man, "Be God, be independent, take your own way, do your own will." And man and women fell away from God.

In his fall, man withdrew his nature from dependence upon God, and made himself a center of his own life and activity. And this world is cursed today because men and women are living for self. The carnal mind is enmity against God, and is darkness and despair.

F. B. MEYER

ACCORDING TO PROMISE

The Promises in Possession

Heaven will much consist in holiness; and it is clear that, as far as the Holy Spirit makes us holy here, He has implanted the beginnings of heaven. Heaven is victory; and each time that we overcome sin, Satan, the world, and the flesh, we have foretastes of the unfading triumph that causes the waving of palms in the New Jerusalem. Heaven is an endless Sabbath; and how can we have a better foretaste of the perfect rest than by that joy and peace that are shed abroad in us by the Holy Ghost?

Communion with God is a chief ingredient in the bliss of the glorified; here below, by the spirit of God, we are enabled to delight ourselves in the Lord and rejoice in the God of our salvation. Fellowship with the Lord Jesus in all His gracious purposes and likeness to Him in love to God and man are also chief constituents in our perfected condition before the throne. The Spirit of holiness is working fellowship and love in us from day to day.

To be pure in heart so as to see God, to be established in character so as to be fixed in righteousness, to be strong in good so as to overcome all evil, and to be cleansed from self so as to find our all in God; are not these, when carried to the full, among the central benedictions of the beatific vision? And are they not already bestowed upon us by that Spirit of glory and of power who even now rests upon us? It is so. In the Holy Spirit we have the things we seek after. In Him the flower of heaven has come to us in the bud; the dawn of the day of glory has smiled upon us.

We are not, then, such strangers to the promised blessings as common talk would make us out to be. Many repeat, like parrots, the word "Eye hath not seen, nor ear heard, neither have entered into the heart of man, the things which God hath prepared for them that love Him" (1 Corinthians 2:9); but they fail to add the words that follow in the same Scripture: "but God hath revealed them unto us by His Spirit." The Holy Spirit has revealed to us what neither eye nor ear has perceived. He has drawn back the curtains and bidden us see the secrets hidden from ages and from generations.

CHARLES H. SPURGEON

SECRET POWER

The Unpardonable Sin

I admit that there is such a thing as resisting the Spirit of God and resisting till the Spirit of God has departed; but, if the Spirit of God has left any, they will not be troubled about their sins. The very fact that they are troubled shows that the Spirit of God has not left them. Satan makes us believe that we are pretty good; that we are good enough without God, safe without Christ, and that we don't need salvation. But when a person wakes up to the fact that he is lost, that he is a sinner, that is the work of the Spirit. When men and women want to be Christians, the Spirit of God surely is drawing them.

If resisting the Spirit of God is an unpardonable sin, then we have all committed it, and there is no hope for any of us; for I do not believe there is a minister or a worker in Christ's vineyard who has not, some time in his life, resisted the Holy Spirit, who has not some time in his life rejected the Spirit of God. To resist the Holy Spirit is one thing, and to commit that awful sin of blasphemy against the Holy Spirit is another thing; and we want to take the Scripture and just compare them. Now, some people say, "I have such blasphemous thoughts; there are some awful thoughts that come into my mind against God," and they think that is the unpardonable sin. We are not to blame for having bad thoughts come into our minds. If we harbor them, then we are to blame. But if the devil comes and darts an evil thought into my mind, and I say, "Lord, help me," sin is not reckoned to me. Who has not had evil thoughts flash into his mind, flash into his heart, and been called to fight them?

One old divine says, "You are not to blame for the birds that fly over your head, but if you allow them to come down and make a nest in your hair, then you are to blame. You are to blame if you don't fight them off." And so with these evil thoughts that come flashing into our minds; we have to fight them, we are not to harbor them; we are not to entertain them. Remember, when an evil thought comes into your mind and evil desires, it is no sign that you have committed the unpardonable sin.

D. L. MOODY

THE TRUE VINE

His Joy in Us

To many Christians the thought of a life wholly abiding in Christ is one of strain and painful effort. They cannot see that the strain and effort only come as long as we do not yield ourselves unreservedly to the life of Christ in us. The very first words of the parable are not yet opened up to them: "I am the true vine; I undertake all and provide for all; I ask nothing of the branch but that it yields wholly to Me and allows Me to do all. I engage to make and keep the branch all that it ought to be." Ought it not to be an infinite and unceasing joy to have the vine thus work all? Each moment let us allow the blessed Son of God in His love to maintain our life.

"That my joy might remain in you" (John 15:11). We are to have Christ's own joy in us. And what is Christ's own joy? There is no joy like love. There is no joy but love. Christ had just spoken of the Father's love and His own abiding in it and of His having loved us with that same love. His joy is nothing but the joy of love, of being loved and of loving. It was the joy of receiving His Father's love and abiding in it and then the joy of passing on that love and pouring it out on sinners. It is this joy He wants us to share: the joy of being loved of the Father and of Him; the joy of in our turn loving and living for those around us. This is just the joy of being truly branches: abiding in His love and then giving up ourselves in love to bear fruit for others.

Let us accept His life as He gives it in us as the vine. His joy will be ours: the joy of abiding in His love, the joy of loving like Him, of loving with His love.

ANDREW MURRAY

FIT FOR THE MASTER'S USE

No Favoritism with God

You may admit that God's abundant grace is near you through Jesus Christ, and yet you may not quite see the necessity of learning how to take. Some people are always telegraphing to heaven for God to send a cargo of blessing to them, but they are not at the wharfside to unload the vessel when it comes. How many of God's richest blessings for which you have been praying for years have come close to you, but you do not know how to lay hold of and use them.

Mark: "They that receive abundance of grace shall reign." The emphasis is not on grace, not on abundance, but on receiving it. The whole grace of God may be around your life today, but, if you have not learned to take it in, it won't help you.

All that God has is within your reach, but you must learn to take it. If a man hears that he has suddenly come into a fortune, and that money is waiting for him in the bank, he goes there by the first train, but he doesn't ask for it as if it were to be made a present to him. He goes in and says, "This is my name. You have money standing in that name, and I have come to claim it."

There are many things in prayer that we cannot be certain of because we have no definite promise to stand upon, but there are also many things in the book that are waiting for us to come for them, and God says, "If you will come and take them, you may have them." You have only to go to God and, supposing you are in a right condition (it may be that you are not), you may open your entire nature to God and believe that, as you claim, God gives. "He that asketh, receiveth." If you want Christ to be your purity, Christ to be your power, Christ to be your salvation, kneel before Him; breathe in what God has promised to bestow; and reckon that, as you open your nature to take, God Almighty gives. You may have no rush of feeling, yet you leave your closet and go forth to your daily life, including the turmoil and temptation, all the time reckoning that what you dared humbly and reverently to claim in the name of Jesus, God Almighty gave.

F. B. MEYER

MOODY'S STORIES
The Fire Alarm

In 1871 I preached a series of sermons on the life of Christ in old Farwell Hall, Chicago, for five nights. I took Christ from the cradle and followed Him up to the judgment hall, and on that occasion I consider I made as great a blunder as ever I made in my life. It was upon that memorable night in October that the courthouse bell was sounding an alarm of fire, but I paid no attention to it. You know we were accustomed to hear the fire bell often, and it didn't disturb us much when it sounded. I finished the sermon upon "What Shall I Do with Jesus?" and said to the audience:

"Now I want you to take the question with you and think it over, and next Sunday I want you to come back and tell me what you are going to do with Him."

What a mistake! It seems now as if Satan was in my mind when I said this. Since then I never have dared give an audience a week to think of their salvation. If they were lost, they might rise up in judgment against me. "Now is the accepted time."

I remember Mr. Sankey singing, and how his voice rang when he came to that pleading verse:

> Today the Savior calls,
> For refuge fly!
> The storm of Justice falls
> And death is nigh!

After the meeting we went home. I remember going down LaSalle Street with a young man and seeing the glare of flames. I said to the young man, "This means ruin to Chicago."

About one o'clock Farwell Hall was burned; soon the church in which I had preached went down, and everything was scattered. I never saw that audience again.

My friends, we don't know what may happen tomorrow, but there is one thing I do know, and that is, if you take the gift of God you are saved. If you have eternal life you need not fear fire, death, or sickness. Let disease or death come, you can shout triumphantly over the grave if you have Christ. My friends, what are you going to do with Him? Will you not decide now?

D. L. MOODY

ACCORDING TO PROMISE

The Rule of God's Giving

The experience of all believers is too much the same effect: we began our new lives of joy and peace by believing the promise-making God, and we continue to live in the same manner. A long list of fulfilled promises is present to our happy memories, awakening our gratitude and confirming our confidence. We have tested the faithfulness of our God year after year, in a great many ways, but always with the same result. We have gone to Him with promises of the common things of life, relating to daily bread and raiment and children and home; and the Lord has dealt graciously with us. We have resorted to Him concerning sickness and slander and doubt and temptation; and never has He failed us. In little things He has been mindful of us: even the hairs of our head have been numbered. When it appeared very unlikely that the promise could be kept, it has been fulfilled with remarkable exactness. We have been broken down by the falseness of man, but we have exulted and do exult in the truthfulness of God. It brings the tears into our eyes to think of the startling ways in which Jehovah, our God, has wrought to carry out His gracious promises.

"Thus far we prove that promise good, which Jesus ratified with blood: still He is faithful, wise and just, and still in Him believers trust."

Let me freely speak to all who trust in the Lord. Children of God, has not your heavenly Father been true to you? Is not this your constant experience, that you are always failing, but He never fails? Well said our apostle, "Though we believe not, he abideth faithful: he cannot deny himself. The rule of His giving is large and liberal; the promise is a great vessel, and the Lord fills it to overflowing. As the Lord in Solomon's case gave him "as he promised him," so will He in every instance, as long as the world stands. Oh, reader, believe the promise and thus prove yourself to be an inheritor of it.

CHARLES H. SPURGEON

FIT FOR THE MASTER'S USE

Christmas Morning

When Christmas morning came, the long-expected morning, the prayers seemed long, and the breakfast was hardly touched when the servant came to announce that all was ready. And father and mother let us helter-skelter in. I can see the table now covered with presents, and the tree in the middle. There was a great heap, and I did not need to ask anybody for them, I just took them. Off the wrapping paper went and onto the floor—one walked knee deep in waste paper. And when the paper was gone, the presents were appropriated: this was mine, and that.

Can you not imagine God lifting the cloth off a great table full of gifts? All is ready. Child, you have been waiting years for it, and the day has come, and there is your gift, and yours, and yours.

What do you want? You have been praying for forgiveness. There it is! Now come up and take it. You have been asking for the assurance of sonship. It is there! Take it. What do you want? Power over passionate thoughts and deliverance from an unholy appetite? Well, the purity of Christ will answer all that. What do you want? "I have a terrible temper, sir. I try to be pleasant at home, but, when I am most determined, I get easily put out and I am ready to kill myself with remorse. If I could only keep my tongue still!" Well, here it is, the patience of Christ. What do you want? It is all ready, it has been here a long time but you have never come for it. Here it is. What is it you want? Well, here it is—all the old, glad strength of earlier days, when you used to leap as the hart. It is here in Jesus Christ.

On Christmas Day, realize that the once-infant Jesus is in heaven and has set the table. He is the table, He is the gift. His human nature, set free in death, is now glorified on His Father's throne. Is not that enough for you? The Lord Jesus is the complement of your need.

F. B. MEYER

ANSWERS TO PRAYER

Waiting for God's Will

December 11, 1850—The special burden of my prayer is that God would be pleased to teach me His will. My mind had also been especially pondering how I could know His will satisfactorily concerning this particular. Sure I am that I shall be taught. I therefore desire patiently to wait for the Lord's time, when He shall be pleased to shine on my path concerning this point.

December 26—Fifteen days have elapsed since I wrote the preceding paragraph. Every day since then I have continued to pray about this matter, and that with a goodly measure of earnestness, by the help of God. There has passed scarcely an hour during these days, in which, while awake, this matter has not been more or less before me. But all without a shadow of excitement. I converse with no one about it. Hitherto have I not even done so with my dear wife. From this I refrain still and deal with God alone about the matter, in order that no outward influence and no outward excitement may keep me from attaining unto a clear discovery of His will. I have the fullest and most peaceful assurance that He will clearly show me His will.

This evening I have had again an especially solemn season for prayer, to seek to know the will of God. But while I continue to entreat and beseech the Lord, that He would not allow me to be deluded in this business, I may say I have scarcely any doubt remaining on my mind as to what will be the result, even that I should go forward in this matter.

Since this, however, is one of the most momentous steps that I have ever taken, I judge that I cannot go about this matter with too much caution, prayerfulness, and deliberation. I am in no hurry about it. I could wait for years, by God's grace, were this His will, before even taking one single step toward this thing, or even speaking to anyone about it; and on the other hand, I would set to work tomorrow, were the Lord to bid me so.

This calmness of mind, this having no will of my own in the matter, this only wishing to please my heavenly Father in it—this state of heart, I say, is the fullest assurance to me that my heart is not under a fleshly excitement and that, if I am helped thus to go on, I shall know the will of God to the full.

GEORGE MUELLER

CHARGE THAT TO MY ACCOUNT

Anathema Maranatha

I f any man love not the Lord Jesus Christ, let him be Anathema Maranatha"
(1 Corinthians 16:22).

This is one of the most incisive and challenging statements in all the
Bible. Incisive because there is no possibility of misunderstanding it. In the
fewest possible words, it declares the inevitable doom of all who do not love the
Lord Jesus. Challenging, first because of its very incisiveness; and second, because of the fact that it contains two untranslated foreign words, *Anathema
Maranatha*, taken from two different languages, and which by their very strange-
ness compel our attention.

Anathema is Greek and means "accursed" or "devoted to judgment." It is the
same word that the apostle uses in Galatians 1:8–9: "But though we, or an
angel from heaven, preach any other gospel unto you than that which we have
preached unto you, let him be accursed. As we said before, so say I now again, if
any man preach any other gospel unto you than that ye have received, let him
be accursed." The man or angel who misleads others with a false gospel is under
the ban of the eternal God—Anathema, "accursed," "devoted to judgment."
He uses the same word again when speaking of himself: he says, "I could wish
that I myself were accursed (Anathema, rv) from Christ for my brethren, my
kinsmen according to the flesh." It implies, then, clearly a definite separation
from Christ, banishment from God, without any hope of restoration.

The other word, *Maranatha*, is a compound word, an Aramaic expression of
Chaldean origin, translated "our Lord come!" or "the Lord comes!" It is a vivid
reminder that the rejected Christ is to return in glory as judge of the living and
the dead.

So, then, the strange compound expression, this Greco-Aramaic term,
"Anathema Maranatha," might really be rendered, "devoted to judgment; our
Lord cometh." Slightly paraphrasing the entire sentence, it would read, "If any
man love not our Lord Jesus Christ, he will be devoted to judgment at the
coming of the Lord." What a tremendously solemn statement and how seriously
we should consider it.

HENRY A. IRONSIDE

GOD'S WAY OF HOLINESS

The Holy Fight

Yet, he that would be holy must fight. He must "war a good warfare" (1 Timothy 1:18), "fight the good fight of faith" (1 Timothy 6:12), though not with "carnal weapons" (2 Corinthians 10:4). He must fight upon his knees, "being sober, and watching unto prayer" (1 Peter 4:7). He must wrestle with principalities and powers, being strong in the Lord and in the power of His might, having put on the whole armor of God, girdle, breastplate, shield, helmet, and sword (Ephesians 6:13–17). This "battle is not to the strong" (Ecclesiastes 9:11), but to the weak; it is fought in weakness, and the victory is to those who have "no might"; for in this conflict "time and chance" do not happen to all. Instead, we count upon victory from the first onset, being made more than conquerors through Him who loved us, and are cheered with the anticipation of the sevenfold reward "to him that overcometh" (Revelation 2:7). And though, in this our earthly course and combat, we have the hostility of devils, we have the ministry of angels in aid (Hebrews 1:4), as well as the power of the Holy Spirit (Ephesians 1:13).

He that would be holy must watch. "Watch thou in all things" (2 Timothy 4:5); "watch ye, stand fast in the faith, quit you like men, be strong" (1 Corinthians 16:13). Let the sons of night sleep or stumble in the darkness, but let us, who are of the day, be sober, lest temptation overtake us, and we be ensnared in the wiles of the devil or the seductions of this wanton world. "Blessed is he that watcheth" (Revelation 16:15). In watching, too, let us "witness a good confession" (1 Timothy 6:13), not ashamed of Him whose badge we bear; let us run a swift and patient race, all the while having our eye upon the coming and the kingdom of our Lord Jesus.

He that would be holy must feel his responsibility for being so, both as a member of Christ's body and a partaker of the Holy Spirit. The thought that perfection is not to be reached here ought not to weaken that sense of responsibility nor to lead us to give way to anything that would "grieve the Holy Spirit of God whereby we are sealed unto the day of redemption." Let us hold to the sevenfold fullness of the risen Christ (Revelation 2:1) and the sevenfold fullness of the Holy Ghost (5:6), for these are the church's birthright.

HORATIUS BONAR

FIT FOR THE MASTER'S USE

The Blameless Life

And do not shrink from holiness, as though it were something unnatural and would divorce you from all that is innocent and right in human life. Spell "holiness" as "wholeness." The holy man is the whole man. The holy woman the whole, complete woman. Sanctification is the deliverance of our nature from the blight of sin and the restoration of the image that the Creator stamped on man in his first creation. The redeemer does not annihilate or resist any natural function implanted by the creator. The holy man is the best father, brother, son, friend, companion, because that is the most natural.

Do not dread sanctification, which is not "it" but "He," not a thing but a person, not a process but a life. Do you want to be sanctified? Let in the sanctifier. When God enters a day, it is a holy day; when He enters a bush, the ground around is holy; when He enters the heart of a man to fill it, he becomes a holy man.

The method of the blameless life is presented in the words "your spirit and soul and body." The apostle prays that God would sanctify them wholly, in spirit, soul, and body.

I pray God, says the apostle, that He may sanctify you wholly—not the spirit without the soul, not the soul without the body, but that body, soul, and spirit should be possessed by the indwelling power of the Holy Spirit of God dwelling in the most holy place of the spirit, shining through the whole nature, making darkness and impurity and evil impossible, and at last irradiating the very body with light and beauty.

F. B. MEYER

SALVATION FROM START TO FINISH

The Faith of Abraham

The blessing of Abraham was justification before God. He was a sinner by nature like all the rest of us. He was born into a state of wrongness and needed somehow to get into a state of rightness if he were to enjoy God's fellowship either here or hereafter. And how did he get there? Simply by faith, simply by believing the testimony of God on a certain matter.

And what was the matter? It concerned the son and heir that should be born to him. God had promised this heir a long while before, and had said that in his seed should all the families of the earth be blessed. But Abraham was an old man, and Sarah his wife long past the natural time of child-bearing, and yet the heir was not born. Was there some mistake about it? Had Abraham misunderstood? He seizes upon an occasion to put that inquiry to God when he is once more assured of it.

"[Abraham,] look now toward heaven. [Canst thou count the stars for multitude? Even] so shall thy seed be" (Genesis 15:5). God was telling Abraham that the seed would come from his loins, and the child would be born of his wife Sarah. Did Abraham's faith measure up to that promise? Yes, it did. "He staggered not at the promise of God through unbelief, but was strong in faith, giving glory to God; and being fully persuaded that, what he had promised, he was able also to perform . . . it was imputed to him for righteousness" (Romans 4:20–22).

That is not to say that Abraham in that moment was made righteous as to his personal experience or character. There were many things thereafter for which he needed to be rebuked of God. But he was made righteous in point of law and in his judicial standing before God.

When in a conflict of arms, an enemy surrenders on the terms of capitulation offered, no change may have taken place in his character, but a tremendous change has taken place in his relation to the foe, and vice versa. And on the basis of this relationship they can get together on a new plan that will work a quiet but thorough revolution in other respects. Something like this is true of every man who receives the blessing of Abraham in the same way.

JAMES M. GRAY

ACCORDING TO PROMISE

Jesus and the Promises

Jesus is the confirmer of the promises. They are "in him yea, and in him, Amen." His coming into our nature, His standing as our head, and His fulfilling of all the stipulations of the covenant have made all the articles of the divine compact firm and enduring. Now, is it not only kind but just with God to keep His promises to men? Since Jesus has rendered, on man's behalf, a full recompense to the divine honor that sin has assailed, the justice of God unites with His love in securing the carrying out of every word of promise.

As the rainbow is our assurance that the world shall never be destroyed by a flood, so is Jesus our assurance that the floods of human sin shall never drown the faithful kindness of the Lord. He has magnified the law and made it honorable; He must be rewarded for His soul-travail, and therefore all good things must come to those for whom He died. It would be an unhinging and dislocation of all things if the promises were now to become of no effect after our Lord has done all that was required to make them sure. If we are indeed one with the Lord Jesus Christ, the promises are as sure to us as the love of His Father is to Him.

Jesus remembers the promises. He pleads with God on our behalf, and His plea is the divine promise. "He made intercession for the transgressors." For the good things that He has promised the Lord will be inquired of by us that He may do them for us; and that this inquiry may be carried out under the most encouraging circumstances, behold, the Lord Jesus Himself becomes the intercessor for us. For Zion's sake He does not hold His peace, but day and night He makes remembrance of the everlasting covenant and of the blood whereby it was sealed and ratified. At the back of every promise stands the living, pleading, and prevailing high priest of our profession.

We may forget the faithful promise, but He will not. He will present the incense of His merit, and the engagements of God on our behalf, in that place within the veil where He exercises omnipotent intercession.

CHARLES H. SPURGEON

BIBLIOGRAPHY

The 365 readings featured in *They Walked with God* are based on more than forty books in Moody Press's Colportage Library, all published during the past one hundred years. The titles follow; parentheses indicate those still in print by Moody Press.

Bonar, Horatius. *God's Way of Holiness.* n.d.

Gray, James M. *Salvation from Start to Finish.* n.d.

———. *Satan and the Saint.* 1909.

Havergal, Frances Ridley. *Kept for the Master's Use.* n.d.

Ironside, H. A. *Full Assurance.* 1937 (in print).

———. *"Charge That to My Account."* 1931.

Meyer, F. B. *Back to Bethel.* n.d.

———. *The Christ-Life for the Self-Life.* 1897.

———. *Five "Musts" of the Christian Life and Other Sermons.* 1927.

———. *Light on Life's Duties.* n.d.

———. *Meet for the Master's Use* (listed as *Fit for the Master's Use* in readings). *n.d.*

———. *The Secret of Guidance.* 1896.

Moody, D. L. *Heaven. n.d.*

———. *Moody's Anecdotes.* 1898.

———. *Moody's Latest Sermons.* 1900.

———. *Moody's Stories.* n.d.

———. *The Overcoming Life.* 1896.

———. *Pleasure and Profit in Bible Study.* 1895.

———. *Prevailing Prayer.* n.d. (in print).

———. *Secret Power.* 1881, 1908.

———. *Select Sermons.* n.d.

———. *Short Talks.* 1900.

———. *Sovereign Grace.* 1891.

———. *Sowing and Reaping.* 1896.

———. *To the Work.* n.d.

————. *The Way Home.* 1904.

————. *The Way to God.* 1884.

————. *Weighed and Wanting.* 1898.

Moody, D. L., Charles Spurgeon, George Mueller, and J. C. Ryle. *The Second Coming of Christ.* n.d.

Mueller, George. *Answers to Prayer.* n.d. (in print).

Murray, Andrew. *Absolute Surrender.* 1897 (in print).

————. *The School of Obedience.* n.d.

————. *The True Vine.* n.d.

Ryle, J. C., Horatius Bonar, D. L. Moody, and C. H. Spurgeon. *Calvary's Cross.* 1900.

Scofield, C. I. *The New Life in Christ Jesus.* 1915.

Spurgeon, C. H. *According to Promise.* n.d.

————. *All of Grace.* n.d.

Spurgeon, Charles H., and D. L. Moody. *The Empty Tomb.* 1896.

————. *The Story of the Prodigal.* 1896.

————. *What Is Faith?* 1924.

Torrey, R. A. *Difficulties and Alleged Errors and Contradictions in the Bible.* 1907.

————. *How to Pray.* n.d.

————. *Practical and Perplexing Questions Answered.* n.d.

————. *Ten Reasons Why I Believe the Bible Is the Word of God.* 1898.

————. *To Shew Thyself Approved.* 1921.